STUDIES IN MEDIEVAL AND
RENAISSANCE HISTORY

Volume VI

D1131669

STUDIES IN
Medieval and Renaissance
History

Volume VI

Edited by
WILLIAM M. BOWSKY
University of California, Davis

UNIVERSITY OF NEBRASKA PRESS · LINCOLN
1969

Publishers on the Plains

UNP

Copyright © 1969 by the University of Nebraska Press

All rights reserved

Library of Congress Catalog Card Number 63–22098

Manufactured in the United States of America

CONTENTS

INTRODUCTION

Studies in Medieval and Renaissance History is a series of annual volumes designed for original major articles and short monographs in all fields of medieval and renaissance history.

The first impetus for the creation of this series came from a belief that there is a need for a scholarly publication to accommodate the longer study whose compass is too large for it to be included regularly in existing media but too small for it to appear in book form. The editors will consider articles in all areas of history from approximately the fourth through the sixteenth centuries—economic, social and demographic, political, intellectual and cultural, and studies that do not fit neatly into a single traditional category of historical investigation.

The editorial board hopes that the *Studies* creates another link between the work of medieval and renaissance scholarship; for many articles pertinent to both disciplines appear in publications consulted almost exclusively by either medieval or renaissance scholars.

While this series is devoted primarily to the publication of major studies it contains occasional bibliographic essays and briefer articles dealing with unpublished archival or manuscript resources. The *Studies* also makes available in translation original articles by scholars who do not write in English.

Studies in Medieval and Renaissance History is not the official organ of any association or institution. Publication in the series is open to all historians whose research falls within its scope and fields of interest.

THE ROMAN
AND FRANKISH ROOTS
OF THE JUST PRICE
OF MEDIEVAL CANON LAW

Kenneth S. Cahn

Queens College
of
The City University of New York

THE ROMAN AND FRANKISH ROOTS
OF THE JUST PRICE OF MEDIEVAL
CANON LAW

INTRODUCTION

In the year 1234, by the authority of Pope Gregory IX, the official collection of canon law known as the *Decretals* was published. In the collection is found a regulation stating that price discrimination was forbidden. Goods sold outside of the market place were to be sold at the price then prevailing in the market place. The just price in any given transaction, then, was not to be determined simply by an agreement between buyer and seller, and certainly not by the overweening power of either of them. It was to be set by the operation of "the law of supply and demand" at a general concourse of buyers and sellers.[1]

The market price was not the only mode of calculating the just price used in the law of the church nor was it the only one employed in the other great bodies of medieval law. According to one, any price agreed upon by buyer and seller was lawful. Another declared that in sales of real estate the income yielded by the property might be used to assess its value. At times the authorities set prices for certain goods.

To provide compensation for those injured by unjust transactions, a principle called *laesio enormis* was often employed in ancillary connection with the just price. It allowed for a certain amount of deviation from the just price, but it set both upper and lower limits to which the deviation might extend. It also prescribed the ways in which the injured party was to be compensated. The various modes by which the amounts were calculated and recompense provided will be fully described below; here it is only necessary to forewarn against a not uncommon misunderstanding of the just price and the *laesio enormis*. Apparently, because they established a type of minimum price, it is assumed that they were aimed at preventing

---

1. There seems little doubt that contemporaries were aware of the operation of that law. See for example Thomas Aquinas, *Summa Theologica*, in *Opera Omnia* (Parma, 1852–73; reprinted New York, 1948–50), II, II, qu. 77, art. 3, obj. 4 and ad. 4, Vol. III, p. 278. For the price regulations found in the *Decretals*, see below, pp. 41–43.

competition—specifically price-cutting.[2] Examination of the law will amply reveal that the just price rules, either with or without the *laesio enormis*, did not prevent a merchant determined to sell at a low price from selling at that figure. One could sell below a just price set by the government or below one set in the market place. (In the latter case, one would be competing with a price which had been set competitively in the first place.) One could, in fact, sell below the lowest limits allowed by the *laesio enormis*, for the law provided only for action by, and compensation for, the injured party. The buyer, in a case where the price was cut, could hardly be described as injured, and the seller, if he were determined to sell at a low price, would not contest a transaction in which he sold at that low price. The just price, then, was set into the law for reasons other than preventing competition.

In examining the canon law and its sources, all of these methods of setting and enforcing the just price will come under consideration. Conspicuously absent will be that concept of the just price which is most frequently associated with the middle ages: that the just price is one which will allow the producer a profit adequate to maintain his status.[3] The omission is unavoidable; the principle was never expressed in medieval canon law. Indeed, the principle does not seem to have been expressed at all until the latter part of the fourteenth century, although the concept of just price had been a real issue for perhaps a thousand years. The first to maintain that there ought to be a connection between price and status was Henry of Langenstein, a theologian whose stature and influence, it may fairly be said, were not among the greatest.[4] One will

2. E.g., M. S. Anderson, *Europe in the Eighteenth Century* (New York, 1961), pp. 78–79: "The still partially medieval character of eighteenth century economic life can be illustrated in other ways. The idea of active competition between manufacturers or merchants as a normal and desirable thing was slow to develop, and governments often attempted to prevent price-cutting. Ideas which had taken root in a pre-capitalist and pre-industrialist age, such as that of the 'just price,' still retained much of their former vitality. Thus Savary des Bruslons, the author of the greatest commercial handbook of the age, *Le Parfait Negociant*, was still able in the 1724 edition to argue that the price of a commodity should be determined by what it was just the vendor should gain."

3. R. de Roover, "The Concept of Just Price: Theory and Economic Policy," *The Journal of Economic History*, XVIII (1958), 418. The author names eleven historians who present the "maintenance of status price" as typical of the middle ages and points out that "the list is by no means exhaustive." Another such list can be found in J. W. Baldwin, "The Medieval Theories of the Just Price," *Transactions of the American Philosophical Society*, N. S. XLIX (1959), 7.

4. Another "minority view" was put forth by Duns Scotus. For a full discussion of

perhaps not be surprised to discover that the views of the more prominent theologians were usually consistent with the declarations of the law of their church.

The canon law influenced not only contemporary Christian philosophers and theologians, but also played a considerable part in modern legislation, and its connection with the modern era has been demonstrated in some cases with more, and in some with less, precision. It has been claimed, for example, that the medieval principle of *laesio enormis* was revived in the Soviet Union in the 1930s. In the same decade, legislation was being passed in America, Great Britain, and Germany, which "restrict[ed] freedom of contract in order to avoid lesion or exploitation of the entire mass of the population."[5] It has also been maintained that there is a connection between the medieval *laesio enormis* and those court decisions in Great Britain and the United States by which contracts have been overturned on the grounds that they "shocked the conscience of the court," but the author concedes that the connection is difficult to demonstrate.[6]

The *laesio enormis* appeared in Dutch law too, according to R. W. M. Dias, and as late as 1950 was still operating in South Africa and Ceylon. Here, the connection between the medieval and the modern law has been demonstrated, such figures as Grotius carrying the law forward in time. Dias makes an additional point, maintaining that *laesio enormis* is found not only in Gregory's issue of 1234, but in some relatively obscure and atypical passages in the Justinian Code, and opens the question of which of the two is the real source of the modern legislation.[7]

An even more fundamental regulation in the *Decretals* has also been traced into modern law. One of the positions taken in that code—that the

---

the theologians' views on the just price see R. de Roover, "The Concept of the Just Price," pp. 418–420, 424, *et passim*.

5. J. B. Thayer, "Laesio Enormis," *Kentucky Law Journal*, XXV (1936–37), 331. The author shows no tangible connection, but merely similarity. B. Eliachevitch (*Traité de droit civil et commercial des Soviets*, 2 vols. [Paris, 1930], II, 86–87) declares that the Soviet code does not contain any special provision concerning rescission of sales in case of *lesion*, but that the Soviet courts were overturning sales on those grounds, one reason being that such sales were apt to mask usurious transactions.

6. Thayer, *op. cit.*, pp. 330–332.

7. R. W. M. Dias, "Laesio Enormis: The Roman Dutch Story," in *Studies in Memory of Francis de Zulueta* (Oxford, 1959), *passim*, especially p. 48. The author's judgment is that the church law is the true source, not because it was first to promulgate the *laesio enormis* but because it was first to state it in a forceful manner and to give it important status.

price in the open market is the just price—has been shown by a number of historians to have had a considerable influence on law and economic theory concerning monopoly. The medieval position has been traced up to and beyond Adam Smith,[8] and it has been concluded "that the conspiracy idea of the antitrust laws goes back to scholastic precedents and is rooted in the medieval concept of just price." [9]

The task of this paper, however, is to trace the origins of this far-reaching concept, not the later developments. The capitulary of 1234, mentioned above, was not the first that sought justice in the market place. Earlier canonists had made the same judgment. Furthermore, a comparison of the texts makes it clear that the *decretal* of 1234 is derived from a Carolingian capitulary of 884 and that both the law of 884 and the law of 1234 contain key words which appear in the Justinian Code.

It is an oversimplification, however, to conclude that the concept went from the Justinian, to the Carolingian, to the canon law. Carolingian legislation issued before 884 seems to carry the same idea and it does not use phrases from Justinian. Again, the Roman (or for that matter the medieval) law on purchase and sale is not so simple that it can be stated in a phrase or two. The discovery of the origins of the just price of medieval law—Romanist, canonist, and Carolingian—is the aim of this investigation. Stated differently, we are measuring in one area the impact of Roman civilization on the medieval and ultimately the modern world. The area to be investigated is not a minor one. That a price is just (or unjust) is one of the most fundamental judgments that can be made upon the most common of all commercial transactions. It is fortunate that in this area the sources exist in such quantity and are of such a nature as to allow the subject to be investigated with a degree of precision.

I. THE THEODOSIAN LINE

In the Theodosian Code it is stated that in each instance the buyer and the seller by mutual agreement fix the price for which property is sold. Set close together under the title of *De contrahenda emptione*, three rules in

---

8. R. de Roover, "Monopoly Theory prior to Adam Smith: A Revision," *Quarterly Journal of Economics*, LXV (1951), 501–502, 507; W. L. Letwin, "The English Common Law Concerning Monopolies," *The University of Chicago Law Review*, XXI (1953–54), 335–361; J. A. Schumpeter, *History of Economic Analysis*, ed. E. B. Schumpeter (New York, 1954), pp. 154–155.

9. R. de Roover, "The Concept of the Just Price," p. 43.

the code have roughly the same force:[1] sales cannot be set aside on the grounds that the price was inadequate. Each of the three rules limits, or rather describes, the scope of this general law. The first excludes from its coverage cases in which the purchaser has brought to bear upon the seller fraud or violence.[2] The second specifies that the rule is to apply only to those who have attained their majority. It declares further that the claim of ignorance of the value of property asserted by an adult is not valid grounds for rescission even if the property is located at a great distance from him.[3] The third restricts the operation of the law to *persona legitima*,[4] which has the definition at law (according to Harper's *Latin Dictionary*) of a being "having legal rights and obligations including free men and the state, but not including slaves."

In 506, less than three-quarters of a century after the promulgation of the Theodosian Code, these three laws appeared complete and *verbatim* in the *Breviarum Alarici*[5]—the *Lex Romana Visigothorum*. In the following century in a consolidated, condensed, and simplified form they appeared in the collection of King Receswinth which is known as the *Lex Visigothorum*. A single rule of law flatly states that no one should attack the validity of a sale on the grounds that he sold at a low price whether that sale be of lands, slaves, any type of animals, or anything else (*res aliquas*).[6] (In a separate rule the validity of sales induced by violence or fear is absolutely denied, price not being mentioned.)[7]

Receswinth's brief rule appears *verbatim* in the Bavarian law, promulgated in the second quarter of the eighth century. In 'the Bavarian law,

1. *Theodosiani libri XVI*, ed. T. Mommsen and P. Meyer (Berlin. 1905) [*Codex Theodosianus*], 3, 1, 1; 3, 1, 4; 3, 1, 7.

2. *Ibid.*, 3, 1, 1.

3. *Ibid.*. 3, 1, 4. This rule, not much altered, is found in C. 4, 44, 16. See below p. 12 n. 1, for full citation.

4. *Codex Theodosianus*, 3, 1, 7: "Iidem AAA Remigio pf. Augustali. Semel inter personas legitimas initus empti contractus et venditi ob minorem adnumeratum pretii quantitatem nequeat infirmari. Dat III Kal April Constantinopoli, Arcadio A IV et Honorio A III coss.

"Interpretatio Cum inter duas quascumque personas de pretio cuiuscumque rei convenerit, quamvis vilius, quam valebat, res fuerit conparata, nullatenus revocetur."

5. *Lex Romana Visigothorum*, ed. G. Haenel (Leipzig, 1849). See also *Breviarum Alarici*, ed. and trans. Max Conrat (Cohn) (Leipzig, 1903).

6. K. Zeumer (ed.), *Lex Visigothorum, edita ab Recesvindo Rege, Monumenta Germaniae Historica* (cited hereafter as *M.G.H.*), *Legum*, Sec. I (Leipzig and Hanover, 1902), Vol. I, pp. 219–220 [V, 4, 7].

7. *Ibid.*, [V, 4, 3]: "Venditio vero, fuerit violenter, et per metum extorta, nulla valeat ratione."

however, a clause is added according to which not only the seller, but also the buyer, is expressly denied the right to escape from the sale.[8] Once the transaction is made, reads the law, it is not to be set aside unless it is determined that the seller has concealed some defect and sold, for example, a slave, which, unknown to the buyer, is blind or leprous or epileptic. (*Sed postquam factum est negotium non sit mutatum, nisi forte vitium invenit quod ille venditor celavit* etc.) The writer of the law seems particularly concerned with making the sale of faulty livestock voidable (*In animalibus autem sunt vitia que aliquotiens celare potest venditor*); nevertheless, they are merely given as examples; the coverage of the law is general (*aut in cavallo aut in qualicumque peculio*). In order to avoid action on grounds of defect, the seller need only inform the buyer of its existence and the sale will stand. The law, then, by stating that hidden defects are the only grounds for rescinding a sale, eliminates high price as grounds for voiding or altering the transaction. Thus, the law was extended in such a manner that, whereas previously the buyer was expressly given the right to do as well for himself as he could, now the seller was named as having the right to sell as dearly as he was able. It should, perhaps, be emphasized that this particular alteration of the law was not due to misunderstanding or even to a somewhat more general interpretation of the Theodosian rule. The section extending the law so as to cause it to protect sellers from actions on the grounds of high prices was a deliberate and novel addition to the original legislation.[9]

In the ninth century the rule covering now both buyer and seller appeared in the collection of capitularies of Benedictus Diaconus.[10] The

8. E. Schwind (ed.), *Lex Baiwariorum, M.G.H., Legum*, Sec. I (Hanover, 1926), Vol. V, pt. 2, p. 437, XVI, 9: "(De venditionis forma) Venditionis haec forma servetur ut seu res seu mancipium vel quodlibet genus animalium venditur, nemo propterea firmitatem venditionis inrumpit quod dicat se vili pretio vendidisse. Sed postquam factum est negotium non sit mutatum nisi forte vitium invenerit quod ille venditor celavit, hoc est in mancipio aut in cavallo aut in qualicumque peculio; id aut cecum aut herniosum aut cadivum aut leprosum. In animalibus autem sunt vitia que aliquotiens celare potest venditor. Si autem venditor dixerit vitium, stet emptio, non potest mutare. Si autem non dixerit, mutare potest in illa die et in alia et in tertia die. Et si plus de tribus noctibus habuerit post se, non potest mutare, nisi forte eum invenire non poterit infra tres dies. Tunc quando invenerit, recipiat qui vitiatum vendidit, aut si non vult recipere, iuret cum sacramentale uno: quia vitium ibi nullum sciebam in illa die, quando negotium fecimus et stet factum."

9. It does not seem accurate then to describe the Bavarian code merely as preserving the Theodosian price rules.

10. Benedictus, *Capitularium Collectio*, Lib. I, chap. 362, in J. P. Migne, *Patrologiae cursus completus. Series Latina* (Paris, 1844–80) (cited hereafter as *P.L.*), XCVII, col. 749.

examples were omitted. At the end of the eleventh century the entire regulation appeared *verbatim* in the very important collection of Ivo of Chartres.[11]

The three Theodosian regulations on the disallowance of sales are also found in several epitomes. Here they stayed much closer to their original form and meaning. Generally speaking, they remain three separate laws, usually present the same qualifications to the force of the law, and are arranged in the same order as they had in their original setting. The only difference between the later and the original versions is in the vocabulary.

The *Epitoma Aegidius*, composed at the beginning of the eighth century, lacks two of the *interpretationes* found in the Theodosian Code. The one it does contain, however, is very similar to the original.[12]

The code which is entitled the *Scintilla*[13] is a little later than that of Aegidius. It was composed at the end of the eighth or early in the ninth century.[14] Its renditions of the *interpretationes* are somewhat briefer and syntactically simpler than the original. The original code states that the sale will stand if no fraud or violence was exerted by the buyer (*Si nihil fraudis vel violentiae eget ille*). The *Scintilla* says that the seller must have acted according to his own free will (*propria voluntate vendiderit*).[15] The second regulation is likewise abbreviated in the later collection but the condition is the same and the same phrase is used to express it; the seller must have attained his majority (*perfecta aetate*).[16] The third is stated in terms similar to the original,[17] but it seems that the special meaning of *persona* at Roman law has been lost.

The *Epitome Codicis Guelpherbytani* which was done in the latter part of the eighth century is remarkable throughout for the brevity of its formulations. For the first qualification of Theodosius (the absence of fraud

---

11. Ivo of Chartres, *Decretum*, Part XVI, chap. 285, in *P.L.*, CLXI, cols. 956–957. See below p. 12. Ivo's version is virtually identical to Benedict's. See n. 10 above.

12. *Lex Romana Visigothorum*, p. 72.

13. The *Scintilla* is also referred to as the *Epitome Codicis Regii Parisiensis Suppl. Lat. 215.* (See *Lex Romana Visigothorum*, p. xxvi *et passim.*)

14. For the dating of these compilations see *Lex Romana Visigothorum*, p. xxiii ff.

15. *Ibid.*, p. 73: "Si quis rem suam etiam minus quam valeat propria voluntate vendiderit, se voluerit revocare quae vendidit, nullatenus permittatur."

16. *Ibid.*, p. 75: "Quicumque perfecta aetate quamlibet dicat, quod rem a se longe positam vendiderit, stabit." (See *Codex Theodosianus*, 3, 1, 4, cited above p. 7 n. 3.)

17. I.e., "Si inter duas personas conveniat, ut res minus, quam valuerit, comparetur, nullatenus refragetur." *Lex Romana Visigothorum*, p. 75.

or violence), it substitutes the presence of good faith,[18] which term probably comprehended the Theodosian qualifications and more. The qualification concerning age is present (*aetas perfecta*) and ignorance of value is disqualified as grounds on which an adult may rescind a sale,[19] as is the case in the original code. That the special Roman meaning of *persona* has been lost seems quite clear and the entry in this epitome is nothing more than a terse statement of the general principle that sales cannot be rescinded on the grounds that the price was too low (*res vindita. p[ropter] vilitatem p[re]cii rescindi non posse*).[20]

The *Monk's Epitome*, or as he called it *Breviarum*, was also done in the eighth century. It simplifies the vocabulary and syntax and holds rather closely to the original meaning. Like the original text it specifies that the presence of fraud provides an exception to the general non-rescindability of sales, but unlike the original it does not mention violence.[21] The second rule carries the same meaning as the original and many of the words are identical.[22] The third regulation is presented simply as a general rule that sales cannot be rescinded on the grounds of low price.[23]

The epitome of Saint Gaul as a whole contains far more adaptations, indeed alterations, than any of the other epitomes.[24] The regulations on price, however, are not very much changed. The sale will stand, the first rule says, if the price has been agreed upon in mutual harmony by the

18. *Ibid.*, p. 73: "Vendicionem bona fide perfectam rescindi non posse." This is the entire entry for *Codex Theodosianus*, 3, 1, 1; cf. above p. 7 n. 2.

19. *Lex Romana Visigothorum*, p. 75: "Qui p[ro]pt[er] rem. sibi incognita[m] vindiccion[em] causatur. non poterit rescindere. qu[id] fecit quia aetas. perfecta. scire potuit. quid vinderit"; cf. *Codex Theodosianus*, 3, 1, 4, above p. 7 n. 3.

20. *Lex Romana Visigothorum*, p. 75.

21. *Ibid.*, p. 73: "Si quis aliquid vendiderit et fraus ibi nulla intervenerit, nullo modo potest re repetere, quod vendidit."

22. *Ibid.*, p. 75; "*Quaecunque persona iam perfecta aetate* aliquid de possessione sua vendiderit et forte repetiit, *quod minus pretii acceperit, non eam poterit revocare, quia aetas perfecta poterit scire quod venderet.*" The italicized words and phrases are found in the original. (See *Codex Theodosianus*, 3, 1, 4, above p. 7 n. 3.)

23. *Lex Romana Visigothorum*, p. 75: "Semel res vendita, quamvis vilius quam valeat, nullatenus revocetur."

24. Haenel reads (*Lex Romana Visigothorum*, p. xxxi): "Etenim totam rem in alium quasi sermonem convertit, ad regionis, ubi vixit, mores at instituta accomodavit, multas leges mutavit, auxit sive amplificavit complures, quae ei videbantur inutiles et a consilio suo alienae esse, omisit, et tantum abest, *Breviarum* ut interpretatus sit, ut novum quasi librum iuris composuerit ex *Breviario* et ex iis, quae addidit, vel omnino mutavit."

buyer and seller.[25] This would seem to mean that the buyer must not have forced the seller to accede to his terms. Concerning fraud, nothing is said. The second rule, like its original model, states that the law refers to adults (*homo iam in plena etate*).[26] The third emerges, as it does in other instances, as a general statement of the law, *persona* being rendered *homo*.[27]

It may be said, then, that the meaning of the Theodosian rules on price are altered to some small degree in the epitomes here considered. The qualifications in the Roman law to the general proposition that low price is no grounds for rescinding a sale are sometimes lost in the later versions. Gone is the Theodosian Code's distinction expressed by the word *persona* which made free adults and the state subject to the law but exempted slaves from it. The other conditions in the presence of which the law would not apply, such as fraud or violence, are not always specifically stated, but even here the epitomes provide that the improper behavior of the buyer may invalidate a sale. The protection of minors from the consequences of their actions as vendors is always present. Most important, the general force of the law and its coverage remain unchanged. The right to rescind sales on the grounds of low price is denied. It is, of course, to the seller that denial is made.

It is not true in all cases that the Theodosian rules were modified. The first of the three Theodosian price regulations appears *verbatim* in Ivo of Chartres' *Decretum*. If there is no fraud or violence, says the *Decretum*, the seller has no grounds for rescission for a sale cannot be rescinded on the

---

25. *Ibid.*, p. 73: "Impē Consī Dat Īd aḡ Inter̄. Cum inter emente[m] et vindentem de qualecunq[ue]: rem fuerit inter eos orta causatio. Ille qui ipsa[m] rem vindiderit si exinde minus p[re]ciu[m] p[en]serit qua[m] ipsa[m] re[m] valebit si addifinitu[m] de ipsa[m] rem conveniencie p[re]cium sic[ut] int[er] eos convenit post ea in p[re]-ciu[m] ipse qui conparat nulla[m] re[m] vinditori addire debit nisi solu[m] q[uo]d conveniencia habuer[it] det in ipsa p[er]maneant."

26. *Ibid.*, p. 75: "Iī. ali Intp̄. Quicu[n]q[ue]: homo iam in plena etate e[st] qui sua[m] causam agere pote[st] si forsitam; aut agru[m] aut villa[m] aut quale[m]-cu[m]que causa[m] vindiderit et postea dixerit q[uod] p[re]ciu[m] minus recipisset qua[m] ipsa[m] rem valebat et forsitam dic[at] illa[m] re[m] aut illu[m] agru[m] longe habui da me ñ nescieba[m] quantu[m] valerat p[er] tales occasiones nec vindicio cadit nec ipsa[m] rem tollere ñ pote[st]."

27. *Ibid.*, p. 75: "Ite alia Intp. Omnem re[m] q[uo]d homo ad alteram vindiderit qua[m]vis vilius fuerit conparata si postea dic[at] ille q[ui] ipsa[m] re[m] vindidit q[uo]d minus preciu[m] pr[end]isset qua[m] ipsa res valebat p[er] hoc ipsa[m] re[m] nullaten[us] retollere pote[st]."

grounds of low price.[28] Thus, Ivo of Chartres has two price regulations deriving from the Theodosian Code. The first, which seems to come directly from the code, refers only to the seller and cases of low prices. The second, which originated in the code, appears in a simpler form in King Receswinth's law, greatly expanded in scope in the *Bavarian Law*, polished up, as it were, in the collection of Benedict Levita and in this version it is found in the *Decretum* of Ivo. In its altered form it not only denies the seller the right to have a sale rescinded on the grounds of low price, but it also denies to the buyer any recourse on the grounds of high price.

II. THE JUSTINIAN LINES

Justinian law appears to be consistent with, and indeed to expand, the principles expressed in the Theodosian Code. Not only is low price denied as grounds for the rescission of a sale, but the *Corpus* seems to allow both the buyer and the seller to obtain the terms most favorable to themselves. It was lawful (and even natural) the law declared, for the seller to charge as much as he could and for the buyer to pay as little as possible and consequently for each party to try to get the better of the other. Fraud might serve as grounds for an adult to have a sale rescinded, but fraud, said the *Corpus*, was judged by the nature of the deed and not by the quantity of the price.[1] Indeed, the principle may have been stated even more firmly. One passage can be translated thus: "In sales and purchases it is naturally allowed to buy a thing of greater value for a smaller price; and to sell a thing of lesser value for a greater price."[2]

In apparent contradiction to these pronouncements are statements found elsewhere in the Justinian *Corpus*. Two passages seem to deny that price is a matter which is to be settled between the buyer and the seller.

28. Ivo of Chartres, *Decretum*, Part XVI, chap. 244, *P.L.* CLXI, col. 950: "De rebus venalibus. Cum inter ementem atque vendentem fuerit res definito pretio comparata, quamvis plus valeat quam ad praesens venditur, hoc tantummodo requirendum est, si nihil fraudis vel violentiae egit ille qui comparasse probatur; et si voluerit revocare qui vendidit, nullatenus permittatur."

1. *Corpus Iuris Civilis*, ed. T. Mommsen, P. Krueger, *et al.* (Berlin, 1880–1922), Digest (cited hereafter as D.), 4, 4, 16, 4. One might also cite the Code (cited hereafter as C.), 4, 44, 10: "Dolus emptoris qualitate facti, non quantitate pretio aestimatur"; or C. 4, 44, 5: "Quod si iure perfecta venditio est a maiore viginti quinque annis intellegere debes consensu mutuo perfectam venditionem resolvi non posse."

2. D. 19, 2, 22, 3.

Instead, they apparently insist, first, that in sales of real estate (*fundus*) there is a certain "just price" (*iustum pretium*) and, second, that the seller, if he sells for less than half that amount, has suffered what was later called a "great injury" (*laesio enormis*). In such a case he would be entitled to receive from the buyer the difference between the selling price and the just price, or if the buyer chose, he might return the property to its seller and have the amount he paid for it returned to him.[3]

In neither of the two passages is the term "just price" defined, and one of the tasks the medieval jurists set before themselves was to discover (or invent) its meaning. Nor was it altogether clear how the "one half" was to be calculated, and this too was the subject of investigation and speculation during the period that followed. These matters will be discussed in more appropriate context. The present concern must be the meaning which the laws in question had when they were set into the *Corpus*.

It is, as has been said, possible to interpret this passage as covering anyone who sells a piece of property at too low a price. Yet, one may suspect that its intended coverage was somewhat more limited. The passage in the law seems to have been written in response to a specific question or questions regarding a particular case. Thus the author of the passage may assume a certain amount of information on the part of the inquirer which may not be obvious to one reading the response only. Any interpretation, therefore, must be to some degree tentative. The fact that those who made the sale are named as "you or your father" (*tu vel pater tuus*) suggests that the sale in question might involve property belonging to a minor. If a rule valid for all sales of property were being stated, it would seem that "*si quis distraxerit*" would have been used.[4] The judgment, then, may have been concerned with protecting a minor from his youth or from his father's errors or even personal interests.[5]

The other case of *laesio enormis* in Justinian's Code also appears to involve the sale of real estate by a minor. In this instance, the father has given the son permission to sell a piece of his (the father's) property. If he sold the property for less than half its worth, the buyer, as in the first case,

3. C. 4, 44, 2. C. 4, 44, 8 (See below pp. 16–17).

4. Several of the passages in this set seem to be answers to inquiries made by interested individuals with particular cases in mind, for example, C. 4, 44, 6: "Idem AA. and CC.: Novisio Gaiano veterano. Non est probabilis causa, propter quam rescindi consensu factum venditionem desideras. quamvis enim duplum offeras pretium emptori tamen invitus ad rescindendam venditionem urgueri non debet."

5. The father, as guardian of the youth, might, for example, in collusion with a "buyer" sell the property for a token price.

has a choice of returning the property and getting his money back or
paying the balance of the just price. One might guess that the parallel
seen by the Roman jurists between this and the first case is that in both a
minor is alienating in a foolishly conceived transaction a piece of property
which will one day be his—a property, moreover, which might provide
his life's income. (That the law was particularly concerned with inherited
properties that provided the necessities of life, there can be little doubt.
Even an adult could not alienate a legacy of sustenance [*fundus ad alimenta
relictus testamento sive ab intestamento*] unless the terms were approved by the
praetor.)

Several passages can be cited which seem to support such an interpretation. They can be found in the section from which *laesio enormis* is
taken (*De rescinda venditione*, C. 4, 44) and in the section on minority
(*De minoribus viginti quinque annis*, D. 4, 4), in which it is declared that one
less than twenty-five years of age is entitled restitution if his property is
diminished.[6] That the Theodosian Code also protected minors against
foolish sales has already been mentioned.[7]

There is still another interpretation of these passages which does not
appear to have been considered and which would give the whole matter
an entirely different meaning at Roman law. *Minus solvere* is generally
translated "to pay less" and taken to mean "to purchase for less." (One
might say, for example, "he paid less than 200" or "he purchased the
goods for less than 200.") This would give "*minus*" a standard classical
definition. However, there are definitions given in the Digest itself of
minus used with *solvere*. In these definitions *solvere minus* does not seem to
imply to pay less in the sense of purchase for less, but rather in the more
mechanical sense of paying less than the price agreed upon, that is
"paying" in the sense of handing over money. (One might say, "The
item was sold for 200. The purchaser paid 100 at the time of the purchase
and he will pay another 100 at a future date.") Thus "pay" in English,
too, is somewhat ambiguous, meaning both purchase for (as, he paid
200 for it, or purchased it for 200) and to make payment (as, he only paid
half of his obligation). It can carry a third signification closely related to
the second and that is "paid in full." (One might say, "the bill has been
paid," and that would imply that payment in full of a certain obligation
has been made.)

It is in the last sense that the Digest, in the section entitled "The
Meaning of Words," seems to define *solvere*. The Digest says, "We say

6. D. 4, 4, 6. (For legacies of sustenance see D. 2, 15, 8 and D. 2, 15, 8, 15.)
7. See above, p. 7.

that he has paid who has done what he has promised to do" (*"Solvere"
dicimus eum qui fecit quod facere promisit*).[8] Holding to this definition would mean that "*minus solutum*" would imply that one has paid (handed to the seller) less than or none of that which he had promised to pay and there are, in fact, three definitions of *minus solutum* in the Digest which indicate that this is an accurate translation. (The following definitions, like the one of *solvere* above, are not extractions which might be misleading taken out of their original context. They are definitions, presented as such, under the title *De verborum significatione* [D. 50, 16].)

Verbum "amplius" ad eum quoque pertinet, cui nihil debetur; sicut ex contrario "minus" solutum videtur etiam, si nihil esset exactum.[9]

The word "amplius" pertains to him to whom nothing is owed; just as, on the other hand, "minus" seems to have been paid even if nothing has been collected.

"Minus solutum" intellegetur etiam, si nihil esset solutum.

Scott: Less is understood to have been paid than is due even when nothing at all has been paid.[10]

Minus solvit, qui tardius solvit: nam et tempore minus solvitur.

Black: He does not pay who pays too late.

Scott: He who is in default pays less than he owes, for less is paid when the time of settlement is deferred.[11]

It should be added that if this interpretation stand, "*pretium*," in C. 4, 44, 2 and 8, very likely means "the amount of payment which was agreed upon by the buyer and seller" and that it keeps this meaning whether modified by *iustum* or *verum*. It has been pointed out in any case that the appearance of the latter two words in the manuscripts is often of doubtful origin. On the other hand, noted below are other definitions of key words in the passage which support this interpretation. The definitions given in the standard dictionaries for *solvere* are many, but when *solvere* is used with money, its meaning seems quite limited and quite similar to the Digest's definitions. (Lewis: "of money or property, pay, pay over, hand over"; Harper: "of obligations, to fulfill"; Black: "to

---

8. D. 50, 16, 176.
9. D. 50, 16, 82.
10. D. 50, 16, 32. *The Civil Law*, trans. S. P. Scott (Cincinnati, 1932).
11. D. 50, 16, 12, 1. Henry C. Black, *Black's Law Dictionary* (St. Paul, 1951); Scott (trans.), *The Civil Law*.

pay, comply with one's obligation to do what one has undertaken to do, to release oneself from obligation, as by the payment of the debt.") It should also be noted that in C. 4, 44, 8 *datum* seems to hold the same place and meaning as *solutum* in 4, 44, 2. (Lewis' first definition of *dare* is "hand over," which is followed by "deliver, give up, render, furnish, pay.")

Translations of the two passages are here offered, not as a positive assertion that they are correct, but because the special definitions of *solvere* and *minus solvere* presented in the Digest warrant consideration of them.

8 Idem AA. et CC. Aureliae Euodiae. Si voluntate tua fundum tuum filius tuus venumdedit, dolus ex calliditate atque insidiis emptoris argui debet vel metus mortis vel cruciatus corporis imminens detegi, ne habeatur rata venditio. hoc enim solum, quod paulo minori pretio fundum venumdatum significas, ad rescindendam emptionem invalidum est. quod videlicet si contractus emptionis atque venditionis cogitasses substantiam et quod emptor viliori comparandi, venditor cariori distrahendi votum gerentes ad hunc contractum accedant vixque post multas contentiones, paulatim venditore de eo quod petierat detrahente, emptore autem huic quod obtulerat addente, ad certum consentiant pretium, profecto perspiceres. neque bonam fidem, quae emptionis atque venditionis conventionem tuetur, pati neque ullam rationem concedere rescindi propter hoc consensu finitum contractum vel statim vel post pretii quantitatis disceptationem:

If with your consent your son sold your estate, fraud from cunning or treachery should be argued, or fear of death or the threat of bodily injury should be disclosed in order that the sale should not be considered valid. But merely that which you indicate, namely that the estate was sold for a price a little low is invalid for the purpose of rescinding a sale. For if indeed you consider the essence of a contract of buying and selling, that the buyer wishing to buy cheaper and the seller to sell dearer approach this contract, and only after much contention, the seller subtracting from what he was asking and the buyer adding to what he was offering, they both consent to a certain price, you will see immediately that neither good faith, which protects contracts of purchase and sale will suffer, nor any other reason allow, a contract concluded by mutual agreement to be rescinded either immediately or afterwards on account of a dispute about the quantity of the price: unless less than half the price which was

nisi minus dimidia iusti pretii, quod fuerat tempore venditionis, datum est, electione iam emptori praestita servanda. D.K. Dec. AA. conss.

agreed upon at the time of the sale has (actually) been handed over (*datum*; paid). The choice of the manner of discharging the obligation is to be retained by the buyer.[12]

2 Impp. Diocletianus et Maximianus AA. Aurelio Lupo. Rem maioris pretii si tu vel pater tuus minoris pretii distraxit, humanum est, ut vel pretium te restituente emptoribus fundum venditum recipias auctoritate intercedente iudicis, vel, si emptor elegerit, quod deest iusto pretio recipies. minus autem pretium esse videtur, si nec dimidia pars veri pretii soluta sit, PP. v k. Nov. Diocletiano A II et Aristobulo conss.

If you or your father sold something of a greater value for a lesser price, it is humane that, with the authority of the judge intervening, having refunded the price to the buyer, you receive the farm that you sold, or, if the buyer chooses, you receive what is lacking of the price. The price, however, seems to be defaulted if half the price has not been paid. (I.e., "handed over, paid over"—Lewis.)[13]

In this case "price" appears to signify simply the amount agreed upon.

Again it is stressed that the above interpretations are merely suggestions. It is possible (though not likely) that the meanings given are correct in one case and incorrect in the other. It can be shown, for example, that the word "*pretium*" is ambiguous and that its meaning changes even in the same paragraph. Most important is the degree of precision with which the word was actually used by the authors of the *Corpus*. *Pretium* has been precisely defined but the dictionary (Harper) also warns that this particular word was often used imprecisely even by the greatest of the Latin writers. In addition to the foregoing, questions of syntax might be raised.[14] But if the word "*solutum*" is used in the *Corpus* as it is defined in

12. C. 4, 44, 8.

13. C. 4, 44, 2.

14. See below pp. 31–32 for *pretium*. On the question of syntax: the "nisi ... datum est" clause is generally taken as modifying the force of the passages preceding it (specifically "neque ... rescindi"). But the rules of grammar would allow it to be taken as directly modifying the force of the passages following it (i.e., "electione ... servanda"). However, the word order that would render such an interpretation would be unusual and therefore the lengthy discussion required to indicate its implications will be foregone.

the *Corpus*, none of these difficulties can imply a significant alteration of the interpretation here suggested for the two passages.

The concept of *laesio enormis* does not seem to have entered into the western European legal systems of the early middle ages. It appears to have been cited first by Brachylogus at the beginning of the twelfth century in his study of the Roman law.[15] If the rule in Justinian's time was concerned with the collection of unpaid obligations, the medieval jurist altered it completely. It is quite clear that Brachylogus was interested in the amount for which goods were sold. For Justinian's "*nisi minus dimidia pretii . . . datum est*" and "*si nec dimidia veri pretii soluta sit,*" Brachylogus substitutes "*si quis rem dimidio iusti pretii vendiderit.*" The case is similar with the other early Romanists. Where the original version used *soluta*, these medieval renditions employ *vendidi* or *distracta*. This was the meaning accepted by those who followed, and even when they used the term "*soluta,*" the contexts make it clear that they understood the law as Brachylogus did.

If Justinian's rules applied only to minors, their scope was expanded to such a degree that what was the exception became the rule. There is no doubt that in Brachylogus' version all sellers are covered (*si quis . . . vendiderit*). Moreover, if *res* is to be understood in its most general sense, the law covers not only the sale of real estate, as seems to have been the case at Roman law, but rather all sales. It is reported that Bulgarus raised the question of whether restitution was to be made in a sale where the selling price was less than the just price but more than half of it. (The source in which Bulgarus is cited was composed in the latter part of the twelfth century.)[16] That question does not seem to have been raised again in the later writings of the legists. With one possible exception, there is no call for adjustment on a low price unless the price was less than one half of the just price.[17]

In the mid-twelfth century, the *Summa Trecensis* presented the *laesio enormis* in the same manner as Brachylogus. If anyone sells for less than one half of the just price, he is entitled to receive the difference between the selling price and the just price or, having returned the sale price to

15. *Corpus Legum sive Brachylogus Iuris Civilis . . .* , ed. E. Böcking (Berlin, 1829), Lib. III, Tit. 13 (10), pp. 98–99. "Illud etiam considerandum, quod, si quis rem minus dimidio justi pretii vendiderit, emptorem vel ad rem reddendam vel ad iustum pretium exsolvendum convenire poterit."

16. *Quaestiones Dominorum Bononiensium*, LXIX, ed. A. Gaudenzi, *Bibliotheca Iuridica Medii Aevi* (Bologna, 1892; rev. ed. 1914), I, 248: "Persuasione et dolo Titii alias non venturus fundum vendidi Seio, bona fide ementi, minus tamen iusto pretio habui, sed plus dimidio vendidi. Queritur si contra eum aliquam actionem habere possim."

17. See below, pp. 28–29.

the buyer, he can recover his property. The choice remains with the buyer.[18] At about that time the law was understood in that fashion by Rogerius[19] and by the author of the *Abbreviatio Codicis*.[20]

At that time Vacarius also presented the law in the same fashion.[21] But Vacarius appears to have sensed that the terminology of the Roman price laws needed clarification and he provided a set of definitions which foreshadowed, as it were, several lines along which these rules would change and develop.

> One price is the true (*verum*) price, another the common (*commune*) price and yet another the special (*singulare*) price. The true price is the price for which the item is sold. The common price is the price for which it can be sold to anyone. The special price is found when something is worth more to one than to others. Consider the slave who is an excellent craftsman and who was sold to one who is a craftsman. The slave is worth more to him than to another who is not a craftsman.[22]

In the middle of the century in a *summa* written in Provençal, the coverage of the law was extended once again. Not only was the seller to be protected when he sold too cheaply, but the buyer was to be reimbursed when he paid more than twice the true value (*si res fuit vendita ultra in duplum quam valeret*). In either case the uninjured party was to choose

18. *Summa Trecensis*, ed. H. Fitting (Berlin, 1894), Lib IV, Tit. 4, 41, 4 pp. 116–117: "Propter intollerabilem deceptionem res[c]inditur: veluti si minus dimidia iusti pretii distracta sit: tunc enim offitio iudicis res[c]inditur vel quod deest iusto pretio restituitur electione videlicet emptori concessa." The editor attributed this work to Irenerius but the attribution is now doubted. On this point see H. Kantorovicz, *Studies in the Glossators of the Roman Law* (Cambridge, 1938), pp. 33–34, where he describes the works of Irenerius; pp. 145–180, where he attributes the *Summa Trecensis* to Rogerius; and especially pp. 152–153, where he discusses other opinions on the identity of the author.

19. Rogerius, *Summa Codicis*, C. 4, 45, in Gaudenzi (ed.), *Bibliotheca*, I, 126: "Propter rei iniquitatem rescinditur venditio, ut puta: minus dimidia iusti pretii vendidit, nam per officium iudicis rescinditur venditio, data electione emptori utrum velit iustum pretium adimplere et rem retinere an restituto pretio rem restituere."

20. *Abbreviatio Codicis* (IV, 44), in Gaudenzi (ed.), *Bibliotheca*, I, 533: "De Rescindenda Venditionis. Minus pretium esse videtur, si nec dimidia pars iusti pretii fuerit soluta. eod, tit. 1. II.

"Substantia contractus emptionis et venditionis est quod emptor viliori comparandi, venditor cariori distrahendi votum gerentes ad hunc contractum accedant, eod. tit. 1. si voluntate (1.8)."

21. Vacarius, *The Liber Pauperum of Vacarius*, ed. F. de Zulueta (London, 1927), Lib. IV, Tit. 46, p. 153: " 'iudicio' Quia si minoris dimidio iusti pretii distracta sit res, venditi iudicio rescinditur emptio, nisi adimpleatur quod iusto deest pretio." *Ibid.*, Lib. IV, Tit. 42, p. 147: "minus pretium videri si nec dimidia pars fuerit soluta."

22. *Ibid.*, Lib. IV, Tit. 46, p. 150.

whether there was to be a return of the merchandise and the purchase price or a sum of money handed to the injured party to bring the selling price (up or down) to the just price. The Provençal *summa, Lo Codi,* containing this version of the *laesio enormis,* was translated into Latin by Richard Pisanus about a decade after its composition.[23]

The interpretation presented by *Lo Codi* was supported by "Hugo-Albericus," who wrote at the end of the twelfth century,[24] and by the author of the *Dissensiones Dominorum* in the thirteenth century.[25]

23. *Lo Codi,* In der Lateinische Ubersetzung Ricardus Pisanus; ed. H. Fitting (Halle, 1906), Lib. IV, Tit. 61, 5, p. 127. "Aliquando contigit quod venditio destruitur, quamvis non sit facta fraus: ut si res vendita est minus medietate quam valeret eo tempore quando fuit vendita. Similiter si res fuit vendita ultra in duplum quam valeret potest destrui vendicio si emptore hoc vult, eadem racione qua dictum est de vendicione." I have not been able to find a full edition of the Provençal version. It would seem that it was supposed to have been published in connection with the Latin edition, but that the project was never completed. Some parts of the Provençal version have been published, but not the section with which this paper is concerned.

24. *Distinctiones,* Collectio Senensis XXVIII, in Gaudenzi (ed.), *Bibliotheca,* II, 152. "Si dolus inest re ipsa, distinguendum est utrum equitate pacti possit tolerari an non, ut siquidem equitate pacti tolerari possit, non agatur, quia licet contrahentibus se naturaliter circumvenire. Si autem talis est deceptio que non possit tolerari equitate pacti, puta si emit plus duplo vel vendidit minus dimidio iusti pretii quod inequaliter factum est, in melius est reformandum; et ideo, proposita actione, ex contractu agetur ut sit in potestate emptoris, vel iustum pretium dare vel quod dedit recuperare, restituta re empta ut C de rescindenda venditione 1. rem maioris et 1 si voluntate [C. 4, 44, 2, and 8] et D de iure dotium si res [D. 23, 3, 12] et D si quid in fraudem patroni [D. 38, 5]," etc. A statement of the principle of the law can also be found in *Quaestiones Dominorum Bononiensium,* in Gaudenzi, *op. cit.,* I, 260, in relation to a specific case.

25. *Dissensiones Dominorum* . . . , ed. G. Haenel (Leipzig, 1834), No. 253, pp. 426–427: "De Resdindenda venditione [C. 4, 44] L. 2. Quando emtor enormiter laesus dicitur? Dissentiunt in C. de Rescind vend. [C. 4, 44.] L. 1 et L. 2 ubi dicitur, quod potest rescindere venditionem, si deceptus sit, etsi minus pretium habeat. 'Minus autem pretium esse videtur, si nec dimidia pars veri pretii soluta sit.' Unde dominus Azo dicit, quod idem sit in emtore, ut si quis rem, quae X valebat, emeret pro XVI, quod emtor, si voluerit, potest rescindere venditionem, quia deceptus est, ultra dimidiam iusti pretii; et hoc ita probat: verum et iustum pretium erat in X et deceptus est in VI, ergo ultra dimidiam iusti pretii, id est, ultra dimidiam X; nec Lex dicit, quod debeat esse deceptus in duplum, sed tantum in dimidiam iusti pretii, ut C. de Rescind. vend. [4, 44.] L.2, et L. Si voluntate tua (8.). Sed Pla. (Placentinus), Al. (Albericus) et M. (Martinus) et Alii Sapientes, dicunt contrarium et dicunt, quod non potest agere, nisis sit deceptus in duplum, et hoc ita probatur. Lex dicit, quod tunc potest rescindere venditionem, si non habet dimidiam iusti pretii. Hoc ita intelligi. si sit deceptus in duplum. Nam deceptus est in duplum, quia ipse venditor debuisset accepisse X et non accepit nisi quattuor. Unde deceptus est ultra duplum, quod debuisset accepisse. Per similitudinem et iste emtor, qui emit rem, quae valebat X, pro XVI, non est deceptus in duplum, nisi XX dedisset; unde non ei subvenitur et ita per consuetudinem adprobatur et ita probo sentiam Alb. (Alberici) et Aliorum."

But also presented in the *Dissensiones* is an interpretation with which its author does not agree—an interpretation, incidentally, which must be considered as broadening the scope of the law so as to include still more transactions. According to this latter interpretation, the seller is covered as before but the buyer is considered injured if he overpays by one half of the just price. Thus, if the just price is ten and the buyer has paid sixteen, a case of *laesio enormis* exists. Now, according to Hugolinus, the selling price must be twenty-one for a *laesio enormis* to have occurred. If this is so, the law, according to the new interpretation, is literally more comprehensive for (to use the same figure) the transaction at sixteen would not be included as an offense under a law which declares an offense at twenty-one. If, on the other hand, offense is declared at sixteen, both sales at sixteen and twenty-one would be included. Doubtless, there would be a great number of actual cases added by shifting the formula for determining the maximum lawful price from two times the just price to 1.5 times the just price. Thus the scope of the law has once more been expanded and the margin for divergence from the just price once more contracted.

Placentinus may have been the first to argue that the buyer had sustained a *laesio enormis* if the selling price was more than half again the just price.[26] Like him, the great Romanists of the thirteenth century, Azo,[27]

26. Petrus Placentinus, *Summa Codicis* (Mainz, 1536), 4, 44, p. 176: "De Rescinda Venditione . . . Iudicis officio venditio rescinditur, puta si venditor ultra dimidio iusti pretii deceptus fuerit. Iusti inquam, tempore venditionis: deceptus, inquam, non per emptoris dolositate[m], sed re ipsa, rescinditur autem iniquitas ista electione emptori praebita, velit ne iustum pretium supplere, et rem retinere: veluti rem restituere, et pretium iniustum a se praestitum recuperare, ut C. eo l.ii [C. 4, 44, 2]. fit et econtrario id est, si emptor ultra dimidiam iusti pretii numeravit, ut C eo l. Solu. mat. si circumscripta [C. 5, 18, 6]." Some difficulty has arisen concerning the proper interpretation of Placentinus' judgment. According to the *Dissensiones* he said that *laesio enormis* occurred when the buyer paid more than double the just price. (See above p. 20 n. 25.) Baldwin ("Medieval Theories," pp. 22–23) says that Placentinus did not expressly maintain that the buyer was to be covered at all. The *Dissensiones* also named Martinus and Albericus as favoring the *duplum*, and Azo favoring the *dimidia*, in regard to the buyer. *Contrario* can be misleading.

27. Azo, *Summa Azonis* (Venice, 1566), 4, 44, 2, col. 417: "Ubi autem decipitur quis re ipsa, non alterius proposito, tenet venditio: sed deceptus ultra dimidiā iusti precii, quod erat tempore venditionis, agit ut non decipiatur ut j eo l ii et l. si voluntate [C. 4, 44, 2 and 8]."

Azo, *Commentarius Azonis* (Lyon, 1596), 4, 44, 2, pp. 508–509: "Rem maioris, Humanum est etc. Ideo dicit, quia aliud est de iure communi, cum liceat contrahentibus naturaliter (se circumuenire): ut D[igestum] de minoribus in causae penult. [D. 4, 4, 16, 4] vel dic, quod contrahentibus licitum est se decipere. non tamen tantum quantum hic dicit. Si ultra dimidia iusti pretii . . . . Vel si emptor elegerit. Habet ergo emptor qui non deceptus est, electionem, suppleat pretium, vel rem restituat . . . . Et ita est cum res valebat XI et ego vendidi V. quia non accepi dimidiam iusti pretii, sed

Accursius,[28] and Odofredus,[29] understood the law to cover both buyer and seller. For both parties the *dimidia* was used in the calculation. An article worth ten might not be sold for more than fifteen nor less than five. If it were, the uninjured party was given a choice. Either the goods would go back to the seller and the purchase price to the buyer or the injured party would receive a sum of money. If the buyer had suffered the *laesio enormis*

pone, e co[n]verso, quod emptor fuit deceptus, et voluerunt quidam ita ponere exemplum, quia si res valebat X et ego vendidi pro XX non decipior ultra dimidiam iusti pretii. Secus si pro XXI. nos non ita. nec enim hic decipitur ultra pretium, sed ultra dimidiam iusti pretii. Si ergo iustum pretium rei erat X et tu dedisti XV non est deceptus ultra dimidiam iusti pretii: secus si XVI quia V erat dimidia iusti pretii, et tu dedisti V ultra quam valeret et plus." See below p. 46 n. 20.

Azo may have altered another rule contained in this section (C. 4, 44) in order to maintain consistency in the use of *laesio enormis*. On the other hand, the employment of the word *paulo* in the Roman text may show that he has caught its real intent. C. 4, 44, 15: "Quisquis maior aetate praedia etiam procul posita distraxerit, paulo vilioris pretii nomine repetitionis rei venditae copiam minime consequatur." Azo says of this passage (*Commentarius*. 4, 44, 14 [*sic*], Quisquis maior): "Paulo vilioris pretii. Secus enim si deceptus esset ultra dimidiam."

28. Accursius, *Corpus iuris civilis Iustiniani: cum Commentariis Accursii* . . . (Paris,1576), C. 4, 44, 2, Vol. IV, cols. 919–920: "Rem. Si rem quae c. valebat. pro xl vendidisti: an rescindere possis venditionem, quaeritur? Respond[eo] quod de rigore iuris, non. de aequitate. sic. refuso pretio quod accepisti: ita tamen ut emptor eligat velit solvere iustum pretium et habere rem: vel rem restituere refuso sibi precio quod dedit, quod quando sit minus preciu[m], in si. dicit: illud scilicet quod est minus dimidia iusti precii. h. Humanum est Secus de rigore iuris, cum licuit contrahentibus sese decipere: ut D[igestum] de mino. 1. in causa ii penul. [D. 4, 4, 16, 4]. Sed ille rigor mitigatur cum est immensa deceptio: sicut & quando inest dolus.

"Sed quae est haec dimidia? Dic in emptore decepto: si res valet dece[m], emit pro xvi. licet alii dicant, emit pro xxi, quod non placet: quia tu[n]c non dimidia[m] iusti precii, sed duplu[m] egreditur. In ve[n]ditore: sicut res valet dece[m], ve[n]didit pro quattor. Et probantur haec fi. huius .1. [C. 4, 44, 2] & infra ea. 1. si voluntate. [C. 4, 44, 8] & infra si ma. [C. 4, 44, 13] . . . ." C. 4, 44, 8, Vol. IV, cols. 922–923: "Si voluntate. . . . quia non est rescindenda venditio propter parvum pretium: quia hoc consueverunt facere emptores, cum venditores primo offerunt vendere magno precio: & emptores offerunt parvam quantitate[m] & postea maiorem, et vendentes detrahunt de eo quod petierant, & ita contendunt invicem, & postea consentiunt: & sic propter exiguitatem precii non poterit rescindi venditio, nisi probes filiu[m] tuum deceptum ultra dimidiam iusti precii."

29. Odofredus, *Lectura Codicis* (Lyon, 1552), 4, 44, 2, quoted by Baldwin, "Medieval Theories," p. 27 n. 59: "Sed laesio est immoderata, licet rigor iuris non patiatur rescindi hanc venditionem, quia licitum est uniquique ab initio contrahere vel non contrahere . . . et quia licitum est contrahentibus invicem se precio decipere: equitas tamen suadet, ut si deceptio est ultra dimidiam iusti precii, quod venditio rescindatur vel suppleatur iustum precium."

he received a refund, bringing the selling price down to the just price. If the seller were the aggrieved, he received a supplementary payment, bringing the selling price up to the just price.

The argument against Azo's mode of assessing the *laesio enormis* was probably based on the employment of the ratio of two to one for both buyer and seller. If a seller sold goods worth ten at the price of four, he had been deceived by more than double (*ultra duplum*) since he should have received ten and he only took four.[30] Thus, it is reasoned, that one who bought that same object for sixteen would not have been deceived by more than double. Such deception would not take place until the price reached twenty-one. Azo, on the other hand, adhered to the word "*dimidia*." The man who purchased at twenty-one had not merely paid beyond half the just price but beyond the just price itself (i.e., beyond the whole price, *ultra pretium*). But deception took place beyond half the just price (*ultra dimidiam iusti pretii*). Since five was half the just price, deception would take place at sixteen. Accursius argued similarly and rejected the view which calculated with *duplum*. Twenty-one was not half, he said, but double. (*Alii dicant emit pro XXI quod non placet, quia tunc non dimidia iusti precii sed duplum egreditur.*)[31] Odofredus called upon the reasoning and authority of Azo in arriving at the same conclusion.[32] He also offered a pragmatic justification for his choice. The law will afford wider protection; much trickery will be avoided.

In connection with *laesio enormis*, another principle of Roman law is often mentioned—a principle which has been called "freedom of bargaining."[33] It is not usually present, at least in this context, in the earlier works of the twelfth century such as Brachylogus, Bulgarus, and Vacarius, nor is it in the *Summa Trecensis*, *Lo Codi*, or Rogerius' *Summa Codicis*. In the latter half of the century, however, and in the thirteenth century, it received a good deal more attention.

The principle of law, as mentioned above, gave both parties to a sale

30. See above, p. 20 n. 25.
31. See above, p. 22 n. 28.
32. Odofredus, *loc. cit.*, cited by Baldwin, "Medieval Theories," p. 23 n. 23: "Sed si vultis exemplificare in emptore decepto ultra dimidiam iusti precii exemplificabitis ita secundum Azo. Rem valentem X emptor emit pro XVI. quia iste emptor deceptus est ultra dimidiam iusti precii, poterit agere ut res empta recipiatur. Alii autem volunt exemplificare in emptore decepto ultra dimidiam iusti precii, sic. Si rem valentem X emptor emit pro XXI sol. Quod non placet: quia in tali exemplo dicitur decipi emptor in duplum, non in dimidiam iusti precii. Ex quo colligetis istud not. quod nimis capito evitatur."
33. By Baldwin, "Medieval Theories," p. 21.

the right to obtain for themselves the most advantageous terms (e.g., *in pretio emptionis et venditionis naturaliter licere contrahentibus se circumvenire*, D. 4, 4, 16, 4). It should be stated immediately that the introduction of the principle of freedom of bargaining to the considerations of *laesio enormis* did not cause the jurists to alter the rules of *laesio enormis*. Although the principle of freedom to bargain may seem in some sense to contradict the restraint imposed by *laesio enormis*, no one used it for that purpose. It was, moreover, present in the writings of those who set the buyer's protection by *dimidia* as well as those who set it by *duplum*.

Although the raising of the question of freedom of bargaining produced no effect on the rules of *laesio enormis*, it seems that the conjunction of the two principles was viewed somewhat differently in the twelfth century than in the thirteenth. In the twelfth century the *laesio enormis* seems to have been regarded as a frame within which legal free bargaining existed —a set of limits within which the freedom of bargaining might take place.

Thus the twelfth-century *Abbreviatio Codicis*,[34] like the *Corpus* itself, described the "fundamental essence" of a sales contract as an agreement made between a vendor who wished to sell high and a purchaser who wished to buy low, the two bargaining till at last they reached an agreement.[35] But the writer added, the price was too low if it was not at least half the just price.[36] In the *Quaestiones dominorum Bononensium* deception (*decipere*) is also declared legal if it is not intolerable, that is beyond half the just price. The case was the same in the *Distinctiones*.[37]

The thirteenth-century Romanists did not change the law or its consequences but they did see and articulate some element of contradiction between the conjoined principles of *laesio enormis* and freedom of bargaining. Thus Azo says the words "*humanum est*" are included in the law of *laesio enormis* because the *ius commune* offers a different principle, specifically, that the contracting parties may deceive each other. But this law, he says, shall not be allowed to operate as it stands. The doctrine of *laesio enormis* shall prevent the full implication of it.[38]

34. See above, p. 19 n. 20.

35. This translation of *substantia* may be found in Sir William Smith, *A Latin-English Dictionary* (London, 1926).

36. *Quaestiones Dominorum Bononensium*, CXXXVIII, in Gaudenzi (ed.), *Bibliotheca*, I, 260: "permissum esse contrahentibus inter se decipere non ex proposito, si tamen deceptio intolerabilis non sit, id est ultra dimidiam iusti pretii."

37. See above, p. 20 n. 24.

38. Azo, *Commentarius*, 4, 44, 2, p. 508: "Rem maioris. Humanum est. etc. Ideo dicit, quia aliud est de iure communi, cum liceat contrahentibus naturaliter: ut

Accursius also speaks of contradicting laws but uses other terms. "Can the sale for forty of an article worth 100 be rescinded?" he asks. "According to the rigor of the law," he answers, "No" (*quod de rigore iuris, non*); "according to equity, yes" (*de aequitate, sic*). "According to the rigor of the law," he continues, "the contracting parties may deceive each other, but in cases of great deception, the rigor is mitigated" (*de rigore iuris, cum licuit contrahentibus sese decipere . . . sed ille rigor mitigatur* etc., C. 4, 44, 2).

Odofredus in his *Lectura Codicis* presented the problem in a fashion quite usual in the twelfth century; deception is legal if the *laesio* is moderate.

To present this matter of the joining of the doctrines of *laesio* and freedom of bargaining as if it were a crucial issue would be quite misleading. The law is unchanged. In one view, however, it is presented as a single principle which includes a set of limits; in the other, as two laws, one of which is, so to speak, imposed upon the other.

The canonists followed the Romanists in the adaptation of *laesio enormis*. The first expression of the principle was made by Alexander III in the decretal *Quum Dilecti* issued sometime between 1159 and 1181.[39] It concerned a particular sale transacted between two clerical bodies. A wood which had been sold by the canons of Beauvais to the abbey of Chaalis was judged by the bishop of Arras to have been purchased for less than one half of the just price (*minus dimidia iusti pretii comparassent*). A bishop had already judged the case and had declared that the land should be returned to the canons. The pope in part upheld and in part rejected the judgment of the bishop. He allowed that the sale could not hold as originally made but the bishop's decision, he declared, was incorrect. The wood need not necessarily have been returned. The buyer had a choice. He could return the property and obtain a refund of the purchase price or he might pay what was lacking of the just price.[40] *Quum Dilecti* was

D[igestum]. de minoribus in causae penult [D. 4, 4, 16, 4] vel dic, quod contrahentibus licitum est se decipere. non tamen tantum quantum hic dicit. si ultra dimidia[m] iusti pretii." "*Ius commune*": the general law common to all, the law which is binding on all peoples or all Roman citizens. See A. Berger, *Encyclopedic Dictionary of Roman Law* (*Transactions of the American Philosophical Society*, N.S. XLIII, Part 2 [Philadelphia, 1953]).

39. Baldwin, however, quotes a canonist who may have been earlier, namely, Johannes Faventinus *ca.* 1171: "Non potest venditionem rescindere. nisi forte minus duplo emisset quam iustum esse pretium deberet." *Summa*, Paris Bibl. Nat. Lat. 14606, fol. 140. Causa XIX, q. 1, pr., in Baldwin, "Medieval Theories," pp. 44–45 n. 14.

40. Gregory IX, *Decretals*, III, 17, c. 3, *Corpus Iuris Canonici*, ed. E. Friedberg (Leipzig, 1879) (cited hereafter as *C.I.C.*), Vol. II, cols. 518–519. See also P. Jaffe and W. Wattenbach, *Regesta Pontificum Romanorum* (Leipzig, 1885–88), Vol. II, No. 13749.

included in Bernard Baldi of Pavia's compilation (*Compilatio Prima*)[41] in 1191 and in 1234 was incorporated into the *Decretals* of Gregory IX.[42] This first pronouncement of *laesio enormis* by the highest church authority was in close conformity with the recently developed Romanist construction of that law. The injured party was the seller; the damages involved more than half. (The term "*laesio enormis*," incidentally, was not actually employed.)

In the second pontifical expression of this law, the term "*laesio enormis*" was used but the pope's ruling was rather less standard. The decretal *Ad nostram noveritis* did not concern a sale but rather an enfeoffment. A monastery had granted an estate in fief to a layman. The layman to whom the fief had been granted was to pay a mortgage on it of eighty pounds. It was discovered, however, that the layman was drawing eighty or more pounds per year from the fief. The pope declared that the monastery had suffered a *laesio enormis* (*enormiter in hoc laesum*). He commanded, therefore, that the revenue received thus far was to be considered ample recompense for the layman's payment of the mortgage and that the fief was to be returned to the monastery free and clear.[43] Peter Beneventanus entered *Ad nostram noveritis* into the *Compilatio Tertia*,[44] and Raymond of Penaforte set it into the *Decretals* which he compiled for Gregory IX.[45]

Unlike *Ad nostram noveritis*, in which the uninjured party was not granted the opportunity of making a supplementary payment and retaining the property,[46] the third decretal, *Quum Causa*, offered these standard alternatives. In the case involved, a monastery had sold properties to two laymen. The price was found to be less than half the just price. The decretal[47] ordered that the purchase price was to be refunded and the

41. *Quinque Compilationes Antiquae*, ed. A. Friedberg (Leipzig, 1882). *Compilatio I*, III, 15, c. 4, p. 31.

42. Gregory IX, *Decretals*, *loc. cit.*

43. Innocent III, *Regesta*, Lib. IX, c. 56, in *P.L.*, CCXV, cols. 868–869.

44. *Compilatio III*, III, 13, c. 2, p. 122.

45. Gregory IX, *Decretals*, III, 13, c. 11, *C.I.C.*, Vol. II, cols. 515–516. (In A. Potthast, *Regesta Pontificum Romanorum* [Berlin, 1874–75], Vol. I, 2729.)

46. It should be stressed, however, that *Ad nostram noveretis* was not concerned with a regular sale.

47. There were, in fact, two letters. The first (*Ne causa*) acknowledged the receipt of the complaint and described the rule of law which would be applied, this being the standard principle of *laesio enormis*. See Innocent III, *Regesta*, Lib. X, c. 145, in *P.L.*, CCXV, cols. 1243–1244. *Ne causa* does not appear in later compilations. The final judgment of the case appeared in the second letter, *Quum Causa*, which repeated the rule of law stated in the first and mentioned also the nature of the testimony which was to be used for the final assessment needed to calculate the supplementary payment.

property returned or a sum was to be paid to the sellers which would bring the price up to the just price at the time of the sale.[48] The decretal *Quum Causa*, like *Ad nostram noveretis*, was entered in the *Compilatio Tertia*[49] and like both *Ad nostram noveretis* and *Quum Dilecti* can be found in the *Decretals*.[50]

The earliest of these decretals comes well after the medieval students of Roman law first put forth their conception of *laesio enormis*. The Romanists understood the law to allow rescission of sales made by responsible agents at extraordinarily low prices (which may not have been the case in the Roman era),[51] and it was in the medieval sense that the popes understood it. It seems quite accurate, therefore, to point to the twelfth-century Romanists as the source from which the church drew in promulgating these decretals.

The three decretals were concerned with protecting the vendor only. Church law was slow in extending the *laesio* principle to the buyer. The first very tentative suggestion of such a possibility was made by Bernard of Pavia nearly a half-century after it was first put forth in medieval Roman law. "Perhaps," he said, after a positive explication of the protection which *laesio enormis* offers to the seller, "Perhaps the same may be said for a buyer deceived by more than half"[52] (*forte idem dici poterit e contrario de emtore ultra dimidiam decepto*). Shortly afterward, Vincentius Hispanus, commenting on *Quum Causa*, also suggested this possibility.[53]

The canonists do not seem at any time to have supported the interpretation which maintains that the buyer must have paid more than double the just price before he has recourse to the law. Bernard Botone shows how the seller is covered and then, citing Azo in a full and clear statement,

48. Innocent III, *Regesta*, Lib. X, c. 162, in *P.L.*, CCXV, cols. 1255–1256.

49. *Compilatio III*, III, 14, c. 2, p. 122.

50. It is split into two parts in Gregory IX, *Decretals*, III, 17, c. 6, and II, 20, c. 42, *C.I.C.*, Vol. II, col. 520, col. 333.

51. See above pp. 13–18.

52. Bernard Papiensis, *Summa Decretalium*, ed. E. A. T. Laspeyres (Ratisbon, 1860), Lib. III, Tit. XV, No. 6, p. 82: "Illud in summa notandum, quod si venditor deceptus sit ultra dimidiam iusti pretii et de ipsa deceptione queratur, in potestate emtoris est vel iustum pretium supplere vel rescindere venditionem ut infra eod c ult. (Gr. c.3 III, 12 et Cod de rescind vend L ult); forte idem dici poterit e contrario de emtore ultra dimidiam decepto."

53. Vincentius Hispanus, *Apparatus to Compilatio III*, Paris Bibl. Nat. Lat. 14611, fol. 93rb, III, 14, c 2. "Quum causa. deceptum. Quid si cives [i.e., the buyers] sint decepti ultra dimidiam in pretia agant. ut refundatur eis de pretio. ut solvatur contractus." Cited by Baldwin "Medieval Theories," p. 44 n. 14.

maintains that a *laesio enormis* had been suffered when the buyer paid more than one and one-half times the just price.[54] Hostiensis citing Azo supported this interpretation twice,[55] and it has been maintained,[56] perhaps correctly, that it was put forth in these terms by Innocent IV.[57]

It is difficult to state with certainty that Innocent was concerned with protecting the buyer. The wording of what seems to be the key passage is a

54. Bernard Botone of Parma, *Glossa Ordinaria* to the *Decretales, d[omi]ni pape Gregorii noni* (Paris, 1507), III, 17, c. 6, fol. ccix: "Ad nostram noveris. dimidiam. Istud sic est intelligendum: ecce, res valet decem vendidisti illa[m] pro q[ua]ttor: patet q[uod] tu es deceptus in sex: sed su[n]t plus q[uam] dimidia iusti pretii, q[uo]d est quinque, & ita est deceptus in dimidia, q[uae] est qu[i]nq[ue] & plus, s[cili]c[et] uno; sufficit si illud plus valet unu[m] bo[logni]nu[m] tm̄ & hoc intellige in venditore q[ui] decipit in pretio, Et sic etia[m] in emptore decepto pone q[uod] res valeat dece[m] & emptor soluit sexdecim, pot[est] age[re] ad p[re]tiu[m] recipie[n]du[m] q[uo]d plus dedit, vel in totu[m] recedere a con[trac]tu: q[uod] sic p[a]tet, q[ui] e[st] deceptus ultra dimidia[m] iusti pretii. soluit em[ptor] sex ultra dimidia[m] iusti pretii, q[uod] fuit decem. Si enim deciperet[ur] in q[ui]nq[ue] tantu[m] no[n] ageret[ur]; q[uia] q[ui]nq[ue] sunt dimidia decem. & ita non est decept[us] emptor in aliquo ultra dimidia[m] iusti pretii. sed q[uia] sex dedit, ultra dimidiam decepti[s] est, ideo aget. Azo. intelligit ista verba ita. Alii dicu[n]t q[uod]necessariu[m] est ut duplu[m] iusti pretii & ultra dederit emptor: ut ecce, res valet decem, et ego emi pro viginti unum, q[uo]d nulla lex dicit: & nihil est quod dicu[nt]: q[uia] hic decipit[ur] emptor in plus qu[am] sit totu[m] iustu[m] pretiu[m], sed primu[m] verius est."

55. Henricus Hostiensis de Segusio, *Summa Aurea* (Lyon, 1537), III, 17, c. 7, fol. 149: "Si in pretio quis deceptus sit non ex proposito contrahentis: si quide[m] ultra dimidia[m] iusti pretii agit deceptus et restituatur scilicet q[uod] rescindat[ur] co[n]tractus: ut suppleat[ur] iustu[m] pretium data elec[tione] decipienti. C. de rescin. vendi. [C. 4, 44, 2] sm Azo. Sed certe l[ex] illa dicit q[uod] electio est emptoris q[ua]n[do] minus dimidia iusti pretii co[m]parat[ur]. j eo cū causam [See above p. 25 n. 40 and p. 27 n. 48.] ergo a contrario si ultra dimidia[m] iusti pretii ut si emptor deceptus sit dabitur electio venditori sicut intellegit Azo. Emit[ur] aut[em] res minus justi pretii si res valet .X. ve[n]dit[ur] p[ro] .V minus uno denario. Sic decipit ve[n]ditor sed si valet .X. emat[ur] p[ro] XV uno denario deceptio est ultra dimidia iusti p[re]tii. Sic decipit[ur] emptor s[ecundu]m Azo. Alii dicu[n]t q[uod] tu[n]c sit deceptio ultra dimidiam iusti p[re]tii q[ua]n[do] res q[uae] valet .X. emit[ur] .XXI. sed s[e]n[tent]ia Azo verior est. . . . "

56. See Baldwin, "Medieval Theories," p. 45 n. 18. He also cites Hostiensis' four-volume *Decretalium Librum Commentaria* (Venice, 1581), III, 17, c. 6, Vol. III, fol. 58[vb]. Quum Causa. dimidiam, a work very difficult to locate.

57. Innocent IV, *Apparatus super Quinque Libris Decretalium* (Strassburg, 1478), III, 17, c. 6, p. e33. "Qum causa [see above p. 27 n. 48] recipio +C+ de rei ven +1+ ii [C. 4, 44, 2] Restituerent+cum quis descipitur ultra dimidiam iusti precii agi potest ut vel rescindatur contractus v[el] ut suppleatur p[re]cium actione ex contractu . . . Est autem decept[us] ultra dimidiam[m] +qui rem valentem +x+ dedit p[ro] quattor.+ dicunt q[uo]d eciam qui rem valentem septem dedit p[ro] quattor." Cf. above p. 18 and n. 16.

bit unusual: "*Est autem decept*[*us*] *ultra dimidiam* + *qui rem valentem* + *X* + *dedit p*[*ro*] *quattor* + *Alii* + *dicunt q*[*uod*] *eciam qui rem valentem septem dedit pro quator.*"

To consider this passage as concerned with the protection of the buyer, it would have to be translated: "He is deceived beyond half who pays (*dedit*) ten for a thing instead of (*pro*) four; others say, it is who pays seven for a thing instead of (*pro*) four." This rendition corresponds with the usual interpretations of *laesio enormis* but it does not match the text too well. For example, *pro* can indeed be translated "instead of" but in price laws it generally means "for." And what would "*valentem*" mean? There are other difficulties with a "buyer's interpretation." It seems rather better to translate it: "He is deceived beyond half who gives (sells, *dedit*) a thing worth ten for four; others say it is he who gives (sells) a thing worth seven for four." With the latter translation, concern would be for the seller. If this is the case, he is speaking of an unusual mode of calculation. The *dimidia*, instead of being one-half the just price, is one-half the selling price. Thus if the sum of the selling price plus one-half the selling price falls short of the just price, a *laesio enormis* exists. The selling price was four. One half of four is two and two plus four equals six, but the just price was seven and so a *laesio enormis* has been inflicted. By the older method (the first of the two cited by Innocent), the *dimidia* is applied to the just price and with a just price of ten, the legal minimum would be five. By the second method described by Innocent, a just price of ten would render a legal minimum of 6.67. Thus what seems to be a tendency to narrow the divergence allowed from the just price apparently continues. The first medieval expressions of the *laesio enormis* were concerned only with minimum prices but soon both *maxima* and *minima* were provided. For goods valued at ten the maximum of sixteen generally prevailed over the maximum of twenty-one. Here Innocent may have substituted for a minimum of five a minimum of 6.67.

Of the legists of the twelfth and thirteenth century about a dozen Romanists, including the most prominent of them, and an equal number of canonists, including five popes, have been cited—all of whom declared the principle that a 50 per cent divergence from the just price is to be allowed. It certainly seems incorrect, therefore, to maintain that the principle of *laesio enormis* originated in the fifteenth century or that it introduced a "new elasticity" or that it stems from a set of ideas expounded in the middle of the fourteenth century which were the "natural outcome of the intense economic activity of the later Middle Ages."[58]

---

58. R. Tawney, *Religion and the Rise of Capitalism* (New York, 1926), pp. 42–43.

After Accursius raised and answered the question of how to calculate half the just price, he posed a question more fundamental: "How should one calculate the just price?" As part of his answer, he cited a passage which appears twice in Justinian's Digest, once in *Ad Legem Aquiliam* and once in *Ad Legem Falcidiam*.[59]

> The prices (values) of things are not to be calculated from the sentiment or interests of individuals, but by the general view (commonly).
> ... pretia rerum non ex affectione nec utilitate singulorum, sed communiter fungi ....
> Pretia rerum non ex affectu nec utilitate singulorum, sed communiter funguntur (finguntur).

In a recent study this principle was held to forbid price discrimination and so it could be concluded that the medieval law was consistent with or

59. Accursius, *Commentariis*, C. 4, 44, 2, Vol. IV, col. 920: "Sed qualiter sciam quando excedit? Respon[deo] non per hoc q[uod] duo vel tres volunt tantu[m] dare, quoniam precia rerum non constituuntur ex adfectione singulorum: ut D[igestum] ad legem Falc[idiam] .l. precia et D[igestum] ad legem Aquil[iam] si servum meum." The passages in question are D. 9, 2, 33 and D. 35, 2, 63:

D. 9, 2, 33: "Paulus libro secundo ad Plautium. Si servum meum occidisti, non affectiones aestimandas esse puto, veluti si filium tuum naturalem quis occideret quem tu magno emptum velles, sed quanti omnibus valeret, Sextus quoque Pedius ait pretia rerum non ex affectione nec utilitate singulorum, sed communiter fungi: itaque eum, qui filium naturalem possidet, non eo locupletiorem esse, quod eum plurimo, si alius possideret, redempturus fuit, nec illum, qui filium alienum possideat, tantum habere, quanti eum patri vendere posset. in lege enim Aquilia damnum consequimur: et amisse dicemur, quod aut consequi potuimus aut erogare cogimur."

D. 35, 2, 63: "Paulus libro secundo ad legem Iuliam et Papiam. Pretia rerum non ex affectu nec utilitate singulorum sed communiter funguntur. nec enim qui filium naturalem possidet tanto locupletior est, quod eum, si alius possiderit, plurimo redempturus fuisset, sed nec ille, qui filium alienum possidet, tantum habet, quanti eum patri vendere potest, nec exspectandum est, dum vendat, sed in praesentia, non qua filius alicuius, sed qua homo aestimatur, eadem causa est eius servi, qui noxam nocuit; nec enim delinquendo quisque pretiosior fit, sed nec heredem post mortem testatoris institutum servum tanto pluris esse, quo pluris venire potest. Pedius scribit: est enim absurdum ipsum me meredem institutum non esse locupletiorem antequam adeam, si autem servus heres institutus sit, statim me locuplatiorem effectum, cum multis causis accidere possit, ne iussu nostro adeat: adquirit nobis certe cum adierit, esse autem praeposterum ante nos locupletes dici, quam adquisierimus, Cuius debitor solvendus non est, tantum habet in bonis, quantum exigere potest. Nonnullam tamen pretio varietatem loca temporaque adferunt: nec enim tantidem Romae et in Hispania oleum aestimabitur nec continuis sterilitatibus tantidem, quanti secundis fructibus, dum hic quoque non ex momentis temporum nec ex ea quae raro accidat caritate pretia constituantur."

even based upon the Roman law.[60] The present concern is with the meaning which the laws in question had at the time they were set into the Digest. It is possible that they were given a different meaning during the middle ages, in which case the identification of the real source of the law in the latter period might be different than it would be were the meaning identical in both periods. A close reading of the laws both independently and vis-à-vis each other and comparison of the two passages with other regulations in the *Corpus* seems in order.

The variant readings of the verb in D. 35, 2, 63 is of no great concern. *Finguntur* and *funguntur* can be translated, in effect, identically. *Finguntur* may be rendered "formed," "made," "supposed"; and "*funguntur*," given the meaning "done," "executed," "administered" as well as a definition for the word as it appears in one of the passages in question (D. 9, 2, 33): "are taken."

Pretia, on the other hand, will receive more than one meaning. It has been shown that the word has been used in the *Corpus* of Justinian to mean several things.[61] In the present context it seems to carry two meanings, the first being "selling price" and the second "value"—in the sense of assessed value (such as, to use modern examples, are made for purposes of taxation or to assess damages and which assessments might or might not match the current selling price). A single sentence in the same set in which the formula "*pretia rerum* etc." appears, provides an example.

> Nonnullam tamen pretio varietatem loca temporaque adferunt: nec enim tantidem Romae et in Hispania oleum aestimabitur nec continuis sterilitatibus tantidem, quanti secundis fructibus, dum hic quoque non ex momentis temporum nec ex ea quae raro accidat caritate pretia constituantur.[62]

Translating *pretia* as "selling price" throughout renders this passage either meaningless or causes it to forbid market fluctuations. (The examples having neither legal nor logical force are omitted so as to bring the two usages into sharp contrast.) "Sometimes places and times will bring a change in selling price . . . selling prices should not be determined from moments of time or from a rare dearness." If, on the other hand, *pretio* is translated as "selling price" and *pretia* as "(assessed) values,"

---

60. Baldwin, "Medieval Theories," p. 21.

61. P. Oertman, *Die Volkwirtschaftslehre des Corpus Juris Civilis* (Berlin, 1891), pp. 39 ff., and Baldwin, "Medieval Theories," p. 20. Satisfactory definitions are in Thayer, "Laesio Enormis," p. 322, and especially p. 332 n. 5.

62. D. 35, 2, 63 (2).

with no other alteration, the passage becomes quite meaningful. "Some-times places and times will bring a change in price ... (assessed) values should not be determined from moments of time nor from rare dearness." In other words, assessments, or rather estimations of value, should not be based on unusual fluctuations of the market.

The estimations are made for specific purposes. Both titles in their entirety (D. 35, 2 and 9, 2) are regulations for the administration of a certain pair of laws. For the cases with which these laws are concerned, assessments of property values for the purposes of a court settlement are necessary or even central. One of them, *Ad Legem Falcidiam* (35, 2), deals with the division of inheritance; the other, *Ad Legem Aquiliam* (9, 2), is concerned with the reparation of unlawful damages.

This fact is clearly indicated by the names of the title-sections—*Ad Legem Falcidiam* (35, 2), *Ad Legem Aquiliam* (9, 2). They are not collections of laws on certain general topics as are most of the sections—e.g., *de servitutibus, de adulteriis, de poenis militum*. The title-heading *De servitutibus* would mean, in effect, "the following is a group of laws concerned with the general topic of slavery," or literally "concerning slavery." *Ad Legem Falcidiam* means, in effect, "the following regulations were devised for the purposes of the *Lex Falcidia*." The rules apply not to cases but to a par-ticular law. The use of "*ad*" is not without meaning. It shows that the rules have been structured for a special purpose as "*ad hoc*," i.e., "for this special purpose" (Black's definition). In this case the *hoc* is the *Legem Falcidiam* and the contents of such a title cannot be laws which are gener-ally valid. If the *Lex Falcidia* is not being invoked, the regulations found under the heading *Ad Legem Falcidiam* are without force.

The areas to which the *Lex Falcidia* can be applied seem quite narrow and certainly do not appear to include the regulation of prices. The law, as it is quoted in the Digest, forthrightly declares its purpose: "After the passage of this law, any Roman citizen who draws up a will shall have the power and the right in accordance with the public law to bequeath as large a sum as he wishes to any other Roman citizen if the will is made in such a manner that his heirs will receive not less than one-fourth of the estate by that testament."[63]

Though such a law would not be concerned with regulating the prices for which property would be sold, it might well be concerned with the evaluation of property. An inheritance might be made up of certain properties not easily divisible, as would be the case if three men inherited

63. D. 35, 2, 1.

an estate which consisted of a single slave. It would then be necessary to set a value on such property so that a cash settlement might be made among the interested parties.

The estimation of values is an important concern of this title and other parts of the title provide a context quite consistent with interpreting the passage in question as being concerned with evaluation. The section contains a set of items which are to be deducted from or added to the total value of the estate.[64] Criteria for evaluation are presented in addition to the ones included in the section here being discussed. Thus is found, "Properties which are in the goods of the deceased are to be evaluated according to the truth of the matter, that is, according to the present price. Fixed or formulated prices are not to be used." [65] It is, in fact, this statement which is directly followed by the regulation in question: "The values of things are not to be calculated from the affection or utility of individuals but, rather, commonly. For a man who possesses his natural son is none the richer simply on the grounds that if someone else possessed his son, he would redeem him at a higher price than anyone else."

Nor do the regulations on calculation end here. Immediately following the statement in question, it is declared that not all market prices may be used for these calculations. The law recognizes that the market may fluctuate sharply at certain times and in certain places,[66] and these unusual extremes of prices may not be employed either.

It seems reasonable to conclude, therefore, both from its use of particular words and from the context into which they are set, that the statement in question does not tell how the proper and legal selling price of an item is to be determined, but rather is concerned with the manner in which its value is to be determined for the settling of a certain type of litigation.[67]

64. D. 35, 2, 39: "Aeris alieni loco deducantur non solum pretia eorum quibus libertas data est et eorum qui etc." See also D. 35, 2, 43; 62; and 69.

65. D. 35, 2, 62 (1): "Corpora si qua sunt in bonis defuncti secundum rei veritam aestimanda erunt, hoc est secundum praesens pretium: nec quiquam eorum formali pretio aestimandum esse sciendum est."

66. See quotes above, pp. 31–32.

67. This conclusion seems to be borne out by many studies in a sort of negative fashion. A number of works on Roman laws of sale have been examined and none of them mention the *Lex Falcidia* (or the *Lex Aquilia*) as part of that law. See G. Hanausek, *Die Haftung des Verkaufers* (Berlin, 1883); J. Mackintosh, *The Roman Law of Sale* (Edinburgh, 1907); J. B. Moyle, *Contracts of Sale in the Civil Law* (Oxford, 1892); V. Scialoja, *Compra, Vendita (Esegesi Tit. I, Lib. XVIII del Digesto) Lezioni Stenografate e Compilate dal Dott. G. Pulvirent.* Anno Accademico 1906–1907 (Rome, 1907); F. de Zulueta, *The Roman Law of Sale* (Oxford, 1945).

Indeed, one might even say in this particular case, it is not a matter in which the courts will determine selling prices or the law determine the mode of setting them, but rather that the market price is used to determine the decision of the court. In itself the statement in question does not demand the operation of a free and open market at all. It does, however, recognize the open market as extant (and apparently legal) and within certain limits[68] allows it to set a value on items for the purpose of the courts.

To show that the *Lex Aquilia* is concerned not with price discrimination but rather with the assessment of damages, it is necessary only to set the extracted passage back into context.

> If you kill my slave, I am of the opinion that my sentiments are not to be taken into account (as for example, if one kills your natural son for whom you would be willing to pay a high price), but only what he is worth to all. Sextus Pedius also agrees that *the value of property is to be reckoned not by the sentiment or interest of individuals, but by the average view* (*pretia rerum non ex affectione nec utilitate singulorum sed communiter fungi*); hence he who possesses his natural son is none the richer because he would buy him for a large price if another possessed him, nor does he who possesses another's son own as much as he could sell him for to his father. *In short under Lex Aquilia we recover our damages* (*in lege enim Aquilia damnum consequimur*); and we are held to have lost what we could have gained or what we are forced to expend.

That the law will employ the market price as it sees fit is shown by comparing the *Aquilia* and *Falcidia*. The formula which is found in the *Lex Falcidia* is practically identical to the form in the *Lex Aquilia* (*pretia rerum* etc.). Yet in the case of the *Lex Aquilia* the amount decided upon by the court may be different than it would have been were the same property being evaluated for the purposes of the *Lex Falcidia*. *Falcidia* uses the present market price (*secundum praesens pretium*); *Aquilia* uses the highest market price of the year (*quanti id in eo anno plurimi fuit*). The latter law says, "If anyone kills a male or female servant or a quadruped (a herd animal) by an unjust injury, he must pay damages equal to the highest amount that the creature was worth during the year."[69] Another passage states, "The law says 'the largest amount that the man was worth during the year': this clause refers to the assessment of damages which were inflicted." The rule then is quite clear. A market price is assumed to exist

---

68. Reference is made to D. 35, 2, 63, (2).
69. D. 9, 2, 2; D. 9, 2, 21.

and is applied in a manner that suits the court. But the law does not seem to have any concern about regulating the price involved in the transfer of goods by sale.

That the law is determined to use the market price and none other is also evident. By "the highest amount the creature was worth during the year" is not meant some unusually high price that an individual in desperate circumstances may have paid for a badly needed object to one either not anxious to sell or determined to take advantage. On this point the law insists (see above p. 34).

Thus, for the *Lex Aquilia* as for the *Lex Falcidia* a (fluctuating) market price is taken as extant, but the law does not seek to establish its legitimacy or to make it mandatory. The texts seem to show that the courts were to use it to settle wills and award damages, in the one case using the present and the other the year's highest market price. It seems reasonable to conclude that the purpose of the formulation (*pretia rerum* etc.) was not to end price discrimination or to establish a legal selling price.

Evaluation of property in the Roman law is not peculiar to the *Lex Aquilia* and *Lex Falcidia*. Scattered throughout Justinian's *Corpus* are many regulations describing the proper mode of ascertaining the value of property.[70] In addition to the evaluations made for damages and the division of estates, are those made for the purpose of dividing property commonly held,[71] estimating the value of jettisoned cargo and other purposes as well. There are a number of "formulae" stating the criteria for these values and the manner in which they are to be obtained.

One of these formulae is "*quanti venire possunt*." (How much [the articles] can be sold for.) It appears three times in portions of the *Lex Falcidia* not considered above.[72] It is also used to evaluate the liability of the master for certain types of purchases made for him by his slaves. It is employed too for certain of the assessments made for proportional distribution of the losses incurred when cargo must be jettisoned at sea in order to save the ship.[73]

This formula, then, like the one discussed above (*pretia rerum* etc.), is used to assess a value for certain types of settlements. In this sense, all these rules concerning value assessments may be called consistent in that

---

70. The most adequate treatment of the subject, perhaps, is that of N. Mathews, "The Valuation of Property in the Roman Law," *Harvard Law Review*, XXXIV (1921), 227–259.

71. D. 10, 3.

72. D. 35, 2, 55. See also D. 35, 2, 45, 1, and D. 35, 2, 73, 1.

73. E.g., D. 15, 3, 5; D. 14, 2, 2 (4).

they govern awards made by the courts and in that none of them regulate the prices at which real estate or merchandise must be sold.

III. THE FRANKISH LINE

The earliest Frankish pronouncement which may perhaps be classified as a price regulation was issued during the reign of Pippin. On March 2, 744, a capitulary declared that the market of each city was to fashion its measures according to the abundance of the time. (*Et per omnes civitatis legitimus forus et mensuras faciat secundum habundantia temporis.*)[1] This brief notice may imply that a standard price was set that was not to be changed. The necessary adjustment to low or high yields would be made by altering the quantity received rather than the amount paid; for example, in times of shortage, the price of a loaf of bread would not be increased, rather would its size be decreased.

Early in the reign of Charlemagne a capitulary was issued concerning things sold for a price which was not just (*quod res venundasset et non iusto pretio*). Where this was the case the buyer and the seller were to come together along with estimators (*existimatores*) and the worth of the property was to be judged. If the price was ruled just, the sale was to stand; if not, the money was to be refunded and the property returned to its former owner. (Improvements made by the buyer might be removed by him or a settlement made between him and the seller.)

This law probably did not have general force. It seems to refer solely to Italy and to that place only at a certain time, that is, immediately after the Frankish invasion. For the value which is to be set upon the lands is that which they were worth, in good condition, before the Frankish invasion (*sicut tunc valebant quando res ipsae bene restaurantae fuerunt, antequam nos hic cum exercitu introissemus*). Moreover, the seller had to show, not only that he did not obtain a just price (*iusto pretio*), but that the sale was the alternative to starvation (*strictus necessitate famis venditionem fecisset*). This particular piece of legislation is in fact one of a set of four *capitulae* which refer rather pointedly to an emergency situation. Contracts by which men sold themselves or their wives and children into slavery are declared invalid. Other types of transactions are suspended pending further judgment. The phrase "*strictus necessitate famis*" appears more than once.[2]

---

1. A. Boretius and V. Kraus (eds.), *Capitularia Regum Francorum* (cited hereafter as *Capitularia*), M.G.H., *Legum*, Sec. II (Hanover, 1883), Vol. I, p. 30, No. 12, chap. 6.
2. *Ibid.*, Vol. I, pp. 187–188, No. 88, pr. et 2.

There is in the Carolingian legislation a general rule concerning price and famine. It was promulgated in 805 and is addressed to all (*ad omnes generaliter*). In case of famine, it is declared, no one should wait for an edict but should pray immediately for God's aid. In the present dearth, it continues, each should aid to the best of his ability and should not sell his grain too dearly. No price is set and no penalty mentioned. Yet an imperial action is threatened that might well be effective both in preventing overcharging or ending it in areas where it might exist. The edict warns that in places where prices are too high, grain from the imperial stores will be sold. Doubtless such a threat would be meaningless in the face of general scarcity, but in scattered cases in which local shortages caused high prices, local sellers might moderate their prices somewhat rather than face the sudden entrance into their markets of large amounts of grain from imperial stores which might break or at least sharply reduce their local market prices.[3]

Not all of the Carolingian pronouncements on price were so general. On a number of occasions laws were promulgated which set specific prices. The first of these (or the first still extant) was promulgated by Charlemagne and reissued by the Council of Frankfurt in 794. It was declared that the prices listed in it were to be held to both in times of plenty and of scarcity (*sive in tempore abundantiae sive tempore caritatis*). All prices were by the "measure"—a standard quantity recently established (*modium publicum noviter statutum*). Oats were set at one denarius per modium, rice at two, rye at three, wheat at four. Prices were also established for bread.

Another set of prices for grain, considerably lower than the first, is also included in the law. These were the prices, the capitulary announced, that would be for the public stores of the king if they were put up for sale. Two measures of oats would be sold for one denarius, a measure of rice for one, of rye for two, of wheat for three.[4]

About a decade later during a year (806) described in the capitulary as one of dearth, the schedule of prices was revised. It appears that the alterations in the schedule were valid for the year of issue only. The price of oats was doubled, a measure being sold for two denarii. Rice was raised to three, rye to four, and wheat to six.[5] The purpose of the higher ceilings,

3. *Ibid.*, Vol. I, pp. 122–123, No. 44, chap. 4.
4. A. Werminghoff (ed.), *Concilia Aevi Karolini* (cited hereafter as *Concilia*), *M.G.H.*, *Legum*, Sec. III (Hanover and Leipzig, 1908), Vol. II, p. 166.
5. *Capitularia*, *M.G.H.*, *Legum*, Sec. II, Vol. I, p. 132, No. 46, chap. 18.

apparently, is to lure a certain amount of grain out of hiding and at the same time to prevent prices from rising too high.

Food was not the only article upon which specific prices were set. Price ceilings were published for articles of clothing. A double cape was to be sold for twenty solidi, a single for ten. Marten and otter capes might bring thirty solidi, sable, on the other hand, only ten.[6] A fine of forty solidi was to be levied on violators, both buyers and sellers. Anyone discovering and denouncing an offender would receive a reward of twenty solidi.

The capitulary on food prices of 806 reappeared during the reign of Louis the Pious. It was placed in the collection of capitularies composed by the Abbot Ansegius in about 827. The wording was altered to some extent and in its later form it seems less a special measure and more a piece of permanent legislation. The clause *praesente anno*, for example, is dropped. On the other hand, it was still described as a famine measure. The prices are the same, wheat being set at six.[7]

In 829 at the Council of Paris it was decreed, in effect, that the fixing of prices was reserved to the emperor. Certain church prelates and nobles, it was declared, were promulgating edicts which forbade the poor to sell their grain and wine at a price higher than those set forth in the edicts. The poor, the council disclosed, were forced to sell their wheat for four denarii. They might, on the other hand, sell it for as much as twelve if their proper liberty was allowed and they were not prohibited by their *seniores* from bargaining with others for the sale of their surpluses.[8] The Emperor Louis, then, by A.D. 829 was apparently willing to allow wheat to be sold on the open market for as high as twelve while a few decades previously his father had set the price first at four[9] and then at six.[10]

It is difficult, however, to judge with precision the real difference between the decrees. The capitulary of 806 had set the price at six, but the order seems to refer to famine conditions (as it does in the collection of Ansegius). The decree of 794, on the other hand, which sets the price at four, clearly states that the rule is to hold for years of good harvest and bad. Again, the law of 794 refers to all (*nullus homo . . . carius vendat*), while the decree of 806 might be understood to cover only those in high church

---

6. *Ibid.*, Vol. I, p. 140, No. 52, chap. 5.

7. Ansegius, *Caroli Magni Ludovici et Lotharii Imperatorum Capitularia*, Lib. I, chap. 126, *P.L.*, XCVII, col. 530; *Capitularia, Ansegii Abbatis Capitularia Collectio, M.G.H., Legum*, Sec. II, Vol. I, p. 411.

8. *Concilia, M.G.H., Legum*, Sec. III, Vol. II, p. 645, No. 50, chap. 52.

9. See above, p. 37 and n. 4.

10. See above, p. 37 and n. 5.

or secular positions who held royal benefices. The decree of 829 expressly grants a free market only to the poor. (However, it certainly does not seem likely that they were being granted an exclusive privilege.) Finally, it should be stressed that the legislation of 829 insists neither that sales be made in the open market nor that the market price is mandatory; it does assume that a market price exists and that the poor would sell at that price. But the law requires only that they should not be forced to sell and that prices should be those freely agreed upon by buyer and seller.

The council's decree mentioned that the potentates were enforcing their local price edicts with beatings (*acribus verberibus flagellatur*). This was not the first time the connection between violence on the one hand and buying and selling on the other was noted. Indeed, the connection had been and would be more direct and less legal. In 787 at Pavia, under the authority of Charlemagne's son Pippin, a capitulary was issued ordering ecclesiastic and military potentates and anyone else traveling to and from the palace, to refrain from carrying off produce and property which they had not purchased or which had not been voluntarily given. It also ordered that in winter time these travelers were to be given shelter so that they would not be forced to perform these unjust acts.[11]

About two decades later another capitulary was promulgated in which the issue was baldly described as the oppression of the poor free man by the powerful. The wording of the latter was somewhat more sophisticated. Not only was it forbidden to take goods by force, but it was also declared unlawful to buy them unless the owner was willing to sell (*ut coacti res eorum vendant aut tradunt*). Perhaps the added distinction was made to forestall attempts to evade the earlier law (or laws) by a literal interpretation. That is, one might force the owner to relinquish his goods, pay him a trivial price and claim, should complaint be made, that one had "purchased" the goods. This seems to be the purpose of the law for the capitulary itself declares that the emperor wishes to prevent the poor from being driven by poverty to begging and stealing. The law, of course, would also prevent forced sale, even at a fair price, of goods which might be badly needed by the owner during a time of shortage. Indeed, as it stands, the law of 805 would allow the seller the right to refuse to sell for any reason including whim.

In 813 the Council of Mainz issued a similar declaration. The terms of the old order are repeated and other prohibitions are added. Neither abbot, bishop, count, vicar, or judge or anyone else is to take advantage of the poor during hard times. Moreover, the law continues, doubtless

11. *Capitularia, M.G.H., Legum*, Sec. II, Vol. I, pp. 198–199, No. 94, chap. 4.

anticipating denials of the employment of coercion, all sales must be conducted in public before suitable witnesses.[12]

Both Charlemagne's capitulary of 805 and the decree of the Council of Mainz of 813 found their way into the collection of Ansegius virtually without alteration.[13] It has been suggested that the council's order was confirmed by Louis the Pious. The issues of 805 and 813 were added to the capitularies of the East Frankish kingdom in 847.[14]

In 850 Louis II promulgated a capitulary which, like the capitulary of 787,[15] was issued at Pavia. The two decrees were similar in more respects than their place or origin. Their wording, to be sure, is quite different. The substance of them, however, is virtually the same.[16] As in the earlier capitulary, those traveling to the royal presence are instructed not to take by force the property of those with whom they lodge en route. There is, however, an added refinement. The earlier decree declares that they must not take what they have not purchased (*non praesumant . . . tollere . . . si non comparaverint*). In the later capitulary they are told that they must not take what they have not purchased for a just price (*nihil . . . tollat . . . nisi . . . precio iusto comparet*). It should be added that nearly the entire set of ten *capitula* to which the one in question belongs is concerned with various matters involving violence and plunder.[17]

In 865 Louis II, now emperor, issued another set of *capitula*, again at Pavia, and again concerning the problem of rapine. One of them ordered that those coming to and going from the emperor's seat should not molest the inhabitants nor take anything from them unless they have paid for it. The inhabitants, for their part, are told that they are not to deny these travelers "roof, fire, water and straw." Then a new aspect is introduced. Nor, says the decree, are the inhabitants to charge the travelers higher prices than they charge their neighbors.[18] The regulation of 865 is the

---

12. *Ibid.*, Vol. I, p. 125, No. 44, chap. 16; Vol. I, p. 312, No. 154, chap. 2 (VII).

13. Ansegius, *op. cit.*, Lib. I, chap. 115, Lib. II, chap. 32, *P.L.*, XCVII, cols. 528, 546; *Capitularia, M.G.H., Legum*, Sec. II, Vol. I, pp. 410, 421.

14. *Capitularia, M.G.H., Legum*, Sec. II, Vol. I, p. 311, No. 154; Vol. II, p. 180, No. 248, chaps. 17, 18.

15. See above, p. 39.

16. *Capitularia, M.G.H., Legum*, Sec. II, Vol. II, p. 87, No. 213, chap. 4.

17. *Ibid.*, Vol. II, pp. 85–88, No. 213, chaps. 1–10.

18. *Ibid.*, Vol. II, pp. 92–93, No. 216, chap. 5: "Episcopus et comes, per quorum transeunt terminum diligenter provideant, ne molestentur incolae aut eorum domos per vim paciantur invadere vel propria diripere absque conlato praecio; sed neque indigenae per solita loca tectum, focum, aquam et paleam hospitibus denegare aut sua carius quam vicinis audeant vendere."

first law, Roman or medieval, that indubitably prohibits price discrimination.

"And each will drink the blood of his own arm." "This means," it is explained, "that each will plunder the substance of his brother; this is the prophecy of Isaiah, (9: 20) and in our time it is fulfilled." This and similar phrases preface a series of fourteen *capitula* issued by Carloman in 884 for the purpose of alleviating the various forms of depredation from which France then suffered.[19] So that every reason for rapine may be removed, declares the thirteenth of these *capitula*, "Parish priests should admonish their flocks not to charge wayfarers more than the price obtainable in the local market. Otherwise, the wayfarers can complain to the priest who is then required to set the price with 'humanity.'" "This text clearly equates just price with market price and does not lend itself to a different interpretation."[20] The usual plea for hospitality is present both here and elsewhere in the set.[21]

Placuit nobis et nostris fidelibus, ut presbyteri suos parrochianos admoneat, ut et ipsi hospitales existant et nulli iter facienti mansionem denegent: et ut omnis occasio rapinae tollatur, nihil carius vendant transeuntibus, nisi quanto in mercato vendere possunt. Quodsi carius vendere voluerint, ad presbyterum transeuntes hoc referant, et illius iussu cum humanitate eis vendant.

It seems likely that the Pavian issue of 864 had the same end as this West Frankish capitulary of 884. The earlier one says that the local inhabitants shall not charge travelers higher prices than they charge their neighbors (*neque . . . sua carius quam vicinis audeant vendere*).[22] The version of 884 says that the prices for the travelers shall be no higher than those obtained in the market (*quanto in mercato vendere possunt*). In both is implicit the notion that the local people know and are paying a price which is the same for all of them; that is, they have perfect knowledge of an extant

19. *Ibid.*, Vol. II, pp. 371–375, No. 287, chaps. 1–14.

20. R. de Roover, "The Concept of the Just Price," p. 421. Vercauteren follows de Roover's interpretation of the capitulary of 884 and cites the capitularies of 774, 850, 865, and 889 as evidence that the idea of the just price was known during the Carolingian era. See F. Vercauteren, "Monnaie et circulation monetaire en Belgique et dans le Nord de la France du VIe au XIe siècle," Settimane di studio del Centro Italiano di studi sull' alto Medioevo. VII: *Moneta e scambi nell'alto medioevo* (Spoleta, 1960), 294–295.

21. *Capitularia, M.G.H., Legum*, Sec. II, Vol. II, p. 375, No. 287, chaps. 12–13.

22. See above, p. 40 and n. 18.

market. In an era characterized by small, comparatively isolated communities, this would not be an unwarranted assumption.

The similarity between the West Frankish and the Pavian capitularies may not be coincidental. Eight years before the issuance of the West Frankish version, Carloman's grandfather Charles the Bald, king of West Francia, had been crowned again at Pavia. Thus the two governments were joined for a time under one ruler.

More regulations of the same or similar type were issued. Two came from Pavia. The first, promulgated in 889,[23] soon after the town had been seized by Guido of Spoleto, was designed tó protect the sellers from the travelers. The second, issued in 891, aimed to protect the populace from the dangerous transient and the transient from price discrimination.[24] Two others in the East Frankish kingdom provided for equal tolls or tariffs for merchants—Jewish, native and foreign[25]—and called for an up-to-date assessment of the monies used to pay.[26]

The West Frankish capitulary of 884 holds a unique place in the history of medieval commercial law. In one sense, it was the culmination of a series of laws promulgated by the Carolingians which perhaps begins with an attempt made in 776 to rectify the terms of a particular set of sales which were seen as unjust. In the intervening years, laws of a more general nature were issued both for the protection of the buyer and the seller. By 865 price discrimination had been expressly forbidden. It was in 884 that the market price was explicitly declared the just price although other of the medieval empire's laws may have been trying to express that principle with such phrases as *iustum pretium* and *dignum pretium*.

In another sense, the capitulary of 884 has a connection with the more remote past. Its fundamental formula "*quanto in mercato vendere possunt*" is quite similar to those phrases often found in Justinian—"*quantum vendere possunt*" and "*quanti venire possunt*."[27] It is fairly certain that the Carolingian law has put the formula to new use. No longer was it used, as in Justinian's time, to assess property values for the courts to use in certain types of settlement. In the Carolingian law it was declared the just price.

Not only did the capitulary of 884 have connections real and apparent

23. *Capitularia*, *M.G.H.*, *Legum*, Sec. II, Vol. II, p. 105, No. 222, chap. 7.

24. *Ibid.*, Vol. II, p. 107, No. 224, chap. 1.

25. *Ibid.*, Vol. II, p. 252, No. 253, chap. 9.

26. *Ibid.*, Vol. II, p. 252, No. 253, chap. 8.

27. See above pp. 35–36. Mathews ("Valuation of Property," p. 238) maintains that it exists in the form *quanti vendere possunt. Quanti venire possunt* and *quanti veniri possunt* seem to be the most common.

with the past, it had an unquestionable connection with the future. In about A.D. 900, it appeared practically unaltered in the *Libellus de Ecclesiasticus Disciplinus* of Regino of Prüm.[28] In the next century Burchard of Worms included it in his collection of laws.[29] Ivo of Chartres' *Decretum* contained it also.[30] Before the twelfth century ended it had been placed in the First Compilation.[31] In 1234 in a form very close to the original, it was entered into the *Decretals* of Gregory IX.[32]

IV. The Crossing of the Lines

The formula *quantum vendi potest* was used not only to judge prices for which goods were exchanged but also to detect the presence of usury. It seems first to have been employed for this purpose by the canonist Simon of Bisignano somewhat before 1180.[1] For that same purpose, Tancredus, no later than 1215, used the same formula together with another which was definitely from Justinian's *Corpus*:

> Res tantum valet quantum vendi potest . . . precia enim rerum non ex affectu singulorum, sed communiter extimatur.[2]

> A thing is worth as much as it can be sold for . . . but the value is to be established not by the affection of individuals, but by the community at large.

28. Regino of Prüm, *Libellus de Ecclesiasticus Disciplinus*, Lib. II, chap. 421, in *P.L.* CXXXII, col. 364.

29. Burchard of Worms, *Decretorum Libri Viginti*, Lib. II, chap. 168, in *P.L.* CXL, col. 653.

30. Ivo of Chartres, *Decretum*, Part VI, chap. 259, *P.L.* CLXI, col. 500.

31. *Compilatio I*, III, 15, C. 2, p. 31.

32. Gregory IX, *Decretals*, III, 17, C. 1, *C.I.C.*, Vol. II, col. 518: "Placuit ut presbyteri plebes suas suas admoneat ut et ipsi hospitales sint, et non carius vendant transeuntibus quam in mercato vendere possunt, alioquin ad presbyterum transeuntes hoc referant, ut illius iussu cum humanitate sibi vendant."

1. Simon of Bisignano, *Summa*, Paris Bibl. Nat. Lat. 3934A fol. 78[va], Causa XIV, q. 4, c.5. "Si quis clericus. Hic queritur si mutavi tibi aureum puta usque ad festum nativitatis et tunc non habeas aureum, hoc vis mihi pro eo frumentum vel huiusmodi dare, an possint tantum de frumento exigere quantum poterat tempore quo mutuavi haberi vel tantum quantum contra communi estimacione habere potest. cum aureus redditur et placet quibusdam tantum me debere accipere. quantum tunc communiter vendi poterit cum aureus debit reddi." Quoted in Baldwin, "Medieval Theories," p. 54 n. 98.

2. Tancredus, *Apparatus* to *Compilatio I*, Paris Bibl. Nat. Lat. 3931A, fol. 71[va], V, 15, c. 18. In civitate. valent. From Baldwin, *op. cit.*, p. 54 n. 100. The work apparently exists only in manuscript.

Bernard Botone used the same words as Tancredus. The phrase "*Res tantum valet quantum vendi potest*" as well as "*pretia enim rerum non ex affectu singulorum sed communiter extimatur*" are found in his Gloss on the *Decretals* and Botone names Justinian's *Ad Legem Falcidiam*.[3] To explain the same bit of text, Innocent IV, a few years later, simply used the phrase "*communis estimacione*."[4] Other thirteenth-century canonists, Vincentius Hispanus, Hostiensis, and Monaldus, have been cited as expressing the same judgment.[5]

Simon of Bisignano had used the phrase "*res tantum valet* etc." in connection with *Si quis clericus*, which is concerned with clerical usury.[6] Tancredus, Botone, Vincentius Hispanus, Innocent IV, and Hostiensis used similar phrases in connection with *In civitate* which was concerned with the giving of higher prices in contracts in which payment was deferred, a contract which might well involve usury as well as speculation.[7] Monaldus employed the phrase under the heading *De usuris*. In each case, calculation was needed to discover whether usury or speculation was present in the transaction in question. The phrase was being used as an evaluating device to ascertain the presence or absence of the condemned practice; it was not being employed as a true price regulation.

In the *Apparatus: Ius Naturale* (1210–1215) was contained a regulation concerning price itself. Clerics were allowed to sell at a profit providing their motivation and behavior were correct and providing they sold for a just price.[8] No declaration as to what constituted the just price seems to be

3. Bernard Botone, *Glossa Ordinaria* to the *Decretales* . . . , V, 19, c. 6. fol. cccclxxii. "In civitate no[n] vale[n]t. Immo v[idetu]r q[uod] tantu[m] valeat. res enim tantu[m] valet q[uan]tu[m] vendi pot[est] . . . p[re]tia e[ni]m rer[um] no[n] ex affectu singulorum sed co[mmun]iter estima[n]tur. D[igestum] ad l[egem] fal[cidiam], [D. 35, 2, 63]."

4. Innocent IV, *Apparatus super Quinque Libris Decretalium*, V, 19, c. 6, p. C–25. In civitate. non valent. communis estimacione.

5. Baldwin, "Medieval Theories," p. 54 n. 102, cites Vincentius Hispanus (*Apparatus in Decretales Gregorii IX*, Paris Bibl. Nat. Lat. 3967, fol. 189, V, 19, c. 6. In civitate. valent.) as expressing a similar judgment. The work exists only in manuscript and he does not quote. The same judgment is found in Hostiensis, *Decretalium Librum Commenaria*, V, 19, c. 6, Vol. IV, fol. 57ra. In civitate. non valent, a four-volume work difficult to obtain, and Monaldus, *Summa Perutilis* (Lyon, before 1516), v⁰ fol. 290 *de usura*, similarly unobtainable. See Baldwin, *op. cit.*, p. 54 n. 102.

6. Gratian, *Decretum*, Causa XIV, q. 4, c. 5., *C.I.C.*, Vol. I, cols. 736–737. The phrase *iusto pretio* is used but not defined.

7. Gregory IX, *Decretals*, V, 19, c. 6, *C.I.C.*, Vol. II, col. 813.

8. *Apparatus: Ius Naturale*, Paris Bibl. Nat. Lat. 15393, fol. 150vb, Causa XIV, q. 4, c. 3, Canonum. studio., quoted in Baldwin, "Medieval Theories," p. 47 n. 36.

included. Nevertheless, in the realm of clerical sales before 1215, a judgment made upon a price is found. In the earlier discussions of sales and purchases made by the clergy, the judgment seems to be rendered upon behavior and motivation only. Not long after the composition of the *Apparatus: Ius Naturale*, Raymond of Penaforte also permitted clerics to sell at a profit if they sold on the open market (*communiter venditur in foro*).[9]

For the purpose of establishing a just price the law might call for witnesses, "good men" or a judge. In the bulls with which *laesio enormis* was brought into the law of the church, the just price was established by witnesses (*per testes*).[10] The author of the *Apparatus: Ius Naturale* called for a good man.[11]

Johannes Teutonicus and Tancredus[12] and the *Decretals*[13] called for witnesses to establish a price from which the extent of a *laesio* could be calculated. Only a little while before Teutonicus had suggested "a judge or someone else."[14] This apparent indifference may be revealing, and indeed, it has been suggested that the naming of an authority or consultant is not in fact a true mode for establishing prices.[15] For the question

9. Raymond of Penaforte, *Summa de casibus* (Rome, 1603), II, 7, part. 9, p. 236; cited by Baldwin, *op. cit.*, p. 47 n. 35.

10. See above pp. 26–27 and n. 48, and pp. 25–26 and n. 40.

11. *Apparatus: Ius Naturale*, Paris Bibl. Nat. Lat. 15393, fol. 151ra, Causa XIV, q. 4, c. 5. "Si quis clericus, mercandi. Quantum vir bonus arbitratur debitos nummos valere tempore solutionis faciende." Quoted in Baldwin, "Medieval Theories," p. 53 n. 88.

12. Johannes Teutonicus, *Apparatus to Compilatio III*, Paris Bibl. Nat. Lat. 3930, fol. 154vb, III, 14, c. 2. "Quum causa. quantitatem. videtur quod non potuerunt (probare) excessum deceptionis quanto probaverunt quantitatem valentie rei. Respondeo hoc modo potuit esse. quia cum res essent vendite decem testes dicerunt quod valebant multo plus quam viginti, sed non taxabant certum pretium rei valentie quod iterum probari debet. vel constitit pape per confessiones partium quod res valebant ultra dimidium iusti precii: sed non conveniebant de quantitate valoris quem monachi debent probare. unde non producuntur hic testes super eodem casu tamen super eodem possunt induci in tali casu. quia ad aliud agitur modo quam prius." Baldwin understands the *decem* to go with *testes*, and says that ten witnesses were being called. The syntax will bear this interpretation. It may be the case, however, that *decem* refers to price thus: "The thing was sold for ten. Witnesses say that it was worth much more than twenty." ("*Pro*" is not necessary, the ablative of price not requiring a preposition. "*Decem*," of course, is not declinable.) Teutonicus is quoted by Baldwin, *op. cit.*, p. 53 n. 90.

13. Gregory IX, *Decretals*, II, 20, c. 42, *C.I.C.*, Vol. II, col. 333.

14. Johannes Teutonicus, *Glossa Ordinaria* to the *Decretum*, Paris Bibl. Nat. Lat. 14317, fol. 156rb, Causa XIV, q. 4, c. 5, Si quis clericus; quoted by Baldwin, "Medieval Theories," p. 53 n. 88.

15. Baldwin, *op. cit.*, p. 28.

of the basis upon which the witnesses or judge are to arrive at their price remains unanswered. In the *Decretals* this was in some sense recognized. The section of *Quum Causa* concerned with the *laesio enormis* had been separated from the section concerning the witnesses and the two halves were entered appropriately.[16]

In addition to the market price (*communis aestimatio*) there seem to be other modes of evaluation. In all but one of these devices for arriving at a just price (the exception, of course, being the use of the market price), the Romanists of the middle ages anticipated the canonists. Bulgarus and others of the twelfth century had called for judges and good men to reveal the price.[17] It was Azo who, among the Romanists, first provided a formula by which those assessors might calculate that elusive and perhaps fluctuating figure.[18] In the first decade of the thirteenth century, he suggested that the price paid for a nearby piece of property be examined. But it might be argued, he warns, that the purchaser of the property used for comparison had bought foolishly or that the property used for assessment did not border the property being assessed and therefore was not suitable for purposes of comparison. "Both these rebuttals," says Azo, "may be refuted."

Nevertheless, he gives an alternative method, clearly useful only for assessments of income-producing property. Drawing upon a Justinian rule concerning public sales of property made for the purpose of paying debts owed to the community,[19] he suggests that the value of property can be established from the quantity of its returns.[20] A price thus estab-

---

16. See above p. 27 n. 50 and p. 27 n. 48.

17. Baldwin, "Medieval Theories," pp. 27–28, and nn. 63–67. Similarly, they had made note of the importance of the time. Thus, for example, Placentinus, *Summa Codicis*, 4, 44, p. 176: "Iusti inquam tempore venditionis." Azo, *Summa*, 4, 44, 2, col. 417: " . . . iusti precii quod erat tempore venditionis."

18. Azo, *Commentarius*, 4, 44, 8, p. 510: " . . . potest esse quod tempore venditionis fuerit X. post XV." He notes that weight, etc., may be changed to cover alterations in price: "sicut per diversa tempora mutantur quae consistunt in pondere, numero vel mensura."

19. C. 4, 44, 16.

20. Azo, *Commentarius*, 4, 44, 8, p. 510. "Si voluntate tua. Finitum. Id est, completum. Mi[nus] dimid[ia] iusti pre[tii] quod fue[rat] temp[ore] vend[itionis]. Ut D[igestum] de iure si. non intelligitur. divi. et ideo dicit, quia potest esse quod tempore venditionis fuerat X. post XV. sicut per diversa tempora mutantur quae consistunt in pondere, numero vel mensura. sed quod hic dicit de iusto pretio, qualiter probabitur? Respon[deo] bene. probabo enim quod res quae non est melior hac, vendita est ultra duplum. si opponatur, ille stulte emit, vel sibi confinis erat fundus, probabo non fuisse confinem: & probabo illum fuisse talem, quem non est

lished is just (*iustum*).[21] Other legists, almost immediately, added a degree of precision. Value, they said, was to be assessed from the income derived from the property over a twenty- or fifty-year period—presumably they meant by capitalizing income at a certain rate. This procedure was drawn from the *Novellae* of Justinian[22] and was suggested in the early part of the thirteenth century by Laurentius Hispanus, Johannes Teutonicus, Tancredus, and Vincentius Hispanus. In the latter part it was described by Hostiensis, but Hostiensis, it is said, preferred the *communis aestimatio*.[23]

Accursius, like Azo, addressed his attention to the problem of discovering the just price when he discussed the *laesio enormis*. After defining the *dimidia* he directly asked the question, "How do I know when it has been exceeded?" (*sed qualiter sciam quando excedit?*).[24] "Not," he says, "by the price that two or three individuals are willing to pay." For, he continues, "the value of things is not constituted from the affections of individuals." He cites for his authority the *Lex Aquilia* and the *Lex Falcidia* (*precia rerum*

---

verisimile stulte emisse. Idem & probatur rei pretium ex quantitate + reditum ut j eo. si quos. [C. 4, 44, 16] & in authent. de aliena. & emphy. & hoc autem concedimus [*Nov.* 120, 9, pr.] & de non alien. reb. eccl. quia vero Leonis. & si vero aliquis [*Nov.* 7, 3, par. 1] & ut D[igestum] de rebus eorum qui sub tut. L. si fundus sit sterilis [D. 27, 9, 13] .... " It is generally agreed that the *non* (on line 8, above) goes with *sibi confinis erat* rather than *probabo* (non) *fuisse confinem* where it is found.

21. Azo, *Commentarius*, 4, 44, 15 [*sic*] p. 511: "Si quos. Et redituum quantitas. Et ita redituum quantitas in iusto pretio aestimatur."

22. *Nov.* 120, 9, pr.; *Nov.* 7, 3. par. 1.

23. Laurentius Hispanus, *Apparatus* to *Compilatio III*, Paris Bibl. Nat. Lat. 3932, fol. 161[ra] and 15398, fol. 162, III, 14, c. 2. Quum causa. probare, quoted by Baldwin, "Medieval Theories," p. 53 n. 91: "Sed qualiter probabit rei pretium, dic quod ex qualitate rei et quantitate redituum. . . . Respondo id est quandoque etiam tanti estimatur res quantum potest de pensionibus colligi in L annis. . . . quandoque autem XX annis." When one period was used and when the other I have no way of telling. Four sources are in manuscript and I have never seen them. I have not been able to obtain the four-volume *Commentaria* of Hostiensis either. Baldwin also cites Johannes Teutonicus, *Apparatus* to *Compilatio III*, Paris Bibl. Nat. Lat. 3930, fol. 164[vb]; Tancredus, *Apparatus* to *Compilatio III*, Paris Bibl. Nat. Lat. 3931A, fol. 185[ra]; Vincentius Hispanus, *Apparatus in decretales Gregorii IX*, Paris Bibl. Nat. Lat. 3967, fol. 90, II, 20, c. 42. Quum causa. articulum; Hostiensis *Decretalium Librum Commentaria*, II, 20, c. 42, fol. 101[ra] Quum Causa, articulum. See Baldwin, "Medieval Theories," p. 53 nn. 91, 93. Perhaps Innocent III should be included in this group. *Ad nostram noveritis* states that the income produced by the property showed the price to be so low as to be unjust. However, no formula is given. Innocent merely says that a year's income equalled the price of the property. Moreover, *Ad nostram noveritis* referred to an enfeoffment. (See above p. 26 n. 43.)

24. Accursius, *Commentariis*, C. 4, 44, 2, Vol. IV, col. 920.

non constituuntur ex adfectione singulorum: ut D[igestum] ad leg. Falc. l. precia. et D[igestum] ad l. Aquil. l. si servum meum).[25]

The price then is to be revealed by a device found in the *Lex Falcidia*. There can be no doubt about the meaning Accursius gives to the passage he cites from that Roman law. In his gloss on the passage *"pretia rerum . . . communiter funguntur"* of the *Lex Falcidia*, he uses the well-traveled passage *"quantum vendi potest"* (what it can be sold for). "A thing is to be estimated by the common price; thus it is said that a thing is worth as much as it can be sold for to the community at large." (*. . . funguntur, id est communi pretio aestimatur res quod ergo dicitur, res tantum valet quantum vendi potest scilicet communiter.*)[26]

Thus did Accursius, the great Romanist of the thirteenth century, accept the just price as it had been defined in church law for three centuries—as it had originally been defined by the Frankish legislator in 884. Stated differently, *"quantum vendi potest,"* a device used for court assessments in the Justinian *Corpus* and converted into a formula for the just price in the Carolingian law, reappears in a thirteenth-century gloss on the Justinian *Corpus* where it performs its Carolingian function.

It is probable that Accursius considered a price established by the legal authorities quite as just and fundamentally of the same type as the market price. He gives several definitions of *communiter funguntur*, the first of which describes the *pretium communis* as the market price and the second describes it as a price established by the community acting as lawmakers rather than as buyers and sellers.[27]

His gloss to the passage in the *Lex Aquilia* is briefer. *"Res tantum valet, quantum vendi potest: intellige communiter,"*[28] is the whole of it; no further considerations are presented. Accursius uses this phrase to explain many other passages in Justinian. He directly cites only the *Lex Falcidia* and the *Lex Aquilia*, however, to provide a formula for the calculation of lawful prices.[29]

It would seem to be incorrect to say that Accursius was, in this regard,

25. *Ibid.*

26. *Ibid.*, D. 35, 2, 63, Vol. II, col. 1397: "funguntur. id est communi pretio aestimatur res Quod ergo dicitur, res tantum valet, quantum vendi potest scilicet communiter ut hic et s, eodem 1. proxi in fin. et s ad legem Aqui[lia]. l. servum [D. 9, 2, 33]. Vel dic, communiter funguntur, scilicet pretia: id est statuunter, et communiter expone ut prius. Vel tertio funguntur communiter, id est, tale pretium imponitur, quod equivaleat rei, ut commune, et quale sit habere rem vel pretium."

27. See p. 48 n. 26.

28. Accursius, *Commentariis*, D. 9, 2, 33, Vol. II, col. 1080, redempturus fuit.

29. See Baldwin, "Medieval Theories," pp. 28–29.

following Azo. Azo, it will be recalled, said that land might be evaluated by examining the price for which a neighboring piece of land has been sold. Accursius, too, has called for the examination of prices for which similar parcels had been sold. The resemblance, however, is deceptive. Azo speaks in the singular (*probo enim quod res quae non est melior hac vendita est ultra duplum*). To stress this use of the singular is not to focus upon a literary or syntactical bit of change. Azo literally means one other sale. He himself recognizes the limited value of this procedure for he provides alternative procedures should the defendant claim that the buyer of that particular piece had bought foolishly (*si opponatur ille stulte emit*). "Prove," he says, "that it was not foolish. Prove (or show) the price of the thing from the quantity of the returns."

Accursius, on the other hand, speaks in the plural (*dic ergo inspici venditiones factas locorum existentium iuxta illum*), and he specifically denies the validity of one or even two or three offers (*non per hoc q[uod] duo vel tres volunt tantu[m] dare quoniam pretia rerum*, etc.). Accursius' solution to the problem of the possibility of a foolish purchase and a therefore misleading price must have been the result of examination of prices obtained in many sales.

In a very real sense then, Accursius' mode is a correction or even a contradiction of one of Azo's methods. (At logic, it is a contradiction.) It flatly denies the validity of employing Azo's guide—a single sale. To argue that Accursius followed Azo in the sense that both were examining sales which had actually been made, would be misleading. Even if Accursius was inspired, so to speak, to his position by reflections on Azo's statement, it would be incorrect to conclude that he is following Azo. To do so would be to fail to distinguish between psychological and legal derivation. Accursius is not broadening the scope of a rule found in Azo; he is denying the validity of a method and substituting an alternative. Needless to say, one can only have a true market price for fungibles. Nevertheless, the more sales that are examined the more closely one approximates it.

Accursius offers another criteria for evaluation which is found *verbatim* in Azo. "Examine," he says, "the quantity of the returns" (*redituum quantitatis*), and adds, "and the quality of the property" (*qualitatem rei*).

Rei qualitatem and *redituum quantitatem*, he suggests, need only be employed in the evaluation of real property (*immobiles*). With other types of goods such as grain, the price is certain (*in mobilis autem rebus, ut frumento est precium certum*). This would seem to mean that the first method, that is, the market price (and perhaps the price established by lawful authority) is the proper price.[30] A summary of the modes of assessment is found in Odofredus. He lists the market price,[31] the value of nearby property,[32] the value of the produce,[33] and the opinion of the men of the neighborhood.[34]

CONCLUSION

Although Justinian's texts were cited by the great legists of the middle ages, it appears that the true origin of the use of the market price as the legal regulator of prices is medieval. The often cited *Lex Falcidia* and *Lex Aquilia* do not seem to have been concerned with regulating the selling price of lands or goods. That they should not have been concerned with the regulation of price seems quite consistent with positive statements found in the *Corpus* and in another great body of Roman law, the Theodosian Code. The latter, indeed, states unequivocally that low price is not grounds for rescinding a sale.

The only Roman regulation which might be construed as a generally applicable price regulation is the one which came to be known as *laesio enormis*. This rule, however, seems to be interpretable in at least three ways. According to the first, sales can be rescinded if the price is too low. This

30. Accursius, *Commentariis*, C. 4, 44, 2, Vol. IV, col. 920: "Sed qualiter sciam quando excedit? Respon[deo]. non per hoc q[uod] duo vel tres volunt tantum dare. quoniam precia rerum non consitituunter ex adfectione singulorum: ut D[igestum] ad leg. Falc. 1. precia [D. 35, 2, 62] D[igestum] ad l. Aquil. si servuum meum [D. 9, 2, 33]. Dic ergo inspici venditiones factas locorum existentium iuxta illum. Item rei qualitatem et redituum quantitatem . . . et hoc in immobilis. In mobilis autem rebus, ut frumento est precium certum."

31. Odofredus, *Lectura Codicis*, 4, 44, 2, fol. 246, col. 3, quoted by Baldwin, "Medieval Theories," p. 28 n. 72.

32. Odofredus, *loc. cit.*, quoted by Baldwin, *op. cit.*, p. 29 n. 77.

33. Odofredus, *loc. cit.*, quoted by Baldwin, *op. cit.*, p. 29 n. 80: "Vel probabit quod tot fructus consueverunt percipi ex illa re sicut ex re que valet. X, quia estimatio rei per reditum fructum estimatur." It has been said that this is virtually the market price (Baldwin, *op. cit.*, p. 29). But the convenience or inconvenience of the location of a farm, for example, might also affect its market value. Perhaps that is among the reasons why bordering lands, which would have a similar location, were listed as a separate criteria. See above, p. 46 and n. 20; pp. 49–50 and n. 30.

34. Odofredus, *loc. cit.*, in Baldwin, *op. cit.*, p. 29 n. 83: "Item probabit quod quando petebat consilium quantum valeret homines dicebant ei quod valebat decem. nam per hoc presumitur ignorare quod valebat. X. quia alias in dubio presumitur quis scire vires patrimonii sui ubi ignoraverat. . . . Et hec que dicta sunt, locum habet in his que certa sunt: ut, fundus vel domus. sed non in his que dubia sunt: ut nomina et condicionalia. nam ibi spectamus quanti invenit emptor."

was the meaning accepted in the middle ages. According to the second interpretation, the law protects only minors. A third interpretation is also possible, according to which, the law was not concerned with prices, but merely allowed rescission of sales in certain cases of unpaid obligations. In either of the latter two cases it seems correct to say that Roman law provided no recourse for adults who paid more or less than the market price. Probably in the *Corpus* and definitely in the Theodosian Code, except where certain types of abuse were present, the seller was explicitly denied recourse on grounds of price.

The Roman law ran a different course in the middle ages. In the Justinian line, laws not concerned with selling price were converted into price regulations and their scope broadened so that they protected not only children but adults, and not only sellers but buyers. The Theodosian line, on the other hand, began as a denial of recourse for sellers on the grounds of low price and this denial was, in the early middle ages, extended to buyers complaining of high prices.

The major changes, both in the Theodosian line and in the Justinian line, occurred in the early part of the middle ages. Of the several bodies of early medieval law which adopted the Theodosian price regulations, it seems to have been the Bavarian code which extended the explicit denial of recourse from sellers to both buyers and sellers. It was a West Frankish capitulary which first employed a Justinian formula as a price regulation declaring that the price on the open market was the just price. The West Frankish regulation, however, was very similar to a number of laws issued earlier at Pavia. The political connection between the West Frankish kingdom and Pavia at that time was close.

The original and the expanded Theodosian principle on the one hand and the principle of Justinian as altered by the Carolingians on the other, entered the law collections of the church. Both lines come together in the collection of Ivo of Chartres and there stand, in essence at least, in contradiction. It was the Carolingian line that was picked by the canonists and Romanists of the following centuries. The Theodosian line was neglected.

When Justinian's *Corpus* was studied again, several rules were interpreted in the Carolingian manner and used as price regulations. But even the ignoring of the Theodosian line did not hide the fundamental Roman position that buyers and sellers might decide on any price and so close a legally valid sale.

Azo and Accursius saw the contradiction within the Roman law itself and said that the words *humanum est* were in the law because *laesio enormis* provided an exception which contradicted the Roman law strictly held.

Indeed, the *laesio enormis* passages may have provided an exception to the general Roman laws of sale. In that case they expressed a principle which was out of harmony with body of Roman law, but which was picked up in medieval law and made central. More likely, the "exception" had not originally been put into the law to contradict it in cases in which the price was "unjust." It may have been inserted to make the law on the rescission of sales consistent with the law's general principle of protecting minors from the dangers of buying and selling. Most likely, it was intended to provide a recourse for unpaid vendors. As to seeing in the law of supply and demand the source of the just price, there is less question. That the market price is the just price and properly the lawful price is a medieval notion to which medieval men made the Roman law conform.

MEDIEVAL URBAN ORIGINS IN NORTHERN CONTINENTAL EUROPE: STATE OF RESEARCH AND SOME TENTATIVE CONCLUSIONS

David M. Nicholas

University of Nebraska

ABBREVIATIONS

AESC	*Annales: Économies, Sociétés, Civilisations*
AHR	*American Historical Review*
AJ	*The Archaeological Journal*
AM	*Annales du Midi*
ASD	*Annali di Storia del Diritto*
ASEB	*Annales de la Société d'Émulation de Bruges*
BDL	*Blätter für deutsche Landesgeschichte*
BGN	*Bijdragen voor de Geschiedenis der Nederlanden*
BJ	*Bonner Jahrbücher*
CAM	*La Città nell'alto medioevo.* Settimane di Studio del Centro Italiano di Studi sull'alto medioevo, VI (Spoleto, 1959)
HMGOG	*Handelingen der Maatschappij voor Geschiedenis en Oudheidkunde te Gent*
IHCD	*International History of City Development*, ed. E. A. Gutkind, 4 vols. (London, 1964—)
MA	*Le Moyen Âge*
RBPH	*Revue Belge de Philologie et d'Histoire*
REA	*Revue des Études Anciennes*
RH	*Revue Historique*
RN	*Revue du Nord*
RV	*Rheinische Vierteljahrsblätter*
SAES	*Studien zu den Anfängen des europäischen Städtewesens.* Vorträge und Forschungen herausgegeben vom Konstanzer Arbeitskreis für mittelalterliche Geschichte, IV (Constance and Lindau, 1958)
SG	*Studium Generale*
SSCI	Settimane di Studio del Centro Italiano di Studi sull'alto medioevo
SZG	*Schweizerische Zeitschrift für Geschichte*
TJ	*Trierisches Jahrbuch*
TZ	*Trierer Zeitschrift*
VJSWG	*Vierteljahrsschrift für Sozial-und Wirtschaftsgeschichte*
WF	*Westfälische Forschungen*
ZRG, GA	*Zeitschrift der Savigny-Stiftung für Rechtsgeschichte, Germanistische Abteilung*

MEDIEVAL URBAN ORIGINS IN NORTHERN CONTINENTAL EUROPE: STATE OF RESEARCH AND SOME TENTATIVE CONCLUSIONS

In the quarter-century since the appearance of F.-L. Ganshof's masterly synthesis of the beginning of town life between the Loire and the Rhine,[1] numerous studies of the earliest phases of medieval urbanism have been published. Recent works include treatments of a general character covering an entire region or a particular urban phenomenon,[2] innumerable local studies, and general reference works, often of largely antiquarian interest.[3] This literature has become so vast that a general analytical survey of the state of research on medieval urban origins has become necessary, with particular reference to the manner in which research conducted since the Second World War has modified the conclusions of earlier scholars.[4]

The focus of attention here will be western continental Europe north of the Alps. This region, bounded by the Mediterranean, the North Sea, the Baltic, and the Alps, forms an obvious geographical unity. This unity corresponds to a certain homogeneity in types of urban life which developed before the twelfth century. The Germanic invasions of the fifth century had a catastrophic effect on most Roman town life west of the *limes*. Corresponding to the decline of the towns, the economy of western Europe

---

1. *Étude sur le développement des villes entre Loire et Rhin au Moyen Âge* (Paris and Brussels, 1943); see also the definitive second Flemish edition *Over Stadsontwikkeling tusschen Loire en Rijn gedurende de Middeleeuwen* (Brussels, 1944).

2. See in particular Hans Planitz, *Die deutsche Stadt im Mittelalter* (Vienna, 1954; reprinted Graz and Cologne, 1965), and Edith Ennen, *Frühgeschichte der europäischen Stadt* (Bonn, 1953).

3. For a general reference work and catalogue of data on town history and origins, see Erich Keyser (ed.), *Deutsches Städtebuch. Handbuch städtischer Geschichte*, 5 vols. (Berlin and Stuttgart, 1939–56). For France see Philippe Dollinger, Philippe Wolff, and Simone Guenée (eds.), *Bibliographie d'histoire des villes de France* (Paris, 1967).

4. For a convenient summary of some earlier opinion on medieval urban origins, see Robert L. Reynolds, "Town Origins," in Kenneth M. Setton and Henry R. Winkler (eds.), *Great Problems in European Civilization*, 1st ed. (Englewood Cliffs, N.J., 1954), pp. 173–205.

became increasingly agrarian during the great Völkerwanderung. Southern France was less severely struck by the invasions than the north, but town life did decline so severely that medieval urban origins in the Midi correspond more closely to those of northern Europe than to those of Italy. Towns revived throughout western Europe north of the Alps at approximately the same time,[5] both in trans-Rhenane Germany, which had never known Roman municipal institutions, and in the west. The contrast between town development in central and eastern Germany and in western Europe illustrates the extent to which the medieval town owes its origins to Germanic antecedents, for Roman centers which persisted across the Germanic invasions were modified under Germanic influence to form an urban type very different from the Roman town.

Italy, in contrast, knew a continuation in many respects of the Roman type of urbanism. Although there is controversy concerning the origins of particular urban institutions in Italy, the circumstances of the origins of the towns themselves are known in most cases. The Italian centers generally date from the Roman period, with little or no break in continuity of settlement even during the Lombard invasion of the peninsula.[6] The commercial advantages presented to the Italian towns by their maritime position and their connections with the east find no counterpart in the north, where trade, even that carried on over long distances, was largely inland. Spain too knew an extraordinary situation on the frontier of Europe in constant struggle with the Moslems.[7] Medieval urban

5. Hektor Ammann, "Vom Städtewesen Spaniens und Westfrankreichs im Mittelalter," *SAES*, p. 111 ff.

6. Gino Luzzatto, *An Economic History of Italy* (London, 1961), pp. 18, 26 ff.; Ennen, *Frühgeschichte*, pp. 233 ff. Toponymic research has shown more continuity of population between Roman and Lombard towns than in the rural areas. There is nonetheless little direct evidence of urban life in early Lombard Italy. See Gina Fasoli, "Aspetti di vita economica e sociale nell'Italia del Secolo VII," *Caratteri del Secolo VII in Occidente*, SSCI, V (Spoleto, 1958), 103–159, and Gian Piero Bognetti, "Problemi di metodo e oggetti di studio nella storia delle città italiane dell'alto medioevo," *CAM*, p. 70 ff. On the general question of continuity with Roman antecedents in Italy, see H. F. Schmid, "Das Weiterleben und die Wiederbelebung antiker Institutionen im mittelalterlichen Städtewesen," *ASD*, I (1957), 85–135.

7. For a general treatment of the growth of towns in Spain, see *IHCD*, III: *Urban Development in Southern Europe: Spain and Portugal* (London, 1967). On points of similarity and differentiation between Spanish towns and those of the north, see J. M. Lacarra, "Les villes frontières dans l'Espagne des XIe et XIIe siècles," *MA*, LXIX (1963), 205–222; and for a bibliographical orientation J. M. Font Rius, "Neuere Arbeiten zur spanischen Stadtgeschichte," *VJSWG*, XLII (1955), 137–151, and J. M. Lacarra, "Orientation des études d'histoire urbaine en Espagne entre 1940 et 1957," *MA*, LXIV (1958), 317–339.

origins in England are also somewhat exceptional, although recent scholarship has tended to emphasize the close parallels of English and continental town development. There is little evidence that settlement continued at Roman town sites in England through the period of the Völkerwanderung, whereas this issue remains in doubt for many continental centers. When the English towns revived in the tenth century, their commercial development received an artificial stimulus from their role as centers of a strong royal administration which attempted to center exchange operations and establish mints in towns whenever possible. Many features of continental urban development therefore are not characteristic of England, as for example the tendency of most important continental towns to develop along waterways, while greater internal security favored the growth of towns on land routes in England.[8]

Between the Germanic and Viking invasions, the medieval development of the towns of northern continental Europe knew no stimulus as powerful as that afforded Italy and no depressant comparable to the Moslems in Spain; the thesis of Henri Pirenne that Moslem control of the Mediterranean over an extended period brought the Mediterranean-oriented trade of northern Europe to a standstill and thereby entailed the end of urban life can no longer be sustained.[9] The invasions of the fifth century, in contrast, which were catastrophic in northern Europe but not in the south, forced a new beginning from which towns might develop under the stimulus of forces peculiar to the medieval situation.

Most leading medieval towns on the Continent originated in "pre-urban nuclei."[10] This term includes towns which originated on the sites of Roman *civitates*, often incorporating their walls or the remains of their buildings, and centers which developed gradually around other nuclei and owed their importance to a variety of forces inherent in their particular situations or environments. Since numerous Roman towns which were destroyed by the barbarian invasions of the fifth century were at best agrarian villages during the middle ages, it is quite apparent that the

8. H. R. Loyn, *Anglo-Saxon England and the Norman Conquest* (New York, 1962), pp. 66 ff., 132 ff.; Peter Hunter Blair, *An Introduction to Anglo-Saxon England* (Cambridge, 1959), p. 277 ff. For a recent survey of opinion on medieval urban origins in England, see John F. Benton, *Town Origins: The Evidence from Medieval England* (Boston, 1968).

9. Henri Pirenne, *Mohammed and Charlemagne* (New York, 1939; reprinted New York, 1957), Part II. For a summary of critical opinion on the Pirenne thesis, see Anne Riising, "The Fate of Henri Pirenne's Theses on the Consequence of the Islamic Expansion," *Classica et Mediaevalia*, XIII (1952), 87–130.

10. The term is Ganshof's; see his *Over Stadsontwikkeling, passim.*

forces leading to the rise of a Roman town, which was essentially a political creation from above, might have little or no effect on medieval urban development. Concentration upon pre-urban nuclei which had no Roman antecedents permits an even closer examination of the forces at work in medieval town formation and of the elements stimulating the rebirth of some Roman centers while others remained dormant. The constitutive topographical elements of the medieval town as a type have been specified as those of the pre-urban nucleus: the fortification, essentially a political, military, or ecclesiastical center, an inheritance in most cases from the Roman urban type; and the Germanic *Wik*, a group of shacks, generally unprotected, along a single street outside the fortification where merchants congregated.[11] Neither of these elements is a town; together they constitute a pre-urban nucleus—an agglomeration which was differentiated economically and topographically, but not yet juridically, from the surrounding countryside.

Places which were prosperous in the early middle ages but did not survive, for example Duurstede and Haithabu,[12] are less instructive than towns developing from pre-urban nuclei. Their sudden decline in the wake of the Viking invasions indicates an artificiality in their prosperity which rendered them unable to adapt to the peculiar conditions of medieval life. Planned urban foundations are not considered for similar reasons. We are concerned here with urban development prior to the formal establishment of the commune or the granting of elementary bourgeois liberties. Most planned foundations are known only from the time of their charters of foundation. They were often artificial creations of lords who were attempting to increase their revenues or give incentives to local peasants. They were a product of a later time and of circumstances completely unlike those characterizing the evolution of pre-urban nuclei into towns. Although some planned foundations later expanded into genuine towns, most were simply agrarian villages whose inhabitants enjoyed bourgeois status. They were towns in a juridical, but not an economic sense.[13]

Two criteria must be satisfied before an agglomeration can be called a town. A permanent, resident settlement must be present. The town can-

---

11. Planitz, *Die deutsche Stadt*, p. 65 ff.

12. Herbert Jankuhn, *Haithabu. Eine germanische Stadt der Frühzeit*, 3rd ed. (Berlin, 1956).

13. See, for example, Hektor Ammann, "Über das waadtländische Städtewesen im Mittelalter und über landschaftliches Städtewesen im allgemeinen," *SZG*, IV (1954), 1–87.

not be defined in terms of its market, for a market was often simply a place in the countryside where peasants came at intervals to sell their produce. In no way did the market imply a permanent settlement. Similarly, the presence of itinerant merchants in a *Wik* does not indicate that a locality has become a town.

Secondly, the town must be differentiated economically, juridically, and topographically from the surrounding countryside. The inhabitants of a genuine town engaged in a form of economic activity, generally commercial, to an extent not characteristic of the surrounding agrarian regions. A juridical distinction between town and countryside reflecting the economic distinction is also implicit in the definition of urbanism. A revolutionary act, the creation of a special market law, with a court and peace of the market, marks the transition from market to town.[14] The personal law of the merchant is transposed to the territorial law of the town.[15] The legal and economic distinctions between town and countryside are complementary. Many scholars, particularly Germans, have defined the town, as opposed to the pre-urban nucleus, in the juridical context of the sworn association (*coniuratio*), even when they see the origins of these unions in economic relationships.[16] Purely economic or legal definitions of the town are unsatisfactory; scholars who have posited exclusively economic origins for the medieval town have been forced to use juridical arguments in defense of their position.[17] Finally, the distinction between

14. Otto Feger, "Auf dem Weg vom Markt zur Stadt," *Zeitschrift für die Geschichte des Oberrheins*, CVI (1958), 10.

15. Planitz, *Die deutsche Stadt*, p. 98 ff.

16. *Ibid.*; Ennen, *Frühgeschichte*, p. 175.

17. This is particularly true of Pirenne and his disciples. Georges Espinas, one of Pirenne's most adamant followers, admits in his discussion of the origins of St. Omer that the *portus* of St. Omer bordered on the abbey of St. Bertin and that the market of 874 was abbatial. Yet Espinas argues that the abbey, as a rural, seigneurial, nonurban entity could not possibly have been the pre-urban nucleus giving rise to the town, for a rigid juridical dichotomy must be maintained between urban and nonurban phenomena. This argument ignores the fact that urban law does not appear until after the development of agglomerations that can be termed towns. Since it is impossible to separate town and countryside juridically until the complete development of the former, and since town proceeded from countryside economically if not juridically, the Pirenne school becomes involved in a logical contradiction by attempting so rigidly to define town in a juridical context while claiming that urban origins were purely economic. See Georges Espinas, *Les Origines du Capitalisme*, III: *Deux Fondations de villes dans l'Artois et la Flandre française (X–XVe siècles). Saint-Omer. Lannoy du Nord* (Paris and Lille, 1946). Cf. the critique of this work by Édouard Perroy, "Les origines urbaines en Flandre d'après un ouvrage récent," *RH*, XXIX (1947), 49–63, and Espinas' reply, "Les origines urbaines en Flandre," *MA*, LIV (1948), 37–56.

town and countryside is symbolized by a physical separation of the two, the construction of a wall around the town. The jurisdiction of the town magistrates normally extended one mile beyond this wall,[18] and the fortification protected the town from dangers and undesirable influences extraneous to itself. The purpose of this paper is to trace the beginning of these distinctions between medieval town and countryside on the European Continent as established by research conducted since the Second World War.

Research conducted since 1945 on medieval urban origins in northern continental Europe has seen some change of opinion on the question of continuity between Roman and medieval town. Most scholars of the prewar generation agreed that the Germanic invasions of the fourth and fifth centuries which ended Roman imperial government in the west did not cause the immediate end of Roman urban institutions. Henri Pirenne saw economic continuity of the west with Rome until the rise of Moslem power around the Mediterranean. In the view of Alfons Dopsch, Roman commercial and urban life continued through the period of Charlemagne.[19]

By 1945 these views had been criticized sharply, and more recent research has tended to return to the older, catastrophic view of the Germanic invasions.[20] Before the third century, most Roman centers in Gaul had been open and unfortified. Of the towns which were fortified before 260, when the Germans broke the Rhine-Danube *limes*, all but two (Lyon and Autun) were on a frontier. The fortified towns included the border settlements of Cologne, Tournai, Avenches, Heddernheim, Ladenburg, Tongeren, Wimpfen, and Xanten, together with most towns along and near the Mediterranean coast.[21] Although these towns were predominantly administrative and military centers, many had important mercantile and artisan settlements as well. *Canabae*, settlements of merchants doing business with the soldiers, even developed around some purely military encampments, generally on the main road leading away from the

18. Winfried Küchler, *Das Bannmeilenrecht* (Würzburg, 1964).

19. Alfons Dopsch, *Wirtschaftliche und Soziale Grundlagen der europäischen Kulturentwicklung*, 2 vols.; 2nd. ed. (Vienna, 1923), II, 365 ff.; see also the abbreviated English translation, *The Economic and Social Foundations of European Civilization* (New York, 1937), p. 320 ff.

20. For an older expression of the catastrophic view of the invasions, see Prosper Boissonnade, *Life and Work in Medieval Europe. The Evolution of Medieval Economy from the Fifth to the Fifteenth Century* (New York and London, 1927; reprinted New York, 1964), p. 26 ff.

21. R. M. Butler, "Late Roman Town Walls in Gaul," *AJ*, CXVI (1959), 25–26.

camp. Noncommercial populations then gathered around these small nuclei.[22]

The temporary breaking of the *limes* by the Germanic tribes in the mid-third century changed all this. The Roman towns were overwhelmed and in many cases burned or sacked.[23] Although the disaster was only temporary, the prosperity of the Roman towns in Gaul had sustained a decisive setback. Population declined drastically. In most cases the outlying areas of the towns, which constituted the most important merchant and artisan settlements, never were rebuilt.[24] Most Gallic towns that the Romans continued to occupy in the fourth and fifth centuries received fortifications for the first time in the later third. These fortifications generally used masonry obtained from the ruins of the buildings of the town—a good indication of the extent of the disaster or at least of the haste with which the walls were constructed. The fortifications generally enclosed a much smaller area than the settlements had occupied before the invasions.[25]

22. Ramsay MacMullen, *Soldier and Civilian in the Later Roman Empire* (Cambridge, Mass., 1963), p. 119 ff. See also Planitz, *Die deutsche Stadt*, p. 16. The archaeological research of Harald von Petrikovits on Neuss has brought about a change of opinion on the nature of Roman garrison towns. Some were larger than has been realized, and the commercial and artisan activities of the *canabae* were more extensive. The *canabae* of Neuss encompassed at least 185 acres, including living quarters and a merchant and artisan suburb. Dependents of the soldiers also tended to live in the suburbs, but there evidently was no purely industrial activity in the *canabae*. See Harald von Petrikovits, *Novaesium. Das römische Neuss* (Cologne and Graz, 1957), and "Das römische Neuss," in *Neue Ausgrabungen in Deutschland* (Berlin, 1958), pp. 380–390.

23. Edith Ennen, "Die Entwicklung des Städtewesens an Rhein und Mosel vom 6. bis 9. Jahrhundert," *CAM*, p. 420 ff.; Robert Étienne, *Bordeaux Antique*, in Charles Higounet (ed.), Histoire de Bordeaux (Bordeaux, 1962), pp. 184–186; Dietrich Claude, *Topographie und Verfassung der Städte Bourges et Poitiers bis in das 11. Jahrhundert* (Lübeck and Hamburg, 1960), pp. 32–33, 43; and more generally Ferdinant Lot, *Recherches sur la population et la superficie des cités remontant à la période Gallo-Romaine*, 3 vols. (Paris, 1945–53).

24. In exceptional cases the reduction of the town area did not have a catastrophic character. The walls of Paris and Senlis were intended merely as citadels. Most of the population remained outside and used the walls only in time of emergency. See M. Roblin, "Cités ou citadelles? Les enceintes romaines du Bas-Empire d'après l'exemple de Paris," *REA*, LIII (1951), 301, and *idem*, "Cités ou citadelles? Les enceintes romaines du Bas-Empire d'après l'exemple de Senlis," *REA*, LXVII (1965), 368–391.

25. Butler, "Late Roman Town Walls," pp. 40–41. The towns which were fortified during the early Empire and received new fortification in the third century show this with particular clarity. Most such towns are in southern Gaul, as for example Autun, Nimes, Orange, and Lyon. Since the towns of northernmost Gaul evidently did not receive two separate fortifications from the Romans, it is at least possible that the Romans occupied them merely as strong points and not as genuine towns, and then

Beginning in the late third century the history of most Gallo-Roman towns is a story of decline. There can be no question of a break in continuity of settlement, however, except perhaps for brief periods immediately following the destruction of the towns by the Germans. All were quickly reoccupied and rebuilt by the Gallo-Romans. But no Roman center regained the prosperity which it had enjoyed under the early empire, with the single exception of Trier, which enjoyed a renewed growth in the fourth century as the seat of the prefecture of Gaul.

Any question of continuity of settlement between the Roman and medieval town, however, must hinge on the barbarian invasions of the fourth and fifth centuries, rather than those of the third,[26] and the object of comparison with the medieval town must be the fortified military and administrative centers into which the Roman towns were transformed in the third century.[27] In one sense, therefore, despite some outward similarities between the two, the problem of continuity between Roman and medieval town[28] is probably malposed, for these rump towns differed as much from the cities of the early Roman Empire as from those of the high middle ages.[29] The decisive moment of break between the towns of antiquity and those of the middle ages as types was the third century, when the construction of town walls began the physical separation of town from countryside.[30]

---

only after the disasters of the third century. See Ernest Will, "Recherches sur le développement urbain sous l'empire Romain dans le Nord de la France," *Gallia*, XX (1962), 101. The second Roman fortification at Metz left out an entire quarter of the area formerly enclosed, although it still contained 173 acres. See Yvette Dollinger-Léonard, "De la cité romaine à la ville médiévale dans la région de la Moselle et la Haute Meuse," *SAES*, p. 196. The only "exception" to this generalization has proved to be no exception; the enormous second wall of Toulouse, enclosing 198 acres, was the work of the Visigoths, not the Romans. See E. Delaruelle, "Toulouse capitale wisigothique et son rempart," *AM*, LXVII (1955), 205–221.

26. For the general chronology of barbarian raids on Roman town sites in Gaul, see Planitz, *Die deutsche Stadt*, p. 24 ff.

27. On the question of whether the Germanic invasions caused a general economic break with Roman civilization, see R. H. Bautier, "Les grandes problèmes politiques et économiques de la Méditerranée médiévale," *RH*, CCXXXIV (1965), 1–28, and especially 1–6.

28. See, for example, the statement of the problem by Dopsch, *Economic and Social Foundations*, p. 363 ff.

29. Fernand Vercauteren, "La vie urbaine entre Meuse et Loire du VIe au IXe siècle," *CAM*, p. 463.

30. Jean Lestocquoy, "De l'unité à la pluralité. Le paysage urbain en Gaule du Ve au IXe siècle," *AESC*, VIII (1953), 172. The important role played by the invasions of the third century in the formation of the medieval town on the continent has been

The problem of continuity of settlement, however, is much more complex. We must attempt by a comparative geographical survey to determine the extent to which late Roman town life survived the Germanic invasions of the fourth and fifth centuries in northern continental Europe.

A leading scholar, Edith Ennen, recently has categorized northern medieval towns into three distinct zones in terms of their degree of continuity with ancient civilization. In southern Gaul, Roman traditions remained comparatively strong, but even there Roman municipal organization as a separate instrument of public authority disappeared almost completely. In northern France and the regions of the Rhine, Danube, and Meuse, Roman civilization largely succumbed to the invaders but did not disappear completely. Northern Germany and the right bank of the Rhine never knew the direct influence of Roman civilization.[31] The break between Rome and the middle ages was clearest where it occurred early; there was much greater continuity in regions where the crisis of the third century was at least partially overcome than in such areas as the lower Rhine region, where the third century meant the real end of Roman civilization.[32]

Some settlement continued throughout the early middle ages at or near most major Roman town sites in southern Gaul, although a few did disappear. Occasionally Roman sites were abandoned in favor of nearby localities. An excellent example of this phenomenon is the case of Cimiez and Nice. Both had been Roman *civitates*, and Cimiez was originally by far the more important of the two. It was a purely administrative center, and access to it was difficult. Nice, a port town, thus gradually supplanted Cimiez as the leading town of the region.[33]

Bordeaux also demonstrates well the fate of Roman town life in southern Gaul. Originally a very prosperous open center, it was severely damaged by the raids of the third century. A wall was built between 278 and 290, evidently from the debris of buildings of the open city which had been destroyed. Bordeaux remained a provincial capital in the fourth

recognized by scholars since at least the time of Ferdinant Lot; see his *Recherches sur la population, passim.*

31. Edith Ennen, "The Different Types of Formation of European Towns," in Sylvia L. Thrupp (ed.), *Early Medieval Society* (New York, 1967), p. 175; translated from "Les differents types de formation des villes européennes," *MA*, LXII (1956), 397–411.

32. See Edith Ennen's review of Claude, *Topographie und Verfassung*, in *Historische Zeitschrift*, CXCVIII (1964), 165–169.

33. Paul-Albert Février, *Le Développement urbain en Provence, de l'époque romaine à la fin du XIV*e *siècle* (Paris, 1964), p. 79 ff.; see also Robert Latouche, *Histoire de Nice*, 2 vols. (Nice, 1951), I, 1 ff.; and especially Paul-Marie Duval, "Rapport sur les fouilles de Cemenelum (Cimiez)," *Gallia*, IV (1946), 77–136.

Northern Continental Europe in the Early Middle Ages: Major Pre-Urban Settlements.

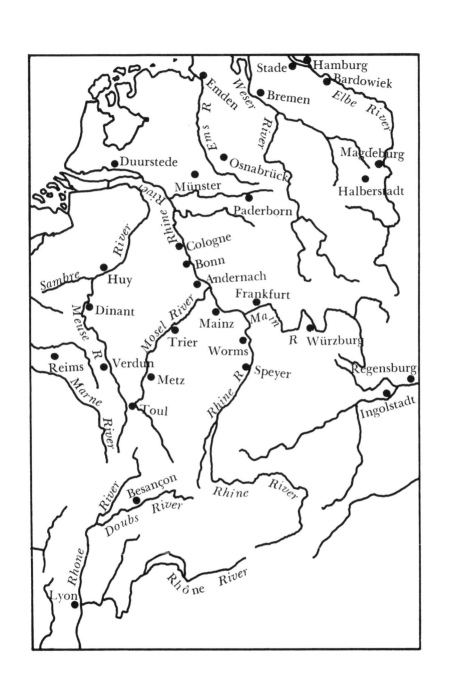

century, with some commercial activity, but the testimony of Ausonius shows a growing ruralization of fourth-century Bordeaux. The town was burned by the Vandals in 414; the population left, but soon returned. But while Bordeaux remained an episcopal seat during the Merovingian period, it had sustained a nearly fatal blow. The town was in the process of an economic transition to a market which was based on a prosperous agrarian regime; many villas surrounding the town were owned by churches and by nobles who lived in Bordeaux for part of the year. This agrarian economy was sufficiently viable and prosperous to sustain a large market and capital. There was a small resident merchant colony at Bordeaux until at least the mid-seventh century, but the crises of the Moslem and Viking invasions ended this gradual evolution away from old Roman forms. In the early ninth century Bordeaux was a mere military stronghold, but from this time the town began to revive.[34]

For all its fluctuations, southern Gaul preserved the Roman municipal tradition more completely than any other area of Europe north of the Alps. These towns never lost their semirural, neo-Roman character, except in such exceptional cases as Marseille.[35] Pirenne's thesis on the role of the Arabs in the break of the west with Roman traditions[36] may have a relevance for the towns of southern Gaul that its promulgator never intended. Beginning with the eighth century, southern Gaul became a frontier area against the Moslems; Moslem pirates ravaged the Mediterranean coast, and Islamic raiders were a constant danger inland. It is difficult to determine precisely the extent to which the towns may have been devastated or pillaged by the Moslems, but the insecurity of the age definitely accentuated the military, noncommercial character of town life in southern Gaul, a character sharply distinguished from the urbanism of the north.[37] The towns of southern France retained the partly rural, partly urban character of the late Roman *civitates*.

Correspondingly, the example of certain towns of southern Gaul illustrates a motif which will become extremely prominent when we

34. Étienne, *Bordeaux Antique*, pp. 184–186, 204, 214–220; Charles Higounet, *Bordeaux pendant le haut moyen age*, in Charles Higounet (ed.), Histoire de Bordeaux (Bordeaux, 1963), pp. 12 ff., 42, 204–208, 220.

35. See E. Baratier and F. Reynaud, *Histoire du Commerce de Marseille de 1291–1480* (Paris, 1951), p. 1 ff.

36. See his *Mohammed and Charlemagne*, Part II.

37. Georges Duby, "Les villes du sud-est de la Gaule du VIIIᵉ au XIᵉ siècle," *CAM*, p. 232 ff.

consider the northern regions: the prosperity of a town in the middle ages often depended in the long run, although perhaps not at first, on the extent to which it broke with its Roman antecedents. Strategic considerations normally determined the selection of town sites by the Romans. But this was not invariably the case; when the Romans built towns on the sites of Celtic *oppida*, they normally transferred the agglomeration from high points and promontories to the plains, or at least the hillsides, so that their towns could participate in some local commerce.[38] The Romans rarely adopted a site, however, which was not of some strategic importance. This is shown clearly in the Roman preference for Cimiez, which declined in favor of Nice when it lost its importance as a garrison. An equally clear illustration is Agde, a Greek colony on the Mediterranean taken over by the Romans. Roman occupation of Greek sites was generally unfavorable for their development as urban centers; following this pattern, Agde declined under Roman occupation while the surrounding countryside prospered. Roman peacetime rule tended to favor dispersal, rather than concentration of the population. The Moslem invasions concentrated population at Agde, but thereby increased the dominance of countryside elements within the town. Agde became a moderately prosperous trading center, but only as a result of its location on the Mediterranean coast.[39]

The Germanic invasions of the fifth century were catastrophic on the Rhine-Danube *limes*. Modern scholarship has generally agreed that few Roman towns survived into the middle ages. At the time of the invasions the Germans had no towns of their own and were hardly in position to maintain those of the Romans. They unquestionably used the towns as fortifications,[40] but only the Gallo-Roman population was familiar with Roman municipal institutions. As Germanic elements gradually assimilated the Roman, the towns declined. The possessors of landed property, who had been the leaders of the Roman municipal aristocracy, left the towns for their countryside estates. The changing economic position of

38. For a discussion of the development of Roman towns at or near the sites of Celtic fortifications, see Planitz, *Die deutsche Stadt*, pp. 11–12.

39. R. Aris and J. Picheire, "Essai sur le développement topographique d'Agde," *AM*, LXXII (1960), 129–135.

40. See Lucien Musset, *Les invasions: les vagues germaniques* (Paris, 1965), p. 241; Fernand Vercauteren, *Étude sur les civitates de la Belgique Séconde* (Brussels, 1934), pp. 49, 109–110, and *passim*; and J. Vannerus, *Le Limes et les fortifications gallo-romaines de Belgique* (Brussels, 1942), p. 18.

the curial class, so often described,[41] meant that Roman municipal life was only a shadow of its former self by the early fifth century, when the Germans struck the border towns in force. Roman imperial officials had generally replaced the decurions in municipal administration by this time.[42] This was the period of great change from the Roman system on the upper levels of urban society.

Yet the Roman settlements were not annihilated; rudimentary agglomerations persisted on nearly every Roman site or in its immediate environs. Demonstration of the continuity of medieval with Roman settlements has been furthered immeasurably by the tendency of recent scholars to concentrate less on written evidence concerning towns than on the gleanings of numismatics, archaeology, and the study of trade routes and trade conditions.[43] Such studies have shown conclusively that the greatest destruction entailed by the Germanic invasions affected the upper classes in the towns. The lower classes, engaged in local trade and industry, had less to lose and thus less to regain. They were hurt badly, but they could recover more quickly than the upper classes. There was continuity of the Roman artisan tradition under the Germanic invaders of northern Gaul. Thus, as would be expected, the *suburbium* of the Roman town was the element which was most fully continued into the middle ages.[44] Merovingian graves found in towns of northern Gaul which had been Roman centers show Roman names and artifacts, presupposing some continuity of settlement.[45] A distinction must be made, however, between the Rhineland, where the change, although often violent, was accomplished within a relatively short time, and the Danube region, where the

41. For the traditional view, see Ferdinant Lot, *The End of the Ancient World and the Beginnings of the Middle Ages* (New York, 1931; reprinted New York, 1961), p. 114 ff. A somewhat more balanced picture of the difficult, but by no means impossible lot of the decurions is given by A. H. M. Jones, *The Later Roman Empire, 284–602: A Social, Economic, and Administrative Survey*, 2 vols. (Norman, Okla., 1964), I, 737 ff.

42. Fernand Vercauteren, "Die spätantike Civitas im frühen Mittelalter," *BDL*, XCVIII (1962), 16.

43. Maurice Lombard, "L'évolution urbaine pendant le haut moyen âge," *AESC*, XII (1957), 7 ff.

44. There are exceptions. Only the Roman civilian settlement at Neuss, not the military and commercial *canabae*, persisted into the middle ages without break in settlement. Ennen, "Entwicklung des Städtewesens," pp. 423–424, following Petrikovits, *Novaesium*.

45. Édouard Salin, *La civilisation mérovingienne, d'après les sépultures, les textes et la laboratoire*, 4 vols. (Paris, 1949–59), I, 368; G. Faider-Feytmans, *La Belgique à l'époque mérovingienne* (Brussels, 1964), p. 112.

transition was much more drastic.[46] No urban cemetery indicating continuity of settlement of the Roman population has been found east of Augst. Of the Roman Danubian settlements only Klosterneuburg seems to have persisted into the middle ages.[47]

These general observations have been confirmed by recent studies of particular towns along the Rhine-Danube *limes*.[48] Regensburg was a fortified Roman camp; evidently it was never a *civitas*, for officials there had jurisdiction only in the territory immediately surrounding the walls. The walls were reduced in size after the disaster of 260; the new fortification enclosed the area forming the central part of the modern city. Between 410 and 420 the garrison of Regensburg was transferred in the wake of the invasions to Manching, near Ingolstadt; the camp was probably abandoned, since there would have been no *raison d'être* for an artisan or merchant settlement after the departure of the soldiers. The site of the camp probably never was destroyed, however, for the walls have been preserved in excellent condition. Regensburg may have passed to Germanic federates of the Romans, and in succeeding years to the Thuringians and Bavarians. Grave finds are ambiguous on the subject of continuity of settlement with Roman Regensburg. The same general vicinity includes Christian graves of the fourth century, Bavarian graves of the seventh, and heathen burial places of uncertain date. A connecting link among these graves must be found to establish continuity; provisionally therefore it seems extremely unlikely that any of the Roman population of the fifth century continued to live on the site of the camp at Regensburg. The subsequent development of Regensburg lends credence to this hypothesis; after it became a residence of the Agilofing dukes of Bavaria

46. See the series of brief talks on this subject given at the fourth meeting of the Kreis für landschaftliche deutsche Städteforschung, April 4–6, 1962, at Trier, published as "Die Frage der Kontinuität in den Städten an Rhein und Mosel im Frühmittelalter," *WF*, XVI (1963), 52–78.

47. Harald von Petrikovits, "Das Fortleben römischer Städte an Rhein und Donau im frühen Mittelalter," *TZ*, XIX (1950), 72–81; *idem*, "Das Fortleben römischer Städte an Rhein und Donau," *SAES*, pp. 63–76, and *Das römische Rheinland. Archäologische Forschungen seit 1945* (Cologne and Opladen, 1960).

48. See W. Schleiermacher, "Die spätesten Spuren der antiken Besiedlung im Raum von Speyer, Worms, Mainz, Frankfurt und Ladenburg," *BJ*, CLXII (1962), 165–173. This study reaches the same conclusion for the middle Rhine as that of Petrikovits for the entire Rhine-Danube area: that after the collapse of Roman provincial administration in the last years of the fifth century, towns which were not abandoned completely reverted to a pre-urban, semiagrarian economy.

in the late seventh century, Regensburg knew no merchant or artisan settlements inside the walls for another two centuries.[49]

There was evidently no continuity of settlement between Roman and medieval Vienna, a fact which further confirms the impression of a cataclysm along the Danube in the fifth century. Roman buildings have disappeared completely, aside from the use of some building stone from their ruins in medieval structures. The Roman street plan left no trace on that of the middle ages.[50]

The invasions were less disastrous along the Rhine. Andernach is an excellent example of a town on the Rhine *limes* which survived. The situation of this town was no more favorable intrinsically for the growth or survival of urban life than that of numerous other Rhineland centers. Toponymic evidence shows that the Romans either found a settlement at Andernach and adopted its name or named their fortification after a Celtic place in the immediate vicinity. Andernach was one of many fortresses along the left bank of the Rhine on the road from Switzerland to the North Sea, guarding a narrow pass in the Eifel range. The construction of the *limes*, however, thrust the border further east, and Andernach lost its military importance. Evidently it then became an open settlement. Andernach regained its importance after the Germans had broken the *limes* in the third century and had made it a frontier town once again. It was later walled. Andernach was on the great Roman military road which paralleled the Rhine; but even more important for its future development was a second road leading south and west into a prosperous agrarian hinterland.[51] Germanic graves have been found along this road and others leading to it, particularly around the ferry across the Rhine south of the Roman fortification, but not within the citadel of Andernach. The Roman garrison left Andernach by 465 at the latest; yet a separate Roman

49. Ernst Klebel, "Regensburg," *SAES*, pp. 87–104. The same data are interpreted with less precision as indicating continuity of settlement between Roman and medieval Regensburg by Karl Bosl, "Die Sozialstruktur der mittelalterlichen Residenz- und Fernhandelsstadt Regensburg. Die Entwicklung ihres Bürgertums vom 9.–14. Jahrhundert," *Untersuchungen zur gesellschaftlichen Struktur der mittelalterlichen Städte in Europa*, Vorträge und Forschungen . . . XI (Constance and Stuttgart, 1966), 97–98.

50. K. Oettinger, *Das Werden Wiens* (Vienna, 1951), pp. 1–6. Although Oettinger admits the force of such arguments as these, he nonetheless maintains a continuity of settlement at Vienna owing to the persistence of the Roman wall.

51. The importance of local trade for the eventual development of major centers, a theme that will be developed in some detail below, was first recognized by Renée Doehaerd, "Au temps de Charlemagne et des Normandes: ce qu'onv endait et comment on le vendait dans le bassin parisien," *AESC*, II (1947), 266–280.

population, living within the walls, was able to maintain itself beside the Germans for a century before the two groups finally merged. Characteristically, these were the lower classes, shopkeepers and artisans, who could trade in modest products with the Germans. There is little evidence of merchants of Andernach engaging in long-distance commerce during the centuries immediately after the fall of the Roman garrison. Andernach specialized in wares that the Germans would want, and while the barbarians were fond of finery and precious metals and textiles, these items did not constitute their major needs. Andernach was able simply to survive, quietly and unspectacularly, by trading in useful products, local in character, which found a ready market among the barbarian warriors and peasants. The presence of Germanic cemeteries near the Rhine ferry is instructive; it indicates that while most Germans still avoided living in towns, they had begun to engage in trade, together with the Romans, with the regions on the right bank. A slow fusion took place which preserved some continuity with Roman antecedents.[52] Andernach thus survived the invasions through its close ties to the surrounding countryside. There is no reason to assume that it was more favored in this regard than other Roman towns which, in default of precise archaeological evidence, and particularly the testimony of cemeteries, cannot therefore categorically be assumed to have succumbed completely to the Germanic invasions.

The city of Bonn shows a characteristic medieval development of a Roman fortification. The medieval settlement was outside Roman Bonn. This does not necessarily indicate a break in continuity of settlement; although the upper classes were decimated, some artisans and merchants remained at Bonn across the period of the invasions. At Bonn, as at

---

52. Karl Zimmermann, "Vom Römerkastell Andernach zur mittelalterlichen Stadt," *RV*, XIX (1954), 317–340. Andernach always remained the center of an essentially local commerce. Zimmermann notes that the *Wik* of Andernach developed south of the town, on the side away from the Rhine; yet he says that Roman roads leading south were losing much of their importance as commercial arteries to the Rhine. The *Wik* was destroyed by the Vikings, and a new market was built east of the town, just south of the Roman road paralleling the Rhine. A town hall and artisan quarters soon were constructed there. The Rhine bends away from Andernach at this point, however, and the new market, although not the later town hall, was nearer to the old *Wik* than to the Rhine. The evidence presented by Zimmermann thus indicates that Roman land routes, over which local trade came from the agrarian hinterland of Andernach, were much more important for the prosperity of the town in the high middle ages than was the Rhine, which carried goods over greater distances; Zimmermann, however, reaches the contrary conclusion. See *ibid.*, pp. 326–327, and especially the map on p. 327.

Andernach, the Roman military road along the Rhine went through the *castrum*. Although most of the Frankish invaders either remained in the German homeland on the right bank of the river or settled in the open spaces on the left bank, there was still a settlement in the Roman *castrum* after the invasions. The agglomeration was entirely too small, however, to fill the space enclosed within the *castrum*. The population concentrated in the southwestern corner of the fortification. Several minor roads leading into the agrarian regions outside the town crossed at this corner; the removal of the settlement thus shows an economic motivation. The settlers of the *Bonnaburg* wished to engage in commercial relations with the peasants in the immediate agrarian hinterland of the fortification, rather than in the long-distance trade which might have been provided by the Rhine or the Roman military road. Bonn affords a classic case of factors other than long-distance commerce influencing the rise of a town, for the Roman camp, the site of a ferry on the bank of the Rhine, was much more favorably located for commerce over an extended area than the inland settlement which developed around St. Cassian's church.[53] The settlers of the *Bonnaburg*, however, maintained no direct contact with the Rhine. The harbors built by the Romans silted.

The center of gravity shifted again, however, in the ninth and tenth centuries. Suburbs arose around parish churches which completely surpassed the *Bonnaburg*, which was destroyed by the Vikings in the late ninth century and never rebuilt. While most Roman towns which persisted into the middle ages remained the nuclei which were gradually absorbed by more economically important settlements in the suburbs, Bonn shows a complete reversal of this pattern. There was a topographical break at Bonn, but no caesura in continuity of settlement. Although Bonn eventually developed some long-distance trade, it survived the Germanic invasions through its local, essentially agrarian commerce.[54]

Instances of the displacement of population away from Roman fortifications also are found in other regions. This often occurred when the Roman town had moved away from a Celtic site which was more easily defended. The Celts had placed their *oppidum* at Besançon on the crest of a hill which jutted into the Doubs River. The Romans moved their camp down the hill to take in only a part of the Celtic citadel. The invasions

53. Edith Ennen, "Die Bonner Märkte," in *Beiträge zur Wirtschaftsund Stadtgeschichte. Festschrift für Hektor Ammann* (Wiesbaden, 1965), p. 56.

54. Ennen, *Frühgeschichte*, p. 85 ff.; Josef Niessen and Edith Ennen, *Geschichte der Stadt Bonn*, 2 vols. (Bonn, 1956), I, 40 ff.

were particularly severe at Besançon; although the topography and walls of the town evidently were left undisturbed, the bishopric provided the only element of continuity of settlement. The population which later grouped at Besançon moved back into the Celtic fortress on the crest of the hill backed against the Doubs. This fortress, rather than the Roman, was the center from which Besançon eventually grew.[55]

Namur affords a parallel case. The high promontory of the Champeau, between the Meuse and the Sambre, had been used by the Celts as a fortification. It was an admirable defensive position, but it was almost inaccessible. The Romans moved their town to the foot of the Champeau. After this settlement was burned during the Germanic breakthrough of the third century, the fortress was again moved to the Celtic site; an extension of the walls incorporated the lowland areas.[56]

Many of the new discoveries and reinterpretations which have been propounded during the past quarter-century on medieval urban origins along the Rhine *limes* and in trans-Rhenane Germany result from archaeological findings[57] made possible by the destruction of so many German cities during the Second World War. There was much less destruction along the Mosel, in France,[58] and in the Low Countries,[59] and our knowledge of the extent to which the Roman town persisted in these regions suffers correspondingly. Metz, where the third-century wall enclosed the unusually large area of 173 acres, knew a flourishing economic

55. Lucien Lerat, "L'Antiquité," in Charles Fohlen (ed.), *Histoire de Besançon*, I: *Des origines a la fin du XVIᵉ siècle* (Paris, 1964), pp. 37–41, 126–127; Maurice Rey, "Le Moyen Age du XIIᵉ au XVᵉ siècle," in *ibid.*, p. 191.

56. Félix Rousseau, *Namur, ville mosane*, 2nd ed. (Brussels, 1958), pp. 21–22, 33–34.

57. See "Archäologische Methoden und Quellen zur Stadtkernforschung und ihr Verhältnis zu den historischen Quellen und Methoden. Protokoll der Tagung des Arbeitskreises für Stadtforschung der Arbeitsgemeinschaft der Historischen Kommission und landesgeschichtlichen Institute Deutschlands in Hamburg vom 2. bis 4. März 1959," *WF*, XIII (1960), 181–194.

58. For a general survey of recent archaeological findings in Roman Gaul, see A. Grenier, *Archéologie gallo-romaine*, 7 vols. (Paris, 1931–64).

59. See H. Van de Weerd, *Inleiding tot de Gallo-Romeinsche Archeologie der Nederlanden* (Antwerp, 1944). Despite the great value of archaeological discoveries for the study of medieval urban origins, the historian often must beware of the conclusions reached by the archaeologist from his data. A recent study of Boulogne sees a complete break in continuity between Gallo-Roman and Germanic populations at Boulogne, largely on the basis of an a priori deduction of the bitter enmity existing between the two groups. The walls of Boulogne remained after the departure of the Romans, but "il semble bien que leurs [Germans'] habitudes militaires ne comportaient pas un souci dévéloppé de la fortification." Ernest Will, "Les remparts romains de Boulogne-sur-Mer," *RN*, XLII (1960), 369–370. See above, p. 67, and n. 40.

life during the late Empire. Much of its prosperity was undoubtedly due to the proximity of Trier, the seat of the praetorian prefecture of Gaul, but Metz also benefited from its position at the junction of the Mosel and the Seille. Gregory of Tours and Paul the Deacon reported that the entire town, except the oratory of St. Stephen, was destroyed by Attila in 451. This seems unlikely, in view of the importance of Metz as a residence of the Merovingian kings in the sixth century, but the archaeological research necessary for a definitive answer to this question has not yet been conducted. Several mints were located at Metz in the sixth century, and there was evidently a commercial settlement by the 590s. The extent to which Metz witnessed a continuity of Roman settlement into the middle ages, however, is uncertain.[60]

Trier, also on the Mosel, was the most important city in Gaul in the fourth century. Long an important commercial and industrial center, it became the imperial capital in 293, as the emperors began living regularly on the frontiers to ward off the Germans. Constantine fortified an enormous area of 704 acres; a complex of churches that was to endure into the ninth century was constructed within and outside the walls. The prosperity of Trier ended suddenly when the prefecture of Gaul was moved to Arles at the beginning of the fifth century. The Franks took Trier four times between 411 and 428. The wall of Trier was too large, and the badly reduced population found it impossible to defend. Some measure of continuity persisted across the invasions, however, despite the misfortunes of the town. A mint was located there in the early fifth century, and the baths along the Mosel were used. Ecclesiastical relations between Trier and Rome are definitely attested in the second half of the fifth century. Some town life continued, but by the sixth century the population had declined to a few thousand from a high of approximately 60,000 in the fourth century. Trier did not completely lose its long-distance commerce; merchants of Trier traded at Metz, and there was a resident Jewish colony at Trier. Merchants of Merovingian Trier were also found in the Mediterranean regions, and there was some trade with Frisian merchants. The invasions did not destroy the commercial life of Trier completely, but they ruined the great economic prosperity of the town.[61]

60. Yvette Dollinger-Léonard, "De la cité romaine à la ville médiévale," pp. 195–201.

61. Ibid., p. 215 ff.; Ennen, "Entwicklung des Städtewesens," p. 433 ff.; Eugen Ewig, Trier im Merowingerreich. Civitas. Stadt. Bistum (Trier, 1952); Theodor Konrad Kempf, "Die Entwicklung des Stadtgrundrisses von Trier," TJ (1953), 5–23.

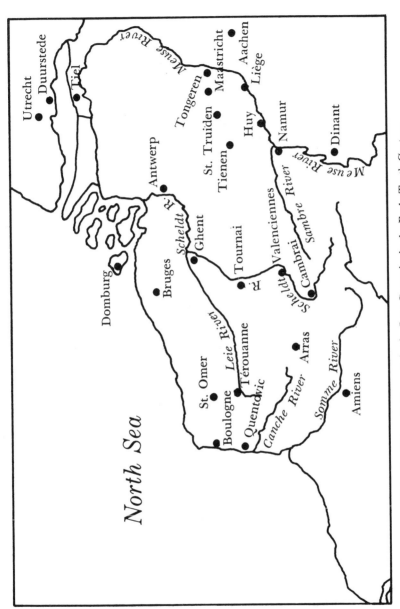

Major Pre-Urban Settlements in the Low Countries in the Early Tenth Century.

There was a limited survival of Roman town life in northeastern France and the Low Countries,[62] particularly along the Meuse River, the most important commercial artery of northern Europe in the seventh century. It is perhaps anachronistic to term what the Romans left "urban," for most of their centers in this region were mere fortresses of twenty-five acres or less. The case of Arlon is instructive. Arlon had been a prosperous center before the disaster of the third century, but the new fortress which was constructed was tiny (300 m. by 225 m.), and the *vicus*, which had been crossed by important overland routes, was excluded. Deprived of protection, the *vicus* disappeared in the confusion of the invasions, and Arlon remained a garrison town throughout the middle ages.[63]

The only Roman *civitates* in northeastern France and the Low Countries were Tongeren and Tournai. Tongeren saw no continuity with Rome; it was an insignificant agrarian village in the middle ages.[64] Tournai is a more complicated case. It was a commercial and industrial center from the early days of the Empire. Despite some destruction by the Germans, there was complete topographical continuity between Roman and Merovingian Tournai. There was also continuity across the early middle ages in the textile and stonecutting industries. The invasions entailed decline, but not disaster.[65]

62. The continuity of the Roman artisan tradition in the Meuse region has been noted by Faider-Feytmans, *La Belgique à l'époque mérovingienne*, p. 112, and André Joris, "On the Edge of Two Worlds in the Heart of the New Empire: The Romance Regions of Northern Gaul during the Merovingian Period," in William M. Bowsky (ed.), *Studies in Medieval and Renaissance History*, III (Lincoln, Neb., 1966), 29, 50. Yet there is a half-century gap between most Roman archaeological finds in this region and the earliest Merovingian artifacts which have been discovered. There seems to have been a similar lag in colonization by the Burgundians, Alemans, and Visigoths. Allowance must be made, however, for changes in burial practices brought about by Christian influences which have confused archaeological research. S. J. De Laet, "La Gaule septentrionale à l'époque romaine à la lumière des fouilles, des recherches et des publications les plus recentes (1935–1950)," *Bulletin de l'Institut Historique Belge de Rome*, XXVI (1950–51), 248–249.

63. Jacques Breuer, *La Belgique romaine* (Brussels, 1945), p. 73 ff. The similar situation at Dinant did not entail the end of the town, since Dinant, on the Meuse, was more favorably located for trade than was Arlon. Josianne Gaier-Lhoest, *L'évolution topographique de la ville de Dinant au moyen âge* (Brussels, 1964), pp. 9–16.

64. Jozef Coenen, "Is de stad Tongeren ooit bisschopsstad geweest?" *Limburg*, XXXII (1953), 29 ff.

65. Franz Petri, "Die Anfänge des mittelalterlichen Städtewesens in den Niederlanden und den angrenzenden Frankreich," *SAES*, pp. 232–236, 245; Paul Rolland, *Les origines de la commune de Tournai* (Brussels, 1931).

While Tournai and the other Scheldt towns were declining, Roman centers along the Meuse probably were more prosperous during the Merovingian period than in the late Empire. Several of these towns have been the subject of exhaustive recent investigation, and thus we can follow the unbroken development from Roman to embryonic medieval town.

After the Romans had occupied Namur, at the confluence of the Meuse and the Sambre, they moved the town to the foot of the Champeau,[66] where it had easy access to the rivers. The Roman *vicus* incorporated this entire quarter and extended across to the left bank of the Sambre; archaeological finds in the Sambre suburb have shown settlement in almost exactly the same area as that later occupied by the medieval town. The *Applé*, the site of the largest horde of Roman coins discovered to date in Belgium, was on the right bank of the Sambre, between the present bridge uniting it to the promontory of the Champeau and the *pointe du Grognon*. The term *Applé*, which recurs in altered form at Dinant and Huy, was derived from the vulgar Latin *applicatum*, a place where boats were docked.

The open *vicus* of Namur was burned in the crisis of the third century; a *castrum* was built on the Champeau which survived into the middle ages and enclosed the entire area of the *vicus*, the settlement on the right bank of the Sambre. There is no break in continuity of the coin finds at the *Applé*. The Merovingians continued to use Namur as a mint (five moneyers are attested there in the seventh century, although they probably did not live at Namur concurrently) and as a market. An almost impregnable location and a situation favorable for commerce maintained the position of Namur across the invasions. The town may even have profited from the disorders in the long run.[67]

In the later Merovingian period the most important town in the Meuse valley was Maastricht, which had been a Roman settlement and had become a bishopric by 500 as chief town of the diocese of Tongeren. By 600 it was the site of an important mint. Maastricht thus saw no more than a brief break with the Roman settlement; grave finds show Christian remains from at least the mid-fifth century.[68]

Huy presents a more difficult case. Along with Namur and Maastricht, it was evidently part of a general Roman defense line at intervals of

66. See above, p. 73.
67. Rousseau, *Namur*, p. 12 ff.
68. See *ibid.*, p. 43 ff., and Petri, "Die Anfänge des mittelalterlichen Städtewesens," p. 242. There unfortunately is no recent study of the earliest history of Maastricht.

approximately twenty miles along the Meuse. There is no direct evidence of Roman occupation at Huy; it was termed a *castrum* in Merovingian documents and thus could have been either a Roman fortification or the site of a stockade erected by the Merovingians. Archaeological evidence suggests a Roman occupation, for Huy was inhabited no later than the beginning of the Merovingian period and had a parish organization too advanced to have developed under Germanic tutelage.[69]

There is also evidence of continuity between the imperial and Merovingian periods along the Meuse at Dinant. As at Arlon, the Roman *castrum* at Dinant was too small to accommodate the entire population except during emergencies. A *vicus* thus developed in the southern part of the modern town. Dinant was crossed by a Roman road, the so-called Chaussée Brunehaut, but it owed its entire commercial position, and as such its survival across the period of the invasions, to its location on the Meuse. Dinant knew something approaching genuine urban life in the seventh century, when it was termed *civitas* by the cosmographer of Ravenna.[70]

The most important Meuse town in the early Merovingian period was probably Verdun, on the upper Meuse. A Roman fortress of approximately twenty-five acres, it had been destroyed by Attila. Verdun may have been abandoned, but if so it made a rapid recovery, for by the sixth century it had an active mint and was a center of long-distance commerce, particularly in slaves. But the question of continuity with the Roman regime at Verdun must remain unanswered for the moment.[71]

At each point along the Meuse where a Roman road crossed the river, therefore, at intervals of approximately twelve to eighteen miles, there was a *castrum* with a mint during the Merovingian period. Verdun was an important center of the slave trade, and by 700 the lower Meuse also had two important merchant settlements: Domburg, on the island of Walcheren, and Duurstede. Coins from the Meuse towns show that there was a lively

---

69. André Joris, *La ville de Huy au moyen âge. Des origines à la fin du XIVe siècle* (Paris, 1959), *passim*, and particularly p. 88; see also Joris' more recent conclusions in *Huy, ville médiévale* (Brussels, 1965), p. 17 ff.

70. Gaier-Lhoest, *L'évolution topographique*, pp. 9–21; see also above, n. 63. On Arlon, see A. Bertrang, *Histoire d'Arlon*, 2nd ed. (Arlon, 1953), pp. 60–61. Although there is no written record of Arlon during the Merovingian period, burial remains of extremely wealthy persons show that it was inhabited.

71. Dollinger-Léonard, "De la cité romaine à la ville médiévale," pp. 208–214; on the slave trade at Verdun, see Charles Verlinden, *L'Esclavage dans l'Europe médiévale*, I [all published] (Ghent, 1955), 214–221.

trade both along the Meuse between Verdun and Domburg and Duur-stede and of the Meuse region with England. Elements of a Verdun design appear on coins struck at Maastricht, Dinant, Namur, and Duurstede, but the money type of Duurstede is definitely attributable to men of Maastricht.[72] There were thus many human contacts among the centers of the Meuse, and this presupposes some commercial contact. There is little direct proof of the continuity of urban life between the imperial and Merovingian periods in the Meuse towns, however, with the single exception of Namur; in particular, the output of the mints is only partially related to the commercial prosperity of the towns themselves, for mints also served the districts surrounding the towns. Commerce could have been carried on, and according to Pirenne's argument[73] was carried on by foreigners: Syrians, Jews, and Arabs. Yet these places regularly were called *urbs* and *castrum*. The latter term implies at least a garrison, and perhaps more, while *urbs* indicates a fairly sizeable and complex agglomer-ation. Shaky and inconclusive though this evidence is, it is certain that some persons on the Meuse were providing food and lodging for the merchants known to have been traveling between Duurstede and Verdun. Some sort of agglomeration thus developed around the points where the boats docked, as at the *Applé* of Namur.

As one proceeds west from the Meuse from Dinant through Bavai to Boulogne, he encounters numerous Roman centers. Some towns that had been *civitates* became bishoprics and capitals of the Frankish kings. Tournai and Cambrai became bishoprics in the fifth and sixth centuries, Arras and Térouanne shortly thereafter. The Roman *civitates* of Cassel and Bavai, however, were neither capitals nor bishoprics during the Merovingian period. They were thus less important than the others or were declining. The fact that the towns in decline were at the junction of some land route with the Dinant-Bavai-Boulogne axis is also significant; none was on a junction with a waterway. There is no evidence, further-more, that either Bavai or Cassel had a mint. They lost their positions as chief towns of their regions to Cambrai and Tournai during the Mero-vingian period. Arras and Cambrai had been textile centers under the Romans, but it is uncertain that this industry was continued on a more than local scale under the Merovingians. Their mints were also less active

72. For this and what follows, see the extremely important study of Jan Dhondt, "L'essor urbain entre Meuse et Mer du Nord à l'époque mérovingienne," *Studi in onore di Armando Sapori*, I (Milan, 1957), 55–78.

73. Pirenne, *Mohammed and Charlemagne*, p. 96 ff.

than those on the Meuse. The cities on land routes, then, apparently were only ecclesiastical or administrative centers at this time.[74]

Two explanations of the rise of Meuse River commerce in the seventh century are plausible. First, the interruption of overland trade between Scandinavia and Byzantium by recurrent German disturbances in eastern Europe forced traders going between the two to use the Meuse route, then join the Rhône to Avignon and thence travel to Italy and the east.[75] Secondly, the Christianization of England and the resumption of English relations with the Continent from at least the early seventh century meant that the Meuse, the most logical artery for English trade, would prosper. This development in turn shifted the axis of the Meuse downstream; while Verdun was the only important commercial center on the river in the sixth century, others developed near the coast in the seventh century. There was thus in the Low Countries a general displacement of town life between the late imperial and Merovingian periods from the land route to the waterway, although the historian must beware of making hasty a priori deductions concerning medieval urban origins from this shift in commercial routes.[76] A triangle can be noted, however, with the Roman land route between Maastricht and Dinant and Boulogne its southern line, the Meuse its northern and eastern edge, and the Atlantic coast its

---

74. Dhondt's conclusion that the rôle of the Chaussée Brunehaut, the Roman road between Cologne and Bavai, in medieval commerce has been overrated has been supported by M. L. Fanchamps, "Étude sur les tonlieux de la Meuse moyenne, VIII-milieu XIV siècle," *MA*, LXX (1964), 205–264.

75. The connection between economic prosperity in the west and trade routes to the Byzantine and Arab worlds, particularly as sources of precious metals, has been emphasized by Maurice Lombard, "L'évolution urbaine," p. 14 ff., and Howard Adelson, "Early Medieval Trade Routes," *AHR*, LXV (1960), 271–287.

76. The argument has been advanced, for example, that streets in German river towns normally ran perpendicular to the streams, thus indicating a tendency for commercial activity to be directed there. See the material cited above, n. 52, and particularly Fritz Timme, "Andernach am Rhein und die topographischen Anfänge der älteren Flussübergangsstädte," *Städtewesen und Bürgertum als geschichtliche Kräfte. Gedächtnisschrift für Fritz Rörig* (Lübeck, 1953), pp. 401–421. Yet not all streets run toward the river even in the towns whose plan Timme reproduces; practically all, however, perpendicularly join the main land route through the town, which in most cases roughly paralleled the waterway but did not regularly bend to follow its course. The town market was invariably on or near the land route rather than on the river, as was the case with the *portus*. Of the towns whose plans are cited by Timme only the case of Brunswick supports his position. Overland trade still was the dominant economic interest of many medieval towns of middle size, even when eventually they engaged in some long-distance commerce.

third, short side. Tongeren, the only large town within this triangle and thus on neither the land nor water routes, declined drastically. Town life ceased within this triangle during the Merovingian period. It continued on the land route, the southern edge of the triangle, but in considerably diminished measure, and actually expanded with renewed vigor along the Meuse. Most of the Meuse centers had known a Roman garrison, but none were important commercial centers for the Romans, who had always placed most of their larger towns on land routes.[77] By this shift in commercial geography the larger Roman centers in the interior were surpassed by the river towns, although they continued to function as political and ecclesiastical capitals.[78]

The role of the bishopric in the preservation of some measure of institutional continuity between Roman municipal administration and the early medieval town has long been recognized. Many diocesan boundaries preserved those of the Roman *civitates* upon which they had been based, but recent research has done little to show the actual working of this

77. Dhondt's hypothesis that the shift of commercial traffic from land routes to waterways was the major factor in the flowering of the Meuse towns in the Merovingian period has been disputed, although unconvincingly, by Fernand Vercauteren, who sees widespread Roman influences, and particularly the Roman road system, as the conclusive element. Vercauteren also regards the Meuse towns as the European meeting place of "Roman and Germanic traditions" of town formation, with the Roman represented by the church, continuing the ancient urban tradition, and the Germanic by the *vicus* or *Wik*. Vercauteren, "De Wordingsgeschiedenis der Maassteden in de hoge Middeleeuwen," Verslag van de Algemene Vergadering van het Historisch Genootschap ... te Utrecht, ... verenigd met Bijdragen en Mededelingen van het Historisch Genootschap, LXXI (Groningen, 1957), 25. The role of Roman land routes in commerce of more than a purely local nature in the Meuse and Rhine regions has also been emphasized by H. Hardenberg, "Romeinse Wegen en Middeleeuwse Geleiderechten tussen Mass en Rijn," *Publications de la Société Historique et Archéologique dans le Limbourg*, XCIV–XCV (1958–59), 173–188.

78. Dhondt, "L'essor urbain," *passim*. Dhondt's interpretation of early town life along the Meuse has been criticized, notably by Franz Petri in "Merowingerzeitliche Voraussetzungen für die Entwicklung des Städtewesens zwischen Maas und Nordsee. Bemerkungen und Ergänzungen zu einer Studie von J. Dhondt," *BJ*, CLVIII (1958), 233–245. Petri sees the economic revival of the seventh century proceeding from a more gradual revival during the fifth and sixth. While Dhondt considers the increased commercial activity of the first half of the seventh century a result of Scandinavian and English trade, Petri emphasizes the unbroken Roman artisan tradition in the Meuse towns during the early middle ages, as shown by pottery, weapons, and grave finds. Although Petri agrees with Dhondt that the Meuse was the most prosperous trading region of northern Europe in the seventh century, he argues that Dhondt underestimates the extent of trade along the Scheldt at this time.

process of continuity.[79] There is little evidence, for example, to show that the bishops helped to retain the curial class as a municipal aristocracy or preserved Roman administrative machinery. Attempts to prove this have been unconvincing even for Italy. The argument used by Gian Piero Bognetti that the presence of a vigorous church life in the old Roman towns indicates that the church took over the municipal institutional apparatus is only supposition.[80] In many areas the bishoprics evidently were so weakened by the invasions that they could play only a passive role, as centers of a small population engaging in rudimentary exchange operations, in the preservation of town life across the transitional period.[81]

The population of the episcopal centers does show some continuity with the Roman towns. Kings and their retainers often lived in or near the towns, particularly during the early Merovingian period. In the towns of central and southern Gaul we find evidence of clerics, *honorati*, and *senatores*, generally members of the old Gallo-Roman aristocracy. The Roman artisanate generally continued to live in the episcopal towns, and distinctions founded on personal fortune were made among various elements of the town population.[82]

The presence of a bishop and his entourage does not of itself constitute a town,[83] and the temporal power of the Merovingian bishops within Roman *civitates* cannot be considered a continuation of Roman practices. This power was based largely upon the growth of church landlordship and the immunity,[84] a Germanic institution, which withdrew episcopal domains from the jurisdiction of the count. The case of Trier demonstrates this very well. All settlement at Trier had congregated around the several churches, some outside the Roman wall, some inside, by the end of the sixth century. In the seventh century the old *civitas* was divided into the *Triergau* and the *Wawergau*. A sphere of episcopal authority had developed

79. See in general E. Ennen, "Die Bedeutung der Kirche für den Wiederaufbau der in der Völkerwanderungszeit zerstörten Städte," *Die Kunstdenkmäler im Landesteil Nordrhein. Kölner Untersuchungen*, Beiheft, II (1950), 54–68.

80. Bognetti, "Problemi di metodo," pp. 59–87.

81. Claude, *Topographie und Verfassung*, pp. 56 ff., 71–72, 180.

82. Vercauteren, "Vie urbaine entre Meuse et Loire," p. 465 ff.

83. See the expression of this rather unsophisticated concept by Friedrich Merzbacher, *Die Bischofsstadt*. Arbeitsgemeinschaft für Forschung des Landes Nordrhein-Westfalen, Geisteswissenschaften, XCIII (Cologne, 1961), 1 ff.

84. Vercauteren, "Vie urbaine entre Meuse et Loire," p. 464. The role of the immunity in the growth of episcopal lordship over towns has also been emphasized by Planitz, *Die deutsche Stadt*, pp. 29–30.

in the *Triergau*, including the city of Trier, from the late sixth century. This area was withdrawn from the jurisdiction of the count. During this period the bishop of Trier apparently assumed some of the administrative functions of the old Roman municipal government, such as the upkeep of buildings and fortifications.[85] The count thus moved his residence from Trier to Bitburg during the seventh century, and the bishop became lord of Trier. Although the temporal authority of the bishop was briefly curtailed by Charlemagne, his successors confirmed all episcopal rights, including the immunity; the later Carolingian period seems generally to have marked the definitive victory of bishop over count in the struggle for control of the towns.[86] There is, then, a clear distinction between the Merovingian and Carolingian periods at Trier. The power of the bishop in the town was the major element of continuity between the two periods of Frankish rule and between them and Roman municipal administration,[87] but this continuity was only achieved as an application of the very Germanic and non-Roman immunity.

The example of Trier clearly demonstrates a fundamental distinction between the medieval and Roman town which always must be borne in mind. The jurisdiction of most bishoprics extended over an entire *civitas* under the Romans, although occasionally in the very late imperial period simple *castra*, having little or no connection with the surrounding countryside, might serve as bishoprics.[88] After the confusion of the invasions, however, the bishops tended to center their activities increasingly in the towns proper.[89] The term *civitas* came to indicate almost exclusively a Roman town which had been a bishopric since at least the Merovingian period, although occasionally a later episcopal foundation might be a *civitas*.[90] Thus, although the bishops tried to bridge the transition between Roman *civitas* and medieval town, the case of Trier shows clearly that this could not always be accomplished.

85. This may also have occurred in some towns in northern France. Planitz, *Die deutsche Stadt*, p. 28.

86. *Ibid.*, p. 30.

87. Ennen, "Entwicklung des Städtewesens," p. 433 ff., after Ewig, *Trier im Merowingerreich*, p. 80 ff.

88. Petrikovits, "Das Fortleben römischer Städte an Rhein und Donau," p. 77.

89. Friedrich Vittinghoff, "Zur Verfassung der spätantiken Stadt," *SAES*, pp. 37–38. On the general subject of the division of the *civitas*, with the corresponding relative decline in the power of the town proper within the overall administrative unit, see Edith Ennen, "Zur Typologie des Stadt-Land-Verhältnisses im Mittelalter," *SG*, XVI (1963), 445–446.

90. Planitz, *Die deutsche Stadt*, pp. 38–39.

In exceptional cases the presence of a bishopric might be a force of topographic and demographic discontinuity. The bishopric of Marseille originally was on the site of the Roman settlement, the *ville haute*. Successive raids during the Merovingian period by the Ostrogoths, Burgundians, Franks, and Mostems brought about a division of the town into *ville haute* and *ville basse*; the latter was near the port, at some distance from the Roman site. The cathedral chapter continued to function throughout the period of the invasions, and in this sense it was a source of continuity with Rome. But during the raids it moved to the abbey of St. Victor, in the suburbs, and only returned inside the walls in the eleventh century. The remainder of the population of the town, meanwhile, had moved from the port to the more easily defended *ville haute*. By its move to the suburbs, the bishopric created a vacuum within the town, although in the case of Marseille this did not entail a complete break in continuity of settlement.[91]

Some bishoprics of post-Roman origin may have been instruments of the surviving Gallo-Roman populations attempting to revitalize Roman towns and preserve order. This is shown clearly by the case of Speyer, which was the most fortunately situated of five fords across the Rhine within a distance of six miles. It was a depot for goods between the Rhine River crossing and the road paralleling the river from Basel through Speyer to Cologne. Grave finds near the abbey of St. Germanus indicate that the Gallo-Roman population survived the invasions, but withdrew into a corner of the Roman town. The Franks preferred to live outside the walls. The Roman town evidently had been largely resettled by 614, when the presence of a bishop is first attested at Speyer. A ducal residence was built in the northern part of the town, and merchants congregated around this structure. In the tenth century the ducal settlement was given to the bishop. In contrast to the general pattern for more important settlements in northern Germany, however, where the merchant agglomeration expanded and eventually dominated whatever population lived in the Roman or episcopal complexes, bishop and *civitas* at Speyer maintained control over the merchant agglomeration. A modicum of continuity was preserved between ancient and medieval Speyer, therefore, through the agency of the bishops. Topographical dualism was not reflected in constitutional dualism.[92]

91. F. Benoit, P.-A. Février, J. Formigé, and H. Rolland, *Villes episcopales de Provence. Aix, Arles, Fréjus, Marseille et Riez de l'époque gallo-romaine au moyen âge* (Paris, 1954), pp. 33–36.

92. Anton Doll, "Zur Frühgeschichte der Stadt Speyer," *Mitteilungen des historischen Vereins der Pfalz*, LII (1952), 133–200.

In summary, the bishoprics may be regarded as a transitional phenomenon between the Roman and medieval town. In some localities they did preserve traces of the Roman municipal organization. In particular, they preserved the position of the walled town as the administrative central point of the *civitas* and thus contributed to the later rise of the towns by providing an already established point around which agglomerations of merchants could gather. Important though the bishops were in this respect, however, originally they were no more so than the counts, the representatives of the king. Many clerics lived in the towns, but even through the Carolingian period there was always a lay population of merchants and particularly artisans, and great lords often resided in the towns in the early Merovingian age. The churches had some property within the towns, but at least before the Carolingian period it was less considerable than town land in the royal fisc and in the hands of various private parties. The lay element in the towns gave way increasingly to the clerical in the Carolingian period; the bishops managed to gain preponderance within the *civitates*, largely through the immunity and landlordship.[93] The medieval town which developed on the European continent in the tenth and eleventh centuries was a reaction against the episcopal city[94] and in many respects was a juridical reversion, albeit greatly expanded, to the type of town prevalent along the great commercial arteries under the Merovingians.

While the bishoprics continued to be the centers of activity of their towns, many new churches and abbeys were founded under episcopal auspices from the sixth century, particularly in the suburbs. Owing to Roman regulations forbidding the burial of the dead within the towns, Roman churches normally were built outside the town walls. These churches could give protection, and settlements, originally agrarian in character, developed around them. Somewhat surprisingly, in view of the Germanic habit of living outside the walls, most German churches were built inside the towns.[95] Roman suburban churches thus often became pre-urban nuclei, while many churches constructed within the towns in the Merovingian period became parish churches when the suburban settlements swallowed up the agglomeration within the walls in the twelfth

93. Vercauteren, "Vie urbaine entre Meuse et Loire," p. 483.

94. Planitz, *Die deutsche Stadt*, p. 98 ff.

95. See in general M. Viellard-Troïekouroff, D. Fossard, E. Chatel, and C. Lamy-Lassalle, "Les anciennes églises suburbaines de Paris (IVe–Xe siècles)," *Fédération des Sociétés Historiques et Archéologiques de Paris et de l'Ile-de-France. Mémoires*, XI (1960), 17–282.

century.[96] This tendency often enables us to trace patterns of settlement. St. Quentin and St. Lambert, built inside the walls of Mainz by the Franks in the mid-seventh and early eighth centuries, respectively, were centers of settlement. The Germans had thus begun to repopulate some Roman towns before the advent of Charlemagne.[97]

Several suburban churches were built at Poitiers and Bourges in the wake of the invasions. During the twelfth century, settlements grew up around these sanctuaries and were walled. Similar agglomerations existed in the Merovingian period at Tours and around the church of St. Remigius at Reims.[98] While the construction of churches in the suburbs of Merovingian towns may be taken as evidence of recovery from the invasions, or at least of a stabilization of the position of the Gallo-Roman element, it in no way indicates the previous existence of a thriving suburban population.[99]

The invasions might have caused the surviving Roman population to remove its churches temporarily from the suburbs to points inside the walls. The suburbs of Metz evidently were destroyed in the fifth century, and the episcopal residence and other churches were moved within the walls, where they kept alive some semblance of urban activity. A similar pattern is shown at Toul, while at Verdun some of the churches remained in the suburbs.[100] Suburban foundations were particularly propitious to town growth if they contained the relics of a martyr. Xanten was one of the few towns where the Merovingians lived within the walls after the departure of the Roman population. This was probably due to the death in the Xanten region of the martyr Victor and the foundation of a church dedicated to him; Christians lived only in the *colonia Traiana*, between two Roman settlements.[101] The only other major exception to this general pattern in northern Gaul seems to have been Trier, where the wall was so

96. Lestocquoy, "De l'unité à la pluralité," pp. 160–162.

97. Heinrich Büttner, "Das fränkische Mainz. Ein Beitrag zur Kontinuitätsproblem und zur fränkischen mittelalterlichen Stadtgeschichte," in *Aus Verfassungs- und Landesgeschichte. Festschrift zum 70. Geburtstag von Theodor Mayer*, 2 vols. (Lindau and Constance, 1955), II, 238–239.

98. Claude, *Topographie und Verfassung, passim.*

99. Roblin's statement on the basis of this church construction that the Paris bequeathed by the Merovingians to the Carolingians had a population of 30,000 is absurd. Roblin, "Cités ou citadelles . . . Paris," p. 309.

100. Dollinger-Léonard, "De la cité romaine à la ville médiévale," pp. 197, 203, 209.

101. Hugo Borger, "Die Ausgrabungen im Bereich des Xantener Domes," in *Neue Ausgrabungen in Deutschland*, pp. 380–390.

enormous that the surviving Roman population was grouped around churches within the walls.[102]

The role of suburban churches in town origins was less apparent in southern Gaul than in the north and in Germany. Roman towns in the south generally were so large that all the space necessary for settlement could be found within the ruined walls. Only at Toulouse and Narbonne did churches become nuclei of settlements outside the *civitates*. In southern Gaul suburban quarters developed only exceptionally from the later tenth century.[103]

A general pattern can be noted for northern and central Gaul and Germany: the agglomerations which grew up around suburban sanctuaries from the Merovingian period had expanded so greatly by the eleventh century that they often surpassed the parent *civitates* in importance. The *suburbium* of the Roman or episcopal town eventually became the central part of the economic complex of the medieval town, but generally at a later date than the suburbs developing around non-Roman *castra*, which assumed primary importance almost from the moment of their inception. The reason for this variation in development was the prevalence of a greater degree of economic activity, albeit limited or on a local scale, in most Roman *civitates* than in the *castra* of temporal magnates at the time of the great European economic expansion. The suburb thus might surpass the original fortified portion of the town in each case, but the process took longer in the Roman and episcopal towns than in the new towns of the middle ages.

Most Roman centers did, then, survive the Völkerwanderung, although in many cases with a break in settlement of some years. By the later sixth century most had been repopulated at least partially. Roman municipal administration had disappeared before the rebirth, but bishops, often of Roman origin, still functioned alongside the counts in the towns. Gregory of Tours speaks of the populations of numerous towns in terms indicating a reasonably large and diverse population.[104] The towns of Merovingian Gaul knew resident merchant and artisan life.

The primitive Germans had no real taste for urban life. Until the eighth century they did not know how, or care, to establish towns.[105]

102. Ewig, *Trier im Merowingerreich*, pp. 79–80.

103. Duby, "Villes du sud-est," pp. 243–244.

104. See the discussion of the value of Gregory's *History* for the study of the Merovingian town by Eugen Ewig, "Volkstum und Volksbewusstsein im Frankenreich des 7. Jahrhunderts," *Caratteri del secolo VII in Occidente*, SSCI, p. 588.

105. Ennen, *Frühgeschichte*, p. 37.

Most agrarian villages in the immediate environs of Roman towns which were located in regions where the Germans managed to penetrate thoroughly bear Germanic names.[106] With the exception of the upper warrior classes, the Germans did not as a rule live in Roman towns, but rather in their immediate environs. They participated in commercial activity from their vantage points outside the walls. All true towns of the middle ages either were located on former Roman sites or developed only in or after the Carolingian period. No pre-urban nucleus developed from Germanic antecedents in the Merovingian age. We can thus speak of Carolingian Frankish, and later Saxon or Bavarian origins of certain towns, but there can be no question of the medieval town on the Continent being basically a Germanic institution. Only certain elements of the medieval town can be attributed definitely to Germanic, even late Germanic, rather than to Roman origin.[107]

In view of the hostility of the Germans to urban life, it seems apparent that when Roman town sites continued to be inhabited through the period of the Völkerwanderung this survival cannot have been due solely to Roman urban traditions or institutions which may have survived the invasions. Other factors favorable to town life were necessary,[108] and these factors led to the rise of an organism completely different in kind from most Roman towns. Topographical continuity, with the Roman town constituting the strong point around which the medieval agglomeration might develop, or at most continuity as an administrative or episcopal center, was normally the extent of Roman urbanism which survived in northern continental Europe. In southern France and Italy, areas less severely hurt by the Germans, there was often continuity of settlement at least until the Arab invasions. The decline in the north was quicker and more complete. As a result, the medieval town of northern Europe cannot be regarded as a continuation of the Roman in any real sense. Even in cases where continuity of settlement can be shown, the Roman town was completely transformed during the Merovingian period by

106. See, for example, Bertrang, *Histoire d'Arlon*, pp. 59–60, and Zimmermann, "Andernach," *passim*.

107. Ennen, "Different Types of Formation," pp. 177–178.

108. Franz Miltner, "Zur Frage der Kontinuität römischer Siedlungen in Österreich," *Miscellanea Giovanni Galbiati*, 2 vols. (Milan, 1951), II, 133. Numerous towns on the *limes* which were destroyed by the barbarians were at best agrarian villages during the middle ages, for example Heddernheim (*civitas Taunensium*), Augst (*Colonia Raurica*), Vindonissa, Carnuntum, Flavia, Solva, Virunum, and Teurnia. Planitz, *Die deutsche Stadt*, p. 25. The factors leading to the rise of a Roman town, which was essentially a seigneurial creation from above, might have little or no effect upon medieval urbanism.

factors only peripheral to the existence of the center under the Romans. The most important factor was usually a commercial consideration enabling the Roman town to survive as a merchant and artisan center where it could not as a mere fortress.

Medieval town sites often are simply near Roman locations but show no topographical continuity with them. Roman towns were generally on land routes, while trade in early medieval Europe was centered on the waterways.[109] Strategic considerations, moreover, motivated the Romans in their choice of town sites. Occasionally such a location was also favorable for commercial development, and in such cases settlement normally continued, although to a greatly diminished extent and under radically different circumstances.

Under no circumstances therefore, even when continuity of topography or even of settlement can be demonstrated, can we speak without serious qualification of a gradual evolution of the Roman into the medieval town. The two urban types were too different. The Roman town had to be destroyed economically and institutionally before the medieval town could begin to evolve as it did. All available evidence suggests that the cataclysm was the Germanic invasions, and not those of the Arabs except perhaps in southern Europe. The merchant element specializing in long-distance trade in the Roman towns of northern Gaul was so small that the towns would not necessarily have declined even if such trade had been cut off, and this disaster never occurred. The break in continuity of settlement, when it took place at all, came in the fifth century. There was partial recovery in the sixth century, and towns of a distinctly "medieval" type had developed by the early seventh, combining fortress and commercial settlement. This occurred before Arab activities, real or putative, could have had an effect in the north. In some areas Roman towns simply had died by this time or were maintained by a handful of priests or administrators. In others, particularly the Meuse centers, the Roman municipal tradition had ended for practical purposes by the early seventh century, but the towns had quickly recovered under the stimulus of locations favorable for commercial activity, either regional or distant. We can thus place the origin of the medieval town as a type in the seventh century along the great commercial waterways and in the eighth in regions crossed by important land routes.[110]

109. Adelson, "Early Medieval Trade Routes," especially p. 278 ff.

110. Hans Strahm, "Zur Verfassungstopographie der mittelalterlichen Stadt, mit besonderer Berücksichtigung des Gündungsplanes [*sic*] der Stadt Bern," *SZG*, XXX (1950), 372–410.

The Pirenne interpretation of town origins postulates a nadir in medieval urbanism shortly before the accession of the Carolingian dynasty to the Frankish throne. The evidence presented in this paper, however, has shown clearly that to speak of an end of town life in the later Merovingian period is a crass oversimplification. While Dopsch and his followers unquestionably overestimate the extent to which the early Carolingian period represents an economic renaissance,[111] the towns in this era were moving toward a new economy based on commerce in goods produced locally. There is no basis in written or archaeological evidence for the supposition that the urban revival which began on the Rhine and Mosel in the sixth and seventh centuries stopped short in the early Carolingian period. A resident settlement of Frisian merchants lived along the banks of the Rhine inside the Roman wall at Mainz from the late eighth century. Cologne knew resident merchant settlements in the early ninth century. Such settlements were developing throughout the upper Rhine regions at the same time. On the Danube, a settlement outside the walls of Regensburg was slowly spreading toward St. Emmeram's in the early ninth century.[112] Town life continued along the Meuse and revived in the Scheldt region. Trade was nonetheless mainly local; few products seem to have had a wide market. The chief transporters and long-distance merchants of the North Sea area during the early Carolingian period were the Frisians; as a result of Frisian commercial activity, *portus* began to appear along the Scheldt.[113] We thus can speak of something approaching urban life and of a modest, but growing, commerce in the great river valleys in the late eighth and early ninth centuries. The old *civitates*, although of predominantly ecclesiastical and administrative character, contained some pre-urban life in the *portus*.[114]

The early ninth century in particular seems to have brought a general prosperity to the embryonic towns. Numerous agrarian settlements began to develop merchant agglomerations in this period.[115] The comparative peace of the Carolingian era entailed a population increase which con-

111. Alfons Dopsch, *Die Wirtschaftsentwicklung der Karolingerzeit, vornehmlich in Deutschland*, 3rd ed. (Cologne and Graz, 1962), II, 102 ff.

112. Planitz, *Die deutsche Stadt*, pp. 42–43.

113. On the Frisians see P. C. Boeles, *Friesland tot de elfde eeuw*, 2nd ed. (The Hague, 1951). On the *portus*, see in more detail below, pp. 110–111.

114. See the summary of F.-L. Ganshof, *La Belgique Carolingienne* (Brussels, 1958), p. 120 ff.

115. See below, p. 96.

tributed to the growth of urban and pre-urban settlements.[116] Agglomerations developed around bishoprics and churches in ninth-century Germany. Carolingian villas and fortresses in Germany were normally constructed along important land or water routes. Although their primary function in the minds of their lords was undoubtedly administrative or military, it would have been inconceivable, in view of their location, that no commercial activity developed around them.[117] Permanent non-agrarian settlements can be proved by written evidence to have existed in the coastal regions of central Germany in the ninth century, and archaeological data shows their existence in the eighth. Such settlements cannot be proved directly for the interior towns before the tenth century, but since there was already clear social differentiation at that time, the settlements must have existed in some form in the ninth.[118] A similar prosperity has been seen for the cities of the Narbonnaise in the ninth century.[119] The cities of Aquitaine had to endure a severe crisis in the eighth century in the confusion entailed by the wars of Pepin against the dukes of Aquitaine, but there was evidently some recovery in the ninth despite Arab raids.[120] Numerous references have been made to the destruction of the walls of Roman *civitates* in the ninth century to obtain building stone for use in other structures, as at Reims, Melun, Langres, and Beauvais. The Pirenne school ascribes this to an alleged difficulty of obtaining and transporting building materials, and this viewpoint may have some validity for the lowland regions of Europe.[121] It is inconceivable, however, given the conformation of European geography and the flourishing condition of trade routes under the Carolingians, that building materials such as stone and clay for bricks would have been of such difficult access over wide areas. A logical explanation, particularly in view of other evidence of town revival in the early ninth century, is that the comparatively peaceful conditions in most regions led townsmen to believe that they could dismantle their fortifications with impunity. The

116. Ennen, *Frühgeschichte*, p. 133, following G. Des Marez, *Études inédites* (Brussels, 1936), p. 56 ff.

117. Edmund E. Stengel, "Die fränkische Würzel der mittelalterlichen Stadt in hessischer Sicht," *Städtewesen und Bürgertum als geschichtliche Kräfte*, p. 40 ff.

118. Walter Schlesinger, "Städtische Frühformen zwischen Rhein und Elbe," *SAES*, p. 349.

119. A. Dupont, *Les cités de la Narbonnaise première depuis les invasions germaniques jusqu'à l'apparition du consulat* (Nîmes, 1942), p. 153 ff.

120. Claude, *Topographie und Verfassung*, pp. 181–182.

121. Vercauteren, "Die spätantike Civitas im Mittelalter," p. 18.

rapidity with which new town walls were built after the Norman invasions must in itself throw the Pirenne explanation of the dismantlings of the ninth century into serious question.

The new prosperity had ended by the later ninth century, however, even before the Viking invaders had struck in full force. The number of charters granted for markets, both rural and urban, declined and reached its low point in West Francia in the tenth century, although this was not the case in East Francia. This decline has been ascribed to a decline in the authority of the West Frankish kings. Markets were regalian rights, and few dukes and counts were sufficiently secure in their own domains thus to usurp royal authority.[122]

That growing political localism and confusion in the late ninth century entailed economic decline cannot be questioned. The Viking invasions, however, were a disaster which temporarily ended much town life in northern and western Europe and delayed the normal evolution of the embryonic pre-urban centers of the early ninth century into genuine towns for half to three-quarters of a century in most areas. The extent to which these raids were brought on by political dislocation following the death of Charlemagne is debatable. In terms of local means of defense against outside attackers, the wars of the Frankish princes cannot have had much effect on an empire which was never under even the vaguest form of "central administration."[123] The most convincing explanation is that the invasions were caused by developments in Scandinavia[124] and that the regions composing the Frankish Empire would have been powerless to stop them even under the most favorable of circumstances.

The extent of the damage caused by the raids has also been questioned. Most writers who speak of total destruction coming in the wake of the Vikings were clergy, who as the wealthiest group in Frankish society were the most severely hurt by the raids, but their accounts cannot be dismissed as mere rhetorical exaggeration. We cannot ignore archaeological evidence, widespread discontinuity of settlement, and the construction of

122. Traute Endemann, *Markturkunde und Markt in Frankreich und Burgund vom 9. bis 11. Jahrhundert* (Constance and Stuttgart, 1964), pp. 70–71.

123. See in general Heinrich Fichtenau, *The Carolingian Empire* (Oxford, 1957; reprinted New York, 1964), and Édouard Perroy, "Carolingian Administration," in Thrupp (ed.), *Early Medieval Society*, pp. 129–146.

124. Marc Bloch, *Feudal Society* (London, 1961), pp. 36–38; Robert Latouche, *The Birth of Western Economy* (London, 1961; reprinted New York, 1966), p. 211 ff.

new fortifications throughout Europe to ward off the Northmen.[125] The invaders struck most severely at towns along major rivers as far south as the Saône and the Mosel; their depredations were less severe in the inland river regions than along such coastal rivers as the Scheldt,[126] but even some towns not on waterways were damaged as the Vikings spread inland.[127]

The Viking, Magyar, and Danish invasions caused a caesura in town life, although it was not as profound as that entailed by the Germanic

125. See in general Ennen, "Entwicklung des Städtewesens," p. 448 ff.; Vercauteren, "Vie urbaine entre Meuse et Loire," p. 475. On destruction and fortification at Bruges, see A. E. Verhulst, "Les origines et l'histoire ancienne de la ville de Bruges (IXe–XIIe siècle)," *MA*, LXVI (1960), 37–63, and especially 60–63; for Arras, see Jean Lestocquoy, "Les étapes du développement urbain d'Arras," *RBPH*, XXIII (1944), 171–172; for Cologne, see Gutkind, *Urban Development in Central Europe, IHCD*, pp. 260–261; and on the depredations of the Danes at Hamburg, see *ibid.*, p. 403, and Heinrich Reincke, *Forschungen und Skizzen zur Geschichte Hamburgs* (Hamburg, 1951), p. 21. For destruction at Angers, see Hektor Ammann, "Vom Städtewesen Spaniens und Westfrankreichs im Mittelalter," p. 126. On Toul, which escaped the Vikings but later was struck by the Magyars, and on Trier, where the Viking invasions were catastrophic, see Dollinger-Léonard, "De la cité romaine à la ville médiévale," pp. 206, 222. The Northmen attacked Paris in 845, 856–857, and 861, ruining the Roman walls of the town; yet Paris was not abandoned completely, for it was used as a residence by Charles the Bald in 863, and the repair of the Roman wall was undertaken only in 885 by Bishop Gozlin; see J. Guerout, "Le Palais de la Cité à Paris, des origines à 1417. Essai topographique et archéologique," *Fédération des Sociétés Historiques et Archéologiques de Paris et de l'Ile-de-France. Mémoires*, I (1949), 113. Valenciennes and Cambrai were attacked in 880–881, although the extent of the damage is unknown. Francine Deisser-Nagels, "Valenciennes, ville carolingienne," *MA*, LXVIII (1962), 87–88. The entire population of Tournai fled to Noyon after the Northmen had captured the town in 881. Paul Rolland, *Histoire de Tournai* (Paris and Tournai, 1956), p. 41. For the cases of Reims, Noyon, Beauvais, and Amiens, see Vercauteren, *Étude sur les civitates de la Belgique Seconde*, pp. 82–85, 170–171, 272–273, 309–310. On Limoges and Périgueux, see Lot, *Recherches sur la population*, II, 244–245, 588. On the Danes at Bremen, see Herbert Schwarzwälder, *Entstehung und Anfänge der Stadt Bremen* (Bremen, 1955), pp. 84–85. At Ghent the settlement was annihilated completely; a second agglomeration developed in the vicinity of a new comital castle. F. Blockmans, "De twee opvolgende Gentsche 'portus,'" *ASEB*, LXXXII (1939), 79 ff. On the Viking depredations at Bordeaux, see Higounet, *Bordeaux pendant le haut moyen âge*, p. 36 ff. For Poitiers, see Claude, *Topographie und Verfassung*, p. 94 ff., and for Bonn, Niessen and Ennen, *Geschichte der Stadt Bonn*, I, 59 ff.

126. Vercauteren, "Wordingsgeschiedenis der Maassteden," p. 25.

127. The Viking invasions evidently forced the population of the commercial *vicus* outside the abbey of St. Truiden to move closer to the monastery, although whether the settlement was destroyed is uncertain. J.-L. Charles, *La ville de Saint-Trond au moyen âge à la fin du XIVe siècle* (Paris, 1965), pp. 114–115.

invasions of the fourth and fifth centuries. The beginnings of recovery were made quickly, however, as settlements grew up around the fortifications which had been erected for defense against the Vikings.[128] These were the last great invasions of western Europe until the end of the middle ages. The physiognomy of the northern medieval town on the Continent begins in many instances with the fortifications erected after the Northmen had destroyed previously existing settlements. The agglomerations which developed after the invasions, however, were of the same type as earlier pre-urban centers. The Viking invasions entailed a break in settlement, but unlike the Germanic invasions they did not result in the creation of a completely new pre-urban type.

We have now considered the periods of early medieval urban development. In these centuries of confusion, towns without a firm economic base did not survive. We must now consider in greater detail the elements of the medieval town on the northern European continent and the forces which brought about its rise as they emerged between the eighth and tenth centuries.

The *sine qua non* of any agglomeration of merchants in an age of devastation and destruction would seem to be some sort of physical protection. In northern Europe the dichotomy of the *castrum* and the merchant agglomeration developing around it characterized the formative period of medieval urbanism.[129] Exceptions to this generalization are rare.[130] Recent research has, however, modified the severity of the views of Hans Planitz and F.-L. Ganshof, both of whom saw *civitas* and *castrum* as structures with no commercial life, in rigid dichotomy to the merchant settlement outside their walls. Yet the essential accuracy of this view for northern Europe has been sustained.[131]

Under such circumstances, it is perhaps surprising that more of the leading towns of northern Europe in the middle ages did not develop on Roman sites, which were admirably suited for defense. Roman *castra* and *civitates*, however, were used only when they were as well adapted to commercial as to defensive purposes. Ghent is a case in point. By far the

---

128. The rapidity of the recovery of Dinant has been emphasized by Gaier-Lhoest, *L'évolution topographique*, p. 25 ff. The long-distance commerce of Dinant may have been crippled permanently, but it soon regained its position as a center of local trade and was again a mint in the time of Louis the Child.

129. See above, p. 58.

130. See material cited below on pre-Carolingian *Wike*, pp. 96–97.

131. See Planitz, *Die deutsche Stadt, passim*, and especially p. 60 ff.; Ganshof, *Over Stadsontwikkeling, passim*; and Ennen *Frühgeschichte*, pp. 123–124.

best defensive position in the region of Ghent is the Blandijnberg, in the southern part of the modern city and the eventual location of St. Pieter's abbey. Since *Blandinium* is the only Gallo-Roman toponym on the present area of the town, a settlement probably existed on the hill in the Roman period.[132] Yet the town developed in the lowlands between the Leie and Scheldt rivers under the shadow of a comital castle erected no earlier than the late ninth century. This area had immense commercial advantages, but no means of defense until the construction of the castle, which postdates the appearance of a settlement there by nearly a century.

Various structures other than Roman *civitates* and *castra* might provide protection for merchants. The most common was perhaps the strong point erected by a local potentate. The princely *castrum* of the early middle ages was neither a castle nor the equivalent of the Gallo-Roman *castrum*. It was a comparatively large and complex structure, with room for the population of the surrounding area to take refuge in time of emergency. Princely *castra* had an area of between two and twelve acres and included the residence of the count, duke, or king, the offices of his officials, a chapel, and other similar accommodations. They became the centers of administration in the castellanies of Flanders, which had the largest and most complex *castra* of western Europe.[133]

The role of the princely *castrum* in town formation is well illustrated by the case of Ghent. Recent research reveals that prehistoric Ghent was an agrarian village around the modern Zandberg, between the Munt, the Botermarkt, and the church of St. Niklaas. A harbor along the rivers is attested in a document of 811, and the foundations thus were laid for the export of local textiles. This industry had grown up as a result of the presence of grazing lands near Ghent.[134] There is no evidence, however, that this harbor, or *portus*, was fortified before the 840s,[135] and a comital

132. Maurits Gysseling, *Gent's Vroegste Geschiedenis in de Spiegel van zijn Plaatsnamen* (Antwerp, 1954), p. 18.

133. P. Héliot, "Sur les résidences princières baties en France du Xᵉ au XII siècle," *MA*, LXI (1955), 27–61, 219–317. The comital castles of Flanders have been seen as adaptations of Roman antecedents by Edith Ennen, "Zur Stadtwerdung im fränkischen Raum," *RV*, XVIII (1953), 7.

134. Gysseling, *Gent's Vroegste Geschiedenis*, pp. 20–21. This interpretation is supported by Hans Van Werveke, "Opgravingen en navorsingen in verband met de oudste geschiedenis van de stad Gent," *BGN*, IX (1954), 33–37. Van Werveke notes that the presence of a sparsely settled agrarian community in the northern section of the *portus* allowed space for the formation of great markets and churches, which would have been impossible had the entire area been thickly settled.

135. Blockmans, "De twee opvolgende Gentsche 'portus,'" pp. 59–60.

castle is attested only from the late ninth or early tenth century.[136] Recent research has indicated that the original *portus* of Bruges took form in the early ninth century, before the erection of the comital *castrum*, in the depression between the modern Steenstraat and the eventual site of the *castrum*, near the modern town hall. The *castrum* was constructed only shortly before 879 as a means of defense against the Vikings. The agglomeration developed at the intersection of an important land route to Ghent and later to Ypres with the old bed of the Reie, which silted during the following century.[137] This view has been challenged, not completely convincingly, in favor of a purely rural origin of Bruges in the vicinity of the churches of St. Salvator and Onze Lieve Vrouw, which thus are claimed to have existed as rural parish churches by the late ninth century, providing some means of protection for the infant community.[138] There seems to be general agreement, however, that at Bruges as at Ghent, a settlement preceded the erection of a comital *castrum*, which was designed in each case as a defensive point against the Viking invaders.

The numerous pre-Carolingian *Wike* in Saxony also often arose without the protection of a fortress, and some of these settlements had grown into genuine towns before they were fortified.[139] Soest was the center of an extremely productive agrarian hinterland which had easy access to the town. No fortification is mentioned at Soest; the settlement first appears in 836 as an agrarian village. Soest may have been more important already than some of its neighbors, by virtue of a flourishing salt-mining industry in its environs. Furthermore, Soest was on the *Hellweg*, the

136. *Ibid.*, p. 81 ff.; Hans Van Werveke and A. E. Verhulst, "Castrum en Oudburg te Gent. Bijdrage tot de oudste Geschiedenis van de Vlaamse Steden," *HMGOG*, N.S. XIV (1960), 56–57.

137. See Verhulst, "Les Origines . . . Bruges," p. 53 ff.; see also Jan Dhondt, "De vroege Topografie van Brugge," *HMGOG*, N.S. XI (1957), 3–30, and Josef De Smet, "De Brugse WIIC-namen," *ASEB*, LXXXV (1948), 112–117.

138. A. C. F. Koch, "Brugge's topographische Ontwikkeling tot in de 12ᵉ eeuw," *ASEB*, XCIX (1962), 5–67, and especially 33–43. Koch sees the origin of the *portus* of Bruges during the Viking invasions, which made the collection of dues by ecclesiastical landlords difficult. The confusion thus entailed economic dislocation, in the midst of which Bruges arose as a merchant agglomeration doing its first trading with the Vikings. See also *idem*, "De ouderdom van de stad Brugge," *ASEB*, LXXXVI (1949), 149–150. The rural element in the early urban history of Brabant also has been emphasized recently; there were settlements of men who might easily pass back and forth between merchant and agrarian activity. Paul Bonenfant, "L'origine des villes brabançonnes," *RBPH*, XXXI (1953), 399–477.

139. Fritz Timme, "Handel und Verkehr im alten Sachsen," *BDL*, XCIX (1963), 28–29.

military road running from Cologne to Magdeburg by way of Dortmund, Soest, and Paderborn. This artery provided the means for export of locally produced articles to more distant markets. Only after Soest had gained this position as an important center of local and regional trade was a Carolingian royal palace erected there.[140] Emden, on the North Sea coast, affords the classic case of a completely unprotected *Wik* which eventually evolved into a town.[141]

Although a fortification was not a necessary precondition for the growth of a trading settlement, the protection which it gave was unquestionably a stimulus to the further development of the town. Valenciennes, for example, was the site of an agrarian settlement in the Roman period, and grave finds indicate that Roman and German lived here in separate settlements throughout the period of the invasions. Valenciennes was not a *castrum*; the important Roman sites in this region were Famars, site of a *castrum* three miles south of Valenciennes, and Escautpont, six miles north, where the Chaussée Brunehaut crossed the Scheldt. A document dated 693 of King Clovis III, however, mentions a royal *palatium* at Valenciennes; a *portus* developed around the *palatium* in the Carolingian period. The royal fortification thus brought about the rapid rise of Valenciennes and the decline of Famars, a situation of which the town was able to take full advantage due to its excellent position on a major waterway.[142]

Settlements most often developed around pre-existing *castra*; former Roman towns afford perhaps the best examples of this genre of pre-urban nucleus. Magdeburg originated around a Celtic *oppidum* which was refortified under Charlemagne and again under the Ottonians.[143] It was the only town east of the Rhine and north of the Main which we know had a walled merchant settlement by the beginning of the eleventh century.[144] Similarly, the growth of Merseburg was due to the construction of a royal fortification along the important road between Frankfurt

---

140. Georg Niemeier and Hermann Rothert, "Der Stadtplan von Soest," *Westfälische Zeitschrift*, CIII (1954), 32–40, 61.

141. Werner Haarnagel, "Die frühgeschichtliche Handels-Siedlung Emden und ihre Entwicklung bis ins Mittelalter," *Friesisches Jahrbuch* (1955), pp. 76–77.

142. Deisser-Nagels, "Valenciennes," pp. 51–90, and especially pp. 53–64.

143. Berent Schwineköper, "Die Anfänge Magdeburgs," *SAES*, p. 397 ff. See also Fritz Rörig, "Magdeburgs Entstehung und die ältere Handelsgeschichte," *Miscellanea Academica Berolinensia*, II, 1 (Berlin, 1950), and Erich Herzog, *Die ottonische Stadt. Die Anfänge der mittelalterlichen Stadtbaukunst in Deutschland* (Berlin, 1964), p. 26.

144. Ennen, *Frühgeschichte*, Map 2.

am Main and Erfurt and the Saale.[145] Stade also originated in a merchant
agglomeration developing at the foot of a fortification.[146] *Wike* often grew up
around Carolingian palaces in Germany;[147] such was the origin of Aachen.[148]

The *castrum* might have been of indirect importance in the development of a town as a place where toll was collected by local potentates.·
Although such tolls might indicate the presence of a resident merchant
settlement, they probably simply stimulated the growth of an exchange
economy by forcing merchants to stop, unload their merchandise, and
surrender either a part of it or a money payment. Tolls thus contributed
to the development of trading agglomerations at the foot of the fortification at such places as Utrecht and Antwerp.[149] The exemption of a
particular group from a toll might have had similar effects. The *familia* of
the abbey of St. Vaast of Arras had such a privilege. After the abbey had
been fortified at the end of the ninth century, various persons, of occupations both agrarian and commercial, came to Arras to enjoy freedom from
tolls that otherwise they would have paid; the abbey eventually was
forced to exclude all *censuales* living outside a radius of twenty miles from
Arras from this privilege.[150]

Recent evidence that many towns of northern Europe were preceded
by agrarian communities on the same site has led to a resurgence of the
Landgemeinde theory of medieval urban origins. This school of thought
tries to derive models, even direct antecedents for the institutions of the
town corporations from prototypes in agrarian villages; the fact that the
inhabitants of most towns of medieval Europe practiced some form of
agriculture was taken as evidence supporting this theory.[151] Leaving aside

145. Herzog, *Die ottonische Stadt*, pp. 45–52.
146. Hans Wohltmann, "Die Anfänge der Stadt Stade," *Hansische Geschichtsblätter*,
LXIX (1950), 46–63.
147. Planitz, *Die deutsche Stadt*, p. 52 ff.
148. See in general Richard E. Sullivan, *Aix-la-Chapelle in the Age of Charlemagne*
(Norman, Okla., 1963).
149. Schlesinger, "Stadtische Frühformen zwischen Rhein und Elbe," pp. 306–307.
150. Renée Doehaerd, "Note sur l'histoire de l'ancien tonlieu d'Arras," *Mémoires
de l'Académie d'Arras* (1943–45). Jean Lestocquoy has noted that of the names of
bourgeois indicating a possible place of origin, most are from an area within twenty
miles of the town. *Fédération Historique et Archéologique de Belgique. 35ᵉ Congrès* ... 1953.
Annales, Fascicule III, 160–162.
151. For the classic formulation of the *Landgemeinde* theory, see Georg von Below,
Der Ursprung der deutschen Stadtverfassung (Düsseldorf, 1892), p. 4 ff. The standard interpretation of more recent proponents of this view was given in the extremely influential
article of Franz Steinbach, "Stadtgemeinde und Landgemeinde. Studien zur Geschichte des Bürgertums, I," *RV*, XIII (1948), 11–50.

the fact that we know very little about the institutions of agrarian villages before the eleventh century, the *Landgemeinde* theory has numerous inherent improbabilities. The most extreme of its proponents, Karl Kroeschell,[152] has charged quite correctly that Ennen and Planitz, in extending the law of the merchants into the law of the *Wik* and thence of the town, fail to explain how the transition occurred between a personal and a territorial liberty.[153] Kroeschell himself, however, confuses motive and result. He first states that the originally servile character of the townsmen in Germany, as dependents of the king, prevented the town from later becoming the model of planned free urban foundations; he ignores the fact that the towns soon became free and were quite able by the eleventh century to serve as such models. He denies Planitz's identification of *vicus* and *Wik*, with both indicating a pre-urban merchant settlement, by citing cases in which Planitz's reading is far more plausible than his own.[154] Kroeschell's difficulty is expressed very nicely when he criticizes Planitz for seeing urban law as a result of social and economic forces rather than considering law and legal history in a vacuum.[155]

A distinction must be made between juridical and physical origins. As an originally rural settlement lost its agrarian character and became commercial, its legal system changed to meet the new conditions. Too many medieval towns on the Continent originated in the union of

152. Karl Kroeschell, *Weichbild. Untersuchungen zur Struktur und Entstehung der mittelalterlichen Stadtgemeinde in Westfalen* (Cologne and Graz, 1960).

153. See the exposition of Planitz, *Die deutsche Stadt*, pp. 55 ff., 75 ff., and in more precise formulation in "Kaufmannsgilde und städtische Eidgenossenschaft in niederfränkischen Städten im 11. und 12. Jahrhundert," *ZRG, GA*, LX (1940), 1–116, and "Die deutsche Stadtgemeinde," *ZRG, GA*, LXIV (1944), 1–85. See also Ennen, *Frühgeschichte*, p. 165 ff.

154. Kroeschell, *Weichbild*, p. 17. The attempt of Ennen (*Frühgeschichte*, p. 131) to separate the *Wik* as a depot for wandering merchants from the *vicus*, a market and artisan settlement, is plausible, but it does not alter the essential accuracy of Planitz's view of the *vicus-Wik* as a place of commerce and trade. Ironically, a misreading of this word was one of the major errors of Pirenne and his disciples, writing before the work of Planitz and Vogel; see W. Vogel, "Wik-Orte und Wikinger," *Hansische Geschichtsblätter*, LX (1935), 29 ff. It caused them drastically to underestimate the importance of commerce in the Carolingian town. Fernand Vercauteren, *Étude sur les civitates de la Belgique Seconde*, portrays a completely passive episcopal town or fortification as characteristic of Carolingian "urban" life. Yet Vercauteren defines *vicus* as a "petite agglomération agricole" in the environs of the town, a definition which is correct only in exceptional cases (p. 393).

155. Kroeschell, *Weichbild*, pp. 22–23. Yet he has difficulty understanding how persons engaged in peasant occupations can enjoy the juridical status of bourgeois; *ibid.*, p. 39 ff.

agrarian communities, among them Brunswick,[156] Dortmund,[157] and Reutlingen,[158] for the phenomenon to be ignored. But this does not permit us to postulate rural origins for urban law; rather the reverse process is often true from the eleventh and twelfth centuries: urban law was granted to agrarian communities in the countryside.[159]

The physical origin of many towns, however, was in agrarian communities. Recent linguistic studies have emphasized the originally close connection of the town with nonurban areas. The Germanic *þur* or *bur* indicated a group of persons congregated into an unfortified community either of peasants or merchants. The Latin *burgus*, occurring from the second century, connoted a small fortification. With the Germanic invasions these conceptions became mixed to indicate a place generally unfortified, with a market, outside a *civitas, castrum,* or similar fortification. When placed in juxtaposition to some other part of the town, *bourg* or *Burg* generally indicated a more recent section; this was invariably true of Roman towns. The *bourgs* of Merovingian Gaul are thus indistinguishable in kind from the *Wike* of ninth-century Germany. The German-Latin *burgus* came to Germany only in the ninth century, and its usage never became common there; *Wik* remained the preferred term. When *burgus* came into general use in Germany in the twelfth century, it connoted not the suburb under the walls, but rather the entire town inside the walls. In France it continued to indicate a suburb.[160] The situation is

156. Planitz, *Die deutsche Stadt,* p. 214, and *passim.*

157. Dortmund evidently was a small merchant center on the *Hellweg* which expanded in the ninth and tenth centuries by the absorption of several agrarian villages in its environs. Luise von Winterfeld, "Die Entstehung der Stadt Dortmund," *Beiträge zur Geschichte Dortmunds und der Grafschaft Mark,* XLVIII (1950), 28 ff.

158. Herbert Kopp, *Die Anfänge der Stadt Reutlingen. Ein Beitrag zur Stadttopographie* (Reutlingen, 1961).

159. Bryce Lyon, "Medieval Real Estate Developments and Freedom, "*AHR,* LXII (1957), 47–61.

160. Walter Schlesinger, "Burg and Stadt," in *Aus Verfassungs- und Landesgeschichte* [cited above, n. 97], II, 97–150, and Schlesinger's more recent statement of his position, "Stadt und Burg im Lichte der Wortgeschichte," *SG,* XVI (1963), 433–444. Schlesinger's arguments explain a number of the inconsistencies of the "Burgus-I" and "Burgus-II" argument of Hans Van Werveke. See by the latter *De Oudste Burchten aan de Vlaamse ende Zeeuwse Kust* (Brussels, 1965), and particularly *"Burgus": Versterking of Nederzetting?* (Brussels, 1965). See the critique of the latter work by John H. Mundy in *Speculum,* XLII (1967), 199–205. Schlesinger also has emphasized the unique character of the dichotomy of *Burg* and the surrounding territory. There was a distinction between its legal nature and the dichotomies of legion camp-*canabae,* legion camp-civilian settlement, and *civitas*-suburban churches. Schlesinger, "Uber mitteleuropäische Städtelandschaften der Frühzeit," *BDL,* XCIII (1957), 36. Although

further complicated by a tendency toward terminological imprecision in Germany, particularly with regard to terms of Romance origin.[161] This process can be seen clearly in areas near the linguistic frontier, as *Burg* ceased to connote simply the settlement and came to include the fortification. There was a pre-urban settlement at Ghent in what was later known as the "Oudburg" by the early ninth century. It seems probable, although at this point the question cannot be answered with certainty, that the streams around the "Oudburg" were man made and that the comital castle was built there after the settlement had developed, in view of the excellent defensive position.[162] The designation *Burg* then spread from the settlement to the *castrum*.[163] Whatever the origins of the term may have been, all *burgi* had a privileged character vis-à-vis the surrounding countryside by the eleventh century as areas throughout which commerce was conducted, not simply as places in which markets were located. *Burgus* and market are independent of each other but are dependent upon the same external factor.[164] Neither indicates a town, but rather an essential component of a town.[165]

---

burgus always implied a wider concept than "fortification," it did not necessarily involve a genuine town. See Lucien Musset, "Peuplement en bourgage en bourgs ruraux en Normandie du Xe au XIIIe siècle," *Cahiers de Civilisation Médiévale*, IX (1966), 177–208, and Jacques Boussard, "Note sur la formation des bourgs et des communes en Normandie," *Annales de Normandie*, VIII (1958), 423–440. See' also in general *Frühe Burgen und Städte. Beiträge zur Burgen- und Stadtkernforschung*. Deutsche Akademie der Wissenschaften zu Berlin. Schriften der Sektion für Vor- und Frühgeschichte, II (Berlin, 1954).

161. Schlesinger, "Burg und Stadt," p. 139 ff.

162. Van Werveke and Verhulst, "Castrum en Oudberg te Gent," p. 12 ff.

163. We are adopting here the terminological arguments of Schlesinger, rather than Van Werveke. The latter sees the term spreading from the *castrum* to include the settlement. The arguments of Van Werveke were anticipated by Mina Mertens, "Les survivances domaniales du *castrum* carolingien de Bruxelles à la fin du moyen âge," *MA*, LXIX (Volume Jubiliare) (1963), 641–655.

164. Endemann, *Markturkunde und Markt*, p. 156 ff.

165. There are few exceptions to the general statement that in the formative period of the medieval town on the Continent the *burgus*, outside the wall, was the merchant center. Two markets were established at Poitiers immediately outside the wall in the *burgus*, but the merchants who frequented them continued to live in the *civitas*. The merchant settlement, however, was still a subordinate part of the total agglomeration at Poitiers; as late as the twelfth century King Louis VII allowed the canons of St. Hilary to dam the river Boivre to make access to the town more difficult. This never would have been permitted had Poitiers been an important merchant center. Claude, *Topographie und Verfassung*, p. 135 ff.

The component role of the agrarian community in medieval urbanism has also been noted, perhaps with too great emphasis, by Heinz Stoob. In addition to the merchant settlement and the fortification, the two "traditional" elements of the medieval town, Stoob sees a third: the local agrarian community with its market.[166] The fact that northwestern Germany developed genuine towns later than the west but before the regions east of the Elbe has been explained as being due to the absence for a longer period of an urban artisan class, which welded the three elements together.[167] This in its turn would seem to tie later town development in northwestern Germany to the absence of Roman antecedents, since the Roman artisan class had continued to live in the towns in the west.[168]

The question of nonurban or agrarian antecedents of the medieval town leads to that of "Germanic continuity." Scholars have seen evidence of settlement on certain sites, particularly in Westphalia, before the Carolingian period and have argued from these archaeological data that the Carolingian and post-Carolingian pre-urban agglomerations were continuations of these Germanic settlements. The strongest case for this theory to date has been made for Paderborn,[169] but even here it is dubious. It has been denied emphatically for Münster.[170] Such coastal locations as Hamburg are special cases; although they were inhabited before the Carolingian period, their example cannot be taken as clear proof of "Germanic continuity."[171] Some *oppida* developed by the Germans as military devices against the Romans may have been a transitional form, leading the Germans away from their distaste for living in close quarters, but they were not an origin of the medieval town. Most of them were destroyed or were mere fortified strong points in the middle ages; they never were true towns. The Germanic *oppida* were a response to stimuli

166. Heinz Stoob, "Die Ausbreitung der abendländischen Stadt im östlichen Europa," *Zeitschrift für Ostforschung*, X (1961), 25–84.

167. Carl Haase, "Grundfragen der nordwestdeutsche Städtegeschichte bis ins 13. Jahrundert," in Wilhelm Rausch (ed.), *Die Städte Mitteleuropas im 12. und 13. Jahrundert* (Linz, 1963), p. 124.

168. Ammann, "Vom Städtewesen Spaniens und Westfrankreichs," p. 111 ff.

169. Bernhard Ortmann, *Vororte Westfalens seit germanischer Zeit. Studie zur Geschichte der "gewordenen" Stadt* (Paderborn, 1949).

170. Joseph Prinz, *Mimigernaford-Münster. Die Entstehungsgeschichte einer Stadt* (Münster, 1960), pp. 99–100.

171. See in general Carl Haase, *Die Entstehung der westfälischen Städte* (Münster, 1960); *idem*, "Zur Entstehungszeit der westfälischen Städte," *WF*, XVI (1963), 125–160, and 'Grundfragen,' pp. 117–118.

different in kind from those producing medieval town life on the continent.[172]

Bishoprics of non-Roman foundation often provided the fortification around which a town later developed. The most conspicuous example is provided by the episcopal *civitates* founded by Charlemagne and his successors for the conversion of heathen tribes brought into the Empire. This practice was continued with even greater emphasis by the Ottonians.[173] Commercial settlements often developed under the walls of the episcopal complexes.

Bremen was a Carolingian royal villa in the eighth century. A bishopric was founded there at the conclusion of the Saxon wars. Bremen basically was a bridge settlement at the last point where the Weser can be crossed conveniently before reaching the sea and as such probably had a *portus*. The catalyst to the economic development of Bremen from agrarian village into town, however, was the foundation of the bishopric, which antedates all direct evidence of merchant activity on the site.[174]

Osnabrück developed around a bishopric founded on the Saxon frontier by Charlemagne in 783. A settlement of traders and artisans had grown up around the episcopal complex by the end of the ninth century. The *Binnenburg* (the cathedral complex, which maintained its own wall until the end of the middle ages) and the *Butenberg* (the market settlement) were surrounded by a common fortification at the beginning of the twelfth century.[175] The first market of Hamburg developed around the mission church founded by Louis the Pious for the evangelization of northern Europe. After the destruction of the church by the Danes in 845, the merchant settlement remained and expanded to the south and west. Prosperity was limited, however, for Hamburg was very much secondary to Stade as a trading center of the lower Elbe. The market was still of very modest proportions when the bishopric returned to Hamburg from Bremen in the tenth century.[176] A bishopric and a royal palace were

172. Ennen, *Frühgeschichte*, pp. 46–47.

173. See in general Robert S. Lopez, "Of Towns and Trade," in Robert S. Hoyt (ed.), *Life and Thought in the Early Middle Ages* (Minneapolis, 1967), p. 43, and Lopez, "La città dell'Europa post-Carolingia," *I problemi dell'Europa post-Carolingia*, SSCI, II (1955), 547–574.

174. Schwarzwälder, *Entstehung und Anfänge der Stadt Bremen*, pp. 57–77; Gutkind, *Urban Development in Central Europe*, 238.

175. Gutkind, *Urban Development in Central Europe*, p. 247.

176. Reincke, *Forschungen und Skizzen*, pp. 7–22; Erich von Lehe, *Die Märkte Hamburgs von den Anfängen bis in die Neuzeit (1911)* (Wiesbaden, 1966), p. 2 ff.

present at Würzburg on the left bank of the Main from the eighth century. A nonagrarian settlement had developed across from them on the right bank no later than the beginning of the ninth century, and the seat of the bishopric was moved across the stream. It is thus unclear whether the bishopric of Würzburg, in conjunction with the royal fortification on the Marienburg, gave rise to the town or merely was founded in a location where a merchant settlement already existed, perhaps as a result of the protection given by the royal castle.[177]

The bishopric of Münster was founded in the late eighth century by the Carolingians as an outpost for the evangelization of the Frisians. The location was extremely favorable for commerce; several roads came from Cologne and the lower Rhine over Dortmund, then united at Münster and proceeded as one road through Osnabrück to the north and northeast. These roads did not use the ford across the Aa River, where the first settlement developed at Münster, but rather stayed on the opposite bank. The roads thus did not contribute to the origin of the town, although they were a major element in its prosperity after the agglomeration had developed. When the Franks came, they found only agrarian activity on the site of Münster; the cathedral complex of the late eighth century was the pre-urban nucleus which evolved into the town. The market and merchant settlement developed along the street in front of this complex, in a settlement pattern typical of the region between Rhine and Elbe, although whether it corresponded to the single-street *Wik* type is uncertain.[178]

Medieval towns also developed around ordinary parish churches of non-Roman origin. Aschaffenburg originated with the church of Liutgard, wife of the East Frankish king Ludwig III (876–882).[179] The "merchants' church" was a particularly fertile source of later urban development. Merchants characteristically erected churches for the protection and safekeeping of their property, and the sedentary merchant settlements naturally congregated around these sanctuaries.[180] Such a church, that dedicated to St. George shortly after 900, was the site of the original *Wik*

177. Karl Withold, "Die frühgeschichtliche Entwicklung des Würzburger Stadtplanes," *SAES*, pp. 363–375; Schlesinger, "Städtische Frühformen zwischen Rhein und Elbe," p. 336 ff.

178. Prinz, *Mimigernaford-Münster*, pp. 7–8, 99–100, 147–149.

179. H. Weigel, "Aschaffenburg—Rheinfrankens Grenzstadt gegen Ostfranken," *1000 Jahre Stift und Stadt Aschaffenburg. Aschaffenburger Jahrbuch*, IV (Aschaffenburg, 1957), 11–32.

180. Paul Johansen, "Die Kaufmannskirche im Ostseegebiet," *SAES*, pp. 499–525.

of Gandersheim, although the settlement was relocated at the modern town as the need for protection grew.[181] A merchants' church played an important, although perhaps not decisive, role in the rise of Erfurt.[182]

The historian, nonetheless, must beware of exaggerated deductions about the role of parish churches as forces of urbanism in the early middle ages. A simple parish church often became the chief ecclesiastical center for a town which developed around it due to factors independent of the church itself. The parish church of St. Martin had served a small agrarian village on the domains of the counts of Flanders. As the city of Ypres grew up south of St. Martin's, across from an island *castellum* established by the counts in the eleventh century, the church of St. Pieter, in the vicinity of the new agglomeration, became dependent on St. Martin's. St. Martin's thus became extremely important due to the growth of the town in its immediate vicinity, but it had nothing to do with the rise of the town.[183]

The abbeys were a peculiarly medieval, and particularly Carolingian contribution to urban history.[184] The abbatial role in urban origins has been underestimated until recent years, and it is quite true that no monastery developed into a town of consequence unless other favorable factors were present.[185] Most abbeys which became pre-urban nuclei were founded outside the ruins of Roman towns in the seventh century, or occasionally in the sixth, and became centers of settlement from the eighth. They were generally wealthier than the bishoprics, which were confined within the old Roman walls. Perhaps for this reason, the later Merovingian kings began to sojourn at abbeys rather than bishoprics.[186] The increasing commerce carried on between the monasteries and their

181. Hans Goetting, "Die Anfänge der Stadt Gandersheim," *BDL*, LXXXIX (1952), 43 ff.

182. Schlesinger, "Städtische Frühformen zwischen Rhein und Elbe," p. 316 ff.

183. A. E. Verhulst, "De Vroegste Geschiedenis van het Sint-Maartenskapittel en het Ontstaan van de stad Ieper," *HMGOG*, N.S. XI (1957), 31–48.

184. Jean Lestocquoy, "Abbayes et origines de villes," *Revue d'Histoire de l'Église de France*, XXXIII (1947), 108–112.

185. See the critique of Pirenne's tendency to denigrate the role of the abbey in urban history by Françoise Lehoux, *Le Bourg Saint-Germain-des-Prés, depuis ses origines jusqu'à la fin de la Guerre de Cent Ans* (Paris, 1951), p. xv. See also in general P. Feuchère, *Contribution à l'étude des origines des villes, les castra et les noyaux préurbains en Artois du IXe au XIe siècle* (Arras, 1949).

186. On the custom of German kings to reside in abbeys or episcopal complexes, see Carlrichard Brühl, "Königspfalz und Bischofstadt in fränkischer Zeit," *RV*, XXIII (1958), 161–274.

dependent estates in the Carolingian period[187] had a definite effect on the population living immediately under the walls of the abbeys. The establishment of monasteries near Roman walls was one of the most important changes in the urban physiognomy of Europe between the fifth and ninth centuries.

Some towns developed around the abbey as a single element, without the involvement of a Roman town. Such centers, as St. Riquier, Abbeville, and Montreuil-sur-Mer in northwestern France, were generally small.[188] This was not, however, invariably the case. Although St. Truiden, twenty miles northwest of Liége, was not one of the greatest medieval towns, it nonetheless grew to a fair size. It had originated in a gradual displacement from the eighth century of the population of the nearby hamlet of Zerkingen toward the walls of the abbey of St. Truiden. This settlement was present a bare half-century after the foundation of the abbey and was already termed *vicus* or *Wik*.[189] Tiel, on the Waal River in the duchy of Guelders, also originated around a monastery which was not attached to a Roman fortification. It was a large merchant settlement by the tenth century.[190] Other cases are less certain; one theory placing the origins of Ghent in the immediate environs of the abbey of St. Bavon has been refuted.[191]

Arras has been the most thoroughly investigated of the towns developing around an abbey near a Roman site. The abbey of St. Vaast was founded in the mid-seventh century near the Roman road which passed close to Arras. Some settlement still persisted in the Roman city. Settlements and parish churches grew up in the vicinity of the abbey and dependent upon the abbot. The monks fortified their complex shortly after the Viking invasions of the later ninth century. The population was too large for these walls, and the market of Arras was established in the vicinity of the *castrum* of the comital castellan. Only the cathedral and its attendant clergy were left inside the Roman fortification.[192]

187. Doehaerd, "Ce qu'on vendait . . . ," p. 266 ff. The idea that local trade eventually gave rise to commerce over greater distances is further developed by Franz Petri, with particular reference to the domanial monastic origins of Nivelles and Gembloux; see his "Die Anfänge des mittelalterlichen Städtewesens," p. 272 ff.

188. Lestocquoy, "De l'unité à la pluralité," p. 164 ff.

189. Charles, *Ville de Saint-Trond*, pp. 105–107.

190. H. Müter, "Het Ontstaan van de stad Tiel," *BGN*, IX (1955), 161–189.

191. Blockmans, "De twee opvolgende Gentsche 'portus,'" p. 52 ff., refuted by Van Werveke and Verhulst, "Castrum en Oudburg to Gent," p. 56–57.

192. Lestocquoy, "Les étapes du développement urbain d'Arras," 163–185. There seems to be general agreement that the urban institutions of Arras, together with most

Tours shows a similar development. The town had been a Roman *civitas*. Some life evidently persisted there across the period of the Germanic invasions, but the *burgus* developed around the abbey of St. Martin. The abbey was fortified after the Viking invasions, thus becoming a *castrum*. The dichotomy of the *burgus*, which was fortified at Tours at an unusually early date, with the *civitas* was lessened through most of the tenth century by the position of the Capetians as both counts and lay abbots of St. Martin's. Settlements developed throughout the century between *civitas* and *castrum*, with the merchant and artisan element centered increasingly in the *castrum*, particularly after the Capetians had surrendered the county while retaining the lay abbacy.[193]

A rhythm thus can be detected in the development of the forerunners of the medieval town. Most Roman towns were still functioning in the fourth century, although their prosperity had diminished considerably. The fifth century was the period of great *débâcle*, the low point of European urban history. From the late fifth century, however, and particularly in the sixth, settlements began to develop both inside the Roman walls and in the *suburbia* around episcopal complexes or parish churches. The abbeys became a prominent feature of the pre-urban landscape from the seventh century, and the castles of secular princes and bishoprics founded by them from the eighth. Merchants generally tended to congregate around abbeys and princely bastions in preference to bishoprics except in cases where the bishopric had been an element of continuity with the Roman municipal system.

The medieval town was primarily a center of trade and commerce, whether regional or carried on over a long distance. It was this economic function above all which differentiated it both from the agrarian village and the Roman town. No medieval site, however well protected, however

---

of the prominent families, had a domanial origin on the estates of St. Vaast. See G. Van Acker, "L'origine des institutions urbaines d'Arras," *RN*, XXXI (1949), 105–125; Lestocquoy, "L'origine des habitants d'Arras aux XIIᵉ et XIIIᵉ siècles d'après les noms de famille," *Cahiers de Civilisation Médiévale*, I (1958), 55–62, and *Les Dynasties bourgeoises d'Arras du XIᵉ au XVᵉ siècle* (Arras, 1945), p. 86 ff. A recent study, however, has indicated that the count may have taken over most abbatial jurisdiction in the merchant agglomeration before the eleventh century; the rural magistracy thus was not a direct ancestor of the urban. A. C. F. Koch, "Continuité ou rupture? De la justice domaniale et comtale à Arras," *RN*, XL (1958), 289–296. Conclusions similar to those of Lestocquoy for Arras have been reached by Edith Ennen for Dinant; see her *Frühgeschichte*, pp. 217–222.

193. Heinrich Büttner, "Studien zum frühmittelalterlichen Städtewesen in Frankreich, vornehmlich im Loire- und Rhonegebiet," *SAES*, p. 183 ff.

favored by political or ecclesiastical circumstances, became a genuine town unless its location was propitious to commercial development.

At times the advantages of sites which gave rise to towns are difficult to perceive. The site of Huy would seem to be extremely poor. The original settlement was on the Hoyoux, a stream which could be navigated only by very small boats. The valley of the Hoyoux was narrow, affording little room for topographical expansion. The settlement nonetheless grew, evidently as a result of its position as the market between two regions specializing in different raw materials. Huy was also the center of a region of important mineral deposits.[194] From local beginnings Huy thus expanded until it attained a bank of the Meuse; the rise of the town then became closely connected with the prosperous Meuse trade. The area on the Meuse was a *portus* by 862, while the *vicus*, the settlement on the nearby Hoyoux around the Church of Notre-Dame, remained a market for agricultural products. Huy thus developed into a town by the combination of a prosperous local market with a site on the Meuse.[195] Valenciennes is an excellent example of the geographical shift from Roman to medieval town. It participated in the general rebirth of trade along the Scheldt under the Carolingians which followed the growth of the Meuse trade in the seventh century.[196] The presence of the royal *palatium* was a factor in the rise of Valenciennes, but the very erection of such a structure along a major waterway is significant. Famars, near Valenciennes and much more favored by land routes, had been a prosperous town under the Romans. It declined as the *portus* of Valenciennes developed along the Scheldt, perhaps at the point where the Scheldt first became navigable. Valenciennes apparently had regular commercial contact with the infant *portus* of Ghent by 830.[197] Ghent too shows a characteristic development. It was crossed by no Roman roads, but it was at the confluence of two great rivers. Such a place was almost inevitably destined to become a commercial center in the middle ages.[198] Similarly, while the foundation

---

194. The importance of nearby mineral deposits in urban development has been noted particularly by Ferdinand Tremel, "Der Bergbau als städtebildende Kraft in Innerösterreich," *Beiträge zur Wirtschafts- und Stadtgeschichte* [cited above, n. 53], 97–115. These towns, however, engaged in little long-distance commerce; the carrying trade was in the hands of bourgeois of towns which did not owe their origin to the mines. On the famous example of Goslar, see Herzog, *Die ottonische Stadt*, pp. 71–72.

195. Joris, *Ville de Huy*, p. 69 ff., and particularly pp. 90–91.

196. See above, pp. 90, 97.

197. Deisser-Nagels, "Valenciennes," pp. 73–74.

198. See material cited above, p. 89.

of the bishopric of Bremen was undeniably a factor of major importance in the rise of the town, the location of Bremen at the last convenient crossing of the Weser before it reaches the sea was decisive for the future development of the town.[199] The location of Erfurt at the junction of land routes at the ford across the Gera was at least as important as the institution of the bishopric there.[200] Although Hamburg was the site of a bishopric, it did not develop commercially into a true town until the twelfth century, for the Elbe, on which it was located, was a frontier waterway,[201] and most merchants preferred the less dangerous Meuse and Rhine routes. Tienen, in the duchy of Brabant, originated in the late eighth century as an agrarian villa of Saint-Germain-des-Prés. At an uncertain date the administrative center of the villa was walled. The site was on a major overland route, and a large merchant agglomeration had developed at Tienen by the late tenth century.[202]

The theory that long-distance commerce conducted in a single-street merchant *Wik* in the shadow of a powerful fortification was the forerunner of the dominant form of commercial activity in the fully developed town received its classic formulation in the "wandering merchant" hypothesis of Henri Pirenne and is still accepted by many scholars. According to this theory, peddlers of uncertain origin traveled throughout Europe with their wares, stopping at various *Wike* to rest and exchange merchandise before moving on. These merchants eventually took up permanent residence in the *Wike*, but their major economic activity continued to be long-distance trade.[203] This hypothesis has glaring weaknesses. It does not account for the population which had to be resident in the *Wike* from their very inception to provide food and lodging for the wanderers and

199. Gutkind, *Urban Development in Central Europe*, p. 238.

200. Schlesinger, "Städtische Frühformen zwischen Rhein und Elbe," p. 326, and *passim*.

201. Gutkind, *Urban Development in Central Europe*, p. 403; Reincke, *Forschungen und Skizzen*, p. 17. Schwineköper's argument that the Elbe was safe for commerce in the tenth and eleventh centuries is not convincing; see his "Die Anfänge Magdeburgs," p. 433. The disaster sustained by the imperial forces in eastern Germany in 983 caused the trade of Magdeburg to move to the west. Merchants of Magdeburg probably participated in the founding of the markets of Halberstadt, Quedlinburg, Merseburg, and Naumberg. Each of these centers was some distance from the Elbe, and only Merseburg, on the Saale, was on another major stream. They were thus less likely than Magdeburg to be pillaged, and all were favorably situated for overland trade. Herzog, *Die ottonische Stadt*, p. 26.

202. Jan Wauters, *Bijdragen tot de Geschiedenis van Tienen* (Tienen, 1962), pp. 15–17.

203. Henri Pirenne, *Les villes et les institutions urbaines*, 2 vols. (Paris and Brussels, 1939), I, 365 ff.

exchange goods with them. It also fails to explain the origin of the wanderers other than to attribute it in vague terms to an increase in population. The obvious explanation, in view of the studies of Doehaerd,[204] Ennen,[205] Lestocquoy,[206] Des Marez,[207] and Schneider,[208] is that the new merchant class came from the countryside surrounding the towns in which the merchants came to center their activities.

Regional research, particularly in Germany, is showing increasingly that although long-distance commerce and industry were the major elements in continued urban growth after a town had become established and prosperous, the towns often were agrarian villages in origin which had risen to pre-eminence by their role in local or severely limited regional trade.[209] Recent work also indicates that the role of transactions involving cash payments in the commerce of the *Wike* has been over-estimated. The great economic revival in these places has left little trace in numismatics.[210] It therefore seems apparent that the part played by long-distance commerce in the rise of the *Wike* and hence of the medieval town has been overemphasized. The progression seems regularly to have been from beginnings in local, agrarian trade to the later great prosperity, based in large part upon the wandering merchant whom Pirenne placed at the beginning of the process.[211]

The desire to avoid exaggerating the importance of long-distance commerce in early medieval urban development must not lead to an error of underestimation. A *portus*[212] on the Continent was invariably a center of commercial activity on a waterway; the rise of the *portus* gives further indication that the urban evolution of a given site hinged directly upon its position on commercial arteries. The *portus* was not the equivalent of the Germanic *Wik* in the strictest sense, although both denoted a depot

204. See material cited above, n. 51, n. 150.

205. *Frühgeschichte*, pp. 217–222.

206. See material cited above, n. 192.

207. See material cited above, n. 116.

208. Jean Schneider, *La ville de Metz aux XIIIᵉ et XIVᵉ siècles* (Nancy, 1950), particularly p. 88.

209. Gabriele Schwarz, "Die Entstehung der niedersächsischen Stadt," *Petermanns Geographische Mitteilungen*, XCV (1951), 161–171; *idem, Regionale Stadttypen im niedersächsischen Raum zwischen Weser und Elbe* (Remagen, 1952). See also Hans Van Werveke, "The Rise of the Towns," in *The Cambridge Economic History of Europe*, III (Cambridge, 1965), 5. See also above, p. 97.

210. W. Jesse, "Wik-Orte und Münzprägung," *Hansische Geschichtsblätter*, LXXIII (1955), 106–116.

211. Petri, "Die Anfänge des mittelalterlichen Städtewesens," p. 272 ff.

212. For this and what follows, see Endemann, *Markturkunde und Markt*, p. 105 ff.

for merchants. *Portus* was a place where boats docked, and often by extension a place where goods were unloaded and commercial activity developed. The *Wik* might develop on an overland route. *Portus* assumed a broader connotation in northeastern France and Flanders than elsewhere, indicating both the harbor and the settlement arising with and in dependence upon it. Occasionally it might indicate a commercial settlement not identical with the harbor, particularly in cases of the simultaneous mention of a market and a *portus* in the sources. The very fact that a *portus* existed does not necessarily connote a settlement of an urban character; by the tenth century there were exclusively rural *portus* apart from towns.[213] The *portus* is often absent, however, in western and southern France, areas where few towns of strongly commercial bent appeared during the early middle ages.[214]

The tendency of the *portus* or *Wik* settlement eventually to dominate the entire town[215] only triumphed in cases where the long-distance merchant element controlled urban economic life. Gandersheim, for example, originated around a merchants' church west of the town, near the important Cologne-Höxter road; this settlement was the *Wik*. The *mercatus*, the local market, was located east of the *Wik* around the imperial monastery of Gandersheim. The Liudolfinger often used this foundation as a residence in the tenth century, and the trade of Gandersheim prospered as a result. The abbey was the nucleus of the later town. When the artificial stimulus to the trade of Gandersheim was removed by the extinction of the Liudolfinger line in 1024, the long-distance commerce of the town declined and the *Wik* was abandoned. Local trade dominated, and the *mercatus* became the economic center of Gandersheim.[216] In towns of local trading interests, therefore, including most Roman *civitates* in southern Gaul, the area within the walls. dominated pre-urban life in the early middle ages, while the *Wik* dominated in cases of more widely extended mercantile activity.

Finally, political circumstances often affected the evolution of particular agglomerations into towns. In addition to planned urban foundations, many towns developed through the efforts of local potentates to favor certain regions. The counts of Flanders evidently were attempting in the eleventh century to fill the void between the settlements along the

213. Pirenne, *Les villes et les institutions urbaines*, I, 115 n. 1.

214. Endemann, *Markturkunde und Markt*, pp. 124, 130.

215. See above, 87.

216. Hans Goetting, "Die Anfänge der Stadt Gandersheim," *BDL*, LXXXIX (1952), 39–55.

Roman road running east to west across the southern part of the county and those on the Scheldt. They built or rebuilt castles, founded collegiate churches with the intention of unifying ecclesiastical administration, and built roads connecting the new centers. The axis of this plan, which may simply have been intended as a series of fortified points on comital domains rather than as an impulse to urbanization, ran between Lille and Bruges through Mesen, Aire, Torhout, Ypres, and Cassel. Towns soon developed around the fortifications along this network.[217]

Use of strong points as princely residences might have furthered urban development. The Germanic kings used Roman towns as residences through the Merovingian period,[218] although the Carolingians tended to sojourn on their countryside estates or at abbeys. The use of a *civitas* as a barbarian capital evidently entailed some increase in population, although this is much more apparent in Italy and Spain than in northern Europe.[219] Yet even here we must beware of hasty generalizations. The extension of the walls of Toulouse in the fifth century after it had become the chief town of the Visigoths had a strategic intent: the king needed to be able to garrison troops near the Roman road and to have easy access to the crossing of the Garonne.[220]

When several princes controlled or resided in a town, however, the result could be deleterious for urban development. At Namur the count held the Champeau and a domain corresponding to the future parishes

---

217. Jan Dhondt, "Développement urbain et initiative comtale en Flandre au XI⁰ siècle," *RN*, XXX (1948), 133–156. Although details of Dhondt's exposition have been modified by subsequent research, his thesis as a whole still stands. Dhondt himself has elaborated on his own conclusions for Ypres, but in terms which suggest that the place might have developed with or without comital assistance into a town. In the eleventh century Ypres was at the last navigable point of the Yper River, which joined the sea by the Yser Gulf. Merchandise in transit to and from central Flanders probably would pass through Ypres. At Mesen, eight miles from Ypres, merchants could reach the Scheldt and the Roman road running across the southern part of the county. The *castellum* of Ypres, which antedated the town, was located at the point where the Yser joined the great fair route between Bruges and Mesen by way of Torhout. *Plans en relief des villes Belges par des ingenieurs militaires français, XVII⁰–XIX⁰ siècle* (Brussels, 1965), pp. 210–215. See also Verhulst, "Sint-Maartenskapittel," p. 32.

218. See above, p. 88.

219. Eugen Ewig, "Résidence et capitale pendant le haut moyen âge," *RH*, CCXXX (1963), 25–72, partially translated as "Residence and Capital in the Early Middle Ages (Ostrogoths and Visigoths)," in Thrupp (ed.), *Early Medieval Society*, pp. 163–173. Ewig's attempt to term these centers genuine capital cities is exaggerated, although their role as princely residences unquestionably made them more prosperous than before.

220. Delaruelle, "Toulouse capitale wisigothique," pp. 213–217.

of St. John the Baptist and St. Aubain. He also became advocate of most episcopal land on the left bank of the Meuse and the right bank of the Sambre, including the *castrum* and the *vicus*. The bishop held the right bank of the Meuse under his direct control. The count obviously would favor the development of the area under his immediate sway, the Sambre region. Namur thus became a town essentially of the Sambre rather than of the Meuse, a development which hurt its commerce immensely. The progress of Namur also was disrupted by its position as the capital of an unusually turbulent feudal principality; the variations in fortune of the counts of Namur stunted the growth of the town still further.[221]

Conversely, relations between princes might have been efficacious for the growth of towns. Very little would seem to have favored the site of Oudenaarde as a town. The counts of Flanders built a fortress there to neutralize that of Ename, near Oudenaarde but across the Scheldt in imperial territory. The fortress of Ename had been constructed in 974 at the point where the Roman military road crossed the river, and a thriving town developed around it. By 1056 at the latest, the count of Flanders had captured Ename and extended his frontier to the Dender River. The fortress of Ename would have been difficult to defend from Flanders, however, since it was on the wrong bank of the Scheldt, and it would be extremely dangerous if it fell into the hands of the count's enemies. The count thus destroyed the fortress and founded an abbey at Ename. With no wall for protection, the town around the fortification declined. Ename had been a normal rest stop for merchants, about one day's journey from both Ghent and Tournai, at the junction of an important land route with a major waterway. Such a place was necessary for the sustenance of itinerant merchants, and the town of Oudenaarde, whose history thus begins around 1060, quickly assumed the function of Ename.[222]

In conclusion, therefore, recent research has modified and nuanced

221. Rousseau, *Namur*, pp. 75 ff., 47 ff.

222. Jan Dhondt, "Het Ontstaan van Oudenaarde," *Handelingen van de Geschied- en Oudheidkundige Kring van Oudenaarde*, X (1952), 50–80, a revision of his earlier "Ontstaan en Wording van Oudenaarde," *Handelingen van de Geschied- en Oudheidkundige Kring van Oudenaarde*, III (1944–45), 1–29. Dhondt's views have been criticized on particular points, but chiefly concerning his positioning of the original settlement at Oudenaarde, rather than in his attributing its rise directly to the decline of Ename. See especially A. Leyman, "Proeve tot verklaring van de bewijste Latijnse Teksten van 1110 en 1117," *Handelingen van de Geschied- en Oudheidkundige Kring van Oudenaarde*, X (1952), 81–93, and G. Gevaert, "Nog over het Ontstaan van Oudenaarde," *Handelingen van de Geschied- en Oudheidkundige Kring van Oudenaarde*, X (1952), 94–112.

interpretations of medieval urban origins in northern continental Europe which were generally held before the Second World War while maintaining them in broad outline. We know now that there was greater continuity of settlement between the Roman and medieval town than was realized by earlier scholars, but less continuity of function. We know that an urban renaissance began almost from the moment the invasions ceased and that true pre-urban nuclei had been formed by the seventh century. The early Carolingian period did not see a severe depression of trade and commerce, but it was closed by a disaster only slightly less profound than that of the fifth century.

Recent work has shown the considerable extent to which agrarian settlements and domanial trade were antecedents of the medieval town and its economic function, but it has left unchanged the juridical distinction which must be made between *Stadtgemeinde* and *Landgemeinde*. The *castrum* element of the pre-urban nucleus was not as inactive economically as was once believed. In centers specializing in local trade it often remained the dominating element of the town. For centers specializing in long-distance commerce, however, the theory that the merchants of the *Wik* were to assume leadership of the towns of the eleventh and twelfth centuries still holds considerable validity.

A firm topographic, demographic, and economic foundation had been established for the development of the medieval town in northern continental Europe by the early tenth century. When the juridical transition to genuine urbanism was made in the eleventh and twelfth centuries, it was only the logical conclusion of a development which had begun with the physical separation of town and countryside during the Germanic invasions of the third century and the functional break with Roman urbanism entailed by the disasters of the fourth and fifth. A distinctly medieval institution had been created which in its essential elements still exists today.

HERBERT OF NORWICH, 1091–1119: STUDIES IN THE HISTORY OF NORMAN ENGLAND

James W. Alexander

University of Georgia

ABBREVIATIONS

Aelfric	B. Thorpe (ed.), *Homilies of the Anglo-Saxon Church . . . Homilies of Aelfric*, 2 vols. (London, 1844 and 1846)
Anselm	F. S. Schmitt (ed.), *S. Anselmi Cantuariensis archiepiscopi opera omnia*, 5 vols. (Edinburgh, 1946–51)
Augustine, *Civ. Dei*	*Aurelii Augustini opera*, Pars XIV, 2: *De Civitate Dei*, Books 11–22, ed. Bernard Dombart and Alphonse Kalb (CC, XLVIII [1955])
Augustine, *Tract. in Jn.*	*Aurelii Augustini opera*, Pars VIII: *In Johannis Evangelium tractatus*, ed. D. R. Willems (CC, XLVIII [1954])
Bartholomew Cotton	*Bartholomaei de Cotton, Historia Anglicana*, ed. Henry Richards Luard (RS, 16)
Bede, *Hom.*	*Bedae Venerabilis opera*, Pars III: *Opera homiletica*, ed. D. Hurst (CC, CXXII [1955])
Bede, *In Luc.*	*Bedae Venerabilis opera*, Pars II: *Opera exegetica. In Lucae evangelium expositio*, ed. D. Hurst (CC, CXX [1960])
Bede, *In. Marc.*	As above, but *In Marci evangelium expositio*
CC	Corpus christianorum, Series latina (Turnhout, Belgium)
CSEL	Corpus scriptorum ecclesiasticorum latinorum (Vienna)
EETS	Publications of the Early English Text Society
Flor. Wig.	"Florence of Worcester," *Chronicon ex chronicis*, ed. Benjamin Thorpe, Vol. II (London, 1849)
GC	Congregation of St. Maur (eds.), *Gallia christiana* (Paris, 1856–99)

Goulburn and Symonds, *Life*	Edward Goulburn and Henry Symonds, *The Life, Letters and Sermons of Bishop Herbert de Losinga*, Vol. I (Oxford and London, 1878)
Gregory, *Hom. in Ev.*	Gregory the Great, *Homiliae xl in evangelia*, in *PL*, LXXVI, cols. 1075–1312
Gregory, *Hom. in Ez.*	Gregory the Great, *Homiliae in Ezechielem*, in *PL*, LXXVI, cols. 758–1072
HE	*Herberti de Losinga primi episcopi Norwicensis epistolae*, ed. R. Anstruther (Brussels and London, 1846)
HF	Martin Bouquet, *et al.* (eds.), *Receuil des historiens des Gaules et de la France*
HS	The sermons of Herbert Losinga, which are edited in Volume II of Goulburn and Symonds, *Life* (cited above)
Hugh the Chantor	Hugh the Chantor, *History of the Church of York, 1066–1127*, ed. Charles Johnson (London, 1961)
Itin. H. I	William Farrer, *An Outline Itinerary of King Henry the First* (Oxford, 1919)
Malmesbury, *GP*	William of Malmesbury, *De gestis pontificum Anglorum*, ed. N. E. S. A. Hamilton (RS, 52)
Malmesbury, *GR*	William of Malmesbury, *De gestis regum Anglorum*, ed. William Stubbs (RS, 90), Vol. II
MGH	*Monumenta Germaniae Historica*
Monasticon	Sir William Dugdale (ed.), *Monasticon Anglicanum*, New ed. by John Caley, *et al.*, 6 vols. in 8 (London, 1817–30)
NR	H. W. Saunders (ed.), *The First Register of Norwich Cathedral Priory*, Norfolk Record Society, XI (Norfolk, 1939)
Old Eng. Homilies	Richard Morris (ed.), *Old English Homilies of the Twelfth and Thirteenth Centuries* (EETS, XXIX, XXXIV, LIII)
PG	J. P. Migne (ed.), *Patrologiae cursus completus. Series graeca*
PL	As above, but *series latina*
PRO	Great Britain, Public Record Office
Regesta I	*Regesta regum anglo-normannorum*, I: *1066–1100*, ed. H. W. C. Davis (Oxford, 1913)

Regesta II	*Regesta regum anglo-normannorum*, II: *1100–1135*, ed. H. A. Cronne and Charles Johnson (Oxford, 1956)
RS	Rolls Series: Chronicles and Memorials of Great Britain and Ireland during the Middle Ages [Published under the Direction of the Master of the Rolls]
VCH	Victoria County History

HERBERT OF NORWICH, 1091–1119:
STUDIES IN THE HISTORY OF
NORMAN ENGLAND

I. THE BISHOP IN HIS DIOCESE

R. W. Southern has written that

> It is quite unlikely that we shall find men of the first rank as original
> thinkers in the shade of St. Bernard, St. Anselm or any other great men
> [of the twelfth century]. But we may find men who are surprisingly
> interesting and sensitive to what is going on in the wider world, yet
> with a strong sense of their own differences. It is only when we know
> more about such men that we shall understand at all fully the dis-
> tinctive place of England in the twelfth-century Renaissance.[1]

Herbert Losinga, bishop of Thetford/Norwich from 1091 to 1119, was one
of these "surprisingly interesting" men. His sermons[2] are the only extant
homilies of his period in England other than one of Archbishop Ranulf
d'Escures and the reports of those of Anselm, and their rarity as well as
their content give them historical value. Herbert's letters, fifty-nine in all,
reveal something about their author and much of his milieu;[3] the bishop's

1. R. W. Southern, "The Place of England in the Twelfth-Century Renaissance,"
History, XLV (October, 1960), 215.
2. *HS*. These are bound with other homilies in a mid-twelfth-century volume in the
Cambridge University Library (Ii.2.19 [s. xii]) and had previously been the property
either of Norwich cathedral or of the priory. Their attribution is clear: "In fine hujus
voluminis est sermo [*sic*] Herberti episcopi fundatoris hujus ecclesiae." See further
M. R. James' appendix of manuscripts to H. C. Beeching, "The Library of the Cathedral
Church of Norwich," *Norfolk Archaeology*, XIX (1917), 95; N. R. Ker, *Medieval Libraries
of Great Britain* (London, 1941), pp. 76–77, and his "Medieval Manuscripts from Norwich
Cathedral Priory," *Transactions of the Cambridge Bibliographical Society*, I, Part 1 (1949), 12.
3. *HE*. The text, badly edited and lacking critical apparatus, is frequently so inaccurate in Latin transcription that a correct reading is impossible without the aid of the
collations printed in Goulburn and Symonds, *Life*, pp. 418–423. The manuscript is a late
seventeenth-century transcript, bound with other English monastic materials relating to
Croyland, Ramsey, Peterborough, Evesham, St. Alban's, Glastonbury, and Durham:
Brussels Royal Library 3723 (7965–73), *Monasteria ordinis S. Benedicti in Anglia*, of which

other writings may include a pontifical[4] and monastic constitutions, but additional works attributed to him either no longer exist or were incorrectly attributed.[5]

Herbert was born around the middle of the eleventh century in Normandy. There seems no reason for the frequent allegation that he was of English birth,[6] for both the Norwich priory register and the house chronicler Bartholomew Cotton are clear on the point: *"qui Normannie in pago Oximensi natus est."*[7] As the canonical minimum age for consecration as a bishop was thirty, he must have been born before 1061.

Herbert's letters are fols. 243–278^v (J. van den Gheyn, *Catalogue des manuscrits de la Bibliothèque Royale de Belgique*, VI [Brussels, 1906], 89–90). The title page, reproduced in Goulburn and Symonds, *Life*, p. 417, shows English provenance (Ex MS. S. Albani) and the legend *Epistolae Herberti Losingae prioris Fiscannensis in Normannia, Abbatis Ramesiensis in Anglia, primi Nortwicensis Episcopi qui floruit circa . . . 1100*. Internal evidence leaves no doubt that the letters are Herbert's.

4. MS. B. M. Add. 28.188 (late eleventh century); Walter Howard Frere, *Pontifical Services Illustrated from Miniatures of the XVth and XVIth Centuries*, Alcuin Club Collections, III (London, 1901), 96–97: "It seems reasonable to conclude that the [Ramsey] Pontifical is that of Herbert de Losinga."

5. John Bale, *Scriptorum illustrium Maioris Brytannie* (Basle, 1557–59), p. 171, gives the following list of works, in addition to the letters and sermons: *De prolixitate temporum; Constitutiones monachorum; Ad Anselmum contra sacerdotes; De fine mundi*. The identical list appears as well in Bale's *Index Brittaniae scriptorum*, ed. R. L. Poole, Anecdota Oxoniensa, Mediaeval and Modern Series, IX (Oxford, 1902), 169, and in Paulin Paris, *Histoire littéraire de la France*, X (Paris, 1868), 267, and in many other secondary works. Herbert may well have written monastic constitutions, but the *De fine mundi* is probably a misreading of Henry of Huntingdon's statement that he heard the bishop preach on the topic (*Historia anglorum*, ed. Thomas Arnold [RS 74], p. xix, and in *HF*, XIV, 265–268; see also John Capgrave, *Liber de illustribus Henricis* [RS 7], pp. 176 and 205. Another sermon of which we have report but whose text has not survived was preached at Ely in 1106 (see below, 142).

6. Ioannes Pitsei, *Relationum historicarum de rebus Angliae* (Paris, 1619), p. 197, was the first to allege English origin for the prelate. See also Thomas Fuller, *History of the Worthies of England*, III (London, 1840), 13 and 166 (which disagree with one another); Goulburn and Symonds, *Life*, pp. 4 and 388 ff.; W. T. Spurdens, "A Memoir of William [*sic*] Herbert de Losinga, First Bishop of Norwich," *Norfolk Archaeology*, III (1852), 142 ff. Among those misled by Goulburn and Symonds was A. J. MacDonald, *Berengar and the Reform of Sacramental Doctrine* (London, 1930), p. 372 n. 6.

7. *NR*, p. 22; Bartholomew Cotton, p. 389. The district is shown in maps at the endpaper in F. M. Powicke, *The Loss of Normandy*, 2nd ed. (Manchester, 1961), and in Edward M. Beloe, "Herbert de Losinga, An Inquiry as to His Cognomen and Birthplace," *Norfolk Archaeology*, VIII (1897), 302. See also Célestin Hippeau, *Dictionnaire topographique de Calvados*, Coll. des docs, inéd. sur l'hist. de France, CVIII: 4 (Paris, 1883), 146, and Paul Joanne, *Dictionnaire géographique et administratif de la France*, Vol. III: *Calvados* (Paris, 1894), *s. v.*

Little is known of Herbert's family. His mother's name is unrecorded, and his father does not appear in the sources until his preferment to the abbacy of Hyde in 1090.[8] Despite the statement of the vitriolic bishop of Ossory that Herbert was *ex monacho monachus*,[9] there is no reliable medieval evidence for the allegation. Herbert had a brother "G."[10] and a cousin named Jordan who was mentioned in a charter of Everard, Herbert's successor in the East Anglian see.[11] Not surprisingly, the family was noble; Herbert mentioned *generis claritatem* as one of the things in life for which he was most grateful.[12]

The surname "Losinga" has occasioned some scholarly debate, since some chroniclers alluded to it as a cognomen labeling the bishop a flatterer.[13] While this attribute would not be rare in a curialist bishop, the interpretation seems specious as both his father (Robert) and Bishop Robert Losinga of Hereford bore the same surname. The attempt to prove English birth, contrary to twelfth-century evidence, by deriving "Losinga" philologically from the Domesday hundred of Lothinga (mod.: "Lodden") has been even less convincing.[14] There seems no surviving evidence for an eleventh-century place name in the Norman Hièmois cognate to "Losinga."

8. Malmesbury, *GR*, p. 385; Bartholomew Cotton, p. 53; H. R. Luard (ed.), *Flores historiarum* (RS 95), II, 24; H. R. Luard (ed.), *Annales monastici* (RS 36), II, 36. The *Flores* is cited hereafter as "Matthew of Westminster."

9. Bale, *Scriptorum*, p. 171. Bale may have based the judgment on knowledge that Herbert's father was abbot of Hyde, although late in life, or perhaps on the chronicle of Robert of Torigni (R. Howlett [ed.], *Chronicles of the Reigns of Stephen, Henry II, and Richard I* [RS 82], IV, 122). While one error does not presuppose another, the good abbot of Mont-St.-Michel also stated that Herbert's father was his predecessor as abbot of Ramsey, and we know this statement to be false on the basis of Ramsey sources.

10. *HE*, ep. 54.

11. Great Britain, Historical Manuscripts Commission, *Report on the Manuscripts of the Marquess of Lothian Preserved at Blickling Hall, Norfolk* (London, 1905), pp. 39–40. Barbara Dodwell of Reading University kindly called my attention to this charter.

12. *HE*, ep. 54.

13. *Flor. Wig.*, p. 33; Malmesbury, *GR*, p. 385 and *GP*, p. 151; Matthew Paris, Ralph of Diceto, John Bromton, and other chroniclers derived their information from "Florence" and William of Malmesbury. C. D. DuCange, *Glossarium ad scriptores mediae et infimae latinitatis*, IV (Paris, 1733), 273, defined the surname as *falsa laus*, with Herbert as his exemplar. Charles de Rémusat, *Sainte Anselme de Cantorbéry* (Paris, 1853), p. 199, and Paris, *Hist. litt. de la France*, X, 267, agree that "Losinga" is a cognomen but do not explain the meaning. It may be significant that Orderic Vitalis (*Historiae ecclesiasticae*, ed. A. le Prévost, Société de l'histoire de France, LXIX [Paris, 1852], 12–13) referred to the new bishop of Chichester, Ralph, as *cognomento Luffa*, but did not in the same sentence describe "Losinga" as a cognomen.

14. Goulburn and Symonds, *Life*, p. 2, and Appendix A.

Details of Herbert's early life are as fleeting and obscure as are those of his family. The future bishop's first recorded ecclesiastical responsibility was as prior of the famous Benedictine house at Fécamp, where he presumably made his monastic profession. His administrative ability in that office contributed to his reputation in mature years,[15] and throughout his life Herbert continued to hold his old religious home in warm affection and as a model of the monastic life.[16]

No evidence survives to explain why William Rufus selected Herbert for the abbacy of Ramsey, a preferment which brought the new abbot to England where his ecclesiastical future lay. Orderic Vitalis, the English-born St. Évroul chronicler, described him as one of the king's chaplains and favorites, promoted for secular rather than for ecclesiastical talents, but supporting evidence for this very possible judgment is lacking.[17] Nor can one accept the uncorroborated allegation of William of Malmesbury that Herbert bought preferment to this mitred abbey.[18] Modern conjecture on Rufus' motives in the appointment also stands in antiseptic isolation from documentary evidence.[19]

Sources disagree on the duration of the Ramsey abbacy, but this

15. *NR*, p. 22; Bartholomew Cotton, p. 389; *Monasticon*, IV, 15; *Flor. Wig.*, p. 33; Robert of Torigni, *Chronicles*, IV, 122.

16. *HE*, epp. 5, 34. The only mention of Herbert in surviving Fécamp documents is a brief and unimportant notice of him acting as prior sometime between 1087 and 1091 [*sic*; this must have been early in 1087] during a pirate attack on the abbey: Arthur Longfors (ed.), *Histoire de l'abbaye de Fécamp en vers francais du XIII* siècle, Annales Academiae Scientiarum Fennicae, B, XXII¹ (Helsinki, 1928), 200–209. There is a spurious document allegedly attested by Herbert as bishop of Norwich in 1084, but he was not consecrated until 1091 nor did he move the diocesan seat to Norwich until 1094; the instrument may be found in Lionel Landon (ed.), *Cartae antiquae, Rolls 1–10*, Pipe Roll Society, N.S., XVII (London, 1939), No. 40 (calendared *Regesta* I, No. 195, where it is noticed as a forgery). For Fécamp, see L. H. Cottineau, *Répertoire topo-bibliographique des abbayes et prieurés*, I (Mâcon, 1939) and Jehan de Povremogne (ed.), *L'Abbaye Bénédictine de Fécamp*, 4 vols. (Fécamp, 1959–63).

17. Orderic, *Hist. eccles.*, pp. 12–15. Orderic also included Herbert in the group of royal favorites who amended their lives after preferment and discharged their responsibilities faithfully.

18. Malmesbury, *GP*, p. 151, implies the charge.

19. Francis Godwin, *Catalogue of the Bishops of England*, appendix in Goulburn and Symonds, *Life*, p. 403, had Herbert obtaining "diverse great preferments" from William Rufus. Fr. Spurdens ("Herbert," p. 149) said he "seems to have held office under Duke Robert [Curthose] as he certainly did under Rufus, who was so pleased with his services that he brought him over to England. . . ." The antiquarian Francis Blomefield, *An Essay Towards a Topographical History of Norfolk*, III (London, 1808), 465, stated that he was chamberlain under William I. While all these ascriptions are possible, they are unsupported by documentary evidence.

problem appears capable of resolution. Some chronicles and annals, including Ramsey's, favor a four-year tenure,[20] others one of three years.[21] The confusion probably arises from the date of Herbert's elevation to the episcopate, since all sources agree that he became abbot in 1087: some chroniclers apparently dated the end of his abbacy from his consecration in 1091, others from his nomination in 1090. Few documents have survived attesting Herbert's activities as abbot: he received a royal charter in 1087 confirming him in "all the customs" of the abbey as his predecessors had held them in the time of Edward the Confessor,[22] and sometime during his incumbency he granted a charter to William Pecche bestowing custody with usufruct over the abbey's lands at Offra (Hunts.).[23] Early in the abbacy William Rufus restored some property in Sawtry (Hunts.) to his jurisdiction.[24] Obviously such surviving instruments as these give us no basis of judgment for comment on Herbert's activities and merits as an abbot.

From Ramsey, Herbert Losinga was raised to the episcopate of the East Anglian diocese, Thetford being its see city at that time. We do not know whether his elevation was accomplished by canonical means, but it is all too clear that a substantial sum of money changed hands. Probably the appointment was solely by royal nomination,[25] and this in itself would have caused no shock in late eleventh-century England. But the fact that the appointment was simoniacal caused not only shock, but outrage, scurrilous lampoons, and his penitential pilgrimage to the pope as well.

The Gregorian reformers had bitterly attacked simony,[26] a particular

20. *Cartularium monasterii de Rameseia*, ed. William H. Hart and Ponsonby A. Lyons (RS 79), III, 174; *Chronicon abbatiae Rameseiensis*, ed. W. Dunn Macray (RS 83), p. 340; *Monasticon*, II, 580.

21. *Monasticon*, IV, 13 and 15; Bartholomew Cotton, p. 389.

22. *Cart. Rameseia*, I, No. 148; *Chron. Rameseiensis*, 208 (No. 181); calendared *Regesta* I, No. 296.

23. *Cart. Rameseia*, I, No. 30 and II, No. 368; *Chron. Rameseiensis*, 233 (No. 239).

24. *Cart. Rameseia*, I, No. 149 and II, 290–291; *Chron. Rameseiensis*, 208 (No. 183); calendared *Regesta* I, Nos. 321 and 322.

25. On royal nomination of ecclesiastics, see Frank Barlow, *The English Church, 1000–1066* (London, 1963), Chaps. I and II; R. W. and A. J. Carlyle, *A History of Medieval Political Theory in the West*, IV (Edinburgh and London, 1950), 25 ff.; Emile Amann and Auguste Dumas, *L'Église au pouvoir des laïques (888–1057)* (Paris, 1948), pp. 190 ff.; Walter Ullmann, *Principles of Government and Politics in the Middle Ages* (New York, 1961), pp. 123 ff. and 135 ff.; and Augustin Fliche, *La réforme grégorienne*, I (Louvain and Paris, 1924), 1–38.

26. There is an excellent survey of contemporary literature on simony in D. Carl Mirbt, *Die Publizistik im Zeitalter Gregors VII* (Leipzig, 1894), pp. 239–371; also valuable

target because it circumvented the free operation of the Holy Spirit in indicating His choice of an elect, and indeed this malpractice was a very effective way to hinder free episcopal and abbatial election. Rome had spoken out repeatedly against the practice, and numerous councils condemning this "heresy" had been held from the mid-eleventh century onward. Herbert was unquestionably aware of the grave nature of his act. He presented the king's greedy agent Ranulf Flambard with one thousand pounds, purchasing the bishopric for himself, and compounded the uniqueness of the transaction—his was the only provable simony among English bishops of his time—by obtaining in the same bargain the abbacy of the New Minster (Hyde) at Winchester for his father, an act of filial devotion startling even under the Red King.[27] The purchase provoked a bitterly satirical poetic attack on the new bishop—"*Crevit in aecclesia monstrum, genitore Losinga*," the doggerel begins[28]—and is one of the few incidents from his life to receive attention from virtually all chroniclers and annalists who noticed the man at all. In a way this is unfortunate, for Malmesbury appears to have been largely correct in judging that Herbert atoned for the errors of his youth by repentance and an exemplary mature life.[29]

It is futile to excuse Herbert's simony by explaining it as a relief

---

is P. Imbart de la Tour, *Les élections épiscopales dans l'église de France du IXe au XIIe siècles* (Paris, 1890), pp. 378 ff. Most of the fundamental tracts and controversial literature are in the *MGH, Libelli de lite*, I–III (Hanover, 1890–97). The relevant conciliar decisions are in [J.] D. Mansi (ed.), *Sacrorum conciliorum nova et amplissima collectio*, XIX and XX, New ed. (Paris and Leipzig, 1902), *passim*.

27. *Flor. Wig.*, p. 33; Malmesbury, *GR*, p. 385 and *GP*, p. 152; Symeon of Durham, *Opera omnia*, Vol. II: *Historia regum*, ed. Thomas Arnold (RS 75), 293. Other medieval chroniclers—Bartholomew Cotton, "Matthew of Westminster," Henry Knighton, etc.— followed these contemporaries of Herbert. John of Oxnede, *Chronica*, ed. Henry Ellis (RS 13), p. 35, noticed the simony but omitted the amount. As the middle ages drew to a close, the amount involved became more inexact in the commentators' reports: John Capgrave (like John of Oxnede, a Norfolk man) simply noted that Herbert bought his see "for a grete summe" in his *Chronicle of England*, ed. F. C. Hingston (RS 1), p. 131. By the seventeenth century the sum had been inflated to 1900 pounds, for which see Goulburn and Symonds, *Life*, pp. 393 and 401 (reproducing Godwin, *Catalogue*, and Neville). On Ranulf Flambard, see R. W. Southern, "Ranulf Flambard and Early Anglo-Norman Administration," *Transactions of the Royal Historical Society*, Ser. 4, XVI (1933), 95–128.

28. The fullest version of the poem was edited by Heinrich Böhmer, "De simoniaca haeresi carmen," in *MGH, Libelli de lite*, III, 615–617. Less full versions are in Malmesbury, *GR*, pp. 385–386; "Matthew of Westminster," II, 26; Bartholomew Cotton, p. 54; Bale, *Scriptorum*, p. 172.

29. Quoting Jerome's pithy statement: Malmesbury, *GR*, p. 386.

payment,[30] as relief was not taken from ecclesiastical fees; it is true that churches were sometimes plundered by royal farmers and other agents during vacancies, but no one claimed this was relief—it was an abuse of regalian right. Equally unconvincing is the attempt to explain the act away by alleging it to have been an invention of monastic chroniclers resentful of the bishop's refusal to champion regular as against secular clergy in their wearisome conflicts.[31] Even the Norwich chronicler Bartholomew Cotton, full of praise and admiration for the bishop, did not deny the simony; he merely passed it off with the incorrect explanation that it was canonically proper to purchase preferment from laymen if there were no other way to obtain the desired position.[32] The new bishop knew better: that he sought absolution of the pope in 1093 indicated quite clearly that he was aware of having committed a gross sin.

Perhaps Herbert's troubled conscience was soothed by the knowledge that he had made a superb investment, for in 1087 the see had been worth at least £403 18s. 6d. annually,[33] and doubtless by the time of the bishop's death in 1119 the value of his holdings was considerably augmented not only by acquisitions during his tenure but also by rising price levels in the early twelfth century. There were, as will appear below, some alienations from episcopal holdings while Herbert held the see, but these were principally to the priory of the cathedral. Furthermore, the Domesday data omit many sources of feudal and of episcopal income; hence the figure I have computed is a minimum estimate, but even if it were representative of all sources of pecuniary wealth it is apparent that the payment to the crown amounted only to somewhat more than two years' income from this see enjoyed by Herbert for twenty-eight years. The speculation is particularly noteworthy when the value of his father's new abbacy at Hyde is included, for the annual income of that holding was £390 4s.[34]

30. Letter from the Rev. J. Gunn, Appendix F in Goulburn and Symonds, *Life*, pp. 412 ff.

31. *Ibid.*

32. Bartholomew Cotton, p. 391.

33. See Appendix I, pp. 228–230.

34. David Knowles, *The Monastic Order in England, 943–1216* (Cambridge, 1950), p. 702. Little is known of Robert Losinga. He is unmentioned in the Hyde chronicle, and Dugdale said of him only that "the oppressed monks were forced to yield obedience to the unworthy Robert, ... his son ... having purchased this dignity ... by way of a provision for his father" (*Monasticon*, II, 249). Even the tenure of the abbot is uncertain; Dugdale had him abbot for two years (*ibid.*) and two pages later for seven years. He apparently died on June 25 (of whatever year) and before the foundation of the priory

Since the metropolitan throne of Canterbury was still vacant following the death of Archbishop Lanfranc (1089), Herbert was consecrated bishop of Thetford by Thomas I of York, probably at the ceremony which also included the elevation of Ralph Luffa to the see of Chichester.[35] As the new bishop of the East Anglians attested a royal charter dated January 27, 1091, as ordinary of Thetford, he was consecrated earlier in the month, in all likelihood on Epiphany.[36]

William of Malmesbury and his fourteenth-century continuator Henry Knighton represented Herbert's consecration as accompanied by highly ominous portents. Part of the episcopal consecration ceremony of the period was the prognostic, an unauthorized custom which had been intruded into the liturgy. The Gospel was opened at random above the head of the elect, and the verse from the top of the facing left page read. Presumably this would indicate the character and career of the episcopal candidate. Herbert's predecessor-but-one, Herfast, had the prognostic *Non hunc sed Barabbam.* The intervening episcopate was brief (1085–1090), so perhaps then William Beaufeu was not the anticipated Barabbas. This set the context for Herbert's prognostic: *Amice, ad quid veniste?*[37] The setting of this passage was Judas' betrayal of Jesus in the garden. The unhappy augury occurs in no other source; perhaps it is simply an imaginative embellishment of William.

---

at Norwich. Herbert enjoined the monks to keep that day as the commemoration of the obits of his mother and father (*NR*, pp. 48–50; see also J. B. L. Tolhurst [ed.], *The Customary of the Cathedral Church of Norwich*, Henry Bradshaw Society, LXXXII [London, 1948], 138: June 25, Anniversarium Patris et Matris Herberti Epyschopi).

35. Hugh the Chantor, p. 7; C. W. Foster (ed.), *The Registrum antiquissimum of the Cathedral Church of Lincoln*, Lincoln Record Society, XXVII (Lincoln, 1931), I, 10. Sir Maurice Powicke (ed.), *Handbook of British Chronology*, 2nd ed. (London, 1961), p. 242, leaves a choice of 1090 or 1091, but since Hugh wrote as though Herbert and Ralph were elevated together (although he errs in likewise including in the ceremony Hervey of Bangor, consecrated in 1092), and since we know Ralph to have been consecrated on Epiphany, 1091, and further as Herbert was in possession of his see by January 27 of that year (see below n. 36), the argument for 1091 is probably correct. The *Handbook's* alternative dates are presumably based on the confused question of Herbert's tenure at Ramsey. Clearly wrong is 1094, as in Henry Harrod's *Gleanings Amongst the Castles and Convents of Norfolk* (Norwich, 1857), pp. 234–235, and in John Britton, *The History and Antiquities of the See and Cathedral Church of Norwich* (London, 1816), p. 16, which as well is mistaken in having the consecration of Herbert take place in Norwich.

36. *Regesta* I, No. 315.

37. Malmesbury, *GP*, pp. 151–152; Henry Knighton, *Chronicon*, ed. Joseph Lumby (RS 92), I, 106. The Scriptures: John 18:40 for Herfast; Herbert's prognostic is Matt. 26:50.

Few documents bear witness to Herbert's activities in the years 1091–1092, for the routine sacramental and administrative ministrations of an eleventh-century bishop seldom found their way into the records. His first attestation as bishop was a royal charter in favor of Bishop John of Bath, dated January 27, 1091,[38] and later in the same year he witnessed another charter by which Bishop Osmund of Salisbury endowed canons in his see city.[39] Again in May, 1092, Herbert of Thetford attested a confirmation of previous grants to the cathedral in Lincoln.[40] At some date between 1091 and 1096 he was among several receiving notification of a royal grant of certain rights to Abbot Aldwin, his successor at Ramsey.[41] As is commonplace in earlier medieval biographical research, these scraps do not permit generalization and judgment on the initial years of Herbert's episcopate. It was in the year 1093 that the bishop's career began to make an impact on the kingdom and on the church at large, and from that time on he has been better served by surviving records and chronicles.

Herbert Losinga sought out the pope in 1093 with the intention of receiving papal absolution from his simony. Some doubt attaches to the precise year of the journey, some sources preferring 1093,[42] others 1094.[43] The chronological problem is a complicated one. Did Herbert actually go to Rome or did the chroniclers use the expression "to Rome" figuratively?[44] If the bishop actually went to the Eternal City, it could have been neither in the last months of 1093 nor early in 1094, for in 1093 Urban II was not in Rome until November 20[45] and Herbert was demonstrably in England both on December 4 and on Christmas Day of

38. *Regesta* I, No. 315.

39. *Ibid.*, No. 319; E. A. Freeman, *The Reign of William Rufus and the Accession of Henry the First*, II (Oxford, 1882), 568.

40. *Regesta* I, No. 328.

41. *Monasticon,* II, 548, for the list of abbots. *Chron. Rameseiensis*, p. 209; *Regesta* I, No. 373.

42. *Monasticon*, IV, 2; "Annales S. Edmundi," in Felix Liebermann (ed.), *Ungedruckte anglo-normannische Geschichtsquellen* (Strassburg, 1879), p. 130.

43. Charles Plummer and J. Earle, *Two of the Saxon Chronicles Parallel* (Oxford, 1892), *s.a.* 1094; Symeon of Durham, *Historia regum*, p. 223; *Annales monastici*, II (Waverley), 203.

44. Malmesbury, *GR*, p. 386 and *GP*, p. 151, used the expression "to Rome," not figuratively *(ubi loci)*; "Annales S. Edmundi," p. 130, says simply, "suscepit Herbertus episcopus pontificium," as does John Bromton, *Chronicon*, in Roger Twysden (ed.), *Historiae Anglicanae scriptores X* (London, 1652), col. 999.

45. See Philip Jaffé, *et al.*, *Regesta pontificum romanorum*, I (Leipzig, 1885), 671–673; before then in 1093 Urban was in Sicily and southern Italy. Perhaps William of Malmesbury assumed that, as Herbert went to see the pope, he must have gone to Rome.

1093, on February 2 and in April of 1094.[46] Therefore, there was not time for the bishop to have made the journey to Rome and return trip to England in the intervals between any of the above dates: the one-way passage from England to Rome took six to seven weeks in the mid-twelfth century.[47] It is possible, of course, that Herbert went to Rome after April of 1094, for the sources which can be precisely dated for the middle· months of that year make no mention of him. Were the expression "to Rome" figurative, however, then these problems of papal and of episcopal itinerary become irrelevant; such a use does occur in the contemporary history of Hugh the Chantor—writing of Thurstan of York's attempt to consult the pope, the York canon stated that he found Rome at Tours ("*Inde profectus . . . Turonis Romam*").[48] As will be shown below,[49] continental evidence makes a date of mid-1093 virtually certain. Regardless of when Herbert saw Urban in that year, he was back in England by December.

The facts of the bishop's meeting with the pope are, as we receive them, simple enough and must omit much soul-searching and weighing of interests by Herbert. We know only that he resigned his ring and staff to Urban II, who absolved the prelate and restored him to office.[50]

One personal problem was solved for the Thetford diocesan, but another emerged which was to plunge him into grave difficulties with his strong-willed and impious king. Herbert had violated the traditional exequatur on three important counts: he had left the kingdom without royal permission (and, if my chronological judgment is correct, even without royal knowledge); he had made his confession to and received reinstatement from a pope as yet unrecognized in England; and the sin for which he sought Urban's absolution involved the king's guilt as surely as it involved his own.[51] England's traditional condition for episcopal

46. In chronological sequence: Eadmer, *Historia novorum in Anglia*, ed. Martin Rule (RS 81), pp. 41–42; *Regesta* I, No. 338; see below p. 129 n. 54; *Memorials of St. Edmund's Abbey*, ed. Thomas Arnold (RS 96), I, 87.

47. Reginald Lane Poole, *Studies in Chronology and History*, ed. Austin Lane Poole (Oxford, 1932), pp. 254 and 264; Charles Homer Haskins, *Studies in Medieval Culture* (New York, 1958), p. 101, where it is noted that "urgent news" could make the journey in four weeks; Lionel Landon, *The Itinerary of Richard I*, Pipe Roll Society, N.S., XIII (London, 1935), 184–191.

48. Hugh the Chantor, p. 69.   49. Pp. 150–152.

50. Bartholomew Cotton, p. 591; Malmesbury, *GP*, p. 151 and *GR*, p. 386; Symeon of Durham, *Historia regum*, p. 223; Roger of Hoveden, *Chronica*, ed. William Stubbs (RS 51), I, 148.

51. Z. N. Brooke, *The English Church and the Papacy* (Cambridge, 1952), p. 162; Barbara Dodwell, "The Foundation of Norwich Cathedral," *Transactions of the Royal Historical Society*, ser. 5, VII (1957), 5–6.

journeys to the pope was royal permission obtained prior to leaving the island,[52] and Rufus was probably inclining at the time toward recognizing the antipope Wibert (Clement III).[53] Both factors involved matters of high policy, but on a more personal level, the bad-tempered king would clearly be annoyed at Herbert's repentance for the deed in which his own culpability was clear. Although not demonstrable, it is at least possible that Herbert's actions in this matter are an important factor in his standing alone among his episcopal colleagues as a proven simoniac, for a potential Pandora's box of appeals to the papacy and of personal embarrassment for the monarch was implicit in the bishop's action.

When the king was present at the dedication of Battle Abbey on Candlemas of 1094, he deprived the bishop of Thetford of his crozier, thus symbolically depriving him of episcopal authority in the realm.[54] There is some confusion regarding the chronology of the act—whereas both medieval and present authority exist[55] for having the deprivation occur because Herbert *intended to* seek absolution of the pope, modern authority (presented, unfortunately, without documentation) also exists for the papal interview taking place *before* the deprivation.[56] Not only does 1093 appear to be the correct date for Herbert's absolution, but it is difficult to

---

52. On the exequatur, see Brooke, *English Church*, pp. 117–146, and Norman F. Cantor, *Church, Kingship and Lay Investiture in England, 1089–1135* (Princeton, 1958), 12–34.

53. Malmesbury, *GP*, pp. 86–87.

54. Symeon of Durham, *Historia regum*, p. 223; *Anglo-Saxon Chronicle, s.a.* 1094; *Annales monastici*, II, 203; *Monasticon*, III, 234. Oddly, the house chronicle (*Chronicon monasterii de Bello*, ed. J. S. Brewer [London, 1846], p. 41) places the year of the dedication as 1095; for this chronicle and its historical value, see H. W. C. Davis, "The Chronicle of Battle Abbey," *English Historical Review*, XXXIX (1914), 426–434 (page 430 notes the inaccurate foundation date). Rose Graham, *English Ecclesiastical Studies* (London, 1929), shows that the early part of the Battle chronicle was written after 1179 and therefore is not contemporaneous with the events described; she further states that the chronicler had "no critical faculty (188)." On the royal power to deprive bishops, see Ullmann, *Principles*, pp. 123 ff.: "As far as principles go, it would be true to say that every office within the kingdom was eventually conferred by the grace of the king. Hence, the withdrawal of grace, resulting in the royal *indignatio*, amounted in law to a deprivation of office." Blomefield, *Norfolk*, III, 466, errs in stating that Herbert had the king's permission to visit the pope. Spurdens, "Herbert," p. 150, thought that Herbert went to Rome for his spiritualities, since Anselm was in exile, but Herbert was consecrated in 1091 and Anselm's first exile began in 1097.

55. Symeon of Durham, *Historia regum*, p. 223; Dodwell, "Foundation," pp. 5–6.

56. Cantor, *Church in England*, pp. 51–52; Heinrich Böhmer, *Kirche und Staat in England und in der Normandie im XI. und XII. Jahrhundert* (Leipzig, 1899), p. 144 n. 6; Charles Duggan, "From the Conquest to the Death of John," in C. H. Lawrence (ed.), *The English Church and the Papacy in the Middle Ages* (London, 1965), p. 82.

believe that Rufus apprehended the bishop in the process of sneaking off to Rome, deprived him, and then permitted him to continue on his way. It is possible, certainly, that Herbert escaped after William II went to Normandy on March 19, 1094, but the weight both of the continental sources and of chronological logic argues against this possibility. The bishop appears, therefore, to have been deprived for the deed rather than for his intention to commit it. While no record survives to inform us either of the date or of the terms of the reconciliation of the bishop with his monarch, it was probably quickly accomplished, for Herbert attested a royal charter in favor of Battle nine days after his disgrace,[57] and his demand on April 29 that he be permitted to assist at Bury St. Edmunds' translation of her patron's relics certainly indicated that he was acting as diocesan ordinary before that time.[58]

A series of documents dated by the editors of the *Regesta* to 1087–1096 in all likelihood relate to Herbert's fall from royal grace. The first precept does not name the bishop of Thetford referred to, but it is directed to the chamberlain and "all reeves of Norfolk and Suffolk" ordering that six warrens be "held in peace" by the bishop.[59] Another directs Ranulf Flambard to permit Herbert "sac and soc and all customs which his predecessors had, and [to] do him justice for the encroachments and wrongs done to him and his men."[60] More clearly linked with Herbert's indiscretion was a royal notification that certain lands have been restored to Herbert, ordering as well that all proceedings brought against the bishop and his men by Ranulf be halted.[61] Barbara Dodwell suggests this last writ may indicate Herbert's return to royal favor, and her judgment is doubtless correct on the matter.[62] It is impossible to date these instruments any more precisely than has been done in the *Regesta*, but if the supposition that they are related to his deposition are correct, a date of 1094 to 1096 would seem reasonable.

Perhaps the last reverberation of the Red King's anger is to be found in a writ issued by Henry I on Christmas Day, 1100, by which certain lands of his church which had been held by the newly incarcerated Ranulf

57. *Regesta* II, No. 348a; later in the year he received a royal precept in favor of the same abbey (*ibid.*, No. 348b).
58. *Memorials of St. Edmund's Abbey*, I, 87.
59. *Regesta* II, p. 411; T. A. M. Bishop and Pierre Chaplais (eds.), *Facsimiles of English Royal Writs to A.D. 1100* (Oxford, 1957), plate xvii (a).
60. *Regesta* II, No. 385b.
61. *Ibid.*, No. 385c.
62. Dodwell, "Foundation," 6 n. 1; but see the note by the editors of the *Regesta*, *ibid.*

Flambard were to be returned to Herbert and all claims against them dismissed.[63] Never again in Herbert's career, when a major conflict occurred between the interests of *regnum* and *sacerdotium* in England, was this curialist bishop to be openly found in any role other than king's utensil.

Herbert Losinga's most enduring monument was the cathedral begun at his initiative in Norwich. There is a lingering, and quite wrong, tradition that Herbert, who was consecrated bishop of Thetford, moved his see city and commenced his cathedral at Norwich to atone for his simony; as Dodwell has clearly disproved this myth, the matter will not be pursued here.[64] Movement of diocesan seats was not novel in Herbert's England—such moves had been authorized at several councils held during the pontificate of Archbishop Lanfranc,[65] and numerous transfers had occurred from rural seats to locations which because of size, location, or prosperity were more suitable as chief cities of dioceses than their predecessors.[66]

The practical objections to the Thetford seat were overwhelming: the diocese did not own the cathedral church there;[67] Thetford was a small town growing neither in importance nor in size; and it was badly situated to be a see city. Furthermore, there had been an atmosphere of impermanence about the East Anglian bishop's diocesan seat: Thetford had claimed the honor since 1072 only, and was preceded by Dunwich and Elmham. Norwich's advantages were patent: it was a port, larger and more important than Thetford, and its economic position was improving

63. *Regesta* II, No. 508.

64. Dodwell, "Foundation," throughout. For examples of the charge, see Thomas Martin, *History of the Town of Thetford* (London, 1779), p. 36, and Britton, *Norwich*, p. 15. Bale's accusation that he moved the see city because of ambition may not be groundless (*Scriptorum*, p. 171).

65. David Wilkins, *Concilia Magnae Brittaniae*, I (London, 1737), 367–378; Mansi, *Concilia*, XX, 5–6 and 449–456; Robert of Torigni, *Chronicles*, p. 122.

66. Crediton to Exeter, Selsey to Chichester, Dorchester to Lincoln, Sherborne to Salisbury, Dunwich to N. Elmham to Thetford, Lichfield to Coventry to Chester, Wells to Bath—all before Herbert's consecration: see John Godfrey, *The Church in Anglo-Saxon England* (Cambridge, 1962), pp. 424–425; Marjorie Chibnall, "Fécamp and England," in de Povremogne, *Fécamp*, I, 369; David C. Douglas, *William the Conqueror* (Berkeley and Los Angeles, 1964), pp. 328–329.

67. *NR*, pp. 22–24; Bartholomew Cotton, pp. 389–390. See also Dodwell, "Foundation," pp. 6–7. She notes that the Thetford church which had served as cathedral was passed on as personal property by Bishop Herfast (*ob.* ?1085) to his sons. Earl Roger Bigod later gave it to the Thetford Cluniacs.

steadily.[68] There seems little reason to advance psychological or disciplinary motivations to explain Herbert's transfer of his cathedral city.

Although only one document exists to demonstrate the probability, the see was in all likelihood moved to Norwich in 1094, for which year some chroniclers give the date April 9.[69] The diocese held property in Norwich before the see's movement, the Church of the Holy Trinity,[70] and land which had been given by the king "for the principal seat of the bishopric."[71]

The first necessity was for the bishop to establish his cathedral, and there is no doubt when this chief church of the East Anglian diocese was founded. Toward the close of 1095 the lands of the cathedral precinct were delineated by Ranulf Flambard, Bishop Walkelin of Winchester, and the leading Norfolk baron Roger Bigod.[72] This survey was followed by a royal writ of early 1096 directing that the land which had been "viewed" and which the king therewith gave to Herbert was for the building of the church and of residences for the bishop and his monks.[73] When William's brother and successor Henry I confirmed the gift, he added the twenty-five shillings rent which the slain monarch had withheld from the original endowment.[74]

The majority of the chroniclers assign the foundation of the cathedral to 1096,[75] Herbert laying the cornerstone inscribed with the name of the

68. *Flor. Wig.*, *s.a.* 1094; Malmesbury, *GP*, p. 151. See also E. Carus-Wilson, "Towns and Trade," in Austin Lane Poole (ed.), *Medieval England*, I; rev. ed. (Oxford, 1958), 223–224.

69. *Flor. Wig.*, *ibid.*; Bartholomew Cotton, pp. 54 and 389; *Annales monastici*, III, 428; "Matthew of Westminster," II, 25 and 30. Dodwell, "Foundation," p. 6 ff., discusses the chronological difficulties inherent in the movement of the see city and the commencement of the cathedral. Gervase of Canterbury, *Historical Works*, ed. William Stubbs (RS 73), II, 68 and 368, gives the year as 1093; Thomas Rudborne, "Wintoniensis historia major," in Henry Wharton (ed.), *Anglia sacra*, I (London, 1691), 264, prefers 1095. Both Gervase and Thomas wrote long after the event.

70. Record Commission, *Domesday Book* (hereafter cited as *DB*), fol. 116*v*; cf. Dodwell, "Foundation," p. 8.

71. *DB*, fol. 117.

72. *NR*, p. 24.

73. *Monasticon*, IV, 13; *inspeximus* in *Calendar of Charter Rolls* (PRO), III, 70. Calendared *Regesta* I, No. 385. Dodwell ("Foundation," p. 8 n. 4) has established this document as belonging to January, 1096.

74. *NR*, pp. 26–28 and 40; *Monasticon*, IV, 15; see also *Regesta* II, Nos. 509, 785, 835 and *Itin. H. I.*, No. 154.

75. "Annales S. Edmundi," p. 130; Bartholomew Cotton, p. 54; *Monasticon*, IV, 1 and 13; Matthew Paris, *Chronica majora*, ed. Henry Richards Luard (RS 57), II, 59;

Trinity and with his own.[76] The great structure was not finished during Herbert's lifetime nor for decades thereafter, but to the first bishop of Norwich must go the credit for beginning one of the most remarkable Norman and Gothic cathedrals of England.

Gifts and endowments were not slow in forthcoming, although they were meager in quantity and, considering the potential of East Anglia, niggardly in amount.[77] Earl Roger Bigod, by any standard a leading baron of the realm, granted land at St. Michael and at Taverham (lying immediately to the west of the cathedral site) but was careful to obtain in return a carucate of land both at Silham and at Wykes.[78] Godwin the deacon gave the church at Cressingham with its appurtenances, promising by the same charter that he would make his monastic profession should his wife predecease him.[79] King Henry presented the manor of Thorpe-next-Norwich[80] and Alan fitz-Flaald gave the manor of Eton in a charter which mentioned the "few possessions" of the cathedral priory (a gift later confirmed by his son William) and the grant was endorsed by Henry I, who added his own grant of part of the royal borough of Norwich, the privilege of prolonging the fair at that city, and the fairs at Lynn and Hoxne.[81] There was an additional grant the instrument for which has

---

"Matthew of Westminster," II, 30. *Annales monastici*, III, 429, placed the foundation in 1097. Dodwell, "Foundation," p. 8, relying on unpublished sources, also refers the foundation to 1096. See also *Ioh. Bramis historiae waldei* (probably a Thetford source) in M. R. James, *A Descriptive Catalogue of Manuscripts in the Library of Corpus Christi College, Cambridge* (Cambridge, 1912), II, 152.

76. *NR*, p. 50. Hubert de Rye, Norfolk noble and benefactor of the cathedral, laid the second stone.

77. Dodwell, "Foundation," throughout and especially p. 10 ff.

78. *NR*, pp. 28–30; *inspeximus* in *Cal. Charter Rolls*, III, 71, and see *Regesta* I, No. 482. Roger later granted both carucates to his Cluniac foundation at Thetford. William II confirmed the Earl's grants to the cathedral: *NR*, *ibid.*; Bishop and Chaplais, *Royal Writs*, pl. xvii (c); *Monasticon*, IV, 13 and 18.

79. Goulburn and Symonds, *Life*, pp. 415 ff.

80. *NR*, pp. 28–30; *Monasticon*, IV, 16–17, which gives the witness list, omitted by the priory register; *Itin. H. I*, No. 26; *Regesta* II, No. 548. For a similar document of 1107, see *inspeximus* in *Cal. Charter Rolls*, IV, 439 (calendared *Regesta* II, No. 786 and *Itin. H. I*, No. 152); Thorpe was to be "quit of aids and scots, as it was when it was in the king's hands and in his demesne." See also Barbara Dodwell, "The Honour of the Bishop of Thetford/Norwich in the Late Eleventh and Early Twelfth Centuries," *Norfolk Archaeology*, XXXIII[2] (1963), 188.

81. *NR*, pp. 42–46. For the royal grants, *ibid.*, pp. 44–46; *Monasticon*, IV, 17. Calendared: *Regesta* II, No. 762 and *Itin. H. I*, No. 243 (which omits mention of the fair rights).

not survived: it must be inferred from a royal confirmation of 1116 [?] by which the king assented to the gift by Ranulf fitzGodric of Newton manor, to which the king added all appurtenant customs.[82]

Herbert was generous in his own benefactions to the cathedral and its priory. His lengthy foundation charter[83] commences rhetorically with a long avowal of his own sinful nature—perhaps it is this which led to the erroneous opinion that repentance for his simony prompted the building of the cathedral and of other churches in the diocese, and it certainly led his previous biographers into the snare of mistaking a literary and devotional device for a *mea culpa*: " [the charter shows] how the penitence of our Bishop for the errors of his past life comes out [and that] his shameful fall was never effaced from his memory."[84]

The foundation charter distinguished carefully between episcopal and monastic holdings, but Malmesbury's statement that Herbert gave nothing from episcopal properties to the monks must be rejected (the charter specifically states otherwise) as must the Norwich records' allegation that the division of episcopal and monastic properties was made so that visitors on diocesan business would not interfere with the monks at their worship.[85] The real reason was probably to keep as much property as possible out of the royal hands during vacancies in the bishopric, as chapter property was not taken over by the king.[86] Further, a bishop's inevitable involvement in secular affairs made such a demarcation desirable.

Herbert Losinga established Benedictine monks to serve as canon clergy in his new cathedral; monastic chapters were virtually unknown outside England, although by no means unusual in that country.[87] While it is possible that Herbert introduced monks because of Lanfranc's (posthumous?) influence and because it was "possibly the best way to

---

82. *Monasticon*, IV, 18 (1107–18; *Itin. H. I* suggests 1116 [No. 363]). *Regesta* II, No. 787, calendars a writ of 1106 directing that the manor of Newton have its meadows quit, as those of Thorpe, of exactions (see also *NR*, p. 36).

83. *NR*, pp. 32–36. *Monasticon*, IV, 19–20 (1281 *inspeximus*).

84. Goulburn and Symonds, *Life*, p. 146.

85. Malmesbury, *GR*, p. 86 and *GP*, p. 151. The statements in the *NR* chronicle narrative (24) and in Bartholomew Cotton (130) are countered by the foundation charter's own statement that the division was to avoid future quarrels between bishop and priory. Even the charter's statement is, I believe, somewhat disingenuous.

86. Knowles, *Monastic Order*, p. 173; see also Margaret Howell, *Regalian Right in Medieval England*, University of London Historical Studies, IX (London, 1962), 5–48.

87. Knowles, *Monastic Order*, pp. 129 ff.; Godfrey, *Church in Anglo-Saxon England*, pp. 308 and 479 n. 27.

fulfill the requirements of the Gregorian reformers for a celibate clergy,"[88] it would be a natural step in England for a bishop who had been successively monk, prior, and abbot before his consecration.

The many grants made to the priory in the foundation charter are detailed and explicit as to their purposes: food, clothing, shelter, and other essentials were amply provided for the monks.[89] To forestall possible objections from his successors, Herbert gave to the bishopric—to balance its property alienated to the monks—the episcopal palace for which he paid £20 of his own money, and several manors.[90]

The royal council held at Windsor in September, 1101, confirmed the bishop's foundation charter, and the king separately issued his own charter of confirmation,[91] as did Archbishop Anselm, who stipulated that Norwich was to be the *caput et mater* of all Norfolk and Suffolk churches with monks serving the cathedral as at Winchester.[92] While in Rome in 1102, Herbert secured a charter of privileges from Paschal II which confirmed all the above instruments and certified Norwich as the replacement for Thetford as the East Anglian see city at the same time approving the establishment of the Benedictines as the cathedral chapter.[93]

88. Douglas Jerrold, *An Introduction to the History of England* (London, 1949), p. 438, is incorrect in stating that the Norwich chapter was not monastic: "Regulars were restored at Worcester, Winchester, and Durham and a strict rule imposed on the congregation of secular canons at Norwich. . . ."

89. For food and clothing: alms given in the cathedral, burial fees, the Pentecost fairs granted by William II, tithes from the episcopal manors (excepting those things pertaining to the bishop's chaplains), Lakenham with its appurtenances (but for the land of Archdeacon Osbern), half of Thorpe wood on condition that it never be alienated without permission (*HE*, ep. 8 to the monk William, forbids him to make any presents from Thorpe since Herbert would take care of the sick and others upon his return to Norwich). For other essentials: Hindringham and Hindolveston as these manors had been held by the bishop, the mill at Norwich as well as the land and meadow there which had formerly been of the episcopal holdings, half the meadow of Thorpe, the bishop's house with appurtenant marsh and eel fishery at Hilgay, the manors of Martham and Hemsby with appurtenances, the churches of St. Leonard (Thorpe) and of St. Nicholas (Yarmouth), the manors of Catton and Newton, the property formerly held by Herbert Ros in Plumstead and Becham, the new mill and the 21 saltpans at Gaywood, and churches at Hoxne (with St. Edmund's chapel), Lynn and Langham (with its tithes).

90. Elmham, Eccles (purchased of the king for £60), and Colkirk. See above p. 134 n. 85.

91. *NR*, pp. 38–40; *Monasticon*, IV, 15 and 17 (*inspeximus*, T. H. II); Wilkins, *Concilia*, I, 381; Mansi, *Concilia*, XX, cols. 1143–44. See also *Regesta* II, No. 547, and *Itin. H. I*, No. 25.

92. *NR*, pp. 40–42; *Monasticon*, IV, 20 (1281 *inspeximus*); *Regesta* II, No. 549.

93. *NR*, pp. 54–56; the bull may be found as well in *PL*, CLXIII, 432, and see also Walther Holtzmann, *Papsturkunden in England*, 5 parts (Berlin, 1932 *et seqq.*), III, 32 and 137 and IV, No. 3; *Monasticon*, I, 410 and IV, 20.

Herbert's other benefactions postdate the foundation charter but cannot be dated precisely. The bishop had kept for himself the less desirable portion of Thorpe manor in order that he might not be a burden to the monks when he was in his cathedral city, but they complained so of this deprivation that to silence them he gave four other parcels of land and a church.[94] Other charters grant the manor of Fring,[95] a mill at Trows so that the monks need not pay to have their grain ground (in return for which mill they were to keep the obit of his father),[96] and a number of churches to be held in frankalmoign.[97] Thus Herbert's gifts to the priory and to the episcopate were extensive; his own munificence was not, however, matched by the generosity of lay patrons who could reasonably have been expected to support his ecclesiastical projects.[98]

We know little of the origins of the sixty black monks established at the Norwich priory.[99] At least one, William Turbe, bishop of Norwich (1147–1174), was a Norman;[100] some may have come from the Rochester chapter[101] and many (if not most) were East Anglians.[102] The first prior was Ingulf, who was still alive in 1121.[103]

The bishop's letters to his monks reveal his great concern for them and great understanding and sympathy for their problems; they also reveal his firmness. He was particularly anxious that the rule not be relaxed among the chapter but for good and exceptional reasons, and the letters touching

---

94. *NR*, p. 48: Pockthorpe and other lands, the manor of Gnatingdon with its customs and appurtenances, a carucate in Mintling, the land of the late deacon Thurstan, and the church of Thornham. *Regesta* II, No. 1159 (1100–16) calendars a notification of Henry I addressed generally to the counties of Norfolk and Suffolk confirming Herbert's donation of Gnatingdon "which he bought from Walter Halthein." This confirms a charter from the unpublished Norwich Register IV, a microfilm of which was kindly supplied me by Barbara Dodwell from the Norwich Cathedral muniments.

95. Norwich Register IV.

96. *NR*, pp. 48–50; and see above p. 125 n. 34.

97. *NR*, pp. 30 and 52; *Monasticon*, IV, 13. The churches were St. Leonard, Thorpe; St. Michael's chapel; and others at Lynn, Yarmouth, Aldeby, Elmham, Hemsby.

98. The list of benefactors in *Monasticon*, IV, 16, has been amplified, and is superseded by, Dodwell, "Foundation," pp. 10 ff.; this article has wise judgments to offer on the patronage situation. Everett U. Crosby, "The Organization of the English Episcopate Under Henry I," *Studies in Medieval and Renaissance History*, IV (Lincoln, Neb., 1967), p. 45.

99. *NR*, pp. 24 and 28; Malmesbury, *GP*, p. 151 and *GR*, p. 386; *Monasticon*, IV, 15.

100. Dodwell, "Foundation," p. 12.

101. Knowles, *Monastic Order*, p. 474 n. 2, where it is suggested that Norwich and Rochester were in confraternity.

102. Dodwell, "Foundation," p. 12.

103. *Monasticon*, IV, 6; see also list of priors in Wharton (ed.), *Anglia sacra*, I, 420.

this topic show both fatherly kindness and awareness of the temptations most likely to assail the monastic as he attempts to follow the way of St. Benedict. He was quite willing to exercise his authority in forthright terms: some have criticized the harshness of his penances, others have complained of his discipline, errant monks might escape the bishop's eyes but not those of God.[104] Yet his sternness could be mitigated by compassion—"receive [Alexander] again into fellowship with you," Herbert wrote to Ingulf, "for as the hardened folly of a habitual offender drives him naturally to despair, so contrarily we may certainly anticipate amendment [of his ways] from leniency shown to a youth."[105]

Some details of the monastic establishment at Norwich clearly demonstrate the bishop's continued respect and devotion for his first monastic home, Fécamp. Both the Norman house and the priory were dedicated to the Holy Trinity and the crest of each monastery bore three mitres. Two letters exist from Herbert to Abbot Roger of Fécamp, thus falling to the period after 1108 when Roger d'Argence succeeded William de Ros in that abbacy.[106] One is primarily concerned with expressing affection for his first house and for its abbot, asserting Herbert's unending fidelity to Fécamp and filial obedience to its abbot.[107] The other is of more concrete interest. He stated that the Fécamp use was the model for that of Norwich, but apologized because secular responsibilities distracted both his memory and his attention. The bishop asked permission to send monks to observe at Fécamp and to report back with information on its customs.[108] The request was probably granted, for the Norwich Customary reflects Fécamp influence.[109]

In his introduction, the editor of the Norwich Customary noted the insertion of a feast for St. Bonitus (January 15), for whom Herbert had a "particular devotion," as one of the few "distinctive features" in the calendar.[110] This is perhaps more interesting than we are here told, for Bonitus had been bishop of Clermont after holding a succession of responsible secular positions, including that of chancellor to King Sigebert III of Austrasia. In 689 Bonitus succeeded his brother St.

104. *HE*, epp. 6, 16, 29, 42, 43, 48, 52, 55.
105. *Ibid.*, ep. 51.
106. *HF*, XIV, 383; but *ibid.*, 226, gives 1107; and *GC*, XI, col. 208, opts both for 1108 and 1109. Roger died in 1139.
107. *HE*, ep. 5; the language is effusive.
108. *Ibid.*, ep. 34.
109. Tolhurst, *Norwich Customary*, pp. xxiv–xvii; Chibnall, "Fécamp and England," in de Povremogne, *Fécamp*, I, 127–135, 369 ff.
110. Tolhurst, *Norwich Customary*, xvi.

Avitus as ordinary, but resigned his see after some years of saintly administration and life because he was assailed by doubts that his election had been canonical. He died in 706 at Lyons after a penitential pilgrimage to Rome.[111] Is it possible that Herbert may have honored a personal patron saint, a bishop whose election, while not simoniacal, had nevertheless been irregular? Further, simony was defined by most Gregorian reformers of Herbert's period not only in its narrowest sense, the buying of ecclesiastical office, but as broadly comprehending any interference with the free operation of the Holy Spirit in designating elects;[112] in this context, Bonitus may be said to have shared Herbert's sin, although in less flagrant form.

Herbert's attention to ecclesiastical building was by no means confined to his diocesan precinct. His smallest structure was a large cross dedicated to St. Michael the Archangel which served as a boundary marker between the king's lands and his own at St. Michael.[113] Lynn priory, dedicated to St. Mary, St. Margaret, and All the Holy Virgins, was constructed around 1100 and was dependent on the cathedral priory.[114] In the following year the bishop replaced, from his own possessions, the small chapel at Yarmouth with a church dedicated to St. Nicholas, which was also dependent on the cathedral priory.[115] Between 1104 and 1107, men from neighboring ports forcibly expelled the chaplain, possibly with the plan of using the edifice, which prompted the bishop to inform King Henry of the incursion. The king deputed Earl Roger Bigod, then sheriff in the county, to drive out the intruders; this was done, and the church restored to the custody of its founder.[116] Finally, the bishop constructed and provided for the maintenance of a leprosarium in Norwich dedicated to St. Mary Magdalene[117] and the hospital of St. Paul, which was in the cathedral priory's holdings.[118]

The diocese of Norwich in Herbert's time did not receive ecclesiastical foundations solely from its bishop. St. Faith's Priory (Horsham) was

111. *Acta sanctorum*, Jan. xv (Brussels, 1863), 351–359.
112. Gerd Tellenbach, *Church, State and Christian Society at the Time of the Investiture Contest*, trans. R. F. Bennett, Studies in Medieval History, ed. Geoffrey Barraclough, VII (Blackwell, Oxford, 1940), 128.
113. *NR*, p. 26; *Monasticon*, IV, 13.
114. *NR*, pp. 32 and 50–52; *Monasticon*, IV, 432. The charter granted a number of lands and income-producing appurtenances: it also exhorted the priory monks to turn out and work on the church.
115. *Monasticon*, IV, 465; *NR*, pp. 30–32.
116. *NR*, p. 32; C. Warren Hollister, *The Military Organization of Norman England* (Oxford, 1965), 229.
117. *NR*, pp. 46–48.
118. *Monasticon*, IV, 13: "in the latter part of Bishop Herbert's time."

founded "with the consent of Herbert the Bishop" by Robert fitz-Walter and his wife in 1105 and dedicated by Herbert.[119] Norwich castellan Hubert de Rye and his wife endowed a prior and three monks at Aldeby,[120] and two cells to the great monastery of St. Alban's were founded as well early in the pontificate: Binham[121] and Windham (Wymondham), which later became an independent abbey.[122]

Roger Bigod founded the most important house established during Herbert's tenure as chief pastor of East Anglia, other than the cathedral priory itself; this was the Cluniac house of Thetford. The earl had planned to make a pilgrimage to the Holy Land, but the beginning of the crusading movement had made this dangerous and his health was apparently declining. Hence he applied to the new monastery the amount of money which a journey to the Near East would have required.[123] Probably in 1103, the foundation was accomplished with the consent of the bishop and granted to the French mother house.[124] While the Thetford Cluniacs apparently used the Church of St. Mary initially, they transferred their *Opus Dei* to a new church dedicated in 1114.[125] The colonizers came from the English Cluniac monastery at Lewes, under Malgod as prior, since Cluny no longer sent colonizers overseas.[126]

119. *Ibid.*, III, 63–67; *GC*, I, col. 245.

120. *Monasticon*, IV, p. 461; Dugdale described the foundation as "small and obscure."

121. *Monasticon*, III, 41, suggested 1104, but Dodwell, "Foundation," p. 15 n. 4, places the foundation before 1093. In 1107 the house received a royal confirmation addressed to Herbert and others (*Regesta* II, No. 828; *Itin. H. I*, No. 194) and another of the same year attested by the bishop (*Monasticon*, III, 351; *Regesta* II, No. 830 [probably spurious]). Herbert appeared only once again in a Binham document, when he and Peter de Valoignes settled the use of common pasture before a royal court at Norwich in 1108: David C. Douglas, *The Social Structure of Medieval East Anglia*, Oxford Studies in Social and Legal History, IX (Oxford, 1927), 241–242; *Monasticon*, III, 348; *Regesta* II, No. 875; *Itin. H. I*, No. 242.

122. *Monasticon*, III, 330; before Sept., 1107, since Roger Bigod, a signatory, died at that time.

123. VCH *Norfolk*, II, 363; *Monasticon*, V, 141. Roger Bigod exemplifies here a stage in the development of the indulgence doctrine and practice.

124. Sir G. F. Duckett (ed.), *Charters and Records Among the Archives of the Abbey of Cluni, 1077–1534*, I (Lewes, 1888), 60–61, royal confirmation 161–162; Martin, *Thetford*, appendix vii, 35–37; *Annales monastici*, III, 430, dates the foundation 1104, but Dodwell, "Foundation," argues convincingly for 1103. See also Malmesbury, *GR*, p. 387 and *GP*, p. 151, and *Monasticon*, V, 148. On Cluniac foundations in England, see Knowles, *Monastic Order*, pp. 145 ff.

125. *Monasticon*, V, 142; *Annales monastici* [cited above n. 8], III, 432.

126. Knowles, *Monastic Order*, p. 151. Incorrect are VCH *Norfolk*, 363, in stating that Cluny could not spare any monks for new filiations, and Martin, *Thetford*, 113, that Abbot Hugh the Venerable did not wish to send his Burgundian-educated monks to a region where language and customs were foreign.

Several of Herbert's letters relate to affairs at Thetford.́ One to Prior Stephen (after 1107, when he was elevated to that office) [127] responded to the prior's request that the bishop consecrate the Thetford churchyard, but he hesitated to do this since the king had made the arrangements by which customary payments from the former churchyard were disposed. The ordinary would, however, perform the desired rite if Stephen would transfer these customs from the old to the new churchyard, barring which he refused until he could consult either with the king or with his justiciars. [128] This correspondence can probably be assigned to 1114, since Herbert referred to the new church, completed in that year. While there is no evidence of royal cognizance of the problem, the king must have granted Herbert permission to consecrate the churchyard—perhaps when he came to Thetford in 1114 [129]—or Stephen must have agreed to the bishop's condition, for Herbert wrote to the prior consenting to consecrate the tract. [130]

Another letter to the Thetford monks is quite interesting. In it the bishop laid a grisly anathema on miscreants who had slain one of his deer in the park at Homersfield, insisting that the excommunication and accompanying curses had as their object the poachers' repentance, not revenge or grief for the loss of an animal. [131] The letter is strikingly similar in content to a dialogue of Gregory the Great in which the killing of a sheep-herding bear is recounted: even some of the identical horrors called down on Gregory's fey monks were invoked against the deerslayers. [132]

Beyond the subjects of Herbert's monastic and ecclesiastical patronage, he is a very obscure figure on the local level in the early years of Henry I's reign, merely witnessing charters [133] and receiving one writ of minor diplomatic importance. This notification, addressed to the bishop, Earl

---

127. *Monasticon*, V, 146. Stephen occurs again in 1130.   128. *HE*, ep. 2.
129. *Regesta* II, Nos. 1057, 1058.   130. *HE*, ep. 7.
131. *Ibid.*, ep. 35. Other letters to Thetford are ep. 36, directing the reeve (*praepositus*) to attend more to ecclesiastical, less to secular, affairs and to stop molesting Dean Bond, and ep. 37 (to the brethren at Thetford) ordering that the dean have his school in peace. Were Athselinus, the *praepositus*, prior at Thetford (the Latin can bear this meaning) the two letters would have an obvious connection, but Athselinus appears in no source as having held that office.
132. Gregory the Great, "Dialogue III," in U. Moricca (ed.), *Gregorii Magni dialogii libri IV*, Fonti per la storia d'Italia, LVII (Rome, 1924), 169–175.
133. Henry confirming his late brother's gift to Bath: *Regesta* II, No. 544 (*ibid.*, No. 573 is another charter to the same, also witnessed by Herbert; see also *Monasticon*, II, 268); *Itin. H. I*, No. 28; cf. *Regesta* I, No. 315. Henry confirming certain English possessions to St. Martin's, Troarn: *Cal. Charter Rolls*, IV, 283; John Horace Round (ed.), *Calendar of Documents Preserved in France* (PRO, 1899), I, No. 470; *Regesta* II, No. 524; *Itin. H. I*, No. 10.

Roger Bigod, and all Norfolk barons, confirmed the gift of a church in Norwich to the monks of St. Peter's, Gloucester.[134] The document is referred by the editors of the *Regesta* to 1100/1101 on the ground that Herbert is styled bishop of Thetford, this implying that after 1101 he ceased to be so designated. Dodwell stated that Herbert ceased to be styled "Thetford" after the papal bull authorizing the transfer of the diocesan seat to Norwich (1102), following which Roger Bigod acquired the former cathedral church in Thetford.[135] Herbert was, however, thus identified in at least two later sources: "Thomas of Ely" so designated him as of 1106;[136] so too did Anselm in a letter to Samson of Worcester dated by Dom F. S. Schmitt to 1108.[137] Hence the limits are somewhat wider for this writ: 1100 to 1107, when Earl Roger died.

Other documentary notices of Herbert from this period relate to his papal mission of 1102 and its attendant events. One of the latter, his attempt to realize his claims to authority over Bury St. Edmunds, while of diocesan importance, involved the bishop in confrontations and problems beyond his diocese and will be treated in the following section. For strictly local matters to mid-1106, Herbert's appearances are again of a routine and uninteresting nature.[138]

There is a fascinating insight into the miraculous—or perhaps into a chronicler's mentality—recorded in the *Liber Eliensis*.[139] In 1106 Abbot Richard of Ely, a Norman and former Bec monk,[140] translated the relics of

134. *Regesta* II, No. 555.   135. Dodwell, "Foundation," p. 7.

136. *Liber Eliensis*, ed. E. O. Blake, Camden 3rd series, XCII (London, 1962), 232.

137. Anselm, V, ep. 464.

138. He received a royal writ of Whitsuntide, 1104, notifying him of a gift to Bury (*Regesta* II, No. 672; *Itin. H. I*, No. 91). At about the same time he attested a charter confirming the establishment of St. John's Colchester as a monastic house: *Regesta* II, Nos. 674 and 777, *Itin. H. I*, No. 92. Herbert received notification in 1105 of a settlement concerning land held by Eye monastery: *Cal. Charter Rolls*, V, 363; *Itin. H. I*, No. 111; *Regesta* II, No. 780 (No. 1144 is another charter for Eye received by Herbert, 1106–1116). A writ of 1106 directed Roger Bigod and Ranulf Passelewe, a leading Norfolk noble, to stop harassing the bishop's land and men at Brisley (Nf), and ordered that he was not to be dispossessed "except by the just judgment of the county court" (*Regesta* II, No. 747; *Itin. H. I*, No. 96). Toward the end of the same year Herbert was among the recipients of a royal writ confirming the gift of a manor to the convent of Malling (Sf): *Cal. Charter Rolls*, V, 56 (*inspeximus*); *Monasticon*, III, 384; *Regesta* II, No. 791; *Itin. H. I*, No. 168.

139. This account is based on the sole source for the incident, the *Liber Eliensis*, pp. 228–233. The propers for St. Etheldreda may be found in the *Breviarium ad usum insignis ecclesiae Sarum*, ed. Francis Procter and Christopher Wordsworth, Fasc. III (Cambridge, 1886), pp. 335–338; the lections are from The Venerable Bede, *Historia ecclesiasticam gentis Anglorum*, ed. Charles Plummer (Oxford, 1896), pp. 243 ff. Bede (*ibid.*, pp. 245 ff.) relates the story of the first translation.

140. *Liber Eliensis*, pp. 234–235; *Monasticon*, I, 461–462.

St. Etheldreda and her companions from the old to the new abbey church in order that the new edifice might be enhanced by the presence of these Anglo-Saxon saints. The Ely chronicler, not surprisingly, stressed Richard's pious desire to provide a more suitable resting place. At this, the second, translation the remains of Etheldreda were found uncorrupted; visual inspection sufficed for this conclusion as hideous misfortunes had befallen those who on the occasion of the earlier exhumation impiously poked the body with sticks and committed other indignities in their examination of the relics.[141] The reinterment accomplished, Herbert— *vir eloquentissimus*—preached with such fervor on the life, death, miracles, and uncorrupt relics of the saint that his audience was moved to weeping: unfortunately, this sermon has not survived, nor was it summarized by the Ely writer. The translation was apparently not entirely pleasing to Etheldreda, for thunderstorms crashed through the air (Anselm is said to have heard them in Kent and thus deduced the dedication of the church to have taken place), windows shattered, traceries of fire which did no damage writhed across the church floor, and, in the main, the Isle of Ely enjoyed a wholly unsettling experience.

Abbot Richard, undaunted, proceeded to the translation of SS. Sexburga and Ermenilda, also holy virgins of the Anglo-Saxon period. This took place peaceably. The last of the holy maidens, Withburga, lay in a tomb which had been cracked four years previously through the carelessness of a workman laboring on the construction of the new abbey; the new sepulchre which had been made for her as a result stubbornly resisted any efforts to make it large enough to receive the relics. The cracked condition of her old tomb permitted the body to be seen, and the bishop of Norwich was among many praising God when the remains appeared uncorrupted; he preached again on the new evidence of sanctity here disclosed, and again drew tears from his congregation. The saint herself solved the problem of whether to move the relics to the new sarcophagus by sealing the cleft in the old one, and all present took this as a sign that she preferred her old to the new tomb, and her relics were borne to the new church in the old cenotaph. It seems not to have been considered that she wished both the old tomb and its old location.

Herbert's activities in 1107 returned to the less extraordinary. Arch-

141. A similar example of saintly displeasure at rude handling of relics was displayed by St. Sergius Martyr, who split a probing finger into three pieces and sent them flying in as many directions: Gregory of Tours, *Historiarum*, ed. Bruno Krusch and Wilhelm Levison in *MGH, Scriptores rerum merovingicarum*, I[1] (Hanover, 1951), 351. See further, on the dangers in disturbing saints' relics, F. Homes Dudden, *Gregory the Great: His Place in History and Thought* (London, 1905), I, 280 and n. 4.

bishop Anselm, following the formal end of the English investiture controversy, proceeded to the first need of the English church: the consecration of elects to dioceses *sede vacante* during his exile. Herbert, who had co-consecrated Anselm and had performed the same function for the royal chaplain Samson to the see of Worcester and the royal chancellor Gerard to the frontier diocese of Hereford in June, 1096,[142] joined in passing the apostolic succession to William Warelwast of Winchester, Roger of Salisbury, Reinhelm of Hereford, William of Exeter, and Urban of Glamorgan.[143] The only evidence of other activity as diocesan bishop in that year was his attestation of a charter in favor of St. Mary's Abbey (Montebourg).[144]

Late in 1107, or early in the following year, an ugly dispute erupted which pitted Herbert against the Thetford Cluniacs. Earl Roger Bigod had died on September 8, 1107, and his foundation claimed the baron's body for burial, but was met with spirited resistance by the bishop who denied the Cluniacs' insistence that the earl had wished to lie at Thetford. Edward Goulburn and Henry Symonds virtually accused Herbert of body snatching against the entreaties of Roger's widow and of his monks (on bended knee),[145] but subsequent litigation judged the ordinary to be correct. The Thetford monks admitted before the royal court that Roger had indeed willed himself and his family to be interred in the cathedral, although the commitment was made before the Cluniacs had been established in the former see city, and their admission was doubtless encouraged by Herbert's producing numerous witnesses who attested that Roger had named Norwich as his burial place.[146] Earl Roger was laid to rest in Norwich cathedral.

The years 1108, after the above unpleasantness, and 1109 again include only routine notices of Herbert on the local level; he attested two charters[147] and received two royal notifications.[148] It is to the year 1110

142. Eadmer, *Historia*, p. 74.

143. *Ibid.*, p. 187; Malmesbury, *GP*, p. 117; *Itin. H. I*, No. 197a.

144. *Cal. Charter Rolls*, IV, 157–158 (*inspeximus*); *Regesta* II, No. 825; *Itin. H. I*, No. 192.

145. Goulburn and Symonds, *Life*, pp. 233–234.

146. *Regesta* II, No. 886.

147. One charter confirming "certain lands and privileges" to Durham and to her bishop (*Cal. Charter Rolls*, V, 454 [*inspeximus*]; *Regesta* II, No. 918; *Itin. H. I*, No. 231), the other granting royal permission to erect the new see of Ely and compensating the bishop of Lincoln, whose holdings were thus reduced, with other grants (Lewis C. Loyd and Doris M. Stenton, *Sir Christopher Hatton's Book of Seals* [Oxford, 1960], No. 419; *Regesta* II, No. 919; *Monasticon*, I, 483; *Itin. H. I*, No. 230). See also *Liber Eliensis*, pp. 249–250.

148. King Henry confirmed the grant by William de Albini of Kilverstone manor to the Thetford monks (*Regesta* II, No. 1084 [1108–1114]); notification also of a division of

that one must turn for material of more than casual interest in Herbert's career.

Many historians of English feudalism have commented on the bishop's dispute with Roger of Salisbury over scutage demanded by the chief justiciar, but it seems doubtful that the document at issue will bear the interpretations placed upon it. The letters to Roger begin with one requesting him to send Archdeacon Walter,[149] one of the three Norwich archdeacons of Herbert's time unnoticed in John le Neve's *Fasti*,[150] back to Norwich, as Herbert could not hold his synod in the absence of this dignitary. This missive also complains of its author's bad health, perhaps the first sign of the illness which came to plague him and prevented him from completing a trip to Rome in 1116. In its initial stages the affliction was primarily an attack on his legs, but by 1116 it had become far more generalized.

As has been stated (see above, n. 80), Thorpe had been given to the bishop of Norwich free of obligations save those owed the crown. Late in 1109, or early in 1110, Herbert Losinga wrote to Roger complaining of several actions recently taken against himself.[151] His lands had been assessed for pleas at a rate of £50 and he had been assessed an additional £60 for scutage (*pro militibus*), when his holdings had lately been diminished and his resources already were so depleted that it was impossible for him to meet the demand with facility. Worst of all was the attempt to assess customary taxes against Thorpe. Herbert reminded Roger that the bishop of Salisbury had seen the original charter, as well as subsequent writs of confirmation, exempting Thorpe from these assessments.

Herbert threatened to take the Thorpe problem before the king on Henry's return to England, and he probably did so since the monarch

---

certain moneys between the abbot of Bury and his prior and monastery (*Monasticon*, III, 153; *Regesta* II, No. 1079; *Itin. H. I*, No. 238).

149. *HE*, ep. 26. Walter occurs as well in the period 1110–1119 (see below n. 150), in *Regesta* II, Nos. 987 and 1089, and in James R. West (ed.), *St. Benet of Holme, 1020–1216*, Norfolk Record Society, II and III (Norwich, 1932), No. 120, and in a charter, probably Herbert's, in favor of the Castleacre Cluniacs (*Monasticon*, V, 53).

150. For the lists, see John le Neve, *Fasti ecclesiae Anglicanae*, ed. T. Duffus Hardy (Oxford, 1854), II, 459–478, and A. J. MacDonald, *Lanfranc: A Study of His Life, Work and Writing* (London, 1926), pp. 122–123. Archdeacons Walter, Richard, and Alveredus attest an agreement between Ralf, *dapifer* of Bury St. Edmunds, and Herbert: Barbara Dodwell, "Some Charters Relating to the Honour of Bacton," in Patricia Barnes and C. F. Slade, *An Early Medieval Miscellany for Doris Mary Stenton*, Pipe Roll Society, N.S., XXXVI (London, 1962), 160–161.

151. *HE*, ep. 26.

issued a precept (May 29, 1110), directing that the manor be "quit of geld and scots as in the time of William I, William II and the King . . . [and] is to be free as in the charters which the Bishop has." Roger of Salisbury was among the addressees, as were the collectors in Norfolk.[152] Herbert had probably paid an aid on the marriage of Henry's daughter Matilda in 1110, but this precept declared the payment was not to constitute precedent for the establishment of new fiscal obligations upon the bishop of Norwich.[153]

Herbert's protest concerning the scutage charge is probably the single most important writing from his hand, as it is one of the only two surviving documents (the other is a royal writ for the bishop of Ely dated 1127) from the reign of Henry I explicitly bearing on the relationship of scutage rates to the duration and financial maintenance of knight service. The letter to Roger, which has received the careful attention of such scholars as Round, Stenton, Chew, Baldwin, Richardson, Sayles, and Hollister, complains of the difficulty in finding the money required; it does not state that the charge is unjust or excessive. Nor is there any internal evidence to support the interpretation, sometimes placed upon this letter, that the bishop could not recover the amount because there were as yet no holdings by knight service in his fee. The only protest is poverty, and the context of other matters discussed in this letter is the same, with the single exception of the Thorpe exaction which is clearly labeled as contrary to justice. The Thorpe problem is also the only one discussed in the letter in the context of innovation; hence neither the geld exaction nor the scutage rate appear to be admissible evidence for novel administrative procedure.

"In some modern books," F. W. Maitland tartly judged, "military tenure has a definiteness and a stability which it never had elsewhere."[154] Herbert's letter has been cited by Round, Stenton, Hollister, and others to establish the existence of scutage early in the reign of Henry I; less certain have been the results of efforts to use the document in determining scutage *rates* prevailing in this reign. There is little point in discussing John Horace Round's calculations of the relation of scutage to knights owed, as C. Warren Hollister's investigations have superseded his conclusions; for

152. *Regesta* II, No. 946. Thorpe continued to be quit of geld in 1130: Joseph Hunter (ed.), *Pipe Roll 31 Henry I* (London, 1929), p. 95.

153. The aid was 3s. per hide: Sidney Knox Mitchell, *Taxation in Medieval England*, ed. Sidney Painter (New Haven, 1951), pp. 164–165.

154. Frederick Pollock and F. W. Maitland, *The History of English Law Before the Time of Edward I*, 2nd ed. (Cambridge, 1898), p. 252.

our purposes, it is sufficient to note that Round believed Norwich's *servicium debitum* to have been forty knights.[155] Helena M. Chew, while she followed Round, did observe that "it seems impossible to reconcile . . . the assessment of 1168 [48¾] with the return of 1166 [33¾]."[156] Sir Frank Stenton utilized Herbert's epistle in calculating a prevailing scutage rate of 30s. per fee in Henry I's reign, and accepted Round's figure—based on 1159 data—of forty knights due from the diocese, although he did note a differing sum in the 1166 *carta* of William Turbe.[157]

Hollister, one of the ablest students of the Norman period in England, is largely in the tradition of Round and of Stenton. He alleged scutage rates to have been "calculated on the basis of the prevailing daily wages of knights" multiplied by the "customary term of wartime military service."[158] Arguing convincingly for the applicability of his formula and for the thesis that the customary annual term of military service in England during the reign of Henry I was sixty days, he introduced Herbert's letter in evidence that the daily maintenance of a knight in the field was 6d.—and this sixpence, multiplied by sixty days, does yield a payment of sixty pounds for forty knights. If Hollister is correct in arguing a thirty shilling per fee scutage, and the other evidence he presented is well reasoned, then Herbert's letter forms an essential part of the usable documentation concerning the questions of scutage and knight service in the reign of Henry I.

The administrative records, however, do not reflect the described forty knights. Herbert's letter makes no mention of the number of knights, and the record evidence for the Norwich assessment of forty comes from the late twelfth and early thirteenth centuries.[159] The *Red Book of the Exchequer* gives the figure of 33¾ fees of the old enfeoffment, the *Black Book of the Exchequer*, 31¾ fees.[160] As the limit of the old enfeoffment was 1135, it is

155. John Horace Round, *Feudal England* (London, 1895), pp. 249 and 270. The reprint edition (London, 1964) is differently paginated, and the references in this edition are to be found on pages 199 ff., and 220. Round's source, which he did not include in his apparatus, was the *Pipe Roll 5 Henry II*, Pipe Roll Society, I (London, 1884), p. 11.

156. Helena M. Chew, *Ecclesiastical Tenants-in-Chief and Knight Service* (Oxford, 1932), p. 19 and n. 2, p. 32.

157. Sir Frank Stenton, *The First Century of English Feudalism*, 2nd ed. (Oxford, 1961), p. 183 and notes.

158. C. Warren Hollister, "The Significance of Scutage Rates in Eleventh- and Twelfth-Century England," *English Historical Review*, LXXV (1960), 579–582. See also *idem, Military Organization*, Chap. VII: "Scutage."

159. *Red Book of the Exchequer*, ed. Hubert Hall (RS 99), I, 22, 76, 81 and II, 40.

160. *Ibid.*, I, 391–392. The *Black Book* return is in *Monasticon*, IV, 18.

possible that there was a diminution in the *servitium debitum* following the bishop's death in 1119, but no evidence survives to indicate this. Dodwell has carefully worked out the Norwich fees in the twelfth century, and has found data which answer the discrepancy noticed by Chew, but which further disrupt Round's and Hollister's use of Herbert's letter to show the relationship of scutage assessments to fees owned. She has shown that the 1166 *cartae* omit the fourteen fees held of the diocese by the honor of Bacton; had these been included in the 1166 returns the old enfeoffment would have been 47¾.[161] That the letter in question is uncertain documentation for the conclusions of Round, Stenton, and Hollister does not of course invalidate their theories; controversy is inevitable concerning any topic for which such fragmentary evidence exists as from the reign of Henry I. There simply are not sufficient records to enable one to pronounce with certainty on the matter; certainly Herbert's plaint conforms with other evidence adduced by Round, Stenton, and Hollister, but it seems difficult to reconcile with Norwich evidence concerning the quota owed by the bishop in the early twelfth century. H. G. Richardson and G. O. Sayles, who also discussed the letter, have a probable answer; they have suggested with admirable caution that the exchequer barons were "only in the initial stages of determining liabilities" and that there was in all likelihood much uncertainty as to what the proper scutage charge was.[162]

Herbert concluded this missive with a suggestion that the queen would uphold his cause with Roger. Probably related, then, to this disagreement with Roger is a letter to Matilda, regent during Henry's absence, which complained with some asperity of the harassment to which secular officials and his neighbors were subjecting the bishop.[163] No evidence survives to indicate whether the queen did indeed intercede with Roger for the bishop, as she was implored to do.

161. Dodwell, "Honour of Norwich," p. 194.

162. H. G. Richardson and G. O. Sayles, *The Governance of Medieval England* (Edinburgh, 1963), pp. 86–88. Cf. Stenton, *English Feudalism*, 182 ff.

163. *HE*, ep. 25. Possibly two other letters of the bishop also relate to this dispute: ep. 30 (to Odo, a student) complains strongly of officials and of neighborly treachery; ep. 50 (to Gislebert) asks the addressee, who is going overseas, to remember his cause before the king as Herbert will remember G.'s before the King of Heaven. In 1109, Henry was absent in Normandy until June second (*Itin. H. I*, No. 51). The last letter could also refer to Herbert's deposition and its attendant complications, for William Rufus was in France from March 19 to December 29, 1094 (Powicke, *Handbook of Chronology*, p. 31). The bishop's other deep difficulties were with the church rather than with the state, although doubtless complaints against officials and neighbors would have been possible in any year.

Notices of Herbert confined to internal diocesan affairs are few after 1110. He received royal notifications of grants,[164] attested a number of charters,[165] and dedicated St. John's Colchester in 1115.[166] In the latter year he also assisted in his last ceremonies as co-consecrator, joining in passing the apostolic succession to Theulf, elect of Worcester, in June and to Ernulf and Geoffrey, elects of Rochester and of Hereford, in December.[167] In September of the same year Herbert's last recorded attendance at the royal court occurred.[168]

The grant of Edwardstone church to Abingdon monastery preceded a cordial letter to the bishop from Archbishop of Canterbury Ranulf d'Escures, in which the primate asked Herbert's kindness to the monks to

164. In 1111: grant of the church at Edwardstone (Sf) to the abbot and monastery of Abingdon (*Chronicon monasterii de Abingdon*, ed. Joseph Stevenson [RS 2], II, 62; *Itin. H. I*, No. 358; *Regesta* II, No. 1089) and a grant of land to the Norfolk house of St. Benet (West [ed.], *St. Benet*, Nos. 121 and 122). In 1114 he was notified that Bishop Hervey of Ely was to have his enumerated liberties at Wicklaw (Sf) as they had been granted by William II: Landon, *Cartae antiquae*, No. 52; *Regesta* II, No. 1049; *Itin. H. I*, No. 327, and see *Liber Eliensis*, pp. 255–256. In the same year Herbert appeared in two charters for his former abbey, Ramsey (*Cart. Rameseia*, I, No. 163 [*Itin. H. I*, No. 362] and *Chron. Rameseiensis*, No. 221 [*Regesta* II, No. 1064; *Itin. H. I*, No. 372]). He appeared only once again in the Ramsey records, in a document which may belong to 1119: *Cart. Rameseia*, No. 168. Falling to the period 1108–1119 are notifications relating to churches in the fee of the bishop of London at Blythburgh and Stowe (Sf) (Historical-Manuscripts Commission, Tenth Report, Appendix IV: *Manuscripts of the Earl of Westmoreland* [London, 1885], p. 451 [*Regesta* II, No. 1218]) and of the grant of a Suffolk church to the canons of St. Osyth (*Westmoreland MSS*, p. 452 [*Regesta* II, No. 1219]). Two royal writs notifying Herbert and others of gifts to Castleacre are calendared in *Regesta* II, Nos. 1195 and 1196.

165. In 1110, a grant to Ramsey: *Chron. Rameseiensis*, No. 199. In 1115, a confirmation in favor of St. Benet of Holme: West (ed.), *St. Benet*, No. 6; *Monasticon*, III, 86; *Regesta* II, No. 1094; *Itin. H. I*, No. 352. From the period 1110–1119, a grant by William of Bacton to Archdeacon Richard: Dodwell, "Bacton Charters," p. 158, No. 1 (cf. Stenton, *English Feudalism*, 92 n.).

166. "Annales Colecestrenses," in Liebermann (ed.), *Geschichtsquellen*, p. 162.

167. Eadmer, *Historia*, pp. 230 and 237; *Itin. H. I*, No. 361a.

168. *Itin. H. I*, No. 347. Crosby, "Episcopate" [cited above, n. 98], p. 7, lists Herbert as provably present at the royal court eleven times in the reign of Henry I; unquestionably he was present but unrecorded far more frequently than this. I would not agree that Crosby's statistical approach (embodied in his table *ibid.*) forms a valid basis for judgment on the relative political importance of English bishops of Henry's time, as the careers of several low-ranking bishops, Herbert among them, establish them as of far more importance than many who rank above them on the statistical table. One of Herbert's letters (*HE*, ep. 15) commends the activities of the priory to Prior Ingulf, and states that the bishop is going to court (Henry's?) without money and virtually without horses, but with God.

be established at Edwardstone.[169] Herbert's acknowledgement and assent, which reflected a kindly and gentle good humor, invited the archbishop to visit Norwich as he had often threatened.[170] We do not know whether the threatened call ever took place.

It is quite possible that Herbert's absence from the records after 1115, and the comparative decline in notices of him after 1110, may be related to advancing age and to increasing physical debility and illness. Certainly his letter of 1110, which mentions a leg ailment so severe that he could not move without assistance, is corroborated by later evidence from the chroniclers, culminating in the 1116 attack (below, pp. 116–117), the horror of which is preserved in the gruesome detailing of the syndrome by the sympathetic Eadmer and the gloating York canon Hugh the Chantor. We shall now return to more active, if no more happy, years and trace Herbert's career as curial bishop, diplomat, legate, and king's man.

II. Curialist and Legate

While Herbert Losinga was a central figure in his own East Anglian diocese, he was a peripheral, although not unimportant, participant in the great controversies affecting England in his lifetime. The late eleventh and early twelfth centuries were exciting and turbulent years, years of the growth and nascent centralization of the Norman monarchy in England and of the great ecclesiastical and spiritual revolution ignited by the Gregorian reformers. During the twenty-eight years in which Herbert was bishop of Thetford/Norwich, a profound readjustment of relations between crown and mitre and between the papacy and national churches was in convulsive progress.[1] As diocesan ordinary, Herbert's involvement with the reform program derived primarily from his simony and resultant repentance, while as Canterbury suffragan, royal diplomat, and papal legate he was ensnared in other aspects of the movement.

169. *Chron. Abingdon*, p. 63.
170. *HE*, ep. 38.
1. Particularly valuable studies of various aspects of the Gregorian reform include the following recent works: Tellenbach, *Christian Society*; T. E. Mommsen and Karl E. Morrison (eds.), *Imperial Lives and Letters of the Eleventh Century* (New York, 1962), pp. 3–51; Augustin Fliche, *La Réforme grégorienne et la reconquête chrétienne* (Paris, 1944) and his more exhaustive *La Réforme grégorienne*, 3 vols. (Louvain and Paris, 1924–37); Cantor, *Church in England*; Brooke, *English Church*; and Alfons Becker, *Studien zum Investiturproblem in Frankreich, 1049–1110* (Saarbrücken, 1955). Still of value are Böhmer, *Kirche und Staat*; P. Imbart de la Tour, *Les élections épiscopales dans l'église de France du IXe du XIIe siècles* (Paris, 1890).

As discussed above (pp. 127–129), the bishop of Thetford sought absolution from the pope for his simony; while with Urban, Herbert was designated *legatus missus* to Normandy to adjudicate a rancorous dispute involving the Abbey of the Holy Trinity at Fécamp. The other protagonist was William "Bona-Anima," Lanfranc's successor as abbot of St. Stephen's at Caen and archbishop of Rouen from 1079 to 1110.[2] His contentious relations with the papacy began upon his accession, when William had not troubled to seek his pallium from Rome, thus eliciting a testy letter from Gregory VII pointing out that the metropolitan was powerless to perform the functions of his office without this symbol.[3] Further, he had chronic difficulties with exempt monasteries in his province and was suspended as a consequence of at least one of the resulting disputes.[4] William exacerbated his uncertain relations with Rome by refusing to recognize Hugh of Lyons as primate of France in 1095, for which he earned another suspension,[5] and by concelebrating the marriage of Philip I of France with Bertrada de Montfort in 1093, a match which displeased the pope since both parties were already married to living spouses; again, the archbishop was temporarily deprived of his ecclesiastical authority.[6]

William's dispute with Fécamp centered on the vexed question of monastic exemption.[7] Exemption was not an innovation of the Gregorian reformers, although it was the topic of bitter opposition on the part of

2. Good brief biographical references for William are in G. H. Williams, *The Norman Anonymous of 1100 A.D.*, Harvard Theological Studies, XVIII (Cambridge, Mass., 1951), 111 ff.; Jean-François Lemarignier, *Étude sur les privileges d'exemption et de juridiction ecclésiastiques des abbayes normandes depuis les origines jusqu'en 1140* (Paris, 1937), pp. 193 ff.

3. *HF*, XIV, 33 and XV, 653; see also Guillaume Bessin (ed.), *Concilia Rotomagensis Provinciae*, I (Rouen, 1717), 74–75. The pall was first given by Gregory the Great as a symbol of authority: Wilhelm Levison, *England and the Continent in the Eighth Century* (Oxford, 1956), pp. 20 ff. From English custom, the use of the woolen stole as an essential function of metropolitan authority had become general practice by the ninth century: Barlow, *English Church*, p. 298, and see also Amann and Dumas, *L'Église au pouvoir des laïques*, p. 217.

4. *GC*, XI, cols. 37 ff.; Bessin (ed.), *Concilia*, I, 75–76.

5. Richer of Sens was included in the suspension: *HF*, XIV, 715–716.

6. *HF*, XIII, 14 and XV, 33; see also Cantor, *Church in England*, pp. 184 ff. and Becker, *Studien*, 86. William was restored through Anselm's intervention in 1106: Eadmer, *Historia*, pp. 177–178; Malmesbury, *GR*, p. 480; *HF*, XV, 33; Anselm, V, epp. 387 and 398 (Anselm to Paschal II, Paschal to William).

7. On exemption, see Lemarignier, *Exemption*, throughout, and his careful essay in Ferdinand Lot and Robert Fawtier (eds.), *Histoire des institutions françaises au moyen age*, Vol. III: *Institutions ecclésiastiques* (Paris, 1962), pp. 57–73; David Knowles, "The Growth of Monastic Exemption," *Downside Review* (May, 1932), pp. 201–231.

anti-Gregorian propagandists during William's lifetime.[8] Following the first grant of the privilege in 628, when Bobbio was freed from episcopal jurisdiction by Pope Honorius, exemption grew from three sources. Both secular and papal authorities had occasionally granted protection to monasteries against outside interference in their affairs, and the specific issue here involved—exemption from diocesan control granted to a monastery—was comparatively rare until the eleventh century.[9] This aspect of reform doctrine was a particularly rich source of controversy not only because the exempt monastery was under direct papal protection but also because the privilege of exemption tended to weaken the authority of diocesan bishops and to cause friction between them and the monasteries.

It is unnecessary to relate the complex history of the Fécamp exemption in the eleventh century, for Jean-François Lemarignier has treated the topic with his customary lucidity and thoroughness.[10] The key document in the house's series of exemption charters is the ducal instrument of 1006 which granted Fécamp autonomy in her relations with temporal powers, ensured free election of her abbot, and forbade any outside domination.[11] This last provision was, as Lemarignier has pointed out, "vague enough,"[12] and it had come to be interpreted as directed against archiepiscopal authority.

The trigger-action for the dispute presently under consideration did not involve Fécamp at all. The ill-starred Robert Curthose, duke of Normandy and brother of William II of England, had granted the manor of Gisors to Philip I in 1089: he had no right to do so as this was in the holdings of the church of St. Mary at Rouen rather than in his own. William of Rouen laid the province under interdict in retaliation for this act of ducal generosity, but the Fécamp Benedictines refused to obey the archiepiscopal discipline, claiming exemption from Rouen's jurisdiction

8. *MGH, Libelli de lite*, I–III; Tract 27 of the "York Anonymous" in Harald Scherrinsky, *Untersuchungen zum sogennanten Anonymus von York* (Würzburg-Aumühle, 1940), pp. 150–151, relates specifically to the Fécamp dispute; Mirbt, *Publizistik, passim*.

9. Knowles, "Exemption," p. 210.

10. Lemarignier, *Exemption*, pp. 34 ff., and 192 ff.

11. For the charter: Charles Homer Haskins, *Norman Institutions* (New York, 1960), pp. 252–255 and Plate 1; Marie Fauroux (ed.), *Recueil des actes des ducs de Normandie*, Memoires de la Société des Antiquaires de Normandie, XXXVI (Caen, 1961), nos. 4 and 9. For discussions, see Lemarignier, *Exemption*, pp. 34 ff., and 253–255, where he argues that the "outside domination" is a later interpolation, and David Douglas, "The First Ducal Charter for Fécamp," in de Povremogne, *Fécamp*, I, 45–46. A collection of the series of charters for Fécamp is in A. du Monstier, *Neustria pia* (Rouen, 1663), pp. 214 ff.

12. Lemarignier, *Exemption*, p. 34.

in the matter.[13] They first sought the protection of Duke Robert, but as he appeared to favor the metropolitan they then appealed to the pope, pleading that the archbishop had exceeded his authority by including their house in the interdict.

Urban II deputed Herbert Losinga, then a penitent at Rome, and Cardinal-Deacon Roger to bear the papal authority to Normandy. The Apostolic See judged William to have included Fécamp in the interdict improperly and his legates accordingly forbade William the use of his pallium, thus depriving him of metropolitan authority.[14] Duke Robert at once interceded for his archbishop, and the legates agreed to restore his pall pending the outcome of an appeal to Rome.[15] Herbert of Thetford departed at this point and returned to England and to his own deposition. The final determination of the conflict was papal affirmation of the 1093 bull, again requiring that the Fécamp privileges be respected by the archbishop of Rouen.[16] When next Herbert encountered the problem of exemption it was in his own diocese, and while the papacy held firmly to its policy as exemplified in the 1093 quarrel, the East Anglian bishop, acting in his own interests rather than as legate, fought vigorously against the policy for which he was a spokesman in 1093.

Of far more consequence than the Fécamp exemption dispute was the selection of the saintly Anselm of Bec as archbishop of Canterbury in 1093. The gentle scholar, yielding to the entreaties of the English episcopate and magnates and to those of the ailing and death-fearing king, was enthroned in the succession to St. Augustine at Canterbury in September

13. *Ibid.*, pp. 193–194; Böhmer, *Kirche und Staat*, pp. 146 and 183; Charles W. David, *Robert Curthose, Duke of Normandy* (Cambridge, Mass., 1920), pp. 81–82.

14. *GC*, XI, instr. xiv, 18–19, and cols. 207–208. The original bull is lost, but modern investigators conclude that 1093 was the year of the suspension: Williams, *Norman Anonymous*, p. 112; Lemarignier, *Exemption*, p. 194; Böhmer, *Kirche und Staat*, p. 144 n. 6.

15. *GC*, XI, instr. xiv, 19; cf. David, *Curthose*, p. 82.

16. J. von Pflugk-Harttung, *Acta pontificum romanorum inedita*, I (Tübingen, 1880), No. 83 (calendared Jaffé, *Regesta pontificum*, I, No. 5957), ann. 1103. Bull of Calixtus II to same intent, *Regesta pontificum*, I, No. 6776, ann. 1119. Of interest to the question of Rouen's authority as head and mother of the churches and abbeys in the province is Tract 3 of the "Anonymous of York" tracts (Böhmer, *Kirche und Staat*, pp. 449 ff.) and Tract 27 cited above p. 151 n. 8. Lemarignier, *Exemption*, pp. 198 ff., shows the attempt to prove that Fécamp was of greater antiquity than the metropolitanate of Rouen by the monks' invention of legends concerning the Precious Blood, Joseph of Arimathea's presence there, and so on; these pleasant stories are related in A. J. V. Leroux de Lincy, *Essai historique et littéraire sur l'abbaye de Fécamp* (Rouen, 1840), pp. 79–138. See now also B. de Mathan, "L'Abbaye de Fécamp dans les cahiers de Dom Lenoir," in de Povremogne, *Fécamp*, II, 260–263.

and consecrated in December, Herbert among the co-consecrators.[17] Anselm did not inherit a sympathetic episcopal bench; a suitably restrained comment is that the English bishop of the time was "not, in general, [a model] of great zeal and of edification."[18] Herbert is the particular exemplification of the general judgment.

The new archbishop was barely in possession of his spiritualities when his troubles with William Rufus began. Anselm and his king quarreled bitterly over the Canterbury temporalities, ecclesiastical jurisdiction, feudal relationships and obligations, relations with the royal advisors, questions of tenure and of ecclesiastical vacancies, the royal refusal to recognize a pope, and an entire range of matters which would today be described as falling under the heading of church-state relations.[19]

As the tenants-in-chief by knight service were the king's natural counsellors, so by analogy were the bishops of their metropolitan, but virtually all were curialists who owed their appointment and status in the realm to the king and who therefore did not care to oppose their patron. Anselm's position was soon worsened further by a deepening division of interest between his suffragans and himself. It is too facile to say that Anselm was interested in serving God and his suffragans in serving Caesar; each was trying to serve God and the king in his own way, but their disparate understandings of what this service meant in the context of their time made a workable symbiosis difficult.

The Rockingham Assembly of 1095, the first dramatic confrontation of issues and personalities in the new pontificate, encompassed rancorous, bitter debate, with William of St.-Calais, bishop of Durham, leading the attacks on Anselm.[20] The traditional royal rights claimed over the English church by the first Norman kings—the *exequatur*—were the central issue.[21] Anselm refused to recognize the Red King's claims, and Rufus hence "determined either to force the archbishop to renounce his allegiance to the pope, or to secure his banishment from the realm."[22] It is unnecessary

17. Eadmer, *Historia*, p. 42; Wilkins, *Concilia*, I, 370.

18. Albert du Boys, *L'Église et l'état en Angleterre depuis le conquête des normands* (Lyons and Paris, 1887), p. 86.

19. For the latest narrative and interpretation of Anselm's troubles with Rufus, see Cantor, *Church in England*, pp. 63 ff., and R. W. Southern, *St. Anselm and His Biographer* (Cambridge, 1963), pp. 150–163.

20. Eadmer, *Historia*, p. 53; *idem, Vita Anselmi archiepiscopi Cantuariensis*, ed. R. W. Southern (Edinburgh and London, 1962), pp. 85 ff.; Wilkins, *Concilia*, I, 373.

21. For comprehensive discussions of the exequatur, see especially Brooke, *English Church*, throughout, and Cantor, *Church in England*, pp. 12–109.

22. Cantor, *op. cit.*, pp. 79–80.

here to follow the proceedings in detail. The principal theme underlying the deliberations was Anselm's dual loyalty, to the pope as metropolitan and to the king as tenant-in-chief, of which he was all too sharply aware. When he was confronted with the choice of renouncing crown or tiara, his suffragans suggested that he rely on the king's good will. Quite naturally, he refused and took the position that since God had given him the archbishopric the king could not deprive him of it. The bishops, including Herbert,[23] supported their royal master but as the lay tenants supported Anselm the king failed to intimidate him. Stalemated, the assembly disbanded and the dispute passed into stages in which there is no evidence of Herbert's involvement. The conflict was not resolved during William II's lifetime, and Anselm finally sought relief from the king's continual hectoring by going into exile on the Continent in 1097.[24] Three years later Rufus met a death as mean, violent, and controversial as his life had been.

Henry, the late ruler's youngest brother, was a member of the hunting party accompanying William when he was slain in the New Forest. Abandoning the king's body in order to seize the kingdom, Henry rushed to Winchester immediately to secure the treasury and the crown. He did so on shaky grounds—his older brother Curthose clearly had the better claim to the throne, but Henry was not only a far abler man, he was present in England as well. To seize opportunity, one must be where the opportunity is. Hardly was he hastily enthroned when a rebellion erupted in favor of his brother, but the ecclesiastical order supported the new monarch rather than the pleasant, weak-willed duke of Normandy, whose amiably chaotic rule of his duchy had permitted evil times for the Norman church.[25] Whereas a sufficient number of barons supported Curthose to give Henry some uncomfortable moments, the king, aided by Anselm and judiciously promising reforms, succeeded in overcoming the threat to his new dignity by agreement with Robert in 1101.[26] Probably

23. Wilkins, *Concilia*, I, 373; only the bishop of Rochester (*solo excepto*) supported the primate; see also Eadmer, *Historia*, pp. 53–67.

24. While in exile Anselm became a determined High Gregorian reformer rather than retaining his former position. For important judgments and discussions on this transformation, see Southern, *St. Anselm*, pp. 160–163; Cantor, *Church in England*, Chap. 3; Böhmer, *Kirche und Staat*, pp. 155–156; Felix Liebermann, *Anselm von Canterbury und Hugo von Lyon* (Hanover, 1886), throughout. Eadmer has chronicled the period in *Historia*, pp. 88 ff., and in the *Vita Anselmi*, pp. 93 ff.

25. On Robert Curthose, see David, *Curthose*.

26. The latest narrative of the rebellion is that of Austin Lane Poole, *From Domesday Book to Magna Carta*, 2nd ed. (Oxford, 1955), pp. 97 ff. See also David, *Curthose*, pp. 131 ff.

linked with this feudal rebellion is a royal precept of August, 1101, addressed to Earl Roger Bigod and others, directing that justice be done to Bishop Herbert against the men of William de Warenne—earl of Surrey and one of the rebels favoring Robert—who had molested the bishop's men and infringed his rights at Thornham, and against any royal ministers who may have aided these rebels.[27]

Anselm had returned quickly from exile upon being notified of Rufus' death, but not quickly enough to officiate at the coronation of the new king. Promptly taking the leadership of the Henrician party, the archbishop set about rallying the nation behind the monarch. He permitted Henry to marry Edith (Matilda), great-granddaughter of Edmund Ironside, thus giving nuptial continuity with the Anglo-Saxon royal house and securing a marriage alliance with her brother the king of Scots.[28] Henry's accession had been immediately followed by promulgation of his coronation charter and, among the many unkept promises therein contained, he pledged to reverse his late brother's ecclesiastical policies.[29]

The king and the archbishop cooperated well in the early months of the reign and it is perhaps not overstating to say that Henry owed his throne to Anselm's staunch support. Despite the promising beginning, Henry's relations with his metropolitan were soon racked upon the issue which gave the Gregorian reform its traditional name—investiture. Henry expected Anselm to do him homage for his archiepiscopal holdings, and Anselm felt obliged to refuse this ceremony. Neither man wished a confrontation over the matter, and the king readily accepted Anselm's proposal that the papal policy on the subject be ascertained: until the pope's wishes were known, the archbishop would enjoy his temporalities without either homage or royal investiture. Paschal II, aptly described by Norman F. Cantor as a "dour old monk," sent messages to England in which he refused to modify Rome's dicta within the kingdom. Investiture of clerics by laymen was forbidden. It appeared that once again the familiar deadlock was recurring but Anselm elected, with royal consent, to persuade Paschal that it would be wise to make an exception in the high Gregorian policy for England.

27. *Regesta* II, No. 542.
28. Anselm also held a council which determined Matilda's eligibility for the marriage, rejecting the popular opinion that she had taken religious vows (Eadmer, *Historia*, pp. 121 ff.; Wilkins, *Concilia*, I, 357–376). Southern, *St. Anselm*, pp. 188–190, discounts Anselm's "glad heart" in supporting the royal match.
29. William Stubbs, *Select Charters*, ed. H. W. C. Davis, 9th ed. (Oxford, 1913), pp. 117-119.

This was not an unreasonable request; the third Norman monarch had shown himself properly respectful and friendly toward the primate and he was sympathetic to those aspects of the Gregorian program which did not limit royal power. Accordingly a mission set out for Rome in October of 1101. Archbishop Anselm's representatives were two monks, Baldwin of Bec and Alexander of Canterbury. Three curialist bishops—Gerard of Hereford (then archbishop-elect of York), Robert of Chester, and Herbert Losinga of Norwich—acted as the king's emissaries.[30]

Why did Henry select Herbert as his spokesman? We know little of the relations between the two men, but the king's selection of the bishop at least reflected an attitude of trust. Herbert's opinion of the king is difficult to assess. In a letter to John, apparently a layman but otherwise unidentifiable, he wrote that "after King Henry nothing in the world is more precious to me than your love,"[31] but such effusiveness was not uncommon in medieval letters and is not to be taken literally.[32] A letter to the king is fawning and adulatory, thanking him for some unspecified favor and acknowledging the writer's total dependence on the royal grace—Henry is even advantageously compared with Constantine and Theodosius.[33] But again, is this sincerity or merely literary convention? In all probability it was sincere gratitude conventionally expressed. Certainly if we are to judge Herbert's relations with his sovereign on the basis of action rather than of letters, there is no doubt that throughout his life, after 1093, the bishop was a dedicated and loyal curialist.

On the way to Rome, Bishop Herbert got ahead of his companions and found himself in a situation demonstrating the hazards of medieval travel, for he was captured by a brigand, Guy of Lyons, a misfortune also suffered by Anselm in 1097 while on his way to Italy.[34] Guy seems to have had a remarkable interest in the English investiture controversy, refusing to release the bishop of Norwich until Herbert swore on relics to act neither against Anselm nor against his interests when he reached Rome.[35]

30. Eadmer, *Historia*, pp. 132–133 and 137; Malmesbury, *GP*, p. 107; *Annales Monastici* [cited above n. 8], II, 41; *Itin. H. I*, pp. 12 and 16. The embassy was still in Rome in April, 1102 (Jaffé, *Regesta pontificum*, No. 5909). Goulburn and Symonds, *Life*, pp. 235 ff., misplaced this mission in 1107, after carefully marshaling the evidence for 1101/1102 and dismissing it.

31. *HE*, ep. 45.   32. See, for example, Southern, *St. Anselm*, pp. 69–70.

33. *HE*, ep. 11.

34. Achille Luchaire, *Les prémiers Capétiens, 987–1137*, Part 2, in Ernest Lavisse, *Histoire de France*, II² (Paris, 1901), 69. Luchaire asked, "Est-ce un legende?"

35. Eadmer, *Historia*, p. 133; Malmesbury, *GP*, pp. 107–108; *Memorials of St. Edmund's Abbey*, I, 354. See also Charles de Rémusat, *Sainte Anselme de Cantorbéry* (Paris, 1853), p. 301.

Subsequent events were to provide practical evidence for the canon law principle that oaths extracted under duress are invalid. Herbert's entourage was not similarly liberated until he enriched Guy by 40 marks, which it was charged he was bearing to Rome as lubrication for the gears of papal decision in the bishop's Bury project (see below, pp. 158–160).[36] I am inclined to doubt this suggestion of bribery—travel costs money, and there is nothing sinister in travelers carrying it. Furthermore, the amount is too small for such a purpose, and Paschal obviously was not the type of pope who would sell favors. One cannot say, however, that Herbert was the type of man who would never have thought of bribing the successor of St. Peter.

The diplomatic mission of the three bishops did not succeed with Paschal, who not only was intransigent in his refusal to make exceptions in his general policy against lay investiture but was nettled that the royal envoys had been so lacking in discretion as even to suggest a modification for England.[37] When the mission returned home late in the summer of 1102, the great reform council so long anticipated by Anselm convened at Westminster. It forthwith considered the papal decisions. The archiepiscopal and royal emissaries brought letters from the pope, among them one each for Anselm and for Henry. The archbishop permitted any who might wish to do so to read his epistle, which refused compromise on the lay investiture issue.[38] The king concealed his own letter and maintained that letters did not count: obedience did.[39] He did not refer to his own disobedience to the papal instruction, which absolutely forbade any lay investiture in England.

The three royal spokesmen then muddied the water further by announcing that the pope had made an oral statement to them, which differed not only from Anselm's but also from the king's letter. Paschal had assured them, and Henry through them, that he would not discipline the monarch so long as only duly ordained men were invested with the crozier and so long as Henry lived an exemplary life in other respects—the message was not in writing in order that other rulers might not learn of it and arrogate similar rights to themselves.[40] The bishops swore the truth

36. Eadmer, *Historia*, p. 134; Malmesbury and *Memorials* as in n. 35.
37. Eadmer, *Historia*, p. 134.
38. Malmesbury, *GP*, p. 108; Eadmer, *Historia*, p. 140. The pope's letter is in Anselm, IV, ep. 222, and in Eadmer, *Historia*, pp. 135–136 (calendared *Regesta pontificum*, No. 5905 [see also No. 5908]).
39. Eadmer, *Historia*, pp. 133–135; Malmesbury, *GP*, p. 108; Anselm, IV, ep. 224.
40. Eadmer, *Historia*, pp. 137–141.

of their report, the monks vehemently denied it, and great confusion prevailed.

Anselm, bewildered and hesitant at being placed in a position where whatever he did would seem to be against papal command, again suggested a solution to the new quandary. Let yet another embassy be sent to Rome to determine the pontiff's true intentions, and in the meantime the truce would continue whereby the archbishop would not excommunicate either the king or any who received his investiture. Henry readily agreed to the suggestion, and cheerfully proceeded to invest Roger the Larderer with the temporalities of Hereford and his chancellor Roger with those of Salisbury.[41] Herbert Losinga and his companions were understandably not utilized for this new mission.

The result of the new confrontation with the pope was not ambiguous: a papal letter to Anselm (December, 1102) affirmed that Alexander and Baldwin had indeed reported the truth, that he stood by his prior letter to Anselm, and that the former royal envoys were to be excommunicated immediately.[42] Another letter written at about the same time to Anselm by Cardinal John (of Tusculum?) referred to Herbert, Gerard, and Robert as "false bishops."[43] Herbert was apparently restored to grace through the good offices of his king, an absolution permitted by Paschal although he insisted that the transgression of the bishops not go unpunished.[44] Anselm, writing to Gerard, imparted his own personal forgiveness to the three cunning curialists.[45]

While at Rome, Herbert pursued a matter of personal and diocesan ambition as well as the king's business discussed above. The bishop planned to bring the wealthy and exempt abbey of Bury St. Edmunds under diocesan jurisdiction, thus continuing a policy begun by his predecessor-but-one, Herfast. There is little point, for the purposes of this study, in carrying the history of the Bury exemption dispute back to 1070, for David Knowles has thoroughly discussed the topic.[46] Herfast, prior to his

41. *Ibid.*, p. 141.

42. Anselm, IV, epp. 280 and 281; Eadmer, *Historia*, pp. 140, 149–151; Malmesbury, *GP*, pp. 491–492; Wilkins, *Concilia*, I, 381.

43. Anselm, IV, ep. 284; Holtzmann, *Papsturkunden*, II, No. 5.

44. Anselm, V, ep. 397 (March 23, 1106); Eadmer, *Historia*, pp. 178–179.

45. Anselm, IV, ep. 250.

46. Knowles, "Exemption," pp. 208 ff. See also Lemarignier, *Exemption*, pp. 146 ff.; R. H. C. Davis, "The Monks of St. Edmund, 1021–1148," *History*, XL, No. 140 (October, 1955), 226–239; V. H. Galbraith, "The East Anglian See and the Abbey of Bury St. Edmund's," *English Historical Review*, XL (1925), 222–228; H. W. C. Davis, "The Liberties of Bury St. Edmund's," *ibid.*, XXIV (1909), 417–431.

consecration a not over-bright royal chaplain, first moved against Bury
in 1070. Perhaps he did, as he stated, wish to move the see city there from
Thetford; this would not have been unusual in the immediate post-
Conquest period, which embraced the transfer of several diocesan seats.[47]
It is perhaps more likely that greed was the hidden motive, however,
for Bury was not only wealthy but had a continuing source of income
from the pilgrims attracted to the shrine of St. Edmund the Martyr.

Herfast's strategy began with an attempt to recover episcopal jurisdiction over the monastery, but unfortunately for his designs Archbishop
Lanfranc gave Abbot Baldwin of Bury permission to seek papal protection
from Rome; hence in 1071 Pope Alexander II confirmed the exemption
and placed the monastery under Canterbury's protection.[48] Lanfranc,
however, disapproved the papal bull since it enhanced papal authority in
England, and therefore confiscated it from Baldwin.[49] The archbishop
delayed for nearly a decade before instituting proceedings in Bury's
behalf, ignoring a tart papal letter of 1073 in which Gregory VII complained of the primate's apparent laxity in the case.[50] A council held at
Winchester in 1081 rejected Herfast's claims on the basis of royal charters
and of precedent, without considering papal documents.[51] There is

47. Above, p. 131. On Herfast's motives in moving to Bury, see *Memorials of St.
Edmund's Abbey*, I, 60 and 345; Lemarignier, *Exemption*, p. 146; Knowles, "Exemption,"
pp. 209–210. Galbraith, "East Anglian See," pp. 227–228, prints a document presenting
the Norwich argument against Bury based on the claim of ancient jurisdiction over the
abbey.

48. The bull is in *PL*, CXLVI, cols. 1363–1364; Lord Francis Hervey (ed.), *The
Pinchbeck Register Relating to the Abbey of Bury-St.-Edmury's, &c.* (Brighton, 1925), pp. 3–4;
Memorials of St. Edmund's Abbey, I, 345–347; *Monasticon*, III, 140–141. Lemarignier
(*Exemption*, p. 147 n. 5) discusses the authenticity of the documents in the St. Edmund's
sources and shows that the papal (rather than archiepiscopal) protection is interpolated.
The bull in Migne recognizes Canterbury's protection of Bury, as do the narratives of
Eadmer (*Historia*, p. 132) and William of Malmesbury (*GP*, p. 156).

49. Eadmer, *Historia*, p. 133. Davis, "Monks of St. Edmund," p. 234, suggested that
Alexander's bull forbidding the move of the East Anglian see to Bury was against Lanfranc's policy of moving sees to more populous or geographically well-situated locations.
I am inclined to doubt this, as Bury was neither particularly populous nor well-located to
be a center of diocesan administration.

50. Hervey (ed.), *Pinchbeck Register*, pp. 49–50; Lanfranc, *Opera omnia*, ed. J. A. Giles
(London, 1844), I, ep. 23; Gregory VII, *Register*, ed. Erich Caspar (*MGH, Epistolae
selectae*, II [Berlin, 1920]), pp. 51–52.

51. Lanfranc's reliance on secular considerations rather than on papal bulls in settling
the matter appears in his letter to Herfast (*Opera*, I, ep. 26). For the documents determining the disposition of the controversy, see *Regesta* I, Nos. 137, 138, 139; Davis regarded
No. 137 as a possible forgery, but Knowles ("Exemption," p. 211 n. 4) is probably

no evidence that Herfast later renewed the attempt against Bury's liberties.

Herbert Losinga revived the issue while with the pope in 1093, but met with no success.[52] In the following year he attempted to pontificate at the translation of St. Edmund's relics at Bury, but the abbot read him the privileges of his house and refused the bishop's demand. Ranulf Flambard and Walkelin of Winchester officiated at the ceremony.[53]

When Herbert was in Rome in 1101/1102 he argued at the curia that the great abbey had been formerly under diocesan jurisdiction and should be restored to that status, but Paschal gave him no satisfaction. Upon his return to England the bishop attempted to have Bury's privileges revoked by the Council of Westminster, but there were dignitaries there who recalled the 1081 decision and the reasons for it. Again he failed.[54] King Henry reconfirmed the Bury liberties and Herbert was shortly inundated with royal writs relating to the abbey and its affairs.[55] He did not again devote his considerable talents to this elusive cause.

---

correct in his assertion that "the fact and substance of the document are certain." The charter in question may be consulted in *Monasticon*, III, 141, and in *Memorials of St. Edmund's Abbey*, I, 347. Also relating to the dispute is David C. Douglas (ed.), *Feudal Documents from the Abbey of Bury St. Edmund's*, The British Academy: Records of the Social and Economic History of England and Wales, VIII (London, 1932), No. 7 (also in *Memorials of St. Edmund's Abbey*, I, 350). The somewhat partisan narrative of the judgment is in *Memorials of St. Edmund's Abbey*, I, 65 ff.

52. Galbraith, "East Anglian See," p. 227, and see the brief note to which this document is appended for an estimate of its reliability. While a forgery, it has value in demonstrating the Norwich claims against Bury.

53. *Memorials of St. Edmund's Abbey*, I, 86–88. Ranulf, who was not created bishop of Durham until 1099, was at this time royal chaplain (*Randulfus capellanus regis*).

54. *Ibid.*, I, 353–355 and III, 5; see also Knowles, *Monastic Order*, p. 586, and *idem*, "Exemption," p. 212. It is doubtful that the St. Edmund's claim (*Memorials of St. Edmund's Abbey*, I, 353) that Herbert wanted to move the diocesan seat to Bury is true, since he had already well begun the construction of his new cathedral and priory at Norwich, of which the St. Edmund's chronicler was aware as he recorded a Bury pledge to aid in the building of the cathedral (*ibid.*, 362). Greed was more likely the motivation, as well as resentment of Bury's exempt status. A diocese was eventually erected there: St. Edmundsbury, founded in 1914 by the Church of England.

55. For the charters, see the following documents which I have correlated thus, while omitting all *Regesta* citations: *FD* represents Douglas (ed.), *Feudal Documents*, and *LB*, Davis, "Liberties of Bury." References are to document, not to page, numbers. Charter of liberties, 1102/1103: *FD*, 21; *LB*, viii; *Cal. Charter Rolls*, II, 258; confirmed *FD*, 22 (probably 1103). Grant of warrens and hunting privileges to Bury, 1103: *FD*, 23; *LB*, ix. Freedom from certain taxes: *FD*, 24; *LB*, x. Grant of land in Stoneham (Sf): *FD*, 26. Bury placed under the king's special protection: *FD*, 28. Bury's freedom from certain taxes:

The Council of Westminster before which the bishop pursued his quest for Bury was probably the most important reform council of Anselm's pontificate. Following the customary Anglo-Norman practice, the king supported those elements of reform which did not infringe royal prerogatives and privileges, and there was ample opportunity for the purely spiritual and moral renewal of the English church. The council deposed the abbots of nine important religious houses (including those of Ramsey, Ely, and Bury) for simony and for other causes,[56] and the conciliar decrees reflect the penetration of the Gregorian reform program into England.[57] Archdeacons had henceforth to be in deacon's orders and not to farm their offices. No one in deacon's orders or above was to be married and in the future even candidates for the subdiaconate (as well as for orders) could not receive ordination without the vow of chastity. Sons of priests were not to inherit their fathers' livings, and priests who persisted in living either with their wives or with concubines were to be avoided by their flocks. The council forbade clergy to act as judges in secular trials and ordered them to refrain from other primarily temporal functions in government and administration, while further restricting abbots and monks from participation in worldly affairs. Other decrees dealt with miscellaneous matters of clerical dress and conduct. Many decrees of this council were renewed at London in 1108[58] and again in 1109,[59] with Herbert present at both.

An interesting letter from the primate to Herbert belongs to the period shortly after the 1102 council. It exhorted the bishop to persevere in promoting obedience to the conciliar decrees, particularly those related to celibacy and clerical incontinence. The diocesan had asked Anselm's advice, which was to expel all clergy of his see who refused to obey the canons of the council, even if his parochial clergy were thus so depleted

---

FD, 27; *LB*, xi. Moneyer and customs at Bury: *FD*, 29; *LB*, xiii. Grant of land formerly held by Peter of Bourges: *FD*, 30. Bury to hold freely 8½ hundreds: *FD*, 32; *LB*, xiv. Freedom of certain Bury lands from taxes: *FD*, 33; *LB*, xii. Confirmation of possessions: *FD*, 35; *LB*, vii.

56. Eadmer, *Historia*, p. 141; Symeon of Durham, *Historia regum*, p. 235; and many others. Aldwin of Ramsey was reinstated in 1107 (Eadmer, *Historia*, p. 187). As mentioned above, he succeeded Herbert Losinga as abbot of Ramsey.

57. The decrees are readily available: for example, see Eadmer, *Historia*, pp. 141–144; Malmesbury, *GP*, pp. 119–121; Wilkins, *Concilia*, I, 382–384; Mansi, *Concilia*, XX, cols. 1149–1154.

58. Eadmer, *Historia*, pp. 193–195; Wilkins, *Concilia*, I, 387–388; Mansi, *Concilia*, XX, cols. 1229–1232.

59. Eadmer, *Historia*, pp. 212–213; Wilkins, *Concilia*, I, 390–391.

in number that monks had to fill parish appointments until secular clergy could be found to replace them.[60]

Some historians have conferred a dignity upon Herbert Losinga which King Henry did not bestow—the royal chancellorship in 1104. While he does appear in some secondary works as holder of the office, none document the assertion.[61] The only evidence for the allegation was presented in the *Life* of Herbert, but it will not bear the interpretation placed upon it by Goulburn and Symonds. The authors discussed the secondary material, arguing on the basis of authority: Henry Spelman and T. Duffus Hardy stated it, therefore it is so. They then presented a charter in the London Tower *cartae antiquae* (Y 31) bearing the inscription, among the witnesses, "... rt ... C ...." which they interpreted [Herbe]rt[o] C[ancellario] to prove their hypothesis. The instrument is a grant of Cheveley manor (Camb.) by Roger fitzRichard to Ralph Pecche (incorrectly inverted by Goulburn and Symonds). While it is not in the published *cartae antiquae* rolls,[62] it is calendared in the *Regesta* and referred to 1133 (1127 at the earliest).[63] This document therefore excludes Herbert as a witness, since he was dead before its signing.[64]

Anselm was driven again into exile as a result of the pope's refusal to permit a relaxation of his policy against lay investiture for England, and during this period (1103–1107) King Henry systematically spoliated the church, causing even his most faithful episcopal servants to turn to Anselm

60. Anselm, IV, ep. 254.
61. Capgrave, *Liber de illust. Henricis*, p. 207 n.; Blomefield, *Norfolk*, III, 469; John Campbell, *Lives of the Lord Chancellors and Keepers of the Great Seal of England*, I; new ed. by John Allan Mallory (Boston, 1911), 56. Others are cited in Goulburn and Symonds, *Life*, pp. 323 ff., and are largely antiquarian authorities.
62. John Horace Round (ed.), *Ancient Charters*, Pipe Roll Society, X (London, 1888); Landon (ed.), *Cartae antiquae Rolls*; J. Conway Davies (ed.), *Cartae antiquae Rolls 11–20*, Pipe Roll Society, N.S., XXXIII (London, 1960).
63. *Regesta* II, No. 1776. There is some doubt of this charter's authenticity.
64. Goulburn and Symonds argued as further evidence for Herbert's chancellorship the results of the careful research of Humphrey Prideaux, dean of Norwich, 1702–1724. Dean Prideaux reconstructed the "Founder's Tomb" in the cathedral, since the original cenotaph had been destroyed in the iconoclasm of the civil war. While Dean Prideaux's published correspondence reveals both industry and imagination in his historical inquiries (*Letters of Humphrey Prideaux to John Ellis*, ed. Edward Maunde Thompson, Camden N.S., XV [Westminster, 1875], especially pp. 121–122), one cannot but conclude that his imagination in this instance triumphed over his industry, for the new epitaph as written by the dean named Herbert chancellor (Goulburn and Symonds, *Life*, pp. 331–332). The original inscription omitted mention of this dignity (John Weever, *Funeral Monuments*, p. 787 ff., appendix in Goulburn and Symonds, *Life*, pp. 406–407).

for protection against the predatory monarch. Among these curialists were Gerard of York, Robert of Chester, Ranulf of Chichester, Samson of Worcester, William of Winchester, and Herbert of Norwich, who jointly wrote the absent archbishop in 1106 begging his return in rather fulsome style, as his sheep were without their shepherd.[65] Anselm replied (not without arch reference to the bishops' past conduct against him) that while he sympathized with their predicament and welcomed their expressions of unconditional support he could not return to England until the investiture conflict were settled, for the king would not permit it unless Anselm betrayed papal policy.[66]

Later in that year a compromise settlement was finally effected, and a council of 1107 confirmed it; the solution was really a royal victory, for while Henry did surrender lay investiture and agree to accept ecclesiastical counsel as to the fitting candidate for vacancies, he nevertheless retained the right to receive homage from the elect *before* he would be invested with his spiritualities and receive consecration.[67] Herbert was present at this council, for he assisted in the consecration of five bishops which immediately followed.[68]

The end of the investiture controversy did not thereby mean the end of conflict for the saintly archbishop; his last years were poisoned by the eruption of a dormant problem whose taproot lay five centuries in the past. The question of primacy over the English church would seem to have been settled on several past occasions, and certainly in fact and by precedent the archbishop of Canterbury was metropolitan of England. But York also had claims, and whenever after the Conquest a new archbishop of either province was to be consecrated the haggling between the two flared up anew, fanned by the pressures, pride, and often by the outright mendacity of the respective chapters, the canons of York and the monks of Christ Church, Canterbury.[69] The recurrence of the feud in 1108 brought Herbert of Norwich into the vortex of events which he did not

65. Eadmer, *Historia*, pp. 171–174; on Anselm's second exile, see *ibid.*, pp. 149 ff. and *idem*, *Vita Anselmi*, pp. 132 ff. The letter is in Anselm, V, ep. 386 (also in Eadmer, *Historia*, pp. 173–174, and Wilkins, *Concilia*, I, 384).

66. Anselm, V, ep. 387 (also in Eadmer, *Historia*, pp. 174–175, and Wilkins, *Concilia*, I, 385).

67. Cantor, *Church in England*, p. 268.

68. Eadmer, *Historia*, p. 187; Wilkins, *Concilia*, I, 386–387; Mansi, *Concilia*, XX, cols. 1227–1230.

69. On the controversy and its history, see Eadmer, *Historia*; Hugh the Chantor, with Charles Johnson's perceptive introduction; Southern, *St. Anselm*, pp. 129 ff.; and Margarete Dueball, *Der Suprematstreit zwischen den Erzdiözen Canterbury und York, 1070–1126* (Ebering's *Historische Studien*, Heft 184 [Berlin, 1929]).

control, but influenced. Again he became his archbishop's envoy, his king's spokesman, and an emissary to Rome.

Of the weight of historical precedence on Canterbury's side there is no doubt. When Lanfranc advanced claims to the primacy shortly after the Conquest, a council held in 1072 decided in his favor and established certain details of the relationship between Canterbury and York. The Humber River was defined as the division between the two provinces, leaving York with only one suffragan (Durham). The northern archbishop and his suffragan(s) were both to attend and to be obedient to any council called in England by the archbishop of Canterbury and he was to consecrate a Canterbury archbishop-elect in Canterbury, while a York elect had to travel to Kent for his own consecration. But the papacy did not confirm these canons, and Thomas of York further made his own profession to Lanfranc alone on the condition that the profession be a personal one only, neither binding York prelates to submission to Canterbury nor binding Thomas himself to any archbishop of Canterbury other than Lanfranc.[70] The problem did not arise again when Thomas died in 1100, for his successor Gerard had been bishop of Hereford and thus did not require consecration—merely enthronement. But when Gerard died in 1108, Thomas II was elected to the York succession, and he refused primatial obedience to Canterbury.[71]

Anselm and Thomas exchanged several letters in 1108, but failed to come to an agreement.[72] Herbert of Norwich traveled to York to confer with the elect and persuade him that he need not make a profession to Canterbury if he would recognize Anselm as primate. Thomas refused, trusting in the king's support.[73]

The York historian Hugh the Chantor at this point in his narrative inserted a patently forged papal letter into his *History of the Church of York*.[74] It purports to be a missive from Urban II empowering Herbert,

70. Malmesbury, *GP*, pp. 41 ff.; Hugh the Chantor, pp. 2–7; Godfrey, *Church in Anglo-Saxon England*, pp. 421 ff.; Donald Nicholl, *Thurstan, Archbishop of York* (York, 1964), pp. 36 ff.

71. For the development of the dispute under Anselm, see Southern, *St. Anselm*, pp. 127 ff. Southern presents a convincing argument that the Canterbury primacy claim had far deeper meaning than being simply a "barren and unedifying wrangle with York," and represented an attempt to return to the wide powers and privileged position of the Canterbury prelate in the days of the see's founder St. Augustine.

72. Anselm, V, epp. 443–445, 451–456, 462, 470, 472.

73. Hugh the Chantor, p. 18.

74. *Ibid.*, pp. 6–7. Helene Tillmann, *Die päpstlichen Legaten in England bis zur Beendigung der Legationen Gualas* (Bonn, 1926), p. 19, objects to the document's genuineness solely on grounds of chronological derangement.

with Cardinal-Deacon R[oger?], as legate in the primacy conflict. The letter is dated 1089, two years before Herbert's elevation to the prelacy, and he is named bishop of Thetford in the document. The instrument clearly misrepresented past papal policy, for it stated that Gregory the Great in his commission to Augustine of Canterbury had decreed precedence to whichever archbishop, Canterbury or York, had been consecrated first, while Gregory's original letter had thus designated those of York and London.[75] While Herbert did consult with Thomas II in 1108, Hugh could hardly have innocently confused this Thomas with his namesake, for there was a different elect, a different pope, no papal letter in 1108 to this sense, and no assistance from Cardinal-Deacon Roger. And certainly Hugh, a contemporary of Herbert and of Thomas II, did not absentmindedly confuse the 1093 Fécamp legation with one to his own house (and probably in his own presence). His motivation for interpolating a forged document is not obscure—the York canon was a strong partisan of his chapter's claims.

While the dispute dragged on, Anselm died (April 2, 1109) after deputing Herbert of Norwich and Gundulf of Rochester to consult with other bishops of the English church concerning the problem.[76] A council convened in 1109 temporarily ended the controversy: the English bishops, all but one being Canterbury suffragans, supported the Canterbury position, as did the king.[77] The extent of the royal support in which Thomas had placed so much faith was meager indeed. At the king's bidding, Herbert of Norwich announced that the York prelate was making his profession because it was the royal will that he do so. Ranulf Flambard of Durham, York's only suffragan, further explained that the king's decision did not intend that the position of York be compromised for the future or that this profession constitute precedent.[78] The elect of York reluctantly made his submission, reiterating (as had Thomas I) that this was a personal act not intended to jeopardize York's liberties, and

75. Gregory the Great, *Registrum epistolarum*, ed. Paul Ewald and Ludwig Hartmann (*MGH, Epistolae*, I and II [Berlin, 1891 and 1899]), II, 312–313; Bede, *Hist. ecclesiasticam*, pp. 63–64; A. W. Haddan and William Stubbs (eds.), *Councils and Ecclesiastical Documents Relating to Great Britain and Ireland* (Oxford, 1869–73), III, 29. Malmesbury, *GP*, pp. 41 ff., prints the relevant papal bulls and conciliar decisions from the time of Gregory I to his own.

76. Anselm, V, ep. 464 (to Samson of Worcester).

77. Eadmer, *Historia*, pp. 207–210; Hugh the Chantor, pp. 23–31; Wilkins, *Concilia*, I, 390–391; Mansi, *Concilia*, XX, cols. 1233–1238.

78. Hugh the Chantor, pp. 29–30; the royal letter (calendared *Regesta* II, No. 916) supports Ranulf's and Herbert's claims.

accepted consecration to his province in 1109, Herbert Losinga among the co-consecrators.[79]

The York controversy smoldered beneath the ashes until the death of Thomas II in the spring of 1114. On May 16 the long widowhood of Canterbury finally ended with the enthronement of Ranulf d'Escures, bishop of Rochester, as the saintly Anselm's successor, and the bishop of Norwich was doubtless present when Ranulf assumed the pallium brought by the papal legate Anselm of St. Saba.[80] Whereas Ranulf's predecessor had been sympathetic to the Gregorian reform program in its entirety, he was one of more moderate inclination. Although no sycophant, Ranulf worked well with the king.

The new archbishop had not long to wait before defending his rights against York. Thurstan, a former canon of St. Paul's, London, and a man of firm character and strong personality, was elected to the northern province shortly after Ranulf's enthronement. Supported enthusiastically by his canons, Thurstan refused to make his profession to Canterbury.[81]

At about the same time another traditional conflict arose to bedevil Ranulf of Canterbury. The exequatur had continued to be English royal policy, despite papal opposition, following the deaths of Lanfranc and of William the Conqueror and however wrong these "ancient customs" may have been from the point of view of Rome, nevertheless they were still royal policy. A renewal of legatine activities in England and in Normandy in 1114 and 1115 caused the king to convoke a council in September of the latter year for the defense of the old tradition in two aspects: that the monarch's permission be obtained prior to admission of papal legates, messages, and jurisdiction, and that no appeals from ecclesiastical courts or episcopal visits to Rome be permitted without royal approval.

King Henry received several letters from Paschal in this year, all complaining with asperity of English conduct toward the papacy. The king had interfered in Paschal's policies and programs, it was alleged—he had forbidden English bishops to attend councils called by the pontiff, he had excluded legates from his lands, he had ignored the wishes of Rome, and he had even permitted translation of bishops without the pope's knowledge, let alone his approval.[82] How, asked Paschal, was he to

---

79. *Ibid.*, p. 29; Eadmer, *Historia*, pp. 209–211; other sources—Ralph of Diceto, "Matthew of Westminster," and others—derive from later centuries.

80. Eadmer, *Historia*, pp. 222–230.

81. Hugh the Chantor, pp. 33 ff.; Eadmer, *Historia*, pp. 237 ff. On Ranulf and Thurstan, and their mutual relations, see Southern, *St. Anselm*, pp. 305–307, and Nicholl, *Thurstan*, especially pp. 49 ff.

82. Eadmer, *Historia*, pp. 228–231 and 238 ff.; Hugh the Chantor, p. 54; Mansi, *Concilia*, XX, col. 1066.

feed his sheep and strengthen his brethren if he knew nothing of their state?[83] The council, held at Westminster and attended by Herbert, advised that envoys be sent to Rome to discuss these grievances with Paschal.

Meanwhile the York controversy had grown in intensity and in bitterness, as Thurstan persisted for more than a year in refusing profession to Canterbury. The York elect, encouraged—even goaded—by his chapter defied ancient custom in 1116 by making Paschal the judge of the quarrel over the primacy, thus compelling Ranulf as well to appeal to the same source of judgment. These appeals followed fruitless attempts to prevent such action. A council had met in Lent of 1116 to consider the feud, but its efforts to make Thurstan submit to Canterbury were in vain—he resigned his appointment to the king rather than yield.[84] The former elect then followed the king to Normandy where, like Anselm, he informed the king that he could not resign to the monarch those things which only God could give: withdrawing his resignation, he repented his error.[85]

Ranulf did not delay in following up Thurstan's appeal to the pope, but left for Rome late in 1116 accompanied by Herbert of Norwich, Abbot Hugh of Chertsey, and William of Corbeil, then a canon of Canterbury.[86] The envoys were to carry out the 1115 council's mandate to secure a settlement of the difficulties with the papacy as well as to achieve a decision favorable to Canterbury in the dispute over the primacy. First the mission was delayed by the illness of the archbishop, who suffered a carbuncle attack so severe that his head swelled horribly.[87] Then, following Ranulf's recovery, Herbert of Norwich was stricken with an incapacity so grave that it prevented him from completing the journey. After he lay ill at Piacenza for several weeks the other members of the party proceeded to Rome and Herbert returned to Normandy.[88]

The embassy did not meet directly with the pope, who was at Benevento, but he replied to their representations by letters—which gave no hint of legatine difficulties—equivocally upholding the dignities of Canterbury without defining what they were. Paschal promised to settle the primacy issue when both Ranulf and Thurstan should be together

83. Eadmer, *Historia*, pp. 232–233.

84. *Ibid.*, pp. 238 ff.; Hugh the Chantor, pp. 41–43.

85. Hugh the Chantor, pp. 46 ff.

86. *Ibid.*, p. 50; Eadmer, *Historia*, p. 238.

87. Eadmer, *Historia*, pp. 239–240; Hugh the Chantor, p. 50; Malmesbury, *GP*, p. 129.

88. Hugh the Chantor (p. 50) gloated uncharitably over the illness; Eadmer, *Historia*, pp. 241–242.

before him,[89] but he died before he could fulfill his intention, and the Canterbury-York dispute dragged on beyond the deaths of Paschal and of his successor. The papacy eventually recognized York's claim to equality with Canterbury, salving the wound to the southern archbishopric by raising Canterbury's incumbent to *legatus natus* of the papacy.[90]

The abortive mission of 1116/1117 was Herbert's last appearance as a diplomat, and the Salisbury council of March, 1116 (on the succession question should Henry die) was his last recorded attendance at an ecclesiastical council.[91] Death overtook him on July 22, 1119, and he was entombed in the cathedral which he founded; among the mourners were his comprovincial bishops.[92] Father Francis Blomefield suggested the interesting thesis that Herbert was never canonized because of his efforts to implement conciliar decrees against incontinence,[93] but we are safer, if not so specific, in following the seventeenth-century antiquarian John Weever who noted that while the monks of his cathedral priory made efforts to have him recognized as a saint, "such impediments were alwaies in the way that it could not be obtained."[94]

Commemorative services were observed for Herbert Losinga at his priory on the Feast of St. Mary Magdalene and on the first day of the octave (July 22 and 23).[95] The last immediately contemporary notice of Herbert appeared on the death roll of Abbot Vitalis of Savigny, who died

89. Paschal's bull is in *PL*, CLXIII, cols. 417–418 (March 24, 1117); other contemporaneous papal letters relating to the topic can be found in Eadmer, *Historia*, pp. 242 ff.; Hugh the Chantor, pp. 54 ff.; Malmesbury, *GP*, pp. 129–130. All these print the relevant bull. The working-out of the controversy after Herbert's death can be traced in Hugh the Chantor and in Eadmer, and see above p. 163 n. 69; and in Nicholl, *Thurstan*, and Cantor, *Church in England*, pp. 300–309.

90. Holtzmann, *Papsturkunden*, II, No. 9; see Cantor, *Church in England*, pp. 312–313, and Southern, *St. Anselm*, pp. 130–132, on the importance of this legatine delegation.

91. The clerical order pledged to accept Henry's son William, doomed to perish in the wreck of the White Ship, as heir apparent; Eadmer, *Historia*, pp. 237 ff.; Wilkins, *Concilia*, I, 393–394.

92. *NR*, p. 56; Malmesbury, *GP*, p. 152; Symeon of Durham, *Historia regum*, p. 254; *Flor. Wig.*, *s.a.* 1119; all later narrative sources—John of Oxnede, Matthew Paris, Ralph of Coggeshall, Bartholomew Cotton, Roger of Hoveden, "Matthew of Westminster," and others—borrow from these contemporaneous chronicles. Bartholomew Cotton, p. 391, tells us of the mourners. A discrepancy in the date is in the St. Edmund's annals (Liebermann [ed.], *Geschichtsquellen*, p. 132), which places the obit in 1117.

93. Blomefield, *Norfolk*, III, 468.

94. Weever, *Funeral Monuments*, quoted in Goulburn and Symonds, *Life*, p. 406.

95. *Norwich Customary*, pp. 153–154. He was remembered in the priory charities in 1284: Herbert W. Saunders, *An Introduction to the Obedientiary and Manor Rolls of Norwich Cathedral Priory* (Norwich, 1930), p. 177.

in September, 1122. When the roll reached the Norwich cathedral priory, the monks inscribed thereon: *"Orate pro domno Herberto episcopo, patrono nostro et fundatore ecclesiae nostrae."* [96]

III. VIR OMNIUM LITTERARUM

Herbert Losinga's letters exist only in a seventeenth-century manuscript in Brussels. Internal evidence leaves no doubt they are his, for virtually all contain at least one of the following indications: they are addressed to Norwich or to individuals we know from other sources to have been at the priory during Herbert's episcopate, they mention himself as bishop, they encourage work on cathedral-building, and they are addressed to, or mention, such of Herbert's contemporaries in England as King Henry, Queen Matilda, Roger of Salisbury, and Ranulf d'Escures. The letters might still be forgeries attributed to the bishop, but their contents are not such as to justify a suspicion of forgery—there would be no purpose in forging such letters as these, as none documents or establishes a right, privilege, precedent, or holding. They are intrinsically important only insofar as they reveal something of the education, interests, and personality of Herbert and thereby permit deeper insight into the man and his times.

The fifty-nine letters do not appear to have been compiled according to any principle or pattern—a not unusual phenomenon in this bishop's period.[1] The existence of one other epistle from Herbert, and the

---

96. Léopold Delisle (ed.), *Rouleaux des morts du XIe au XVe siècle*, Société de l'histoire de France, CXXXV (Paris, 1866), 315. On confraternity, see Knowles, *Monastic Order*, pp. 472–475, and Godfrey, *Church in Anglo-Saxon England*, pp. 250–251.

1. The letters (ed. R. Anstruther) are collated in Goulburn and Symonds, *Life*; the texts are often unintelligible without the collations, and the edition is not critical even by mid-nineteenth-century standards of amateur editing. C. R. Cheney (*English Bishops' Chanceries, 1100–1230*, Publications of the Faculty of Arts of the University of Manchester, III [Manchester, 1950], 120–121) discusses the letters of Anselm, Gilbert Foliot, and Arnulf of Lisieux and comments that "all three [collections] include correspondence . . . , selected on principles which defy explanation." There is no comprehensive study of medieval letter-collections, but interesting analyses can be found in the works cited in the immediately following notes, and in Southern, *St. Anselm*, pp. 67 ff.; Frank Barlow (ed.), *The Letters of Arnulf of Lisieux*, Camden, Third Series, LXI (London, 1939), lxi ff.; *The Letters of John Salisbury*, ed. W. J. Millor and H. E. Butler, I (London, 1955), xxxviii ff.; Adrian Morey and C. N. L. Brooke, *Gilbert Foliot and His Letters* (Cambridge, 1965), pp. 8–31; Joseph de Ghellinck, *L'Essor de la littérature latine au XIIe siècle*, 2nd ed. (Brussels and Paris, 1955), pp. 110 ff.; Jean Leclercq, *The Love of Learning and the Desire for God* (New York, 1962), pp. 179 ff., and *idem*, "Le genre épistolaire au Moyen Age," *Revue de Moyen Age latin*, II (1946), 63–70. [Concerning the manuscript of Herbert's letters, see above, p. 119 n. 3.]

implication of yet another, establish that the collection is not complete,[2] but the absence of evidence makes a final decision impossible whether, like those of Anselm and Arnulf of Lisieux, these letters were collected by the author and his disciples;[3] or by the disciples without Herbert's assistance; or, as in the cases of Gilbert Foliot and Grosseteste, by a chancery staff;[4] or by some other means. The only internal evidence bearing on their collection can be discounted: Herbert demurred from collecting his letters, disavowing any intent to preserve the wandering thoughts of old age.[5] Literary convention demanded such modest demurrers, and thus his hesitancies are not to be taken at face value.[6]

The letters are miscellaneous. Sixteen concern education and learning, eight are devoted to affairs of the religious life, another eight relate to diocesan administration, six are addressed to erring monks or clergy, five request books or favors, three discuss the building of Norwich cathedral, four involve personal troubles, two concern public affairs, and the remaining seven treat of varied matters. The collection contains no letters written before Herbert's elevation to the episcopacy.[7] Few epistles are addressed to important persons on important matters—one flowery letter thanked Henry I for some favor, two others were for Queen Matilda (one asked her intercession in a fiscal problem, the other was a prayer composed by Herbert for her), one to Anselm, another to Ranulf of Canterbury asking him to visit, none to a pope.

The bishop revealed himself, perhaps more than he intended, in these letters. Conscientious as diocesan administrator, stern yet gentle with his inferiors, obsequious toward his betters, interested in correct latinity, he was also mendacious and grasping, compassionate and sensible, and not without a sly and cunning sense of humor. He failed to return a borrowed psalter and declined to pay for it, since *"non est monachorum habere argentum."*[8] He likewise borrowed a horse from Bishop Robert (probably of

2. Herbert's letter is in Anselm, V, ep. 386; one is inferred in *ibid.*, IV, ep. 254.

3. Southern, *St. Anselm*, pp. 67 ff.; Barlow (ed.), *Letters of Arnulf*, pp. lxi ff.

4. Cheney, *Bishops' Chanceries*, pp. 120–121.

5. *HE*, ep. 1.

6. See, for example, Ernst Robert Curtius, *European Literature and the Latin Middle Ages* (New York, 1963), pp. 83–85, and P. C. Spicq, *Esquisse d'une histoire de l'exégèse latine au moyen age*, Bibliothèque Thomiste, XXVI (Paris, 1944), 71.

7. As inferred in epistle 1, in which Herbert stated that all letters from his younger days had been lost.

8. *HE*, ep. 46. Cf. the *Regula monachorum* of Benedict of Nursia, ed. Justin McCann (London, 1952), Chap. 33.

Chester) and in a thank-you note explained that he was not returning the mount: Herbert indeed remembered that Robert had asked for its return, but he was obeying his colleague's heart rather than his mouth, and the beast would be restored to its former owner in the life to come![9]

The mischievous humor was given free rein in a letter to one Gislebert, who had sent the bishop a gift of five pears and five quinces. The gift was appreciated but should have symbolized a New Testament number, rather than either the five bodily senses or the Decalogue of the Old Dispensation. The present should have included 13 (Our Lord and the Apostles), 24 (the elders in Revelation), 153 (the draught of fishes), or *maxima* 144,000 (the number of the saved in Revelation) fruits.[10] Curiously, he did not suggest one (the unity of the Godhead), two (the divine and human natures in Christ), or three (the Trinity).

Herbert could have warm sympathy for those entrusted to his pastoral care when family troubles assailed them, and genuine concern for those even rightly accused of wrongdoing.[11] He could be quite sharp in his intolerance of error and of evil, but the general impression acquired from a reading of his missives is one of understanding and kindness.[12]

Many letters are to students, as might be expected of a bishop most interested in the classics and in education. While abbot of Ramsey he established a monastic school at that house,[13] although nothing is known of it beyond the fact that it was not the first school there, as instruction had been carried on as early as the tenth century.[14] No hint survives to explain precisely what happened to the Ramsey school of the Anglo-Saxon period thereby necessitating a new foundation after 1087, but perhaps the turbulence of the Norman settlement made such gentle pursuits as learning seem relatively unimportant and the school may simply have fallen into neglect.[15]

While nothing of importance can be established concerning the

9. *HE*, ep. 19.   10. *Ibid.*, ep. 50.

11. For example, *ibid.*, epp. 27 and 31.

12. *Ibid.*, epp. 6, 16, 29, 42, 43, 48, 52, 55.

13. Goscelin, *Vita S. Yvonis episcopi Persae*, in *PL*, CLV, col. 81. The relevant passage is omitted in the transcription of the *Vita* in *Chron. Rameseiensis*, pp. lix ff.

14. We know little of the Anglo-Saxon school at Ramsey. The house chronicler claimed that the liberal arts were taught *temp.* Prior Aednoth and that (*ca.* 1041–42) theological studies were pursued. For this school, see *Chron. Rameseiensis*, pp. 42, 112–114, 153.

15. For the effects of the Conquest on English monasticism, see Knowles, *Monastic Order*, pp. 103–106; Douglas, *William the Conqueror*, pp. 317–345 and 327–329; Sir Frank Stenton, *Anglo-Saxon England*, 2nd ed. (Oxford, 1955), pp. 650 ff.

Ramsey school, other than Herbert's refounding of it, this is not the case for the Norwich monastic school, despite the fact that the standard (indeed, the only) book-length history of subuniversity education in medieval England judges that there was no school there in Herbert's time, dismissing the documentary evidence as "romance."[16] It is true that a sixteenth-century source must be used with great caution to establish twelfth-century events, but Herbert's letters to students corroborate the later evidence.

The *Valor ecclesiasticus* was the result of a meticulous investigation of the financial condition of the English monasteries at the Dissolution, compiled by commissioners at the command of Henry VIII. It is a survey which has been shown to be generally reliable, and the few errors and instances of fraud in the *Valor* do not include Norwich information.[17] The relevant passage from the *Valor* reads as follows:

> Twenty-one pounds [to be distributed thus]: To 13 boys resident each year within the monastery for instruction there . . . , for each at the rate of £1 6s. 8d. for food and clothing annually; and for the wages of a master to teach these boys £2 13s. 4d. per year; and for the wages of a servant [to attend] these boys £1 yearly; so founded [*sic fundat*] by Hilbert [*sic*: the context makes it clear that Herbert is the intended benefactor], late Bishop of Norwich, founder of this monastery. . . .[18]

The evidence of the *Valor* is straightforward, and it does not stand in isolation. The bishop's letters also indicate the existence of a school at Norwich, not merely the existence of some boys in whose education Herbert was interested. One specifically adjures the students at Norwich to obey their schoolmaster.[19] Another is to a youth at the priory who, it is implied, was a teacher and himself being instructed by Herbert.[20] Yet another implies the existence of formal instruction at the house.[21] It is also true that two letters indicate youths being sent away from the house for

16. Arthur F. Leach, *The Schools of Medieval England* (London, 1915), pp. 224–225.

17. On the *Valor*, see especially Alexander Savine, *English Monasteries on the Eve of the Dissolution*, Oxford Studies in Legal and Social History, I (Oxford, 1909), throughout and especially pp. 3–4, 16 ff., 33; and David Knowles, *The Religious Orders in England*, Vol. III: *The Tudor Age* (Cambridge, 1959), 241 ff.

18. *Valor ecclesiasticus temp. Henr. VIII*, Record Commission (London, 1817), III, 287. Savine, *English Monasteries*, pp. 232–233, accepts the genuineness of this evidence for the school at Norwich. Another translation is in Saunders, *Rolls of Norwich Priory*, p. 24.

19. *HE*, ep. 39.

20. *Ibid.*, ep. 49.

21. *Ibid.*, ep. 53.

study,[22] but this need not contradict the probability of at least basic education at Norwich. Further, the letters last mentioned are not addressed to the students who were usually the recipients of Herbert's correspondence on pedagogical matters. The evidence thus seems to demonstrate the strong probability of a school at the priory, a likelihood of some importance, for Arthur F. Leach was wrong when he stated that there was "no . . . doubt . . . that all the cathedral and collegiate churches kept schools" at this time.[23]

No documents survive to inform us of the curriculum at the priory school during the early twelfth century, but much can be inferred from Herbert's letters viewed in the wider context of medieval education at this period.[24] The specific references to Herbert's academic program at Norwich are so scant as to be more frustrating than enlightening were there not excellent secondary works which permit the historian to place Herbert's all-too-brief allusions within the general pattern of the intellectual history of the period immediately preceding the "renaissance of the twelfth century."

The bishop mentions as objects of study only logic,[25] Augustine and the Bible,[26] grammar,[27] the trivium and quadrivium,[28] Donatus and Servius,[29] Ovid[30] and Aristotle.[31] Other than Augustine and the Bible, all were among the *auctores* and in the liberal arts curriculum. Despite Herbert's mention of the quadrivium, none of its disciplines specifically appear in his letters: this may indicate that the quadrivium was not actually taught, which in turn may reflect Norwich's sharing in the general neglect of

22. *Ibid.*, epp. 20 (to Samson and Roger) and 29 (to Thurstan).

23. Leach, *Schools*, p. 115.

24. Among the innumerable works in this area, the following have been of most value in the preparation of this study: R. R. Bolgar, *The Classical Heritage and its Beneficiaries* (Cambridge, 1958); Marie-Dominique Chenu, *La théologie au douzième siècle*, Études de philosophie médiévale, XLV (Paris, 1957); Pierre Courcelle, *Les lettres grecques en occident de Macrobe à Cassidore*, Bibliothèque des Écoles Francaises d'Athènes et de Rome, F. CLIX, nouv. ed. (Paris, 1948); M. L. W. Laistner, *Thought and Letters in Western Europe, A.D. 500–900*, 2nd ed. (Ithaca, 1957); Emile Lesne, *Histoire de la propriété ecclésiastique en France*, Vol. V: *Les écoles*, Memoires et travaux publiés par des professeurs des facultés catholiques de Lille, F. L (Lille, 1940); G. Paré, A. Brunet, and P. Tremblay, *La Renaissance au XIIᵉ siècle: Les écoles et l'enseignement*, Publications de l'Institute d'Études Médiévales d'Ottawa, III (Paris and Ottawa, 1933).

25. *HE*, epp. 41, 53.   26. *Ibid.*, ep. 43.

27. *Ibid.*, and ep. 20. The students *ad grammaticam descendisti*.

28. *HE*, epp. 20, 49.   29. *Ibid.*, ep. 9.

30. *Ibid.*, ep. 39. Neither here nor elsewhere are specific titles ordinarily mentioned.

31. *Ibid.*, ep. 49.

these subjects during Herbert's lifetime.[32] There seems no reason to doubt that the educational program at the priory was typical of that of the Benedictine centuries, since Ovid, Donatus, and Servius were standard "texts" in the mònastic schools of that period.[33]

What did the East Anglian ordinary mean by encouraging the study of Aristotle and of logic? There is no doubt that if he was acquainted with Aristotle at all it was in Latin translation, and the *logica vetus* included only two parts of the *Organon*, the *Categories* and the *On Interpretation*.[34] Herbert was clearly within the old logic in urging students to master the *Categories*, but what did he mean by the *topicas differentias*?[35] He could not have meant Aristotle's *Topics*, for—despite Boethius' translation[36]—it formed part of the *logica nova* and was not utilized in the West until the mid-twelfth century. There are three strong possibilities to explain Herbert's reference: the *Topics* of Cicero (a rhetorical work), the *De topicis differentiis* of Gerbert of Aurillac, and the identically titled work of Boethius. There is little doubt that Boethius is intended: Herbert's period was the "century of Boethius,"[37] "*aetas Boetiana*."[38]

Not surprisingly, most of the bishop's references to secular learning name classical Latin men of letters rather than Greek or Latin philosophers. His manner of approach indicated both his conformity with the prevailing academic practices of his time and his awareness of the con-

32. Lesne, *Hist. prop. ecclés.*, V, 571 ff. and 610–611; Chenu, *Théologie*, p. 48; Paré, *Renaissance*, pp. 97 ff.; E. K. Rand, *Founders of the Middle Ages* (New York, 1957), pp. 223 ff. For the meagerness of the curriculum at one of the great centers of learning at about Herbert's time, see Loren C. MacKinney, *Bishop Fulbert and Education at the School of Chartres*, Texts and Studies in the History of Medieval Education, ed. Astrik L. Gabriel and J. N. Garvin (Notre Dame, 1957).

33. Lesne, *Hist. prop. ecclés.*, V, 571 ff. and 610–611; A. J. MacDonald, *Lanfranc*, 27 ff. Compare Charles Homer Haskins, *The Renaissance of the Twelfth Century* (New York, 1957), pp. 368 ff.

34. On this, see especially Bolgar, *Classical Heritage*, pp. 149–162; Paré, *Renaissance*, pp. 31 ff., 101–104, 160–163; Courcelle, *Lettres grecques*, throughout; J. T. Muckle, "Greek Works Translated Directly into Latin Before 1350," *Medieval Studies*, IV (1942), 34 ff., and V (1943), 104–105. Other important elements of the old logic included Porphyry's introduction to the *Categories*, a number of commentaries on Aristotle and on Porphyry by Boethius, and the *Topica* of Cicero. Herbert mentions none of these.

35. Both in *HE*, ep. 49; *ibid.*, ep. 53, he exhorts to the study of logic but is otherwise not specific.

36. Lorenzo Minio-Paluello, "The Genuine Text of Boethius' Translation of Aristotle's *Categories*," *Medieval and Renaissance Studies*, I (1941–43), 151 and 171; Étienne Gilson, *A History of Christian Philosophy in the Middle Ages* (New York, 1955), p. 603 n. 2.

37. R. W. Southern, *The Making of the Middle Ages* (New Haven, 1953), p. 174.

38. Chenu, *Théologie*, p. 142.

tinuing conflict in tradition over the propriety of a Christian pursuing pagan learning.[39] Despite the rich vein of controversy over the aptness of secular learning for clerics, the empirical solution was unavoidable for a civilization building, as all must, on its own past: the classics had to be permitted because they were necessary as texts in the trivium. The compromise had been made long before Herbert's time—classical studies as an *ancilla theologiae* were acceptable as a basis for the study and expression of holy things.[40]

An ambivalent attitude toward the classics appears strikingly in the bishop's writings. On the one hand he encouraged the use of classical authors: his students were to memorize Donatus with all the grammatical rules of Latin,[41] they were encouraged to read Ovid[42] and to work up "the authors," those secular and pagan writers whose works served as models and as texts for the trivium.[43] No two surviving lists agree on the identity of all *auctores*, but most include Donatus, Aesop, Boethius, Ovid, Sedulius, Virgil, Juvenal, Lucan, Horace, and Statius.

Not only did Herbert suggest elements of a program of learning to the young boys of the priory school, he also took a direct hand in their education, teaching,[44] admonishing, passing judgment on their work. He promised to appraise their work upon his return from a journey[45] and in at least one instance must have been sent a poem, for he derogated Odo's efforts in stinging sarcasm: "I call on Jesus to assist me, that I may chance

39. Of the vast literature on this topic, I have found the following most useful in the preparation of this study: Laistner, *Thought and Letters*; Bolgar, *Classical Heritage*; Leclercq, *Love of Learning*; David Knowles, *The Evolution of Medieval Thought* (Baltimore, 1962), pp. 59–68; M. L. W. Laistner, *Christianity and Pagan Culture in the Later Roman Empire* (Ithaca, 1951); idem, "The Christian Attitude Toward Pagan Literature," *History*, XX (1935), 49–54; Jean Leclercq, *L'Humanisme bénédictin du VIIIe au XIIe siècle*, Analecta monastica, I [Studia Anselmiana, XX] (1948).

40. See note above, and Haskins, *Renaissance*, Chap. 4; Beryl Smalley, *Study of the Bible in the Middle Ages*, 2nd ed. (New York, 1952), pp. 13–16 and 26; Helen Waddell, *The Wandering Scholars* (New York, 1955), pp. xiii-xxxiii; Southern, *Making of the M. A.*, p. 171.

41. *HE*, ep. 9, which also directs the study of Servius and of Sedulius.

42. *Ibid.*, ep. 39; but ep. 53 counsels against Ovid. For the popularity of Ovid in Herbert's time, see E. K. Rand, *Ovid and His Influence* (Boston, 1925), pp. 112–113, and Haskins, *Renaissance*, p. 107, where Ovid is called the second most popular secular Latin poet in the twelfth century.

43. *HE*, ep. 20. For the *auctores*, see (among others) Edwin A. Quain, "The Medieval *accessus ad auctores*," *Traditio*, III (1945), 215–264; Lesne, *Hist. prop. ecclés.*, V, 593 ff.; Chenu, *Théologie*, p. 351 ff.; Curtius, *European Literature*, pp. 48 ff.

44. *HE*, ep. 9.

45. *Ibid.*, epp. 20, 47.

upon a criticism worthy of the products of so subtle an intellect, and . . . to ornament it judiciously and in appropriate language . . . . These noble compositions . . . your poems, which I regard as so much rubbish. . . ."[46] He continued in 'the same letter to remorseless criticism of Odo's grammar and expression. This Odo is probably to be identified with the Odo referred to in another letter as knowing only the names of books and not their contents.[47] In a gentler vein the bishop wrote to Odo and William [Turbe?] in criticism of their verse: it was mechanically acceptable but lacked depth of meaning.[48] Throughout his letters to students Herbert showed careful attention to literary detail, a clear comprehension of grammar and of rhetoric, a sharp eye for form and idiom, and a still sharper wit and pen.

It would give less than a complete picture of Herbert's attitude toward the classics to leave the impression that he was an advocate of their use, even as handmaids of theology—he held some hesitation about their propriety for himself as priest and as bishop, or at least he affected to do so. It is not necessarily an argument against his sincerity to note that his expression of these doubts is derivative from patristic and postpatristic writers, but it at least raises the question of whether Herbert was saying conventional things in a conventional way because he felt it his duty to his young charges to warn them against becoming enamored of pagan writers at the expense of Christian ones.

In three letters to students Herbert refused entreaties to write in verse. It was the office of a bishop to be concerned with the things of God, not to indulge himself in secular literature and its delights. His thought here precisely paralleled that of Lanfranc, also contained in a letter.[49] The impropriety of a bishop lecturing on classical authors was forcefully called to mind in Gregory the Great's famous letter to Desiderius of Vienne and was also a teaching both of Augustine and Jerome.[50] More

46. *Ibid.*, ep. 30. Odo even erred in sending thirty-six verses, since thirty signifies the pleasures of the flesh, six the labors of this world.

47. *Ibid.*, ep. 49.   48. *Ibid.*, ep. 39.

49. *Ibid.*, epp. 32, 39, 47. In the first Herbert pointed out that Moses, Isaiah, the Apostles, Jerome, Augustine, Ambrose, and Gregory the Great wrote prose rather than verse. Compare Lanfranc's ep. 33 (*PL*, CL, col. 533) and Milo Crispin's *Vita beati Lanfranci* (ibid., cols. 30–31) where the archbishop's renunciation of *studiis litterarum* is recounted.

50. Gregory I, *Reg. epistolarum*, I, 357–358 and II, 303; the former citation is the great pope's refusal to chain the words of Scripture to the grammar of Donatus. See also Augustine, *Epistolae*, ed. A. Goldbacher (CSEL, XXXIV), pp. 666 and 697–698 and *De doctrina christiana*, in *PL*, XXXIV, col. 68; Jerome, in *PL*, XXV, cols. 141, 585, 1058. No attempt is made here to present an exhaustive listing of the idea, but these are the

dramatic was Herbert's vision against episcopal study of the classics, a reverie clearly derived from earlier sources.

Herbert had been oppressed by a dream one night when he had fallen asleep after considering the students' interest in classical literature. Hobgoblins assailed him, but they were driven off by the appearance of a woman who asked of the cleric what his vocation be. He replied that he was a Christian and a bishop. The apparition warned that mouths and hearts filled with Vergil and Ovid had no business fulfilling priestly functions and that it was particularly unseemly for a successor to the Apostles thus to sully his profession. She went on to enumerate the many blessings of his life and career, from his noble birth to his "rich stores of knowledge," all of which came solely from the grace of God; then she demanded of Herbert what he intended as reparation for his lapse from grace. Calling to mind Jerome and Boethius, the aging prelate confessed that not only had he read heathen authors, he had also emulated their conduct. Responding to the bishop's willingness to submit to punishment, the lady replied that his genuine repentance was sufficient, and Herbert thereupon resolved to speak and write only of Christ.[51] Unquestionably the prototype of this vision was Jerome's well-known dream, to whose didactic elements was added Boethius' personification of Lady Philosophy.[52]

Less important and less exalted than Herbert's teaching on the classics and his ideas of a proper curriculum was his exercise of academic discipline as revealed in his letters to students. They show both that the bishop was an exacting taskmaster and that the nature of students has changed as little as has that of masters over the centuries. Herbert lamented, he cajoled, he threatened, he complained, he grumbled: the students lacked zeal for study, they were lazy, vain, self-indulgent, gluttonous.[53] He also

---

sources with which Herbert was most likely to have been familiar, as he used them in his homilies.

51. *HE*, ep. 28. Goulburn and Symonds (*Life*, p. 47 n. k) have shown undue innocence in their comment on this particular literary convention: "Not that we would imply that the vision was an intentional fiction, but only that in his dream he fell unconsciously into a similar train of thought."

52. Jerome, *Epistulae*, ed. Isidore Hilberg (CSEL, LIV), I, 22:30, pp. 189–191; cf. epp. 21 and 70, and Rand, *Founders*, 107. Boethius, *Philosophiae consolationis*, ed. W. Weinberger (CSEL, LXVII), p. 1. For other visions against classical learning, see Lesne, *Hist. prop. ecclés.*, V, 594 ff.

53. *HE*, epp. 20, 24, 40, 41, 53. Letter 41 is specifically addressed to William Turbe, later (1146–74) bishop of Norwich; probably the other letters addressed to William are also to the future prelate. On William, see David Knowles, *The Episcopal Colleagues of Archbishop Thomas Becket* (Cambridge, 1951), pp. 31–34, and the sources there cited.

attended to the nonacademic side of the boys' lives. Employing a nautical symbolism he suggested Christ as their pilot in life's sea, and added that the students must crucify their fleshly desires.[54] Youth was dangerous because of its temptatiohs to drinking, gluttony, and whoring, a suggestion found less explicitly stated by Gregory the Great.[55] The ordinary also wrestled with the problem of the gifted child. Writing to a student who apparently had complained that the bishop was retarding his studies, he urged the student to exercise charity toward those less quick-witted than himself and advised him to read on his own and thus increase his knowledge beyond the required material.[56]

How learned a man was this teacher of others? Was he truly "one in advance of his times in respect of intellectual gifts and attainments,"[57] *vir magnanimus et admodum litteratus* and *vir omnium litterarum tam secularium quam divinarum imbutus scientia?*[58] What can be established with certainty concerning his own reading and educational background?

The bishop mentioned the following secular writers by name: Seneca (ep. 45), Cicero (*ibid.*), Donatus, Servius, Ovid, Aristotle, Josephus (ep. 10), Suetonius (ep. 5, asking for its loan: he erred, however, in thinking it was not to be found in England), and Trogus Pompeius (ep. 6). In addition he utilized Aesop and Plautus' *Amphitryo*[59] and expressed himself in ways closely paralleling Ovid (*Tristia* I: 8), Vergil, and Cicero. One cannot conclude that the bishop had read these authors and made them his own, however, for he could have used florilegia. Perhaps ominously for Herbert's reputation, the most extensive printed discussions of florilegia demonstrate that they contained excerpts from the classical authors to whom Herbert referred.[60]

Furthermore, "in any estimate of the influence of classical authors in our period, full account must be taken of the large body of quotations

54. *HE*, ep. 22.
55. Gregory I, *Dialogii*, p. 79.
56. *HE*, ep. 42.
57. Goulburn and Symonds, *Life*, p. 347.
58. Malmesbury, *GR*, 386; Bartholomew Cotton, pp. 389–391; Robert of Torigni, *Chronicles*, p. 122; *NR*, p. 22.
59. In alluding to classical authors as fit matter for Christian education, Herbert used fable 12 from Book III of the *Phaedrus*: perhaps the students will find a pearl in the dungheap (*HE*, ep. 30). Aesop's fables were in florilegia: E. M. Sanford, "The Use of Classical Latin Authors in the *libri manuales*," *Transactions and Proceedings of the American Philological Association*, LV (1924), 241. For Plautus, ep. 45: John, the addressee, is to be *alter ego* with Herbert, not as Mercury impersonated Sosia, but as John and Elijah.
60. Sanford, "Use of Classical Latin Authors," pp. 190–248 (esp. 241–247); Berthold L. Ullman, *Classical Authors in Mediaeval Florilegia* (Chicago, 1932), throughout.

which came at second hand, through the Fathers [and] the Latin grammars and glossaries."[61] The library at Ramsey when Herbert was abbot there contained Priscian, whose grammar contained "ten thousand lines of quotations from the ancients, . . . quotations to which many readers were indebted for whatever acquaintance they possessed with these authors."[62] Of classical authors referred to by the bishop, Ramsey also possessed Vergil, but the other classics listed from that abbey's catalogue come from a fragment of as late as the close of the thirteenth century since it includes works of Grosseteste and of Stephen Langton. There is thus no way to ascertain whether they were there as early as the time of Herbert's incumbency. When the bishop was monk and prior at Fécamp, that house's library apparently possessed nothing from the classics.[63] Judgments on the holdings of the Norwich priory library in Herbert's time are impossible, since a fire in 1272 destroyed almost all its books.[64] It can be inferred that Norwich held Donatus, Servius, Ovid, and other works which Herbert goaded the priory students to study, or there would have been no point in his having written letters urging this reading.

Argument from silence is risky and treacherous, but it is true that there was a wide currency of classical works in Herbert's time and it is also possible that—library catalogues aside—Herbert had borrowed some classical works, as he at least asked the loan of Josephus and in another instance of Suetonius. Perhaps his correspondent was so incautious as to lend the bishop the requested works.[65] Further the contemporary encomiums of Herbert as a man of respectable learning cannot be entirely

61. Haskins, *Renaissance*, p. 113.

62. *Ibid.*; James W. Thompson, *The Medieval Library*, new ed. (New York, 1957), p. 122.

63. Genevieve Nortier, "La Bibliothèque de Fécamp au Moyen Age," in de Povremogne, *Fécamp*, II, 222–237; Lesne, *Hist. prop. ecclés.*, Vol. IV: *Les livres* (1938), 584 ff.

64. Beeching, "Library of Norwich," pp. 68 and 93–102; Ker, "Norwich Manuscripts," pp. 5–6 and 12–13, and *idem*, *Medieval Libraries*, pp. 76–77.

65. *HE*, ep. 10. James S. Beddie, "The Ancient Classics in the Mediaeval Libraries," *Speculum*, V (1930), 4, suggests some of the difficulties inherent in working with surviving library lists of the period. "Account was taken only of the number of manuscripts, rather than the works contained therein; and volumes were regularly listed by the name of the first work contained, in cases where several works are found in one manuscript those after the first being allowed to go uncatalogued. The volumes are often found cited by brief titles, which are sometimes indefinite. . . ." See further, for the availability of the classics, *ibid.*, pp. 3–20, and the same author's "Libraries in the Twelfth Century," in *Anniversary Essays in Medieval History by Students of Charles Homer Haskins* (Boston, 1929), pp. 1–24; Paré, *Renaissance*, pp. 153 ff.; Haskins, *Renaissance*, pp. 93–126; Lesne, *Hist. prop. ecclés.*, IV, throughout.

discounted. This is particularly true of William of Malmesbury, who lost no opportunity to call attention to less attractive elements of the man's character. But it is impossible to prove that the bishop had read any classical author whatever in his entirety, as there were alternative methods of acquiring at least a superficial acquaintance with the classics, and it is true that his letters simply refer to these authors, they are not permeated with the easy and intimate familiarity which his sermons demonstrate with the Fathers' works. He had some claim to be a stylist, but his surviving letters do not support contemporary judgments praising his secular learning. It would be pointless to argue that, had letters written in his pre-episcopal days survived, this judgment would be reversed, but it is at least an undemonstrable possibility.

Herbert Losinga's sermons, and to a much less degree the letters, demonstrate the validity of J. M. Campbell's dictum that "patristic sources were so dominant in certain works of pre-Conquest and Norman England that if the thought and phraseology undoubtedly patristic (and biblical phrases as interpreted by the Fathers) were subtracted from such works, there would be nothing of major significance left."[66] As is usually the case with Herbert, he again exemplifies the general tendencies of his time: indeed, deleting all such patristically derived material from his sermons would leave him with only two original teachings—that quaternity symbolizes eternity, and that the Godhead was composed of four persons rather than three, a startling piece of theology which doubtless reflects a copyist's error.

The problems involved in assessing the intellectual debt owed the Fathers by the bishop are similar to those previously discussed in tracing his classical sources. While Herbert's patristic learning was extensive, was it acquired through firsthand acquaintance with the Fathers' writings, or was it mediated through such postpatristic writers as Isidore, Bede, Rabanus Maurus, Aelfric, and others? If the same patristic allusion occurs in more than one possible source, how can one determine which was the work utilized by Herbert? There is no certain way of knowing, hence the following sections will list a number of likely possibilities, in inverse chronological order, for the sermons' teachings.

Another problem with sources appears less difficult. As the prelate's sermons are altogether based on others' writings, I have assumed that where his phraseology or ideas are even remotely similar to those of a Father of the church, he was unoriginal; that his allusions are similar in

66. J. M. Campbell, "Patristic Studies and the Literature of Medieval England," *Speculum*, VIII (1933), 470.

substance and in wording to earlier material leaves no reasonable doubt that he was not coincidentally discovering the same exegetical tools. Indeed, so firmly was he in the tradition of western Latin homiletics that on those few occasions where he did venture on his own, the passages stand out like virtue among medieval kings. Parallel with this apparent difficulty is that many of the bishop's ideas, while similar to or obviously derived from patristic sources, were current in homiletics of his day: there is thus the additional possibility that he got his ideas from his own contemporaries, although this does not seem to be a defensible thesis. Rather, he and his contemporaries were using the same sources and participating in the same intellectual environment.

There is the additional problem of florilegia. Compendiums of patristic writings were quite common from the fifth century onward, whether arranged topically or, as in the famous *Catena aurea* of Thomas Aquinas, according to the sequence of biblical passages. At least one such patristic florilegium was at Fécamp when Herbert was there, the *Liber scintillarum* of Defensor of Ligugé,[67] but only two references of the bishop are possibly attributable to this collection, both in the letters. Appendix II (p. 231) lists the writings of the patristic and postpatristic age available at Fécamp, Ramsey, and Norwich during Herbert's incumbencies at each. While availability does not prove access, the constant citation of some of these materials in the sermons would strongly suggest that he had not scratched the dog's ear during Lent.

The homilist's favored Fathers were Augustine, Gregory the Great, and Jerome. For the postpatristic period, Isidore and Bede held the place of honor. Although he frequently expressed ideas strikingly similar to those of eastern doctors, there is no evidence that he knew even the Greek alphabet, and in any case his possible Greek sources were all available in Latin well before his time, usually in Jerome's or Rufinus' translation.[68] Once again, it is unnecessary to assume firsthand acquaintance with

67. Genevieve Nortier, "Les bibliothèques médiévales des abbayes bénédictines de Normandie," *Revue Mabillon,* Ser. 3, No. 206 (Oct.–Dec., 1961), 339.

68. The myth dies hard that Greek was not uncommon among learned men of the West during the earlier middle ages. On the topic, and for careful compilation of the available translations to the mid-twelfth century, see Courcelle, *Lettres grecques*; Albert Siegmund, *Die Überlieferung der griechischen christlichen Literatur in der lateinischen Kirche bis zum zwölften Jahrhundert*, Abhandlungen der Bayerischen Benediktiner-Akademie, V (Munich, 1949); Bernhard Bischoff, "Das griechische Element in der abendländischen Bildung des Mittelalters," *Byzantinische Zeitschrift* (1951), pp. 27–55 (or in Bischoff, *Mittelalterliche Studien*, II [Stuttgart, 1967], 246–274); Laistner, *Thought and Letters*, pp. 76–77 and 238 ff.; Milton Anastos, "Some Aspects of Byzantine Influence on Latin

the teachings of the Greek fathers, for numerous florilègia of their works circulated in the Latin west.[69]

Herbert's use of apocryphal materials in his sermons was unusual in the homiletics of his period. Probably because of these legends' condemnation by the church,[70] they appear but rarely in contemporary sermons. Although most of the New Testament Apocrypha had not been originally written in Latin, they were circulating in that language well before 1100.[71] These stories add literary charm to the bishop's sermons, and the prayer which he composed for the queen is' entirely based on the apocryphal *acta* of St. John the Evangelist.

This sketch of Herbert Losinga's sources demonstrates that he exemplified the monastic culture of the "Benedictine Centuries," that culture composed of Scripture, the patristic heritage, and the classical tradition.[72] "It would be desirable, were it possible, to examine the intellectual background of each [twelfth-century] writer on the basis of his citations, his travels, and the books to which he had access," Charles Homer Haskins wrote.[73] As we have now presented what is known of Herbert's life and travels and suggested his own intellectual sources and the library materials available to him, the remainder of this study will set forth in some detail the scholar-bishop's' use of his sources, his method of expounding his text, and the range of his patristic knowledge.

IV. Homilist and Exegete

The historical value of Herbert Losinga's sermons lies not in their originality, for he was no intellectual innovator and probably "could not conceive of Scripture being understood in any way other than . . . it had always been understood,"[1] but rather in this, that apart from one of Ranulf d'Escures, his are the only extant sermons of an English bishop of

---

Thought," in Marshall Claggett *et al.*, *Twelfth-Century Europe and the Foundations of Modern Society* (Madison, 1961), pp. 137–139; Leclercq, *Love of Learning*, pp. 96 ff.; Muckle, "Greek Works," throughout. Less satisfactory for the period with which this study is concerned is George R. Stephens, *The Knowledge of Greek in England in the Middle Ages* (Philadelphia, 1933).

69. Siegmund, *Überlieferung*, pp. 139–161; Robert E. McNally, *The Bible in The Early Middle Ages* (Westminster, Md., 1959), pp. 35–36.

70. McNally, *Bible in M. A.*, p. 25.

71. Siegmund, *Überlieferung*, pp. 34–47.

72. Leclercq, *Love of Learning*, p. 76.

73. Haskins, *Renaissance*, p. 70.

1. McNally, *Bible in M. A.*, p. 29 (writing of tradition and exegesis).

this period. Therefore their uniqueness gives them an importance which their content alone would perhaps not justify. Only fourteen remain; if there were ever any more in the Norwich library, they were destroyed either during the anarchy[2] or during the great fire of 1272.

The sermons follow the general structural pattern recognized over a century ago as the principal pastoral elements of medieval sermons.[3] They reveal an "immense and almost intuitive knowledge of Scripture,"[4] although he seldom used passages not found either in the Mass propers or in the monastic diurnal,[5] and the bishop directed his interpretations to the needs of his hearers, most probably monks. He employed *exempla* to illustrate his teaching, and shared the general custom of speaking of past occurrences as being present or future. Personalizing the biblical stories, the bishop exhorted his auditors as if they were present at the incident being discussed. He retold the biblical account verse by verse and then in his own words, explaining the meaning of the festal proper and its significance for the congregation and frequently elucidating his exegesis by cross-references to parallel or similar scriptural accounts and to prophecies. There were constant enlargement and embellishment of biblical descriptions through frequent references to what the Fathers said about the incident or occasion and use of their ideas and symbolisms. His hearers were frequently exhorted to emulate biblical examples and precepts. Herbert always extracted a moral meaning from his text, no matter how he had to torture it to do so.

Exegesis in his day was largely determined by traditional practices, indeed "dominated by an inordinate reverence for the antiquity and authority of the Greek and Latin Fathers of the Church."[6] From the

2. Thompson, *Medieval Library*, p. 303. The author states that most of the collection from Herbert's time was destroyed during the anarchy rather than during the fire of the late thirteenth century.

3. John Mason Neale, *Mediaeval Preachers and Mediaeval Preaching* (London, 1856), introduction.

4. *Ibid.*; and see Southern, *Making of the M. A.*, pp. 217–218.

5. Unlike his former abbot, Jean of Fécamp (or of Ravenna), for whom see Jean Leclercq and Jean-Paul Bonnes, *Un maître de la vie spirituelle au XIᵉ siècle, Jean de Fécamp*, Études de théologie et d'histoire de la spiritualité, IX (Paris, 1946), 56 ff., where his intimacy with the whole range of biblical writings is discussed. For John, see further Leclercq, *Love of Learning, passim*. He was abbot of Fécamp from 1031 to 1078 and thus must have had some influence on the youthful Herbert, but there is no obvious link between the writings of this sensitive and gifted spiritual master and those of the bishop of Norwich.

6. McNally, *Bible in M. A.*, p. 11. This short book is the work of a master who has steeped himself in the study of patristics and of medieval exegesis throughout a most

seventh century to the time of Abélard, Rupert of Deutz, and Anselm of Laon, exegetical method centered in the repetition and dissemination of the Fathers' writings, a far from useless approach as it gave later centuries the "riches of Christian antiquity."[7] Postpatristic authorities were generally those who themselves relied heavily on the Fathers, such as Isidore of Seville, Bede, and Rabanus Maurus. Florilegia of the patristic commentators circulated widely and were primarily used as aids in making sermons[8]—hence the difficulty in determining Herbert's sources. In his sermons, the bishop of Norwich epitomized an age then drawing to a close, an age primarily of transmission rather than of exegetical innovation.

To say that Herbert's exegeses are traceable ultimately to the Fathers is to say that his allegories are thus attributable, for his period has been accurately categorized as one in which exegesis was "essentially and universally allegorical."[9] Not apparent in his sermons is his acquaintance with secular classics—indeed homilies are hardly the ideal vehicles for pagan learning—yet his rhetorical style is not without eloquence and subtlety. Certainly they are the products of an educated mind: "since the content of Scripture is encyclopedic, it calls for an encyclopedic knowledge in the student; hence all the resources of late-antique culture are brought to bear upon Bible reading."[10]

The earlier medieval homilist's dependence upon allegorical interpretation of the Bible derived from his judgment that strict literalism was somehow superficial and unsophisticated, that the exegete must search beneath the surface of the "lifeless literal sense" to the spiritual treasure

---

fruitful career. See further the following works on medieval exegesis: Henri de Lubac, *Exégèse médiévale: les quatre sens de l'Écriture*, Théologie et études publiées sous la direction de la Faculté de Théologie S. J. de Lyon-Fourviere, XLII (Paris, 1959–61), Parts 1 and 2; Smalley, *Study of the Bible*, which concentrates primarily on the period following that dealt with in Fr. McNally's work; Spicq, *Esquisse*, far more than a mere sketch as modestly promised in the title. G. R. Owst's two studies, *Literature and Pulpit in Medieval England*, 2nd ed. (New York, 1961) and *Preaching in Medieval England* (Cambridge, 1926), while suggestive for the present study, primarily concentrate on the thirteenth and later centuries. Frederic W. Farrer, *History of Interpretation* (New York, 1886), while based on wide reading in the sources, is marred both by a hostile attitude toward medieval exegesis and by a too-obtrusive anti-Romanism.

7. Spicq, *Esquisse*, pp. 11 and 72 ff.; see also McNally, *Bible in M. A.*, pp. 11–12, 29–30.

8. McNally, *Bible in M. A.*, p. 30.

9. Spicq, *Esquisse*, p. 16.

10. Smalley, *Study of the Bible*, p. 26; Bolgar, *Classical Heritage*, pp. 102–103.

beneath.[11] He did this through either the fourfold method—historical, allegorical, tropological, anagogical—or the older trichotomy (historical, tropological, mystical senses).[12] Herbert, while preferring the quaternal exegesis, also utilized the triune. His sermons will be discussed first through digesting allegorical exegeses of his texts, arranged in the order in which the feasts for which they are the propers fall progressively through the Christian year. Then what little he offered in the discipline of theology will be examined, followed by his hagiological excurses.

In the bishop's sermon for the Nativity, he presented only two pieces of symbolism, one unique, the other common. I find no patristic or medieval parallel to his exegesis of John 1:1-3, "In the beginning was the Word...." Noting that the word "was" appeared four times in the Prologue, he pointed out that this symbolized the fact that there never was a time when the Son did not exist.[13]

In preaching that all elements of creation rejoiced at Christ's birth, Herbert used a most popular allegory found as early as Gregory of Nazianzus, used in one of the most majestic of medieval hymns by Venantius Fortunatus, and frequent in sermons of the middle ages.[14] So common is this theme in Christian homiletics and hymnology that further documentation of its appearance would be redundant.

One of the richest mines of the bishop's sources is his homily for the Epiphany. Setting up the sermon for this feast in the usual medieval manner, he taught that the Adoration of the Magi, the baptism of Christ,

11. McNally, *Bible in M. A.*, p. 56; but of course allegorizing must be orthodox both in teaching and in expression (Spicq, *Esquisse*; Lubac, *Exégèse*, Part 2, p. 120).

12. Indispensable to the study of allegory are Lubac, *Exégèse*, and Spicq, *Esquisse*, throughout; McNally, *Bible in M. A.*, pp. 53–62; see also H. Caplan, "The Four Senses of Scriptural Interpretation and the Mediaeval Theory of Preaching," *Speculum*, IV (1929), 282–290. The fourfold approach appeared as early as the second century (Clement of Alexandria [*ob.* before 215], *Stromata*, in *PG*, IX, col. 348) and was popularized by, among others, Jerome, Cassian, Gregory the Great, Isidore, Bede, and Rabanus Maurus. The threefold method apparently began with Origen (G. L. Prestige, *Fathers and Heretics* [London, 1940]; Johannes Quasten, *Patrology*, 3 vols. [Westminster, Md., 1960–62], II, 92–93).

13. *HS*, p. 6: "Habes quater erat. quia non erat quando filius non erat." Vincent Hopper, *Mediaeval Number Symbolism: Its Sources, Meaning, and Influence in Thought and Expression* (New York, 1938) does not include this interpretation of quaternity.

14. *HS*, p. 8. Gregory of Nazianzus, *Oratio* 37, chap. x, in *PG*, XXXIII, col. 322. The Easter hymn *Salva, festa dies* in F. J. Raby, *A History of Christian Latin Poetry from the Beginning to the Close of the Middle Ages* (Oxford, 1953), p. 93, applies the gladdening of nature to the Resurrection; see also Orientius' poem in this vein, *ibid.*, pp. 83–84. Rabanus Maurus, Christmas sermon, in *PL*, CX, col. 16. Aelfric, I, 108.

and the miracle at Cana all occurred on the same day (the baptism thirty, Cana thirty-one years after the Epiphany).[15] After retelling the Gospel Epiphany story, the homilist explained the gifts of the three Magi as signifying Christ's lordship (frankincense), His kingship (gold), and His mortality (myrrh).[16] These were frequent interpretations in the development of medieval homiletics, and they were found in the preaching of Herbert's contemporaries Ivo of Chartres and Peter Damian as well as in an unattributed collection of English sermons of the period.[17] If we examine earlier centuries, without exhausting all examples of it through the first millennium of the church, we can see this symbolism's popularity in the imagery used by Aelfric, Rabanus Maurus, Isidore of Seville, Gregory the Great, Synesius of Cyrene, and the late fourth- and early fifth-century writers Prudentius and Juvencus, who seems to have originated this teaching.[18] The bishop of Norwich then moved to tropology: his auditors should offer tears for their past offences instead of frankincense, a good life in lieu of gold, and mortification of bodily lusts as their myrrh.[19] The same virtues were encouraged in the identical context by Ivo of Chartres, Peter Damian, Rabanus Maurus, and Gregory the Great.[20]

Another aspect of Epiphany symbolism which left much room for the homilist's ingenuity was the significance of the three Magi. Herbert, and he appears to be unique in this, preached that they represented those whom God had "predestined, foreknown and called from the three parts

15. Gregory Dix, *The Shape of the Liturgy*, 2nd ed. (Westminster, 1954), pp. 357–358. Late in the fourth century, both in the East and in the West, Epiphany "became the commemoration of the other manifestations of Christ—to the Magi, at His Baptism, and at Cana of Galilee."

16. *HS*, pp. 38–40.

17. Ivo carn., serm. *In Epiphania Domini*, in *PL*, CLXII, col. 574. Peter Damian, sermons for the Epiphany, in *PL*, CXLIV, col. 510, and CXLV, col. 152. *Old Eng. Homilies*, II, 45 ff. See also Ruth Ellis Messenger, *Ethical Teachings in the Latin Hymns of Mediaeval England* (New York, 1930), pp. 87–88.

18. Aelfric, I, 116–118. Rabanus, in *PL*, CX, cols. 18–19. Isidore, *Allegoriae quaedam sacrae scripturae*, in *PL*, LXXXIII, col. 117. Gregory, *Hom. in Ev.*, x (Epiphany), cols. 1112–1113. Synesius, Hymn 7, in *PG*, LXVI, col. 1611. Raby, *Christian Poetry*, p. 49 (Prudentius). For Juvencus, see Bernhard Bischoff, "Wendepunkte in der Geschichte der lateinische Exegese im Frühmittelalter," *Sacris Erudiri*, VI (1954), 215 and 250 (reprinted *idem, Mittelalterliche Studien*, I [Stuttgart, 1966], 205–272).

19. *HS*, pp. 40–42.

20. Ivo carn., serm. x (Epiphany), in *PL*, CLXII, col. 574. Peter Damian, Hom. i on the Epiphany, in *PL*, CXLIV, cols. 510 ff.; the interpretation of gold and incense is slightly variant although in the same sense. Rabanus, in *PL*, CX, col. 19. Gregory, *Hom. in Ev.*, col. 1113.

of the world."[21] Lanfranc also wrote that they came from the three parts
of the earth, but far more common was the attribution of the three royal
worshippers to the four quadrants, as found in Aelfric, Orosius, and in
Augustine of Hippo.[22] Isidore taught that they simply represented the
gentiles, although he did raise the symbolism of the four quadrants in
another context, in speaking of the soldiers parting Christ's garments,
which prefigured *quatuor partes mundi*.[23]

Herbert again used a very common allegory in his exposition of the
Cana wedding miracle: the six wine vessels represent the six ages of the
world, a concept which derived from Christian antiquity. The days of
creation were seen to parallel the ages of history, delineated by "major
interventions" of God, and found another parallel with the "ages of
man" imagery which originated with Augustine. This last applied to
God's treatment of man in a similar progression, that is, the first age saw
man treated by God as if the race were in infancy, and so on.[24] The
customary division points for the six ages were from Adam to Noah, Noah
to Abraham, Abraham to David, David to the Babylonian captivity, the
Captivity to the Nativity, and thence to the end of the created world.

The bishop of Norwich's homilizing on the six ages was in conformity
with this formula but for the sixth, which he altered in such a way as to
conclude, contrary to the statement with which he began his allegorizing,
with eight ages. The final three ages in his interpretation were from John
the Baptist (here synonymous with Advent) to the coming of Elijah, from
Elijah to the new heaven and the new earth, and thence throughout
eternity.[25] Herbert's sixth and seventh age are the received sixth age, for
the coming of Elijah is not equated theologically with the end of the
present world.

This allegory was so popular in the history of patristic and medieval
thought that cataloguing all its appearances would be as wearisome to the
reader as to the writer. The eleventh-century English homilist Aelfric
used it, preceded by (to choose a representative sampling) Bede, Isidore,

21. *HS*, p. 42.

22. Lanfranc, *Eulogium*, in *Opera*, II, 22. Aelfric, I, 130. Orosius, *Historiam adversum paganos*, ed. C. Zangemeister (CSEL, V), p. 82. Augustine, *Tract. in Jn.*, IX, 98; *idem*, serm. cciii, in *PL*, XXXVIII, col. 1035.

23. Isidore, *Allegoriae*, in *PL*, LXXXIII, col. 130. For Bede's use of the theme, see McNally, *Bible in M. A.*, p. 26.

24. Augustine, *Civ. Dei*, x, 14 (*PL*, XLI, col. 292), and xxii, *fin.*; *idem*, *De vera religione*, xxvi (*PL*, XXXIV, cols. 143–144); *idem*, serm. ccxvi (*PL*, XXXVIII, col. 1081). See also Chenu, *Théologie*, pp. 72 ff.; McNally, *Bible in M. A.*, pp. 43–44; Lubac, *Exégèse*, Part I, 47–48.

25. *HS*, pp. 62–64. He also counted an eighth age in his St. Paul sermon, *ibid.* p. 310, when the general resurrection would take place (cf. Augustine, *Civ. Dei*, xxii, *fin.*).

Gregory the Great, Augustine, Jerome, Victorinus, Lactantius, and the early Fathers Cyprian of Carthage and Irenaeus.[26] The apocryphal *Epistle of Barnabas* was the earliest extant Christian writing to employ the hexameral interpretation.[27] It is not only impossible to state with certainty which of these (or others) was Herbert's source, it is also immaterial, since again he represented the traditional in his intellectual approach. In this sermon he interpreted "Galilee," where Cana lay, to mean a place of transmigration, following Bede, Gregory, and ultimately Jerome,[28] urging his hearers to remove themselves from their sins to purity of life. And the changing of the water to wine signified, again as was common in medieval exegesis, the fulfillment of the Old Testament in Christ.[29]

Nature symbolism reappeared in the Candlemas sermon. After relating the Gospel story of the Purification and attendant events, the bishop explained the spiritual meaning of the turtledoves and pigeons offered at Mary's presentation. The turtledoves indicated the innocence of the Blessed Virgin and of the Lord; should one of these birds lose its mate, it does not seek another. The pigeon, which remains meek even when fighting in defense of its young, represented simplicity.[30] This allegorizing was common in Herbert's time, appearing in bestiaries and in contemporaneous English sermons,[31] and can be traced back through the early

26. Aelfric, I, 58 ff. (Epiphany) and 74 (Lent I) applies this allegory to the laborers in the vineyard. Bede, *Hom.*, L. I, 14, pp. 99–102; *idem, Opera de temporibus*, ed. Charles W. Jones (Cambridge, Mass., 1943), L. XVI: *De mundi aetatibus*, p. 303; *idem, Opera*, L. IV: *Opera rhythmica*, ed. D. Hurst (CC, CXXII), Hymn i, pp. 407–411. Isidore, *Quaestiones in Vetus Testamentum*, in PL, LXXXIII, col. 213; *idem, Etymologarium sive originum*, ed. W. M. Lindsay (Oxford, 1911), L. V, xxxviii. Gregory, *Hom. in Ev.*, xix, cols. 1154–1155. Augustine: *Tract. in Jn.*, IX, 93–94; *De catechizandis rudibus*, in PL, XL, cols. 190–193; *Quaestionem in Heptateuchum*, in PL, XXXIV, col. 821; *Tract. in Jn.*, XV, 153–154; *Civ. Dei*, xxii, 30, pp. 856–866; *De diversis quaestionibus*, in PL, XL, col. 42–44; *Ennarrationes in Psalmos*, in PL, XXXVI, col. 1132; serm. cclix, in PL, XXXVIII, cols. 1197–1198; and see above p. 187 n. 24. Jerome, *Epistulae* (CSEL, LVI), p. 278. Lactantius, *Diviniarum institutionem*, L. xv, 14, in *Opera omnia*, ed. S. Brandt and G. Laubmann (CSEL, XIX), pp. 628–630. Victorinus, *Opera*, ed. J. Haussleiter (CSEL, XLIX), p. 4. Cyprian, *Ad Fortunatem*, in *Opera omnia*, ed. Wilhelm Martel (CSEL, III), I, 318–319. Irenaeus, *Contra haeresis*, L. V, in PG, VII, col. 1200.

27. Quasten, *Patrology*, I, 89; Farrer, *Hist. of Interpretation*, p. 170.

28. *HS*, pp. 56–58. Bede, *Hom.*, II, 7 (*In vigilia Paschae*), p. 229. Gregory, *Hom. in Ev.*, col. 1172. Jerome, *Opera exegetica*, ed. P. Antin (CC, LXXII), Vol. I: *Liber interpretationis hebraicorum nominum*, 140.

29. *HS*, p. 60. McNally, *Bible in M. A.*, p. 67; Lubac, *Exégèse*, Part i, 344 ff.

30. *HS*, p. 78.

31. Florence McCulloch, *Mediaeval Latin and French Bestiaries*, University of North Carolina Studies in the Romance Languages and Literatures, XXXIII (Chapel Hill, 1962), 111 and 178. *Old Eng. Homilies*, II, 49.

medieval and patristic periods to classical Rome. To choose a representative catena of writings, the imagery was used by Aelfric, Rabanus, the Venerable Bede, Isidore in his *Etymologies*, by Augustine, and by the anonymous writer of the early Christian *Physiologus*.[32] The ultimate source is Pliny, whose *Natural History* here served as *ancilla theologiae*.[33] Herbert's only symbolism in his Ash Wednesday[34] sermon is so universal as to require no source documentation: he taught that ashes were the outward manifestation of death and of repentance.

Alternating textual citation with derived allegory, Herbert's sermon for Palm Sunday draws heavily upon the exegeses of the Venerable Bede. Following the great Northumbrian's, and ultimately Jerome's, teaching, he interpreted Bethany to mean the "house of obedience," as Christ entered there in obedience to His Father's will.[35] Of the many readings on the account of the two disciples sent ahead into the village, the bishop chose that which had them symbolize those sent to preach the Old and New Testaments, men full of love for God and for their fellow men, the interpretation also of Peter Damian.[36]

The multitudes greeting the Lord with palms and flowers signified the countries of the world acknowledging the resurrection of Christ and of His faithful, led by the examples and doctrines of the patriarchs and Prophets, an interpretation similar to those of Aelfric, Rabanus, and

32. Aelfric, I, 142. Rabanus, *De universo*, in *PL*, CXI, cols. 248–249. Bede, *In Luc.*, I, 64–65; Bede, *Hom.*, I, 12, p. 84, and 18, pp. 129–130 (the first citation is the lection for the third nocturne of the Purification in the *Breviarium ad usum Sarum*, Fasc. III, p. 142). Isidore, *Etymologarium*, L. XII, vii, 1 and 60–61. Augustine, *Tract. in Jn.*, VI, 54–55, 59, 63; *Civ. Dei*, xvi: 24, p. 527 and 43, p. 550. Francis J. Carmody (ed.), *Physiologus latinus versio Y*, University of California Publications in Classical Philology, XII, No. 7 (Berkeley and Los Angeles, 1941), 131 and 133–134. The *Physiologus* was extant before the time of Justin Martyr, Origen, and Clement of Alexandria (*ibid.*, p. 97) and was in Latin *temp.* Herbert (Siegmund, *Überlieferung*, p. 128).

33. Pliny, *Natural History*, X.

34. Herbert's editors here made one of their few blatant errors in translation. The title of the homily is *Sermo in .IIII^{ta}. feria ante Quadragesimam*, which Dean Goulburn and Father Symonds translated as "Wednesday before Lent," despite the clear application of the sermon's total content to Ash Wednesday. Medieval Latin *Quadragesima* can mean "the first Sunday in Lent," thus making the Wednesday before Lent I Ash Wednesday.

35. *HS*, p. 120. Bede, *In Marc.*, III, 571. Jerome, *Lib. interp. heb. nom.*, p. 135. Cf. Phil. 2:8.

36. *HS*, p. 120. Peter Damian, serm. for Palm Sunday, in *PL*, CXLIV, col. 545. But Aelfric taught (I, 206 ff.) that they symbolized learning and good example in teachers sent by God: Bede (*Hom.*, II, 3, p. 201) and Jerome (*Commentarius in Evangelium secundum Matthaeum*, in *PL*, XXVI, col. 153) that they signified the Jews and the Gentiles. Numerous other interpretations exist.

Jerome.[37] Those casting their garments in the path of Jesus symbolized the martyrs placing their bodies in the path of faith, thus paving the way by which the hearts of the faithful are turned to their Savior. This was a most common allegory, found in (among many others) Aelfric, Rabanus, and Gregory.[38] The worshippers who cried *salutem in excelsis* signified the pure and innocent, as only they follow Christian truth.[39] More popular was the teaching that these children represented those saints who preceded the Gospel and those who followed it.[40]

Most interesting is Herbert's treatment of the episode in which the tables of the money-changers were overthrown and the dove-sellers rebuked. To him, this represented the expulsion of the Jews from the cognition of Christ's incarnation, and the condemnation of the Jewish priests who tried to subvert the laws of Moses to suit their own purposes.[41] The usual interpretation, and indeed the obvious one, was Christ's condemnation of simony.[42] There seems no reason to doubt that the bishop's allegorizing was original here because to be traditional would have been to condemn that which he was himself: a simoniac.

Medieval homiletics, contrary to the modern practice, emphasized the foot-washing rather than the institution of the Mass when treating of Maundy Thursday. Following the teaching of Bede and of Augustine, the East Anglian ordinary told his hearers that the soul has its feet, that is its temptations to walk in earthly and temporal defilements, and that these feet are to be washed by sacramental Penance.[43] This is a brief sermon, at the end of which Herbert acknowledged that the day's offices were indeed lengthy; hence the sermon is shorter than the importance of the feast really deserves.

Just as Herbert preached the rejoicing of all created things in Christ's birth so again he employed this figure for his Easter sermon, applying it to the Resurrection. The incidents at the empty tomb provided tempting

37. *HS*, p. 120. Aelfric, I, 214. Rabanus, serm. for Palm Sunday, in *PL*, CX, cols. 29–30. Jerome, *In Matt.*, col. 154.

38. *HS*, pp. 120–122, Aelfric, I, 212. Rabanus, *op. cit.* Bede, *Hom.*, II, 3, p. 203; *In Marc.*, III, 573; *In Luc.*, V, 342. Gregory, *Hom. in Ez.*, col. 985.

39. *HS*, p. 122.

40. As in Rabanus, in *PL*, CX, cols. 29–30, and Jerome, *In Matt.*, col. 153.

41. *HS*, p. 122.

42. As, for example, in Bede (*In Marc.*, III, 579; *Hom.*, II, 187) and Gregory the Great (*Hom. in Ev.*, col. 1145); Herbert's deviation from the customary exegesis is the more telling because he knew both these masters' works here cited.

43. *HS*, p. 142. Bede, *Hom.*, II, 5 (*In caena Domini*), p. 217. Augustine, *Tract. in Jn.*, LVI, 4–5, pp. 468–469. Bede made the connection, as Herbert did, of the Maundy lavabo with Baptism.

opportunities for allegorizing and the homilist's presentation exhibited marked similarities to those (among many other possibilities) of Aelfric, Bede, and Gregory the Great. The angel sat on the right side of the tomb, thus signifying that the Lord had passed from mortality to immortality, from present to future life.[44] His white garment symbolized the meekness of Christ and the graciousness with which He remits sins,[45] while his countenance prefigured the Day of Judgment when the Son of God will appear in glory and majesty. The priory monks were to bring good works to the tomb as their burial unctions and spices.[46]

Three other symbolisms used by the bishop occur in the letters and in the report of a sermon not otherwise known, rather than in the printed edition of his homilies. These are the Pauline doctrine of the division of history into the old and new dispensations, the Augustinian threefold demarcation of redemptive history, and the nautical similes found in his epistles.

The Pauline "two epochs" application is to be found in Romans, Gal. 4:4–5, and Heb. 1:1–2. Put most simply, the apostle divided the history of salvation into the first age, when men were under the law, and the second, the time of grace, with Christ's advent as the delimitation. Herbert reflected this doctrine in several instances. Henry of Huntingdon wrote that he had heard the bishop preach on the end of the world, saying "the truth will last longer than the type, the light than the shadow, the thing signified than the indication, the time of grace than the time of law."[47] In his Maundy Thursday sermon, he interpreted that feast day as "*finis legalis. et inchoatio est evangelici sacrificii,*" and in that for the feast of St. Paul he applied the interpretation transmitted by Henry of Huntingdon to Saul's persecution of the Light.[48]

Augustine added an age to the Pauline eschatology, that before the law,[49] and Herbert stated this teaching as well in a letter to Odo

44. *HS*, p. 162. Aelfric, I, 222 (Easter). Bede, *Hom*, II, 7 (*In vig. Paschae*), pp. 227–228. Gregory, *Hom. in Ev.*, cols. 1170 and 1217. See also Rabanus, in *PL*, CX, cols. 34 and 35.

45. As in n. 44, but that Aelfric has the angel's robes signify glory, and Bede and Gregory imply rather than explicitly state Herbert's idea.

46. *HS*, p. 160. Aelfric, I, 222. Bede, *In Marc.*, IV, 639. Gregory, *Hom. in Ev.*, col. 1170.

47. Henry of Huntingdon, *De contemptu mundi*, in *Historia anglorum*, p. xix; also in Capgrave, *Liber de Illust. Henricis*, pp. 176–177. Another sermon not in the surviving Norwich MS is reported in the *Liber Eliensis* (above, 142).

48. *HS*, pp. 146 and 300.

49. Augustine, serm. cx, in *PL*, XXXVIII, col. 638 (triennium autem, tria sunt tempora: unum ante Legem, alterum sub Lege, tertium sub gratia); *Epistulae*, ep. 155; *De Trinitate*, IV, Chap. 4, in *PL*, XLII, cols. 892–893; *Enchiridion*, in *PL*, XL, col. 287. On the three ages and other elements of medieval historical theology, see Chenu, *Théologie*, pp. 62–89.

encouraging him to embrace the monastic life with more fervor: "*ante legem et sub lege laboriose nostri praelati sunt patres, sui Salvatoris a longe salutantes praesentiam, et nostrorum temporum suarum virtutum insigniis praefigurantes plenitudinem.*"[50] This triune division of history, like the "six ages" and the twofold interpretation, a response to the Christian desire to interpret historical process as a redemptive process, was common in medieval exegesis, and (among many others) it appeared in a sermon collection roughly contemporaneous with those of Herbert, in the "York Anonymous," Aelfric, Bede, and Gregory the Great.[51]

One of the most common symbolisms in the western literary tradition is the comparison of life and its turbulence with the uncertainty of a sea voyage. This simile is in three of Herbert's letters. He lamented to Abbot Richard of St. Alban's that the abbot had simply sat in safety on the shore and watched as the bishop tossed about like a ship in a storm, offering no succor.[52] In writing to Norman the Sacristan he symbolized some misfortune by representing it as shipwreck after he relied on calm seas and fair breezes—ignoring the perils of submerged rocks he was dashed on Palinurus after having been seized by Scylla and Charybdis and was now an outcast on an alien shore.[53] In yet another letter he again referred to Scylla, Charybdis, and Palinurus when comparing life to a sea journey in which Christ should be one's pilot.[54] Nautical metaphors abound in medieval literature, and among many using them were the bishop's contemporaries Ivo of Chartres and John of Fécamp, his near-contemporary Aelfric of Eynsham, and Boniface, Columban, Gregory I, and Cyprian of Carthage.[55]

50. *HE*, ep. 13.

51. Williams, *Norman Anonymous*, p. 9. *Old Eng. Homilies*, II, 3. Aelfric, I, 312 (also in *Old Eng. Homilies*, I, 89). Bede, *Hom.*, I, 14, p. 96. Gregory, *Hom. in Ev.*, col. 1228.

52. *HE*, ep. 10.

53. *Ibid.*, ep. 12. Homer's *Odyssey*, xii, is the first appearance of Scylla and Charybdis, which occur throughout Greek and Roman literature. Palinurus, Aeneas' steersman on the voyage from Troy to Italy following Troy's fall, was lost overboard because of Neptune's requirement that one life be given the god in return for his calming of the storm, an act of grace which saved many lives. Palinurus was murdered by mainlanders and the cape where this is alleged to have taken place (C. Spartimento) received his name: Vergil, *Aeneid*, iii, 11. 337 ff.

54. *HE*, ep. 22.

55. Curtius, *European Literature*, pp. 128–130; Owst, *Literature and Pulpit*, pp. 68–69; and many other secondary works treat of nautical metaphors. For some representative ecclesiastical users, consult the following: Ivo of Chartres, ep. 165, in *PL*, CLXII, col. 169. Leclercq, *Jean de Fécamp*, pp. 143, 168, 189–190. Aelfric, II, 386 ff. and 393 ff. (also in *Old Eng. Homilies*, II, 43 ff. and 161 ff.). Boniface, epp. 31–33, 38, in *Die Briefe des heiligen Bonifatius und Lullus*, ed. M. Tangl (*MGH, Epistolae selectae*, I). Columban *Epistolae*, ed.

Herbert employed *exempla* in five of his sermons, those for Christmas, Epiphany, Purification, Ash Wednesday, and St. Michael and All Angels. The last is a structurally peculiar homily; the *exemplum* occupies more than half the sermon and simply repeats, as he acknowledged, the major portion of Gregory the Great's sermon on angelology.[56]

The history of *exempla* for this period has received excellent studies.[57] It can be said that Jesus introduced them in the form of parables into Christianity, and they were certainly common among the Fathers. Gregory I not only enthusiastically encouraged their use and himself set the example, but as well wrote, in his *Dialogues*, a thesaurus of sermon-stories for later homilists. In the patristic and early medieval periods the sources of these tales, histories, fables, parables, moral lessons, or descriptions, which served to emphasize doctrinal, religious, or moral points— were primarily biblical and the acta of the Fathers, martyrs, and saints.[58] By Herbert's time preachers drew but seldom on the Bible for *exempla*, but often on apparitions, fables, natural history, visions, and so on.[59] The bishop of Norwich used one *exemplum* whose source is purportedly history, two apparitions, and one vision. In some measure they satisfied one or another of the manifold specific intentions which *exempla* might assume: to illustrate the consequences of obeying or disobeying a moral precept, to prove an assertion, to "arouse fear in the sinful or to stimulate the godly," and probably to "revive languid listeners" and "to eke out a scant sermon"[60]—the Candlemas and Ash Wednesday sermons would be less than ten printed pages each were the *exempla* excised.

The *exemplum* appended to the Christmas sermon postulates a city in the Greek east where Christians and Jews lived in harmony. Common association brought some leaven of Christianity to the Jews and especially to their children, and as a result a Jewish boy received Communion on Easter with his Christian playmates. Upon his return home he made the

W. Gundlach (*MGH, Epistolae merowingici et karolini aevi*, III), pp. 156–160. Gregory, *Reg. epistolarum*, I, 354–355; *Regula pastoralis*, ed. H. R. Bramley (Oxford and London, 1874), pp. 322, 356–368, 404. Cyprian, *Ad Donatum*, in *Opera omnia*, I, 5–6.

56. Gregory, *Hom. in Ev.*, xxiv, cols. 1246–1259. This passage is also the matins lection for this feast in the Sarum Breviary (*Breviarium ad usum Sarum*, Fasc. III, pp. 867 ff.).

57. Joseph A. Mosher, *The Exemplum in the Early Religious and Didactic Literature of England* (New York, 1911), and J.-Th. Welter, *L'Exemplum dans la littérature religieuse et didactique de Moyen Age* (Paris and Toulouse, 1927). Also of value, although concentrating primarily on later centuries, is T. F. Crane, *Medieval Sermon-Books and Stories*, Proceedings of the American Philosophical Society, XXI (Philadelphia, 1883).

58. Spicq, *Esquisse*, pp. 177–178.

59. Welter, *Exemplum*, p. 33, and Mosher, *Exemplum in England*, p. 33.

60. Mosher, *Exemplum in England*, p. 8.

serious error of telling his parents, and the father, enraged, fired up his furnace and hurled the child into it. The mother, who had instigated the horrible deed, repented and ran to the Christians who, having been told of the act, immediately rushed to the furnace, broke it open, and found the boy alive. Following his liberation from the fire the child told his rescuers that the Blessed Virgin and her Son had preserved him from the terrible end to which he had been abandoned. The Christians then visited punishment upon the members of the Jewish community who would not accept Christ: *combusti sunt*, in the very furnace which was to have been the fiery tomb of the child.[61] The didactic purpose of this jolly tale is clearly stated: it demonstrates how Christ looks after His own, in contrast to the usual interpretation of it as illustrating the protective power of the Blessed Virgin.[62] It seems unnecessary to add that this *exemplum* has not the remotest connection with Christmas.

    The Judaeo-Christian tradition is rich in stories of believers escaping from similar uncomfortable situations, from the children in Nebuchadnezzar's furnace (Dan. 3) to Gregory the Great's monk unharmed in the oven,[63] and beyond. As far as I am aware, the story used by Herbert Losinga first appeared in the *Ecclesiastical History* of Evagrius Scholasticus, a historian well described as "credulous and addicted to miracles."[64] Appearing first in the West in Gregory of Tours, the *exemplum* was very popular in the Norwich bishop's own time:[65] William of Malmesbury used it, it is in a collection of Marian miracles from the English twelfth century, and in at least one Norman writer contemporary with Herbert.[66] It seems unnecessary to cite all the users of the story: it was one of the most popular of all medieval sermon-stories.[67]

61. *HS*, pp. 30–32.

62. E. A. Wallis Budge, *One Hundred and Ten Miracles of our Lady Mary* (Oxford, 1937), pp. 156–158.

63. Gregory I, *Dialogii*, pp. 184–185.

64. Evagrius Scholasticus, *Historiae ecclesiasticae*, in *PG*, LXXXVI², col. 2770. Berthold Altaner, *Patrology*, trans. Hilda C. Graef (New York, 1960), p. 277.

65. Gregory of Tours, *Libri miraculorum*, Vol. I: *De gloria martyrum*, ed. Bruno Krusch and W. Arndt (*MGH, Scriptores rerum merovingicarum*, I, Part 2), 494–495 (also in *PL*, LXXI, cols. 714–715). R. W. Southern, "The English Origins of the Miracles of the Virgin," *Mediaeval and Renaissance Studies*, IV (1958), 176–216, throughout.

66. Stubbs printed the table of contents in his introduction to Malmesbury, *GR*, I, cxxv (*Liber de mirac. BVM*, C. I: *Quomodo pueram judaeorum ab incendio clibani liberavit*). T. F. Crane (ed.), *Liber de miraculis Sanctae Dei genetricis Mariae*, Cornell University Studies in Romance Languages and Literature, I (Ithaca, 1925), Chap. 31, 39–40. Durand of Troarn, *Liber de corpore et sanguine Christi*, in *PL*, CXLIX, cols. 1420–1421.

67. Eugen Wolter, *Der Judenknabe*, Bibliotheca normannica, I (Halle, 1879), collects a number of these legends and comments upon them. His list may be expanded on the

The bishop's next *exemplum*, ending his homily for the Feast of the Epiphany, teaches the scriptural and monastic lesson that he who cares for the poor cares for Christ in their guise.[68] A wealthy man, most generous with his material possessions, invited a poor stranger into his home to share the evening meal. Ministering to his needs he was about to present the stranger with water in which to wash his hands when the man suddenly disappeared. The following night the Lord appeared to the rich man and announced that it had been He Himself who had been received as a stranger the evening before. As Herbert acknowledged, this anecdote, also used by Aelfric, derived from Gregory the Great.[69]

The two remaining *exempla* seem to be original with the bishop of Norwich, although that concluding the Purification sermon is similar to many Marian legends in circulation during his period. A man lay gravely ill, and the Virgin, appearing to him as a physician, laid her hand upon his chest and he promptly recovered. Not unnaturally, the newly cured person asked the identity of his attendant. The Virgin disclosed herself and returned to the company of the saints.[70] While doubtless a variation of the Mary healing *exempla*,[71] this form seems to be Herbert's own, his didactic purpose being to show that the Holy Mother is present with, and leads, all believers.

The second anecdote whose source remains undiscovered concerns "wicked men punished by fiends" and warnings from the dying.[72] Herbert related the gruesome tale of a young man, his king's confidant, who abused his position by encouraging the evil, while trampling upon the good, men in the royal entourage.[73] This courtier fell moribund and the king, hastening to the bedside, exhorted the young bravo to repent and make his confession. He refused, judging that it would be hypocritical for him to confess in fear of death those things which he had not confessed in time of health. The wretch fell daily into illness more critical, and the

---

basis of the citations above, although the monograph is exhaustive for the material published before 1879 (but he did overlook Herbert's use of the exemplum).

68. *HS*, pp. 70–72. Cf. Benedict, *Regula*, chap. 53.

69. Aelfric, II, 286. Gregory, *Hom. in Ev.*, col. 1183.

70. *HS*, pp. 88–90.

71. See, throughout, the following for exhaustive cataloging of Marian legends: Southern, "English Origins." Crane, *Sermon-Books*. Welter, *Exemplum*. Mosher, *Exemplum in England*. Budge, *Miracles of Our Lady*. Albert Poncelet, "Miraculorum B. V. Mariae quae saec. iv–xv Latine conscripta sunt," *Analecta Bollandiana*, XXI (1902), 241–360. Adolfo Mussafia, *Studien zur den mittelalterlichen Marienlegende*, Sitzungsberichte der Kaiserliche Akademie der Wissenschaft in Wien, Phil.-Hist. Classe, 5 parts (1887–1898).

72. Mosher, *Exemplum in England*, p. 28.

73. *HS*, pp. 108–112.

ruler's continued admonitions and consolations went unheeded. Despairing of salvation, he rejected the monarch's repeated pleading that he make a good confession, and revealed that he had seen a vision in which two foul apparitions had presented him with the record of his few good deeds while numerous unwholesome entities catalogued his many evil acts. As the deplorable acts far outweighed the commendable, his despair appeared justified and indeed the wicked counsellor was not disappointed in his expectations, for his soul was borne off in triumph to hell as he expired. Curiously, the moral drawn by Herbert from this grisly story is the futility of despair.

Since the only surviving sources for the theology of Herbert Losinga are the sermons, and since his sermons were not the vehicle for speculative or learned theology, we cannot expect to find argument and elucidation of theological principles in these pastoral homilies. He asserted, stated, postulated: he did not explain or develop. It is possible to find contemporary uses, patristic and biblical sources, credal statements, and conciliar decisions as the sources of virtually every doctrinal teaching of the bishop.

Trinitarian doctrine was worked out in the first four and a quarter centuries of the church's history, largely as a response to heretical movements. The customary words of the orthodox apologists, such as Irenaeus, Athanasius, Hilary, and Augustine, were the ones used in Herbert's sermons: the Trinity was transcendant, coequal, coeternal, consubstantial, identical in substance with distinction of persons, and so on. The very words used by the Fathers as they groped toward expression of truth beyond human understanding became enshrined in the theological lexicon of the middle ages, and Herbert's use of them, so frequent as to require no documentation, was to be expected.[74] He also taught a doctrine postpatristic in definition, the Dual Procession of the Holy Spirit, that is, that the Holy Spirit proceeds from both the Father and the Son rather than from the Father alone,[75] a dogma still not accepted by the Eastern Orthodox church. Herbert preached little on the Father in the fourteen surviving sermons, expounding instead on the other two persons of the Trinity.

There was little unusual in Herbert's Christology, the unique citation

74. Of the vast literature concerning the development of Trinitarian doctrine through the Council of Chalcedon, I have found the following most helpful: J. N. D. Kelly, *Early Christian Doctrines* (New York, 1958); G. L. Prestige, *God in Patristic Thought* (London, 1959); Altaner, *Patrology*; Quasten, *Patrology*, Vols. I–III.

75. *HS*, p. 6. On the doctrine, see Prestige, *God*, pp. 250 ff., and Joseph Tixeront, *Histoire des dogmes dans l'antiquité chrétienne*, 2nd ed., Vol. III: *La fin de l'age patristique* (Paris, 1912), 335 ff.

being one referring to Jesus' birth. Preaching on the festival of the Nativity, he taught that Christ was "born of the Father."[76] The "born" is unusual and, if taken narrowly, unorthodox as it is at clear variance with both the Nicene Creed and the Athanasian symbol, which use "begotten." But as this homily opened with the symbolism referred to above in which the bishop preached the eternity of all three persons of the Godhead he was using *nasci* in its broadest meaning, i.e., the verbal form of any generative act. It was also unusual for him to state the presence of God the Father in the Virgin's womb sharing in the act of Christ's conception,[77] for the credal statements of the church clearly teach the sole operation of the Holy Spirit in this function. I doubt that this teaching was intentionally unorthodox: probably it was either a literary device to emphasize the cooperation of the persons of the Trinity in the Incarnation or a scribal error.

In two homilies Herbert asserted that there were three elements in Jesus: Godhead (or, in the Nativity sermon, mind), soul, and flesh.[78] This triune division occurs in an anonymous collection of sermons from Herbert's time, in Priscillian, Isidore, Eucherius, Augustine, Jerome, Cassian, and Ambrose, and appears first to have been utilized by Irenaeus of Lyons and by Origen.[79] The interpretation is Pauline in origin.[80] More common was the often-reiterated principle occurring in Herbert's homilies that Christ has two natures, divine and human, a teaching which obviously requires no supporting evidence for its currency in the Christian tradition. The bishop taught that at the Crucifixion only the human nature of Jesus endured the Passion, not the divine nature, in which he repeated a teaching of Aelfric, Rabanus Maurus, Gregory the Great, and Augustine.[81]

Herbert's teaching on the life of Christ adheres closely to Scripture except where he touched upon some incidents involving the life St. Mary the Virgin, which will be dealt with below. It is interesting that this

76. *HS*, p. 6: "de patre filium nasci."

77. *Ibid.*, pp. 6–8.

78. *Ibid.*, pp. 8, 174–176.

79. A. O. Balfour (ed.), *Twelfth Century Homilies in MS. Bodley 343* (EETS, CXXXVII), p. 88. Lubac, *Exégèse*, Part 1, 194–195. Farrer, *Hist. Interpretation*, pp. 196–197. Irenaeus, *Contra haereses*, III:22, in *PG*, VII, col. 956 (in Latin *temp.* Herbert: Siegmund, *Überlieferung*, p. 90; Courcelle, *Lettres grecques*, p. 185).

80. Lubac, *Exégèse*, Part 1, 194–195.

81. *HS*, p. 14: "Ita in cruce salvatoris divinitas mansit impassabilis. et humana natura succubuit passioni." Aelfric, I, 120. Rabanus, in *PL*, CX, col. 16. Gregory I, *Hom. in Ev.*, col. 226; *Moralia*, in *PL*, LXXV, cols. 895–896. Augustine, *De Trin.*, IV, Chap. 4, in *PL*, XLII, cols. 889–892.

preacher, so given to allegorizing and moralizing, resisted the temptation when he recited the wonderful works (*magnalia*) of Christ in his Pentecost sermon—he simply listed the incidents, rather than explaining their mystical or moral meanings, unlike his former abbot John of Fécamp in his *Confessio theologica.*[82] His identifications of Jesus with Old Testament prophecies are the customary ones (as found in Isaiah, for example).

Herbert's teaching on the Holy Spirit is referrable to the conciliar and credal statements of His role in the Godhead but for the interpretation he referred to the Pentecost *glossalalia*—here he was particularly unscriptural, as were his possible sources. The bishop stated the gift of tongues to mean one universal language rather than a diversity of speech, an interpretation used in his own time by an unknown English homilist and by Aelfric nearly a century earlier.[83] The Venerable Bede introduced this idea to the West by transmitting Rufinus' translation of a sermon by Gregory of Nyssa; Gregory seems to be the earliest source for it.[84] Herbert's exposition of the operations of the Holy Spirit is otherwise literal retelling of scriptural narratives, recounting His role as inspirer of prophets, apostles, and so on.

The bishop's ecclesiology is again quite brief, concerned only with the necessity for unity with the church and the meaning of the Petrine commission, and the sermons contain only one sentence relating to the episcopal office. As would be expected, he taught that Christians must be in communion with the institutional church, the Body of Christ.[85] This ancient doctrine is traceable ultimately to conflicts in the early centuries of the church, when those in heresy claimed to be as truly Christian as those within her communion. It was necessary, Hilary of Poitiers taught, to be united with the church on the grounds of her authority, her teaching, her sacraments, and her visible unity.[86] There were many statements of this requirement and the reason for it, perhaps the strongest being those of Cyprian of Carthage, who taught that Christ and the Holy Spirit were not

82. *HS*, pp. 260–264. Leclercq, *Jean de Fécamp*, pp. 139–140 (and in *PL*, CI, col. 1065, where it is tentatively [but incorrectly] ascribed to Alcuin).

83. *HS*, p. 260. *Old Eng. Homilies*, II, 117–119. Aelfric, I, 318; he identified this language as the tongue common to all men before the beginning of the Tower of Babel.

84. Bede, *Expositio actuum Apostolorum et retractio*, ed. M. L. W. Laistner (Cambridge, Mass., 1939), pp. 14 and 16, 98; see also M. L. W. Laistner, "Bede as a Classical and Patristic Scholar," in Chester G. Starr (ed.), *The Intellectual Heritage of the Early Middle Ages* (Ithaca, 1957), p. 106. Gregory of Nyssa, *De Spiritu Sancto sive in Pentecostem*, in *PG*, XLVI, cols. 698–699.

85. *HS*, pp. 256–258.

86. Kelly, *Doctrines*, pp. 409 ff.

operative but in the church: *"salus extra ecclesiam non est,*[87] *christianus non est qui in Christi ecclesia non est."*[88] Herbert's admonition was not rare; so common was it indeed that it is impossible to make an intelligent guess as to his source. The teaching was part of the milieu and of the prior ecclesiological tradition of the church.[89]

What was the foundation of this church with which organic and sacramental union was prerequisite to salvation? He preached that its bedrock was Peter's confession of faith: "Thou art the Christ, the Son of the living God," a dictum common among later twelfth-century canonists, used by Orderic Vitalis and by Aelfric, by the Carolingian divine Rabanus Maurus, Isidore of Seville, Augustine of Hippo and many, many others.[90]

The bishop of Norwich referred only in passing, and vaguely, to the importance of his own office: *"Magna res episcopalis potestas ...."*[91]

He preached on only three of the seven sacraments: Baptism, the Eucharist, and Penance. Not only the numbering but even the definition of the sacraments was still tentative in Herbert's day, and not until after his own death in the twelfth century was the first definite list of sacraments established.[92] Vagueness of definition rendered such precision impossible before then—for example the great Augustine offered the definition *"sacramentum est sacrum signum."* The so-called "sacraments of initiation" (Baptism, Confirmation, the Eucharist) were those most commonly cited in the patristic and early medieval periods; Penance was first called a sacrament by Gregory the Great. It seems hardly necessary to add that his referring to these alone in his surviving sermons does not imply that Herbert accepted only three of these rites as sacraments.

The homilist's sole doctrinal teaching on the function of Baptism is so common, permeating Christian history from the Bible itself, that it needs

---

87. Cyprian, *Epistulae* (CSEL, III[2]), ep. 73.

88. *Ibid.*, ep. 55. See also his *De catholicae ecclesiae* (CSEL, III[1]), pp. 209–233.

89. Tixeront, *Hist. des dogmes*, III, 361 ff.

90. *HS*, p. 268. Brian Tierney, *Foundations of the Conciliar Theory* (Cambridge, 1955), pp. 26 ff. Aelfric, I, 368 and II, 390. Orderic, *Hist. eccles.*, I, 228. Rabanus, St. Peter sermon, in *PL*, CX, cols. 332–333. Isidore, *Etymologarium*, L. VII, ix. Augustine, *De Trin.*, in *PL*, XLII, col. 864; *idem*, Pentecost serm., in *PL*, XXXVIII, cols. 1239, and serm. for SS. Peter and Paul, in *ibid.*, cols. 1348–1349; but *Tract. in Jn.*, p. 685, states Christ to be the rock on which the church is built.

91. *HS*, p. 106. In *HE*, ep. 35, he drew the analogy between the relations of husband to wife, and bishop to the people of his church, judging the latter superior to the former because it is of a spiritual, rather than of a temporal, nature.

92. P. Pourrat, *The Theology of the Sacraments* (St. Louis, 1910), pp. 258 ff. This paragraph is based on Pourrat.

no supporting evidence as to sources. Baptism, he taught, symbolizes a washing of the soul and "drowns" both original and actual sin.[93] His poetic and popular exegesis of the baptism of Christ, presented in his Epiphany sermon, attempts to confront the question why Christ, who knew no sin, should have been baptized by John the Baptist in Jordan. In conformity with the interpretations of Lanfranc, Aelfric, Rabanus Maurus, and Bede the Venerable, he taught that, rather than Christ deriving any sacramental benefit, His baptism imparted to water its subsequent power of conferring this sacrament.[94] This application began in the Greek east, occurring in the works of John Chrysostom, Gregory of Nyssa, Gregory Nazianzus, and Cyril of Jerusalem.[95]

The bishop's teaching on the Eucharist involved two traditional doctrines: the Real Presence and the inefficacy of unworthy reception. Most explicitly, he defined the consecrated elements as the Body and Blood of Christ, in substance although not in appearance. The sacramental Body is the historic Body which was crucified, lay in the tomb, arose from the dead, was exhibited to the Apostles, and ascended into heaven.[96] The host and the wine were received and their physical attributes subject to dentition, but the substance (Christ) is not affected by reception and ingestion. He preached here a doctrine current in Christian thought from its beginnings—the Real Presence—but in language reflecting the recent theological battle over the nature of the Eucharist as fought by Berengar of Tours and Lanfranc.

The earliest explicit teaching that the Eucharistic Body was identical with that which suffered and was resurrected was probably that of Ignatius of Antioch (ca. 35–ca. 107), and it was a recurrent theme throughout the patristic and early medieval periods.[97] Not all theologians held this strict literalist interpretation, but rare indeed was denial or qualification of the doctrine of the Real Presence. So long as the doctrine—the

93. Kelly, Doctrines, pp. 193 ff. and 428 ff., for the patristic period; Tixeront, Hist. des dogmes., III, 371 ff., for the early medieval teachings on Baptism. HS, p. 54.

94. HS, p. 42. Lanfranc, Opera, II, 22. Aelfric, II, 40. Rabanus, Epiph. serm., in PL, CX, col. 18. Bede, Hom., I, 7, p. 50 and 12, p. 81.

95. Chrysostom, In homiliam de Baptismo Christi et de Epiphanias, in PG, XLIX, cols. 365–366. Gregory of Nyssa, Hom. in Baptismum Christi, in PG, XLVI, cols. 591–594. Gregory Nazianzus, Oratio 39, in PG, XXXVI, col. 351. Cyril, Catechesis, Chap. 11: De Baptismo, in PG, XXXIII, col. 442.

96. HS, pp. 180–188: "non fantastice, set substantialiter."

97. Kelly, Doctrines, pp. 196 ff., 211 ff., 440 ff.; Tixeront, Hist. des dogmes, III, 375 ff.; E. B. Pusey, The Doctrine of the Real Presence (London, 1883), assembles an imposing catena of patristic citations embracing the doctrine (pp. 315 ff.). See also Darwell Stone, A History of the Doctrine of the Holy Eucharist, I (London, 1909), throughout.

literal transformation of the elements into the Body and Blood of Christ—
was seen with the eyes of faith there was little disagreement on the
teaching.[98] The violent controversy over Eucharistic belief between
Lanfranc and Berengar came from their common use of dialectic in
sacramental theology.

Reduced to its essentials the dispute between the learned monk and the
archdeacon of Angers turned on what, if any, change in the elements was
affected by the consecration in the Mass. Berengar held that, as the
physically measurable and perceivable qualities of the bread and wine
were unchanged, so too was their substance: the Mass was therefore
merely a representation, bringing the symbolic presence of Christ but not
bringing the thing symbolized. Lanfranc on the contrary advanced the
thesis that there was no difference between the symbol and what it
represented—that while the physical qualities of the elements remained
unchanged their substance (essence) was transformed by the consecration
into the Body and Blood of Christ.[99]

While Herbert Losinga did not attack the straw man who was Berengar, he opted clearly for his first English archbishop's position: the sacrament involved a conversion of substance. It is surprising neither that he
reflected the orthodox position on this issue so recently a subject of debate,
nor that he cautioned when speaking of the Eucharist against inquiring
too closely into the mystery: "We seek the rational explanation, but the
highest reason is to trust God's will and word"—do not reason concerning
that which is beyond reason.[100]

He also preached the conventional position on valid reception of the
Communion—following Paul (I Cor. 11:29–30), the unworthy receive the
Blessed Sacrament to their own damnation, the righteous to salvation.
With Augustine, he offered Judas as the example that reception of the
sacrament is not efficacious for the wicked.[101]

In his Palm Sunday sermon, the bishop applied Passover symbolism
to the Eucharist, making the obvious and traditional link between the

98. The ninth-century dispute between Paschasius, who maintained the doctrine
taught by Herbert, and Ratramnus did not have important effects beyond its own time;
for the dispute, see Stone, *Eucharist*, pp. 226–233.

99. Particularly acute on this controversy is R. W. Southern, "Lanfranc of Bec and
Berengar of Tours," in R. W. Hunt, *et al.* (eds.), *Studies in Medieval History Presented to
Frederick Maurice Powicke* (Oxford, 1948), pp. 27–48; cf. A. J. MacDonald, *Berengar and
the Reform of Sacramental Doctrine* (London, 1930), throughout.

100. *HS*, p. 190; *ibid.*, p. 6, also describes the Nativity as beyond reason.

101. *Ibid.*, pp. 190–192. Augustine, *Tract. in Jn.*, L, 437 and LXII, 483. See Stone,
Eucharist, throughout.

Old and the New Testament sacrifices. He emulated Gregory I in preaching that blood is sprinkled on both doorposts (Exod. 12) when the Eucharist is received with the heart as well as with the mouth.[102] Herbert found as the spiritual meaning in the Passover events that one should meditate upon the sacrament and upon the Incarnation, then went on to allegorize that in eating the head of the lamb one should understand perceiving the divinity of Christ, as with Aelfric, Bede, and Cyril of Jerusalem, an early possible (but unlikely) source.[103] Again following Bede, the meaning of roasting the lamb was that the mysteries of the Incarnation should not be diluted by the weak waters of human learning (as in boiling),[104] and to eat the feet of the lamb was to seek and imitate the human nature of Christ, as taught also by Aelfric, Bede, and Cyril.[105] Again as in Bede and Aelfric, the lamb's viscera signified the hidden commandments of Christ's teachings. This allegorizing seems rather tortuous when compared with the biblical similes representing Christ as the Passover Lamb fulfilling the Exodus Passover, but simplicity was not among the bishop's homiletic virtues.

His teachings on the sacrament of Penance are spare but sufficient to place his doctrine in the development of sacramental confession in the western church, since we are again fortunate in having brilliant studies of the history of Penance, both from a historical and from a theological point of view.[106] It is true that "our knowledge about the Church's theology of penance [in the first and second centuries] remains bafflingly obscure."[107] In part this uncertainty derives from the question whether sin committed after Baptism could even be remitted, but it seems clear that by the time of the second-century Father Hermas at least one remission was permitted although there is no certainty as to the formal machinery for its implementation.[108] The first mention of Penance as a prerequisite for Communion

102. *HS*, p. 128; the simile is also in the contemporaneous *Old Eng. Homilies*, I, 126. Gregory, *Hom. in Ev.*, col. 1178.

103. *HS*, p. 130. Aelfric, II, 280. Bede, *Hom.*, II, 4, pp. 210–211; *idem, In pentateuchum commentarii*, in *PL*, XCI, col. 306. Cyril of Jerusalem, *Catechesis*, in *PG*, XXXIII, col. 726.

104. *HS*, p. 130. Bede, *In pentateuchum*, col. 306.

105. *Ibid.*

106. Oscar David Watkins, *A History of Penance*, 2 vols. (London, 1920) (this work prints the relevant texts discussed in its narrative); R. C. Mortimer, *Origins of Private Penance in the Western Church* (Oxford, 1939); Paul Anciaux, *La Théologie du Sacrement de Pénitence au XIIe siècle* (Louvain and Gembloux, 1949). See also the pertinent material in Altaner, *Patrology*; Quasten, *Patrology*; and Paul Galtier, *L'Église et la rémission des péchés aux prèmiers siècles* (Paris, 1932).

107. Kelly, *Doctrines*, p. 198.

108. Watkins, *Penance*, I, 57–70.

appears in the postapostolic Didache, although this is in all probability liturgical rather than sacramental confession.[109] Penance in the early years of the church was public, although there is controversy whether the confession of specific sins was as well, but by the late fourth century the practice of private confession to a priest was gaining ground, particularly as the practice was encouraged by Gregory of Nyssa and by John Chrysostom, and Rome during the reign of Pope Innocent II saw the connection of Penance with Lent which became so marked a feature of western homiletics.[110]

As a result of English and Irish influences, the early middle ages witnessed the general introduction of the system of private confession and private penance into penitential practice: now sacramental confession and sacerdotal absolution could be repeated.[111] By the early ninth century it was the "general practice [to confess] at the beginning of Lent,"[112] so it is hardly startling that Herbert's entire Ash Wednesday sermon exhorted his listeners to make their confession and receive absolution.[113] The bishop urged confession before communion, and preached that the descent of the dove at Jesus' baptism symbolized the remission of sins by the church in which the Spirit still dwells.[114]

Herbert's penitential theology is that of his age. Despite the fact that he exhorted rather than explained, his exhortations imply the doctrine. In his Ash Wednesday sermon he promised absolution to follow the congregation's sacramental confession. In a letter to William Turbe he castigated the future bishop for confessing through an intermediary, and in another he granted absolution, having read the confession, to William, specifically invoking the power of the keys (John 20:23 and Matt. 16:19).[115] Here we see Herbert acting as the agent of God, assuring the penitent of the absolution which God gave. Confession to him was necessary because the priest must know the gravity and nature of the offenses in order to assign proper penance and to judge the contrition of the sinner.[116]

109. *La Didaché*, ed. Jean-Paul Audet, Études bibliques (Paris, 1958), Chap. 14, p. 240. Siegmund, *Überlieferung*, p. 65, shows that the Didache was available in Latin well before Herbert's time. Quasten, *Patrology*, I, 33, and Watkins, *Penance*, I, 73–74, for the judgment.

110. Watkins, *Penance*, I, 326 ff. and 415, and II, 537 ff. Dix, *Shape of the Liturgy*, pp. 355–356; Tixeront, *Hist. des dogmes*, III, 387 ff.

111. Watkins, *Penance*, II, 537 ff., 644 ff., and throughout.

112. *Ibid.*, p. 713.

113. *HS*, pp. 92–108. The same exhortation is in the contemporaneous *Old Eng. Homilies*, I, 25 ff., and II, 71 ff. Balfour (ed.), *Twelfth Cent. Hom.*, pp. 40–42 and 50–54.

114. *HS*, pp. 24, 50–52 (also in Bede, *In Luc.*, 84), pp. 140–142.

115. *HE*, epp. 41, 42.   116. Anciaux, *Pénitence*, pp. 31–43.

The bishop's hagiography dealt only with the saints of Scripture, and his treatment of these figures is based on biblical, apocryphal, and patristic sources. In only one instance did he reflect theological controversies of his time, in mentioning the Immaculate Conception—and he suggested, rather than argued, the opinion. His only other excursion into hagiographic theology also involved St. Mary, but this—the perpetual virginity—was interlaced with patristic and early medieval authority and was hence not a matter of contemporary controversy.

Herbert insisted that devotion to the Virgin really belongs to her Son,[117] but his preaching did not reflect this theological position. He well deserved the description of himself as a "pious client of the Mother of God,"[118] although he appeared to be unduly credulous. As the Blessed Virgin's place in the church's devotional life increased, the problem of the spare Bible narrative concerning her arose. The lack of scriptural material dealing with her life after the birth of Jesus was to some extent compensated for by allegorizing the Old Testament, especially the Song of Songs, and to a further extent by the utilization of apocryphal writings. Less important during Herbert's lifetime was the growth of romance and devotional invention, although its beginnings were already to be detected in the works of Anselm, Eadmer, and Bernard of Clairvaux.

So little does the Bible say of St. Mary that even the names of her parents are not canonically attested, but by Herbert's period tradition had fixed their names as Anna and Joachim, and so the bishop named them.[119] Like Elizabeth and Zacharias, he taught, they were of pure life but beyond childbearing age; however, in answer to their prayers, they were granted the girl Mary whom they raised with the aid of the Holy Spirit.[120] The legend of Anna and Joachim had been ever

117. *HS*, p. 330.

118. Francis M. Miltner, "The Immaculate Conception in England up to the Time of Duns Scotus, II: The First Champions in England of the Doctrine of the Immaculate Conception," *Marianum*, I (1939), 203. The same appellation is applied by H. Thurston, "Abbot Anselm of Bury and the Immaculate Conception," *The Month*, CIII (1904) 564.

119. The original source for their names is the apocryphal *Protevangelium Jacobi*, which Altaner (*Patrology*, p. 67) judges to have been written before 200. The *Protevangelium* is in J. C. Thilo (ed.), *Codex apocryphus Novi Testamenti* (Leipzig, 1832), pp. 167–173. From it is apparently derived the ninth-century Latin *Pseudo-Matthaei Evangelium*, printed in Konstantin von Tischendorf, *Evangelia apocrypha* (Leipzig, 1876), pp. 54 ff., and J. A. Fabricius (ed.), *Codex apocryphus Novi Testamenti* (Hamburg, 1703), pp. 19 ff., where it appears under the title *Evangelium de Nativitate Mariae*. This work was at Fécamp in Herbert's time; see Appendix II, p. 232. Cf. Quasten, *Patrology*, I, 119.

120. *HS*, pp. 330–332.

more widely taught from the time of Justin Martyr forward, and had merged into the tradition of the medieval church well before Herbert's time.

The popularity of the Feast of the Immaculate Conception (December 8) was first manifest in England in the eleventh and early twelfth centuries, although it did not originate there.[121] In the words of the official dogmatic definition (Pius IX, *Ineffabilis Deus*, 1854) the central belief is that "from the first moment of her conception, the Blessed Virgin Mary was . . . kept free from all stain of original sin" in order that she might be a more perfect vehicle for bearing the Godhead in human form. The feast appears to have begun within Greek ecclesiastical jurisdiction and first appeared in definite form in the West in the ninth century. Coming to England in the eleventh century, the liturgical celebration of the conception became ever more popular in the twelfth, particularly after its sanction by the 1129 Council of London. But in Herbert's day, the doctrine, which had enjoyed widespread approbation among the Anglo-Saxons,[122] was in temporary disfavor, probably due to the Norman settlement with its attendant scorn of things English. While Herbert was thus teaching something controversial he was not unique, for Anselm's great disciple Eadmer was the seminal English theologian of the Immaculate Conception, and he was Herbert's contemporary.[123]

There is a contradiction in the bishop's presentation of the doctrine. In his sermon for the Feast of the Assumption the doctrine is quite plain: speaking of the Virgin, he described Mary "*cui nulla de propagine macula*

121. I find the following works most helpful for the development of the doctrine in the prescholastic period: Edmund Bishop, "On the Origins of the Feast of the Conception of the Blessed Virgin Mary," *Liturgica Historica* (Oxford, 1918), pp. 238–259. Mirella Levi d'Ancona, *The Iconography of the Immaculate Conception in the Middle Ages and Early Renaissance*, Monographs on Archaeology and Fine Arts Sponsored by the Archaeological Institute of America and the College Art Association of America, VII (New York, 1957), 6 ff. A. W. Burridge, "L'Immaculée conception dans la théologie de l'Angleterre médiévale," *Revue d'histoire ecclésiastique*, XXXII (1936), 570–597. "L'Immaculée conception," in A. Vacant and E. Mangenot, *Dictionnaire de théologie catholique*, VII¹, 845 ff.; this article, by X. le Bachelet and M. Jugie, contains extracts from relevant documents. R. W. Southern, "English Origins," pp. 176–216. Jean Fournée, "L'Abbaye de Fécamp et les origines du culte de l'Immaculée-conception en Normandie," in de Povremogne, *Fécamp*, II, 163–170, is disappointing.

122. Southern, "England in the Twelfth-Century Renaissance," pp. 207 ff.

123. On Eadmer's Mariology, see Southern, *St. Anselm, passim*, and especially pp. 290 ff., and P. Godfried Geenan, "Eadmer, le prèmier théologien de l'Immaculée Conception," *Academia Mariana internationalis: Virgo Immaculata*, Vol. V: *De Immaculata Conceptione in epocha introductoria scholasticae*, Acta congressus mariologici-mariani Romae anno MCMLIV celebrati (Rome, 1955), 90–136.

inhesisset."[124] But in the Christmas homily he preached that the Holy Spirit came upon her, freeing her both from original and from actual sin.[125] This purification from original sin would clearly have been unnecessary had she not shared this attribute of mankind in general. Ingenious, imaginative, and somewhat devious explanations have been originated to explain the contradiction,[126] but they appear unconvincing. Perhaps one of the references is a scribal error; there are others in the manuscript. Or possibly, although it is unlikely since the sermons probably came from the same liturgical year, his Marian theology evolved—were this so, it might reflect the changing response of the bishop to the influence of others, for Anselm opposed the doctrine while Eadmer espoused it.[127] There appears to be no satisfactory way to reconcile the contradiction without abandoning the evidence, which allows no basis for reconciliation.

The bishop shared in the general tradition of patristic and early medieval Christianity in ascribing perpetual virginity to St. Mary, utilizing what had become virtually a liturgical formula for expressing the opinion: *virgo concepit. virgo peperit. virgo permansit.*[128] To catalogue all the appearances of this tradition would be purposeless: a representative sampling of Herbert's possible sources must include his contemporaries Eadmer, Anselm, Ivo of Chartres, John of Fécamp and his near-contemporaries Aelfric and the Blickling (Norfolk) homilist.[129] Gregory of

124. *HS*, p. 330.

125. *Ibid.*, p. 2. The contradiction was marked as well by Miltner, "Champions," pp. 202–203, and Thurston, "Abbot Anselm," pp. 562–564.

126. For example, Miltner, "Champions," pp. 202–203: "But surely such a pious client of the Mother of God, as we know Herbert to have been, did not suppose that up to the time of the Annunciation she was still subject to sin . . . ? [Herbert here referred to a] special and privileged purification in Mary at the time of the Annunciation [a purging of concupiscence], *caro peccati.*" See also Thurston, "Abbot Anselm," p. 564: "surely he did not mean to suggest. . . ." Perhaps he did.

127. Anselm, *De conceptu virginale et de originale peccato*, in Anselm, II, 149–153. Eadmer, *Tractatus de conceptione B. Mariae virginis*, in *PL*, CLIX, 301–318 (where it is assigned to Anselm, but see Palemon Glorieux, "Pour revaloriser Migne," *Mélanges de science religieuse*, IX (1952), Cahier supp., 63). I have used the Migne citation as the newer edition by Frs. Thurston and Slater (Freiburg-im-B., 1904) is virtually unobtainable.

128. *HS*, pp. 2–8, 74–88, 350. For a liturgical use, *Breviarium ad usum Sarum*, Fasc. III, pp. 131 ff., where the versicle for the Purification is: "Virgo concepit. virgo peperit: et post partum virgo permansit." Other versicles and responses, and the lections from Bede, are in the same sense. For the frequency of the teaching, see Altaner's and Quasten's patrologies, and Tixeront, *Hist. des dogmes*, III, 422 ff.

129. Anselm, *De excellentia virginis Mariae*, in *PL*, CLIX, cols. 557–580, where it is incorrectly attributed to Eadmer (Glorieux, "Migne," p. 62); *idem*, *Oratio ad sanctam Mariam*, in Anselm, III, 15. Ivo of Chartres, in *PL*, CLXII, col. 570. John of Fécamp, in

Tours made the formula a confession of faith and both the great Pope Gregory and Augustine of Hippo used it in their catechetical and homiletical writings.[130] The opinion, on which Jerome wrote a treatise, appears to have originated in the *Protevangelium Jacobi* and was transmitted to the Latin West through the *Transitus* of the pseudo Melito of Sardis.[131]

Following Gregory I, the bishop taught that the Virgin had suffered no pain in childbearing because there had been no lust in her conception of Christ.[132] She was attended by angels at her delivery, a detail which first appeared in the *Protevangelium*, as did the opinion that she nursed Jesus.[133] His further preaching on Mary's role in the childhood and early manhood of Christ adhered closely to the biblical narrative. It was not until the baptism of Christ was discussed that the homilist presented His mother again in contexts derived from apocrypha and tradition rather than from canonical sources.

According to Herbert, Mary was present at Jordan when the Holy Spirit descended, and at Cana it was really she who performed the miracle since she compelled Christ to convert the water to wine for the wedding feast.[134] In the same sermon, he asserted that Mary was present at all the works—miracles, instructions, and so forth—of Jesus, and he then returned to scriptural accounts in his narratives of her presence during the Passion and the Crucifixion, departing from the biblical sources only to allege, as did Eadmer, that it was to her that her Son first appeared after the Resurrection.[135]

Herbert's preaching on the Assumption is ultimately based on apocryphal sources. No connection with the bishop's sermons can be demonstrated, but it is interesting that a tenth-century Norfolk homilist recounted

---

PL, CI, cols. 1047–1048 (here attributed to Alcuin, but see Glorieux, "Migne," p. 55). Aelfric, I, 144 ff., and II, 10 and 66. *The Blickling Homilies of the Tenth Century,* ed. Richard Morris (EETS, LXIII), II, 155.

130. Gregory of Tours, *Historiarum,* in *MGH, Scriptores rerum merovingicarum,* I, pt. 1 (ed. Bruno Krusch and Wilhelm Levison), p. 4. Gregory, *Hom. in Ev.,* cols. 1197–1198 and 1283; *Moralia,* in *PL,* LXXVI, cols. 89–90 and 288. Among the many possible citations from Augustine, Herbert was most likely to have been familiar with *De cat. rudibus,* in *PL,* XL, col. 339; and the sermons, in *PL,* XXXVIII, cols. 343, 995–996, 1004, 1009–1010.

131. Jerome, *De perpetua virginitate beatae Mariae adversus Helvidium,* in *PL,* XXIII, cols. 181–216. *Protev. Jacobi,* in Thilo, *Cod. apoc. NT,* pp. 167 ff. Pseudo Melito, in *PG,* V, cols. 1236–1237. See as well Bernard Capelle (ed.), "Vestiges grecs et latins d'un antique *transitus* de la Vierge," *Analecta Bollandiana,* LXVII (1949), 21–48.

132. *HS,* p. 8. Gregory, *Moralia,* in *PL,* LXXVI, col. 288.

133. *HS,* pp. 8 and 332. *Protev. Jacobi,* in Thilo, *Cod. apoc. NT,* pp. 247–248.

134. *HS,* pp. 332–334: "dum coegit filium ut faceret miraculum."

135. *Ibid.,* p. 336.

a virtually identical group of Dormition legends, although the Blickling homilies contain much more detail than do Herbert's sermons.[136] Deriving in part from the church's condemnation of New Testament apocryphal material, the apostolic age had not seen authoritative acceptance of the idea of the Assumption of the Blessed Virgin.[137] Despite this official disapproval, the Assumption and associated events had become common stock by Herbert's time, and it is neither unique nor irregular that he used these apocryphal materials in his sermons, because he was probably utilizing them for devotional purposes rather than to establish doctrine, and there was a wide latitude for pious opinion in the medieval church.

The Apostles, he taught, were present when the body of the Virgin was entombed. This is a one-phrase summation of apocryphal writings legion in number, which state that the Apostles, scattered throughout the world, were miraculously returned to the Holy Land to attend her at her death.[138] He also omitted the incidents attendant upon her body's transit to the tomb, such as that of the impious Jew who presumed to attack her bier, with his resultant withered hand, and others. While the Virgin's body was permitted to suffer death, it was not allowed to undergo corruption, for as Christ took His flesh from hers it was obviously unsuitable that the body of the mother of Christ should share in the general fate of the dead: she was immortal both in body and in soul. The apocryphal Assumption legends, while agreeing with Herbert that Mary's flesh did not endure decomposition, state the reason for this as her virginity rather than her motherhood of God.[139] As the remains were assumed to heaven angels attended her, and she was received in heaven by her Son and exalted above all created beings. Mary still intercedes, and the bishop's congregation was urged to flee to her loving advocacy and abandon their temporal, sinful distractions.

136. *Blickling Homilies*, I, 137 ff., and II, 147 ff.

137. McNally, *Bible in M. A.*, p. 25. See now for this topic Walter J. Burghardt, *The Testimony of the Patristic Age Concerning Mary's Death* (Westminster, Md., 1957), throughout, and the sources there cited; Joseph S. Bruder, *The Mariology of St. Anselm* (Dayton, 1939), pp. 70–78; and—with great caution—Carolus Balić, *Testimonia de assumptione beatae Virginis Mariae ex omnibus saeculis*, Bibliotheca Assumptionis B. Virginis Mariae, I, Part 1 (Rome, 1948), throughout.

138. *HS*, pp. 338–352. See also *Early English Homilies from the Twelfth Century MS. Vesp. D. XIV*, ed. Rubie D.-N. Warner (EETS, CLII), pp. 43–44. "Melito," *Transitus*, in *PG*, V, col. 1238. Pseudo Matthew, in Tischendorf, *Evang. apoc.*, p. 135. For *transitus* literature generally, see Burghardt, *Testimony*, pp. 13 ff., and M. R. James, *The Apocryphal New Testament*, 2nd ed. (Oxford, 1955), pp. 194–228.

139. *HS*, pp. 338–352. Capelle, "*Transitus*," pp. 45–48. "Melito" and psuedo Matthew as in n. 138 above.

The bishop composed a remarkable prayer, addressed to St. John the Evangelist, for Queen Matilda.[140] This prayer, which provided a comprehensive review of the apocryphal literature on the Beloved Apostle, may be compared with the great Anselm's prayers to John, which are more spiritual and devotional, nonapocryphal and nonlegendary.[141] Apparently unique in early twelfth-century devotional writings,[142] this overly emotional and treacly sentimental supplication does not reveal Herbert at his finest as a composer of spiritual pieces: it lacks both the dignity and the insight of his sermons.

It was a tradition antedating the earliest of the great Latin Fathers— Tertullian, Jerome, Augustine—and probably beginning in the East between A.D. 150 and 180, that John was the Cana bridegroom, and was there called from marriage to celibacy by Christ. The suggestion is found in the lengthy prayer purportedly recited by the saint as he prepared for death, in a passage where the apostle praised God that He had thrice saved him from marriage, and while John did not explicitly state Cana as one of the three, the tradition of the early medieval church had so interpreted this thanksgiving.[143] Herbert did not neglect to salute John in this context: "friend of Christ . . . at whose nuptials He converted the water to wine. . . ."

The bishop also referred to the coolness of John's virginity preserving him from the heat of boiling oil into which he had been cast, a legend which, although known both to Tertullian and to Jerome, was not from the Acts of John.[144] The incident allegedly took place during the Domitian persecution, and does not appear to have been known to the Greeks—it is absent both from the *Apostolic History* and the pseudo Melito—but it did appear roughly contemporaneously with Herbert in Orderic Vitalis and in Aelfric's sermon for the Assumption of St. John the Apostle.[145] Herbert's special touch here is the teaching that the saint's virginity saved

140. *HE*, ep. 18. There is no firm evidence for Goulburn's and Symonds' allegation (*Life*, p. 298) that "he acted as [the queen's] spiritual counsellor," if by that they intended to imply some official relationship (such as chaplain).

141. Anselm, *Oratio* xi and xii, in Anselm, III, 42–50.

142. But, in nondevotional writings, the Joannine material appears in Orderic Vitalis, *Hist. eccles.*, II, Chap. v; on p. 222, Orderic acknowledged "Melito" as his source.

143. *De S. Johanne lib. V*, in Fabricius, *Cod. apoc. NT*, pp. 585–586. Quasten, *Patrology*, I, 135.

144. Tertullian, *De praescriptione haereticorum*, in *Opera*, II, ed. E. Kroymann (CSEL, LXX), 45–46. Jerome, *In Matt.*, in *PL*, XXII, col. 149.

145. Orderic, *Hist. eccles.*, II, 288–289. Aelfric, I, 58. Orderic relates all three apocryphal legends referred in the text to Herbert.

him from the fiery doom. While this connection is unique, it is true that church tradition placed great emphasis on John's chastity.[146]

Throughout the prayer, Herbert addressed John as having raised the dead, and there are repeated incidents of this nature throughout the apocryphal Acts of John, the most famous of which perhaps is the raising of Drusiana. The stories were repeated by pseudo Melito, and many appeared in Aelfric's sermons.[147] According to a further apocryphal legend, Aristodemus, the high priest, demanded that John prove the rightness of his faith by drinking a cup of poison, after the identical potion had demonstrated its potency by killing others. John, after invoking God's protection and power, drank the liquid and was unharmed. Aristodemus then required the further miracle that the poison's victims be restored to life before he would accept Christ. The disciple gave the high priest his cloak and, invoking Christ as he did so, instructed him to place it over the corpses. The dead were resuscitated, and Aristodemus and many others accepted Christianity and destroyed their idols and temples. Herbert referred to these incidents in a phrase, rather than emulating Aelfric in rehearsing the entire story.[148]

As John restored the dead to life, so he restored the lapsed to right faith, and the bishop of Norwich recalled this as well to the queen's mind. There were two brothers who sold their inheritance and distributed the resulting money to the poor, but having done so, and seeing their former servants richly adorned, they repented their generosity bitterly. John, observing this, directed them to bring him sticks and pebbles, which he turned into gold and precious stones, with which he bade the brothers buy back their inheritance. The Beloved Apostle then told them the parable of Lazarus and the rich man, and warned that they no longer possessed the healing gifts and miraculous powers of Christians: they had instead the worldly gifts for which they had yearned, and John counseled them at length on the folly of accumulating this world's riches. The brothers then witnessed John raise a dead youth to life; thus inspired, they asked that the apostle receive them back again as disciples. He advised them to pray for thirty days that their gold and jewels be restored to their previous condition, his own intercession aiding their orisons. The precious

146. Aelfric, I, 438. Augustine, *Tract. in Jn.*, 124, p. 687. Jerome, *Adversus Jovinianum*, in *PL*, XXIII, col. 258. "Melito," *Act. Jn.*, in *PG*, V, col. 1232.

147. "Abdias," in Fabricius, *Cod. apoc. NT*, pp. 531–590 (for Drusiana, pp. 542 ff.). "Melito," *PG*, V, cols. 1241–1244. Aelfric, I, 60, 66–68, 74.

148. Fabricius, *Cod. apoc. NT*, pp. 575 ff. "Melito," *PG*, V, cols. 1247–1248. Aelfric, I, 72–74.

things returned to their former lowly state, and the brothers again did wonders in God's name.[149]

Herbert's concluding hagiographical reference to John summarized the legendary account of his death, in which Christ is said to have appeared to his disciple—the only apostle, incidentally, to die a natural death rather than a martyr's—and promised his reward to come. John then offered the Holy Sacrifice and received viaticum, and entered a prepared grave, "returning his body and soul to Christ."[150] The bishop added a minor detail to the apocryphal material: the saint was, he said, in full eucharistic vestments as he said his last Mass.

John the Baptist did not receive the full legendary treatment accorded the Evangelist in Herbert's teachings: there was little not based directly on the Gospels. He did allege the Baptist to have been of noble birth, an idea probably derived from Ambrose as mediated through Bede.[151] The bishop also used the simile of Christ as the Light, John the lamp, since Christ shone by His own *lux*, the Baptist—*lucerna*—by that of the Lord, a comparison drawn as well by Augustine.[152]

The preacher's homilizing on Peter and Paul followed apocryphal sources where not based on Scripture. Saul, he said, stoned Stephen the Protomartyr alone, because in holding the coats of those who actively did the deed he took on their responsibility, an idea which may have come from Augustine.[153] Passing in detail through the biblical account of the conversion and subsequent life of Paul, and summarizing the least of the apostles' general principles of ethics and morals, he moved to a presentation of the last days of the great missionary and of Peter, utilizing common apocryphal sources with Orderic and with Aelfric. Both Peter and Paul were martyred at Rome, a belief which had become part of the tradition of the church and which appeared in the *Sarum Breviary* lection for matins of the octave of SS. Peter and Paul.[154] This suggestion occurred as early as *ca.*

149. Fabricius, *Cod. apoc. NT*, pp. 560 ff. "Melito," *PG*, V, cols. 1243–1247. Aelfric, I, 62–68.

150. Fabricius, *Cod. apoc. NT*, pp. 581 ff. "Melito," *PG*, V, cols. 1249–1250. Aelfric, I, 74 ff.

151. *HS*, p. 268. Bede, *In Luc.*, p. 21. Ambrose, *Expositio evangelii secundum Lucem*, in *Opera*, IV, ed. M. Adriaen (CC, XIV), 14. The reading from Bede was the seventh lection for the third nocturne of matins for the feast of St. John Baptist: *Breviarium ad usum Sarum*, Fasc. III, pp. 345 ff.

152. *HS*, pp. 286 and 292. Augustine, *Tract. in Jn.*, II, 15–16; XXIII, 232–234; and XXXV, 317–318. See also the Sarum lection, *Breviarium ad usum Sarum*, Fasc. III, p. 383.

153. *HS*, p. 298. Augustine, serm. for St. Stephen's Day, in *PL*, XXXVIII, col. 1429.

154. Aelfric, I, 370 ff. *HS*, p. 318; their dual martyrdom was in Rome in order that

170 in the writings of Dionysus of Corinth, whose now lost work is preserved by Eusebius.[155]

Together Peter and Paul caused the death of Simon Magus, the sorcerer, when the' wizard tried to fly as the last of a series of diabolically inspired miracles. This story, used as well by "Abdias," seems to have originated with one Marcellus, who claimed to have been a disciple of the two saints and a witness to the events which he described.[156] Shortly, following this incident, Peter was martyred, and Herbert assigned to Nero the responsibility for this deed (omitting, however, the majestic *Domine, quo vadis?* episode); and after the fisherman's death, the bishop alleged, Paul instructed his successor [sic] Clement.[157] I find neither a source, nor a similarity in contemporary works, for this detail.

One night after Peter's crucifixion, when Paul was evangelizing alone in Rome, he was preaching in a house which became overcrowded, leading at least one hearer, Patroclus (an attendant of Nero), to climb into the rafters from which a falling beam plummeted him to the floor, with fatal results. The apostle revivified the youth by prayer, and he returned to his emperor who had already heard of the accident. Nero asked for an explanation and Patroclus related that Paul had prayed to Christ that his life return. The courtier then added that the Lord would judge Nero at the end of the world, adding further insults and taunts which caused the affronted caesar to demand that Paul be brought into the imperial presence. The apostle to the gentiles disputed with the crowned buffoon, using such sound doctrine that the emperor, confounded and frustrated, in fury ordered Paul's head struck off. The noble Roman lady Plautilda gave him a handkerchief as Paul went to his martyrdom, and he promised to return it, stained with his own blood, after his death. After his decapitation, Paul appeared to warn Nero of his own impending horrible death and judgment. The legend is derived from the pseudo Linus, Marcellus, and "Abdias," who have the details of the passion of Paul beginning with the confounding of Simon Magus.[158]

---

the city should be deprived of neither—he attributed this idea to *beatus ambrosius*, but probably meant Augustine's sermon ccii. See *Breviarium ad usum Sarum*, Fasc. III, p. 441.

155. Fragment preserved by Eusebius of Caesaria, in *PG*, XX, 207 and 210.

156. *HS*, p. 314. The *De actibus Petri et Pauli* is in Fabricius, *Cod. apoc. NT*, pp. 632–653; at the conclusion of the work the author wrote: "Ego Marcellus Discipulis Domini mei Apostoli Petri, quae vidi scripsi. 'Abdias,'" in Fabricius, *ibid.*, pp. 430 ff. and 449 ff.

157. *HS*, pp. 316–318.

158. *HS*, pp. 318–322. "Abdias," as cited in n. 156, above. Marcellus, *De actibus Pauli*, in Fabricius, *Cod. apoc. NT*, pp. 651 ff. For the legends of Patroclus and of Plautilda, also used by Orderic, see the pseudo Linus in Léon Vouaux (ed.), *Les actes de Paul et ses lettres*

The good bishop added to his apocryphal source material, narrating that Nero hid in a forest after his deposition and then was murdered by his freedmen, his cadaver thereafter becoming sustenance for wolves. He agreed with Aelfric in this account, but not with Suetonius (VI, 49), who had the lecherous fiddler dead of his own trembling hand. Perhaps the abbot of Fécamp never sent the Suetonius for which Herbert had asked.[159]

No writings of Herbert Losinga relating to postbiblical saints have survived, although it is clear that he did not believe that sanctity ended with the apostolic age. On the Feast of All Saints he preached that the saints who might have been neglected during their festal celebrations now might be fitly venerated together, and his hearers were not on this day to let pass the opportunity to multiply the number of those who would intercede for them, an exhortation found in less crass form in the Sarum collect for All Saints.[160] As the bishop did not expound on postbiblical saints, so also he did not preach about postbiblical miracles (the *exempla* excluded). No miracles occurred in his own age, the bishop averred, despite his having witnessed one at Ely, because the whole world had become Christian and they were therefore no longer necessary.[161] The miracles now being wrought by the established sacramental and spiritual channels of the church were more astounding than the nonsacramental miracles of the early church. Herbert's explanation for the redundancy of miracles was that of Aelfric, Gregory, and Augustine.[162]

V. THE MONASTIC TRADITION

Since Herbert Losinga had been monk, prior, and abbot before his elevation to Norwich, where he established a black monk priory, one would be justified in expecting his letters and sermons to have much material of interest for the history of monasticism. Unfortunately, one would be quite wrong. Other than his exchange of letters with Abbot Richard, the bishop's surviving writings contain only commonplace teachings and moral precepts.

---

apocryphes, Documents pour servir a l'étude des origines chrétiens: Les apocryphes du Nouveau Testament, publiés sous la direction de J. Bousquet et E. Amann (Paris, 1913), pp. 280 ff. ("Linus" says that Patroclus fell from a window, pp. 304 ff.)

159. *HS*, pp. 322–324, and *HE*, ep. 5. Aelfric, I, 384.

160. *HS*, pp. 394–396. *Breviarium ad usum Sarum*, Fasc. III, pp. 964, 979–980.

161. *HS*, p. 212.

162. *HS*, pp. 220–224. Aelfric, I, 304–306. Gregory, *Hom. in Ev.*, cols. 1090–1091, 1215–1216; *Moralia*, in *PL*, LXXVI, 420–421. Augustine, *De vera relig.*, in *PL*, XLII, col. 142.

The monastic virtue *par excellence* was humility, and Herbert insisted that this attribute must characterize the life and conduct of the Christian. He not only used this argument to justify Jesus' description of John the Baptist as the greatest of men, but he also returned to it frequently in his sermons.[1] Just as the Bible stresses this virtue throughout, so too does the Rule of St. Benedict.[2] It would be futile even to attempt documentation of the frequent advocacy of humility in patristic and early medieval religious writings, for it was ubiquitous—indeed, one seventh-century florilegium has fifty-three entries under "humility."[3]

The monk-bishop gave due attention to asceticism as well. While he was by no means an advocate of extreme self-mortification, Herbert did emphasize the value of self-denial, always in a positive sense—mere fasting, abstinence, and formal worship were not sufficient for the Christian: they must be accompanied by spiritual and moral virtues.[4] A teaching which permeates the Bible, this association of negative and positive good is a standard theme in Christian moral theology, as illustrated, for example, by twelfth-century English sermons, the great Anselm's *Cur Deus homo*, the sermons and saints' lives of Aelfric, Rabanus Maurus, Bede, Gregory the Great, Augustine, and the second-century *Shepherd* of Hermas.[5] Again, an exhaustive catalogue of this principle is both beyond reason and pointless—Defensor lists seventy-five entries under "abstinence" alone.[6]

The bishop's expostulations concerning sin followed neither the conventional seven deadly sins nor the equally traditional eightfold categorization, a not unusual phenomenon.[7] His exposition of the sins most fatal to

1. *HS*, pp. 82, 288–294, Ash Wednesday Sermon, and throughout either directly or by implication or litotes. See also *HE*, ep. 23.

2. Benedict, *Regula*, chaps. ii, v, vi, vii, xx, xxxi, liii, lx, and elsewhere.

3. Defensor of Ligugé, *Liber scintillarum*, ed. Henri M. Rochais (CC, CXVII), IV, 18–22.

4. *HS*, pp. 98–100, 144 (where the positive aspects of fasting are from the *Regula*, chaps. iv, xlix, lxii), 424, and throughout.

5. *Old Eng. Homilies*, I, 37–39. Anselm, II, 86–87. Aelfric, I, 180; *idem, Lives of Saints*, ed. Walter Skeat (EETS, 82), II, 290 ff. Rabanus, *PL*, CX, col. 22. Bede, *Hom.*, I, 217. Gregory, *Regula pastor.*, p. 242. *Augustine*, serm. *De utilitate jejunii*, in *PL*, XL, cols. 711–712. Hermas, *Le Pasteur*, ed. Robert Joly, Sources chrétiennes, LIII (Paris, 1958), 224 ff. Hermas was in Latin before Herbert's day: Courcelle, *Lettres grecques*, p. 82, and Siegmund, *Überlieferung*, p. 86.

6. Defensor, *Lib. scint.*, X, 47–54.

7. On the seven virtues and vices, see Adolf Katzenellenbogen, *Allegories of the Virtues and Vices in Medieval Art*, Studies of the Warburg Institute, X (London, 1939), throughout; and Morton Bloomfield, *The Seven Deadly Sins* (Lansing, 1952), throughout. See also Messenger, *Ethical Teachings*, pp. 16, 18–19; Wulfstan, *Homilies*, ed. Dorothy Bethurum (Oxford, 1957), p. 187. Hermas, Vision III, 8, pp. 119–120. The sources here

the soul was patristic rather than medieval in its sources, in that he inveighed against incest and unnatural vice, and in another context named apostasy and adultery as the worst sins.[8] The reference to apostasy is probably to be understood in a monastic context, that is the renunciation of religious vows without due dispensation, rather than the renunciation of the faith itself: apostasy in the latter sense was not an English problem in Herbert's day.

Patristic authorities seemed to regard apostasy (or idolatry), homicide, and adultery as particularly heinous, some writers even placing them beyond the church's power to absolve.[9] While Herbert did not mention murder as in the patristic trichotomy, he did place it after adultery and apostasy with theft, false witness, and sacrilege.[10] It is not very important that the condemnation of abnormal vice is in a letter to the Norwich monks, for although the derogators of the middle ages would probably have had a splendid time with this charge, the epistle in which it is found is overflowery and poetic, and includes condemnation of some faults which can hardly have been practiced at the priory, such as worshipping Jupiter.[11]

The bishop clearly regarded some sins as worse than others. In his reference to purgatory he described it as a place where those who have kept the faith and committed no mortal sins (*criminalia peccata*) are purified by fire and thereafter admitted to heaven. The Fathers had laid the foundation of the doctrine of purgatory, that state where the guilt of sin unexpiated at death is satisfied, both on the basis of Scripture and of common sense; that is that most people live neither wickedly enough to deserve damnation nor well enough to enjoy the beatific vision immediately upon death.[12]

---

cited do not agree on the identification of the seven, and this is but the smallest sampling of the sevenfold approach.

For the eight mortal sins and their opposites, see *Twelfth Cent. Hom.*, p. 40; *Early Eng. Homilies*, pp. 16–19; *Old Eng. Homilies*, I, 103, 105–107; John T. McNeill and Helen M. Camer (eds. and trans.), *Medieval Handbooks of Penance* (New York, 1938), pp. 101 ff. and 153; Gregory, *Moralia*, in *PL*, LXXVI, cols. 364–365; Nilus of Ancyra, *De octo spiritibus malitiae*, in *PG*, LXXIX, cols. 1146–1162. For undifferentiated lumping of sins, see (e.g.) McNeill, *Handbooks*, 18 ff., for a summary of patristic texts.

8. *HS*, pp. 24–26, and *HE*, ep. 6.

9. Kelly, *Doctrines*, pp. 217, 436; Watkins, *Penance*, I, 11 ff., 72, 124, 134, 330 ff., 454 ff.

10. *HS*, p. 26.

11. *Ibid.*, pp. 412–414.

12. Quasten's and Altaner's patrologies, throughout. II Macc. 12: 39–45; Matt. 12:31 ff.; I Cor. 3:11–15.

As the bishop's preaching on morals was hortatory as well as admonitory, so also was his teaching on sin. He seldom warned against sins without requiring the embrace of the good works which were their opposites.[13] He was emphatic that repentance and good works must not be delayed, following both the scriptural precept that tomorrow may be too late and the moral teachings presented by, among others, an anonymous homilist of his own time, Aelfric, Rabanus, the pseudo-Bede, Gregory I, and the mystical *Shepherd*.[14]

He warned against accumulating temporal goods instead of the good works which yield a treasure of spiritual wealth. In a passage chillingly reminiscent of Anselm's letter to a royal nun who wished to leave the convent, he urged his congregation to "reflect upon your ancestors. They are dead, and will not return to this . . . life. . . . Death knocks at the door of your castles, and do you [despite this] fill them with wealth?"[15] Yet more melancholy, "your body is corruptible and mortal . . . in a short time your flesh will become a cadaver, and the cadaver putrescence, and the putrescence a worm, and the worm dirt. This is the common end both of princes and of the lowly."[16]

The bishop's teaching on the poor was also unoriginal, within the broad tradition of Latin moral theology, and ultimately derived from biblical counsels. He stressed the obligation of charity so continually that citations would be pointless, a judgment which applies as well to the literature of rich and poor in Christian tradition.[17] He did not try to "enlarge the eye of the needle so more camels could go through," but taught that the poor would judge his hearers in heaven, that charity to the poor is charity to Christ, and that the "church's poor people are the Body of Christ."[18] Herbert did present one unusual teaching on the impover-

13. *HS*, pp. 24 ff., 98–100, 144–146, etc.

14. *Ibid.*, pp. 106, 134, 424, 366–368, and 420, offer Armageddon as symbolic of the battle between good and evil in the souls of the faithful on earth. *Old Eng. Homilies*, I, 21. Aelfric, II, 602. Rabanus, in *PL*, CX, cols. 104–105. "Bede," Hom. cii, in *PL*, CX, cols. 503–504. The attribution to Bede is in Migne (above), in Neale, *Medieval Preachers*, pp. 15–16, and in *HS*, p. 134 n. 1 (probably following Neale), but see Eligius Dekkers and A. Gaar, *Clavis Patrum latinorum* (ed. alt.), *Sacris Erudiri*, III (1961), No. 1368. Dudden, *Gregory*, 253: "The approach of the judgment and the duty of penitence were [Gregory's] favorite themes." Hermas, Vision III, 102 ff.

15. *HS*, p. 424.

16. *Ibid.*, p. 104. Anselm, IV, ep. 169, to Gunnilda, daughter of King Harold. The saint asked, "Considera: quid est gloria mundi?" and recalled her parents, brother, and friends. "Ubi sunt? Vermis et pulvis sunt."

17. But see, for England, Brian Tierney, *Medieval Poor Law* (Berkeley and Los Angeles, 1959).

18. The first quoted phrase is Sidney Painter's, in seminar. *HS*, pp. 426, 70, 90, 122. Cf. Benedict, *Regula*, chap. liii.

ished, namely that the appearance of Jesus to the disciples after His Resurrection signified His dining with those who send a portion of their meal to the poor, an interpretation which appears to be uniquely his.[19]

The conventional interpretation of the parable of the sower (Matt. 13:8–23), applying it to marriage and chastity, was also Herbert's. He defined three states of human relationship: marriage, which he valued as good; continence, which was better; and best of all, virginity.[20] With the parable as a point of departure, he taught that in heaven virgins would be crowned a hundredfold, the continent sixtyfold, the married thirtyfold. The imagery was also employed by Aelfric (who, unlike Herbert, acknowledged his source: *Augustinus Magnus sic docet*), Bede's contemporary Aldhelm of Sherborne, Gregory I, Jerome, and Augustine.[21]

Elsewhere the Norwich ordinary advanced virginity as equally important with right faith and righteous living in earning salvation. His great primate Anselm also taught that *virginitas melior sit coniugio*, as did his abbot at Fécamp, John of Ravenna.[22] Herbert did not, of course, deplore marriage. That he regarded the virgin state more highly implies no invidious or pejorative attitude toward marriage: it is simply a reflection of the monastic and biblical (e.g., I Cor. 7) precept that wedlock, like possessions, interferes with the nonattachment to earthly affections necessary to enable complete devotion to God.

His only reference to canon law involved a question of marriage as well, and his decision was both obvious and ordinary: a woman could not remarry while her present husband lived.[23] No other particulars were given.

Most of Herbert's letters dealing with the religious life are concerned primarily with discipline within the house. He showed an acute awareness of the potential dangers and temptations of the celibate calling, especially for the young, combined with an understanding, yet firm, insistence upon obedience to the rule. Many of his letters reveal Herbert as compassionate and sensible: flexible in nonessentials, rigid in essentials.

19. *HS*, p. 202.

20. *Ibid.*, pp. 354–356 and 412. See a catena of scriptural and patristic citations in Defensor, *Lib. scint.*, XIII, 64–67.

21. *HS*, p. 412. Aelfric, I, 148 and II, 70 and 95. Aldhelm, *De laudibus virginitatis*, in *PL*, LXXXIX, cols. 116 ff. Gregory, *Regula pastor.*, pp. 320, 330. Jerome, ep. 23 in *Epistulae*, III, 82. Augustine, *Civ. Dei*, XV: 26, p. 494; *De sancta virginitate*, in *PL*, XL, col. 422; serm. cxcvi, *PL*, XXXVIII, col. 1020.

22. *HS*, p. 28. *Cur Deus homo*, in Anselm, II, 128, among many possible citations. John of Fécamp (among Alcuin's "dubia"), *PL*, CI, col. 1079.

23. *HE*, ep. 3. Such a marriage, he said, would be contrary both to the Bible and to canon law.

The monk-bishop had the perfect Benedictine attitude toward the monastic vocation: it does not mean sadness, deprivation, and rigidity, but the holy joy which grows from obedience to the Holy Rule. Following the rule, Herbert particularly emphasized humility, chastity, and obedience.[24] Despite his evident love for the monastic life, and perhaps because of his experienced insights into its living, he warned an anchorite of the temptations of arrogance, envy, pride, anger, and vainglory.[25] This letter gives an interesting insight into the bishop as a judge of human nature, for these defects are those which might appear as personality weaknesses in a hermit either when resentful or when smug in reacting to his solitude and deprivations.

The bishop was uncompromising on the issue of those who willingly left the conventual life. As Dom Cuthbert Butler has written, "once a man had definitely devoted himself to the monastic life, it was at all times looked on as a moral obligation, and its abandonment was regarded as an apostasy." Related to this duty was stability, the promise to remain attached to the monastery of his profession unless the monk be given permission to move to another.[26] Herbert advised Odo by letter to remain in the priory, to take the Cross that he might earn the Crown. Less gentle is a letter to "G.," declaring that unless he returns forthwith to the monastic life he will be excommunicated. Among many other criticisms, the bishop charged that drinking had replaced learning in the errant monastic.[27] The monk Thurstan likewise received an episcopal tongue-lashing and was not only ordered back to the priory but commanded to share the money he had made outside the house with the brothers.[28] "*Monachus qui in terra possessionem querit, monachus non est.*"[29]

It would appear from his letters that the bishop's principal concern with the activities of his black monks was disciplinary. He complained of thievery, sloth, gossiping, waste of material possessions of the priory, and the unwarranted taking of privileges by the brothers.[30] Godfrey, a member of the priory community, received particularly scathing and detailed attention for his relaxed attitude toward the rule: he was indolent, spent too much time in idle talk, and indulged his body too frequently. For

24. For example, *HE*, ep. 57. Benedict, *Regula*, throughout.
25. *HE*, ep. 56 (to Wido the anchorite).
26. Cuthbert Butler, *Benedictine Monachism*, rev. ed. (New York, 1961), pp. 122–124. Cf. Benedict's *Regula*, throughout.
27. *HE*, epp. 13, 55; the latter casts disapproving reflections upon English character.
28. *Ibid.*, ep. 29.
29. Gregory I, as quoted in Defensor, *Lib. scint.*, XL, No. 22, p. 130.
30. *HE*, ep. 52; cf. also epp. 17, 48, 57.

example, he took too many baths and had his blood let more frequently than was necessary, which was not a medical objection, but a condemnation of sloth since medical treatment was followed by an easier routine for a while.[31] Godfrey's lapses were the more deplorable as the priory was providing both for his father and for his seven-year-old son. The bishop was hardly less displeased by his monks' failure to work as enthusiastically as he thought they should on the building of Norwich cathedral.[32]

He also appreciated goodness in the community. He wrote to Felix that he never sent the monk letters because he did not require counsel, and the bishop's letters were reserved to the sinful.[33] Herbert also showed capacity for forgiveness. A letter to Ingulf, prior of Norwich, prayed him to forgive a lapsed monk and permit him to remain in the community, and a similar missive to Bishop Richard (of London?) requested him to forgive the priest Hunfrid against whom his ordinary held just but here unspecified grievances.[34] Aware that no disciplinarian is beloved solely on the basis of his discipline, Herbert defended himself, arguing that he was neither inconsiderate nor excessive in his exercise of authority, requiring of the monks only what was salutary for their own spiritual lives.[35] This letter is primarily concerned with breaches of the regulations forbidding conversation except under prescribed conditions, and may well reflect the probability that the house had a good proportion of young men, a likelihood reinforced by the number of episcopal letters to Norwich dealing with study and warning of youth's temptations.

The unedifying and unbecoming conflict between secular and regular clergy is one of the less attractive features of monastic history in the early twelfth century. The bickering in England began somewhat after the conquest; indeed Anselm had used his office to enhance the position of monastics vis-à-vis seculars and regarded himself as defender of the regulars, a role in which he wished his bishops to join.[36] At the base of

31. *Ibid.*, epp. 16, 36. The *Regula*, throughout, forbids unnecessary conversation as well as laziness; Chap. 36, discussing baths, orders that they be granted to the healthy, and especially to the young, but seldom (*tardius concedatur*). Knowles, *Monastic Order*, pp. 465–466, quotes the *Regularis Concordia* as permitting baths on fixed days through the year. Perhaps Herbert's complaint is even more pointed when viewed against Professor Knowles's judgment that "even so the bath would seem to have made its way but slowly to England," not appearing at Abingdon until between 1120 and 1131.

32. *HE*, epp. 14, 51.   33. *Ibid.*, ep. 23.

34. *Ibid.*, epp. 51 and 31. If this Bishop Richard were English (and Hunfrid is an English name), this letter would be to Richard de Belmeis, bishop of London from 1108 to 1127; if Norman, to Richard of Bayeux.

35. *Ibid.*, ep. 48.

36. Cantor, *Church in England*, pp. 294 ff.

this controversy lay the attempts of the Gregorian reformers to spread the monastic way of life—celibacy, the rule of prayer, poverty, and so on— throughout the entire clerical order, secular as well as regular. The clergy not under monastic vows were naturally unenthusiastic both at this challenge to their accustomed ways and to the implication that the life of the monks was somehow more favored by God than was their own, and they did not hesitate to rebel with vigor against what they regarded as the presumption of the champions of monachism. For their part, the monks disapproved of the seculars' way of life, which so sharply contrasted with their own.

Following Anselm's death, Abbot Richard of St. Alban's urged Herbert of Norwich to take up the dead primate's leadership of the monastic order.[37] His letter to the bishop, showing the meanness of human nature rather than the charity and love of the ideal monk, is a good example of some monastics' querulousness at his time. Richard's style is aptly described by Goulburn and Symonds as "fulsome"; his missive can be dated between the spring of 1109, when Anselm died, and April, 1114, when Ranulf d'Escures acceded to Canterbury.

Satan, the abbot wrote, had inspired the canons (seculars) to seek positions of authority in the church and had prompted them to attack the monastic order, fostering dissension and schism within the Body of Christ. They had failed sufficiently to appreciate the fact that there was no more secure path to heaven than that of the monastic life; indeed they had even been so arrogant as to suggest that there were better ways (unspecified) to achieve salvation. Richard advanced a superb proof for the excellence of the monastic way: at the approach of death both lay and clerical nonmonastics become monks rather than priests or canons. Who attacks monachism attacks a way of life which Christ revealed and which the Fathers advocated.[38] The monks have endured these attacks meekly; now that the great defender of their order is dead, would Herbert

37. The only other English abbot of that name in Herbert's time was Richard of Ely, who translated the remains of the Anglo-Saxon saints at the dedication of his new abbey and died in 1107 (*Liber Eliensis*, p. 230 n. 3). Richard of St. Alban's was present at this translation (*ibid.*, p. 229) and held his abbacy until 1119. When Herbert was consecrating churches and ordaining clergy in the diocese of Lincoln, he was with this Richard (*Gesta abbatum monasterii sancti Albani*, ed. Henry Thomas Riley [RS, XXVIII], IV¹, 148–149). Richard's letter is *HE*, ep. 59. Richard probably chose Herbert to replace Anselm as advocate of the monastics because there was only one other monk-bishop at this time— Ranulf d'Escures of Rochester—and he had just been elevated in 1108 (Knowles, *Monastic Order*, appendix xii, p. 709).

38. Cf. Lubac, *Exégèse*, Part 1, 578 ff., and Defensor, *Lib. scint.*, pp. 149–152.

pour forth some drops of heavenly nectar, sing a new celestial melody, and so nauseatingly on—would he write a tract in defense of monasticism to succor his oppressed brethren? After further sticky effusion, Richard closed with the none-too-subtle suggestion that the bishop of Norwich would be a marvelous choice to succeed the venerated Anselm.

Perhaps it could logically have been expected that Herbert—monk, prior, abbot, monk-bishop over a Benedictine community which he founded, extoller of the monastic life—would have willingly assented to Richard's request. But this would be to overlook his own position as a bishop, and therefore at least in part a secular; his bitter experiences with the Bury monks in his quarrel over exemption; and the possibility that another letter written to Abbot Richard, if he be identical with him of St. Alban's, flayed him for looking on while Herbert stood in need of support and encouragement. His coolly negative reply was such as to disprove the allegation that he began the hostility between regular and secular clergy in his diocese.[39]

Summarizing the abbot's request, he promptly refused to launch an attack against priests who also offer the Eucharist and are the shepherds of Christ's flock. Then came a sensible refutation of Richard's rancorous sniping: all orders of the church, from subdeacons through primates and popes, had been subjected to monks and to the monastic way; hence "it would be absurd for us to condemn what we are." The dignity of the secular clergy and hierarchy has been "wholly transferred" to the monks, and Herbert, although himself an example of this transference, profoundly disapproved of this development. All clergy serve the one God, and praise should be awarded good priests, just as evil monks should not be honored because of good monks' lives and examples; provided only that the conduct of monk and secular priest be godly, they are on an equal plane. The letter closed with a reminder that the abbot had not sent, as he had apparently promised, some work of Augustine and a lectionary.[40] If the squelched Richard made a reply, it has not survived.

VI. The Place of Herbert Losinga in Anglo-Norman History

In the strictest sense, any figure of Herbert's period, survived by so few writings and so little noticed in the fragmentary records of the reigns of William Rufus and Henry I, must remain ephemeral despite the most thorough efforts to make a genuine biographical study of the man. The

39. Britton, *Norwich*, p. 17.
40. *HE*, ep. 60.

difficulties inherent in historical research for the turn of the twelfth century in England make it necessary, rather, to produce a study of the bishop and his times. Even so, many questions of both interest and importance must remain unanswered. We would like to know much more than we do about his thoughts and opinions concerning the major issues of his time: for example, Herbert said nothing about the Gregorian reform, Anselm, the primacy disputes in England, the kings whom he served, the popes whom he opposed, and the changes already begun in his time which embodied the intellectual revolution forming part of the twelfth-century renaissance. We cannot even judge whether his learning and intellectual ability were superior or inferior to those of others in his time and place, as he is the only English bishop of less than archiepiscopal rank whose writings have survived. Obviously he cannot bear comparison with Lanfranc or Anselm either in originality or in learning. Nor can he be compared with continental bishops of his period, for many of these have left us more works on the basis of which to judge them.

Fortune has served Herbert better than it has his episcopal colleagues in England, however, and while his sermons and letters are sparse in quantity and tantalizingly meager in content, they do permit Herbert to be placed with some confidence in his proper place in medieval intellectual history, as his actions so permit him to be placed in political and ecclesiastical history. What little can be established concerning his personality shows him to have been a pleasant, humorous man, yet with the ability to be firm and unyielding. A man of some intelligence and literacy, he was also highly practical, and had the ability to learn from experience: in no important instance did he make the same mistake twice.

Despite the unpromising beginning of his episcopate, Herbert turned out to be a more than adequate bishop. While all chroniclers who notice him mention his simony, they also praise him as an excellent ordinary, a judgment substantiated by his own house's chronicle and by his letters. One cannot conclude that saintliness of life is the basis for the laudatory opinions, however, although no scandal tainted his career after his simony (his lying misrepresentation of the pope's words in 1102 was not widely enough known to constitute scandal). Careful administration seems rather to be the foundation for the praise. He both commenced the great cathedral at Norwich and established a priory there which endured for almost four and a half centuries. The Norwich Cathedral Priory was never one of the great religious houses of medieval England, although it did produce one chronicler of significance, Bartholomew Cotton (*ob.* 1298), and several bishops: William Turbe (Norwich, 1147–1174), Ralph of Wareham (Chichester, 1218–1222), Roger Skerning (Norwich, 1266–1278), Thomas Brunton (Rochester, 1373–1389), and Alexander Tottington (Norwich, 1407–1413). Despite these men, it cannot be said that the priory was ever of national importance, and it seems, unlike most other large medieval English monasteries, not to have had a "great age." Its reputation in the later middle ages suggests a decline more than normal in a general age of monastic decline in England. We cannot tell, of course, how many black monks found spiritual solace and godly living at the priory, and it was for these purposes that Herbert founded his monastic chapter.

Herbert's activities as diocesan add little to our knowledge of the Norman period. His charters, and other records, show that he exercised conscientious, detailed supervision over the administration of his see and over the affairs, as well as the spiritual life, of the priory. His determined efforts to remove Bury St.-Edmunds from exempt status and return it to diocesan control demonstrate both his hostility to exemption in his own diocese and his ability to pursue a goal relentlessly for a decade. The failure of these efforts exemplifies both the efficacy of papal judgment (1093, 1102) and of a royal council's determination of ecclesiastical disputes (1102). And that Herbert attempted to have a royal council overturn two papal decisions of a strictly ecclesiastical nature tells us something of his opinion concerning where real power lay in England.

The bishop's career as a secular public figure serves to demonstrate clearly the equivocal position of a medieval prelate as a servant of both God and king. His appeal to the pope for absolution from his simony in 1093 foreshadowed the flood of appeals to the papacy which was so dominant a characteristic of English church history by the later twelfth century. His violation of the exequatur in so doing had results which also demonstrated the lack of wisdom in flouting royal policy, and Herbert did not again make the pope the judge of matters affecting the king. He was always hereafter the king's man against both his pope and his archbishop. In the primacy disputes between Canterbury and York, Herbert backed his own archbishop: but so did the king, and what was therefore a natural position for a Canterbury suffragan was thereby politically enhanced by royal support. While there is no way to support the opinion, I suspect that when Herbert lied for the king at the council of 1102, it was at royal command. The king's intercessions with Anselm to secure Herbert's absolution for this piece of chicanery lend weight to this suspicion.

The bishop appeared often in the records as public figure, attesting writs and charters, seeking relief from scutage owed by the diocese, and representing his king as a diplomat on two occasions. That he was not without skill in conciliation is also suggested by Anselm's use of Herbert as an envoy to York. We cannot conclude that the pope's use of this penitent bishop as a legate argues his great diplomatic skill, for his selection was probably due to coincidence: he was in Italy in 1093 when a legate was needed, he was a Norman and a former monk and prior of Fécamp (involved in the dispute which Herbert was deputed to adjudicate), and Normandy was on his way home. Further, he was not endowed with the great powers of a *legatus a latere*, simply those of *legatus missus*. And certainly the legatine commission is not evidence that Herbert was a high Gregorian. While he did indeed support reform when the king's interests, the English "ancient customs," were not involved, his entire career after 1093 found him consistently supporting royal as against papal prerogatives and claims.

We can perhaps make some judgments about Herbert Losinga as a diplomat and politician. He must have possessed qualities of dependability and of loyalty to his superiors to have been selected by the king and the archbishop for sensitive assignments, and there is no evidence that he failed to serve his masters well, whether on missions for king, archbishop, or pope. In fact, Henry's choice of Herbert to go to Rome in 1116 would imply that he had performed satisfactorily, from the king's point of view, on his 1101/1102 mission. The bishop of Norwich may not have fulfilled the classic definition of a diplomat—"a man sent to lie abroad for his country"—when with the pope, but he certainly perjured himself in council after his return. He was one of that faceless legion whose place in public life is to execute faithfully the policies of those in authority over them and to lie both when told to do so and when it suited his own interests. There is no evidence to indicate that he ever initiated any important governmental or ecclesiastical policy, although—with the exception of the "political" aspects of the Gregorian reform—he was quick to implement the policies and commands of others. He was a deputy rather than an initiator, a good and faithful servant (at least of his earthly king), and was assigned roles in church and state which, while secondary, were by no means inconspicuous.

One man's corpus of writings does not give us the basis for generalizing upon the extent of penetration of patristic and early medieval learning among the higher clergy of Norman England, but we can assess Herbert's place in the intellectual history of the early twelfth century. Seldom original, but often interesting, this bishop holds a place in intellectual history approximating that which he holds in ecclesiastical and political history: peripheral, but not insignificant. His relative importance is enhanced by the fact that, with the exception of the obvious giants, the prescholastics have not received the full attention given by intellectual historians to theologians and exegetes of the mid-twelfth century and after.

The bishop's scholastic foundation at Norwich did not have influence beyond his diocese. Apparently, it was not an intellectually progressive establishment. The curriculum which we have inferred from his letters is much the same as that found at Chartres about a century before Herbert's time: the *auctores* and *logica vetus* encouraged, the quadrivium mentioned but probably not really taught. In brief it was a school of liberal arts, and probably not a very advanced one. It can be assumed that instruction continued at Norwich until the Dissolution. As some students appear from the context of the bishop's letters to have been studying away from the priory school, instruction there was probably quite elementary in character, merely basic education, the students being sent elsewhere for more advanced learning.

The sources will not permit much hypothesizing concerning Herbert's own intellectual attainments. One cannot accept the universal encomium of his own age that he was learned in secular as well as ecclesiastical literature: such praise was virtually a formula description for clergy of his time who showed even the most casual interest in education and in letters. His own description of himself as a man of deep learning can also be discounted—it may certainly be true, particularly since it was expressed in a letter written to people who knew him, but without firm supporting evidence of other than a narrative nature it cannot be accepted. It seems probable that his classical references are at least in part based upon florilegia, as the monastery where he was educated and spent his youth then had no classical works of which we know. But that he asked for the loan of Suetonius indicates his interest in direct exposure to at least one classical author, and I doubt that this is the only one. It cannot be proved, but it is more than likely that he had read numerous classical authors, although there is no way to tell which ones. Had he not had some acquaintance with the classics, it would have been quite unusual for a man of his position in his time.

Herbert Losinga was as conservative and traditional in his homiletics and his exegesis as he was in his pedagogy. He was not an original exegete, and made no important innovations or original interpretations. It is even difficult to discover his sources for patristic and early medieval doctrines and allegories, so common are his exegeses. But I think it can be safely judged that the following works, known to have been available to Herbert at Fécamp, Ramsey, or Norwich were utilized by the bishop, for they appear to be frequently cited: Augustine's epistles, the *De catechizandis rudibus*, the *De Trinitate*, his sermons, and the *Tract. in Jn.*; Bede's homilies and exegetical works are reflected again and again throughout the sermons; he was obviously steeped in Gregory the Great's teachings, particularly in the homilies on the Gospels and on Ezekiel, the *Moralia*, and the *Dialogues*. Although he appears to have used Isidore's *Etymologiae* and Eusebius but seldom, he could well have read them at Fécamp and Ramsey. The pseudo Matthew version of the apocryphal *Protevangelium of James* was probably the source of much of his teaching on the Virgin. This is all one can state with reasonable certainty, for we know these sources to have been available to him.

Of works which cannot be demonstrated to have been in libraries to which he had access, Herbert apparently had read Augustine's *City of God*, Bede's commentaries on the Pentateuch, and further *transitus* legends and apocryphal materials, although one cannot judge with certainty which specific pseudo *acta* he used. Quite possibly he was acquainted with the sermons of Rabanus Maurus. Although it is dangerous to speculate, it is probable that he had read more widely in the patristic sources than is here indicated. The frequent appearance in the apparatus of Aelfric's *Catholic Homilies* is not intended to mislead: there is no evidence that Herbert knew English, although it is likely. He and the abbot of Eynsham used the same sources, and Aelfric is cited simply to demonstrate this, in other words to underscore the fact that Herbert was no innovator, even in England.

Any study of the writings of a man such as Herbert must be somewhat tentative in its conclusions, for it is obvious that he preached more than fourteen sermons in his four years as abbot and twenty-eight as bishop. Perhaps our conservatism in judging him is justified, however, despite the chroniclers' high opinions of this bishop: only Henry of Huntingdon in later years thought him worth quoting—although John Capgrave at least thought him illustrious—and his writings seem not to have been utilized materially in either the English or continental religious controversies of the sixteenth and seventeenth centuries. What made him noteworthy in his own epoch, and neglected since, was that he epitomized a period drawing to a close. His more original contemporaries have been well served by subsequent scholars: John of Fécamp, Anselm, Lanfranc, Peter Damian, Ivo of Chartres, Eadmer, and others. Herbert Losinga exemplified prescholastic hermeneutic: he operated within traditional patterns both of homiletics and of exegesis, interpreted virtually everything within the context of received authority, and homilized allegorically rather than theologically. He appears to have used no unusual sources, and there are few surprises in his sermons and letters. In only one instance did he reflect a theological development of his time: his Marian theology was more advanced than that of any immediate contemporary but Eadmer. His letters regarding monastic life are of some interest, not because they state conventional monastic and moral theology, but because they reflect the difficulties encountered in enforcing the Benedictine rule among his priory monks: they point up a sometimes overlooked (although not by G. G. Coulton) aspect of religious community living in the twelfth century.

Herbert Losinga,

> vir omnium litterararum tam secularium quam divinarum imbutus scientia. . . . Fide integer, spe erectus, quicquid agebat quicquid loquebatur, sapientia disponebat, confirmabat veritate, caritate saporabat, temporabat modestia, et misericordiae bonum cujus maxime visceribus affluebat, superponebat judicio ut eandem ipse consequi mereretur (Bartholomew Cotton, 389),

was an upholder of older ways on the eve of exciting innovation and creativity. To think of the period characterized as the renaissance of the twelfth century only in terms of the Anselms, Abélards, the Victorines, and so on, is to warp the true picture: there were also many such men as Herbert Losinga, and to ignore them is to permit a false historical portrayal of a most vigorous period of growth and transition.

APPENDIX I

AN ESTIMATE OF THE VALUATION OF THE BISHOPRIC OF EAST ANGLIA, 1091

The value of the lands held by the bishopric when Herbert bought the see can only be approximated. In the following tabulation the lands either mentioned in the *First Register of Norwich Cathedral Priory* (column headed *NR*) as belonging to the see *temp*. Herbert, or as alienated either by the bishop or a successor, are assumed to have been in the holdings of the see when Herbert bought it. The other columns denote late thirteenth and early fourteenth century evidence:

> *FA:* PRO, *Inquisitions and Assessments Relating to Feudal Aids . . . A.D. 1284–1431*, III, V, VI (London, 1904–1920).
>
> *LF:* Great Britain, Exchequer, *Liber feodorum (Book of Fees, Commonly Called the Testa de Nevill)*, I (London, 1920).

I have used only the earliest page references per holding for the *Book of Fees*.

> *DB:* *Domesday Book seu liber censualis Willelmi primi regis Angliae*, II (London, 1783).

I have used this to establish 1087 holdings of the bishopric. References here are to folio rather than to page numbers; folio numbers in the 300s indicate Suffolk holdings, others are in Norfolk.

As lands acquired by Herbert Losinga obviously were not part of the holdings of his diocese in 1091, their value has not been tabulated here. My method has been to compare the *DB* lands of the see with later holdings. When I have found (e.g.) a manor held in 1087, then appearing in later sources in the holdings either of Herbert or of an episcopal successor, I have assumed that the land involved was not alienated between 1086 and the later date; such alienation could of course have occurred and the property then reverted to the bishopric, but in the absence of evidence I have deliberately discounted this possibility. The amount calculated is conservative; probably more *DB* holdings remained the property of the diocese than is indicated by surviving evidence.

Place names are modern, not *DB*. The standards for modern use have been Eilert Ekwall, *Concise Oxford Dictionary of English Place-Names*, 2nd

228

ed. (Oxford, 1940), and William Page, VCH *Norfolk*, II and VCH *Suffolk*, I and II. All places identified are shown in the map in *Valor ecclesiasticus*, III.

HOLDING	DB	LF	FA III	FA V	FA VI	NR	1087 EVALUATION £	s.	d.
Becham	128	...	436	...	...	58	13		
Beighton	194	...	545	...	...	110–112	7	13	4
Billockby	201	...	398	...	...	...		20	
Blakeney	189	III, 70	...	...	...	...			16
Blickling	196b	...	390	...	...	70	8	25	
Blofield	194–195	132	457	...	...	86	8		
Bradeston	200	...	418	...	...	...			10
Catton	200	...	473	...	...	36			15
Clippesby	201b	...	398	...	...	...		20	
Cockthorpe	198b	...	548	...	...	110		30	
Colkirk	191b	...	404	...	...	36	9	2	
Cressingham	197b	...	449	...	...	70	9	50	
Eccles	194	128	424	...	...	36		60	
Egmere	192b	...	421	...	...	...		45	4
Elmham	191b	...	...	...	...	...	32		
	380	132	455	...	...	58	10	36	8
Frings	(See Sedgford, to which this manor is appurtenant)								
Gunton	194	...	436	...	...	...	4		
Helmingham	196	...	415	...	...	...	4	10	8
Hemblington	199	...	472	...	...	142		2	
Hemsby	195	...	...	...	...	36	29		
Hindolveston	192b	...	...	...	...	36	13	9	8
Hindringham	192, 198b	...	420–421	...	...	36	17	10	
Holkham	194b	...	420	...	...	...	22	22	4
Homersfield	379, 380	...	...	...	...	110	17	19	4
Hunstanton	179b	...	525	...	...	...		10	
Langham	194, 198	...	461	...	...	...	20	1	4
Langley	195b–196	...	433	...	...	...	4		1
Marsham	200b–201	...	486	...	533	83	9		
Martham	200b–201	...	...	...	...	36	8	14	2
Melton	198	...	511	...	...	...		40	5
Mendham	379b	...	...	63	...	...		60	
Mintling	197b	...	453	...	...	48		30	
N. Burlingham	199b	...	419	...	...	...	37	10	
Ormesby	197	...	...	...	...	66		8	
Plumstead	199	...	472	...	...	58		40	5
Raveningham	197	...	...	...	...	112	3		
Rollesby	201	...	398	...	...	...			
Saxlingham	191b–192	...	511	...	...	...		20	
Scratby	197	...	397	...	...	...		33	32
Sedgford	193b	136	410	...	...	52, 58	24	80	
Silham	379b	...	...	...	...	26		60	
S. Burlingham	199b	...	418	...	...	...		30	15
S. Walsham	194b	329	...	...	...	...		4	

(Table—*continued*)

HOLDING	*DB*	*LF*	*FA* III	*FA* V	*FA* VI	*NR*	1087 EVALUATION £	s.	d.
Stratton	193, 197	...	412	...	...	...	4	42	
Swafield	193	...	486	...	552	...		7	4
Swanton	192	...	511	...	...	110–112	8		
Taverham	196	...	419	...	...	...		20	
Thornage	192	...	...	...	...	86	30	32	
Thornham	191	III, 410	...	...	...	80	16		
Tofts	191–191b	...	426	...	...	...		60	
Trows	125	...	...	...	...	48–50		30	
Witton	200b	418	...	...	...	...		30	16
						Total	£403	18*s*.	6*d*.

APPENDIX II

Below are the patristic and postpatristic sources known to have been available to Herbert at Fécamp, Ramsey, and Norwich. The list includes only the materials which might have been sources for his work: it is not a comprehensive catalogue of all holdings. I have further omitted all indefinite citations, e.g., "Ambrose," "*Homiliae*," "Commentaries on the Bible." For Fécamp and Ramsey, no listings from later than the eleventh century have been included. The sources for the bibliographical information are:

H. C. Beeching and M. R. James, "The Library of the Cathedral Church of Norwich," *Norfolk Archaeology*, XIX (1917), 67–116.

N. R. Ker, "Medieval Manuscripts from Norwich Cathedral Priory," *Transactions of the Cambridge Bibliographical Society*, I, Part 1 (1949), 1–28.

———, *Medieval Libraries of Great Britain: A List of Surviving Books* (London, 1941), pp. 76–77.

Emile Lesne, *Hist. de la prop. ecclés. en France*, Vol. IV: *Les livres* (Lille, 1940), pp. 584–585.

Genevieve Nortier, "La bibliothèque de Fécamp au Moyen Age," pp. 221–237, in Jehan de Povremogne (ed.), *Fécamp*, II. See also her article "Les Bibliothèques médiévales des Abbayes bénédictines de Normandie," *Revue Mabillon* (1957), pp. 1–33, and (1961), pp. 332–346.

James W. Thompson, *The Medieval Library* (New York, 1957), p. 122, for Ramsey.

WORK	LOCATION
Augustine, *Contra Faustum*	Fécamp
———, *De cat. rudibus*	,,
———, *De consensu evang.*	,,
———, *De Trin.*	,,
———, *Enchiridion*	,,
———, *Epistolae*	,,
———, *Tract. in Jn.*	,,
Bede, Commentaries on Acts, Revelation, Luke, Mark	,,
———, *De tabernaculo test.*	,,
———, *De temp.*	,,
———, *In epp. can.*	Norwich
Benedict, *Regula*	Fécamp
Cassian, *Collations*	,,

(Table—*continued*)

WORK	LOCATION
Chrysostom, *Homeliae*	Fécamp
Defensor, *Liber scintillarum*	,,
Eusebius, *Hist. eccles.*	Fécamp, Ramsey
Gregory the Great, *Dialogues*	Fécamp
———, *Hom. in Ev.*	,,
———, *Hom. in Ez.*	,,
———, *Epistolae*	,,
———, *Moralia*	,,
———, *Reg. pastar.*	,,
———, Homilies	Norwich
Isidore, *Etymologiarium*	Fécamp
Jerome, *In Marc.*	Norwich
———, *De vir illustr.*	Fécamp
———, *Epistolae*	,,
Pseudo Matthew, Sermons on the Assumption	,,
Vitae Patrum	,,
Vitae Sanctorum	,,

A CENTURY OF CONTROVERSY
ON THE FOURTH CRUSADE

Donald E. Queller

University of Illinois

Susan J. Stratton

University of Southern California

A CENTURY OF CONTROVERSY ON THE FOURTH CRUSADE*

Returning to a problem declared fruitless and unworthy of further consideration by several generations of distinguished scholars requires some audacity. Near the very beginning of the controversy over the diversion of the Fourth Crusade, Comte Paul Riant in 1878, after offering his interpretation, declared the matter closed unless new documents were discovered. In 1897 the Russian scholar P. Mitrofanov supported Riant's plea for a cessation of the debate. All those acquainted with the question are familiar with Achille Luchaire's dictum of 1907: "... we will never know, and science has truly something better to do than to discuss indefinitely an insoluble problem." More recently, in 1962, Edgar H. McNeal and Robert Lee Wolff in the prestigious Pennsylvania *History of the Crusades* have urged that Luchaire's plea makes excellent sense, and Hans Eberhard Mayer in 1965 declared the literature on this subject unfruitful and the question insoluble.[1] In the face of this opposition, however, scholars have continued their debates. On the simplest level they cannot do otherwise, for anyone who writes on the Fourth Crusade can only examine the evidence, interpret it as best he can, and thus join the controversy. On a more philosophical plane, moreover, we now understand that science does not progress so much by the accumulation of new evidence, as by the acquisition of fresh insights, which grasp the relevance of evidence not previously used or look at the old evidence from a new point of view. Since Ernst Gerland offered a thorough review of the scholarship on the Fourth Crusade in 1904, valuable new insights have

* The authors are grateful to Dr. Janet Rabinowitch for her copious notes on the Russian authors, since neither of them have the use of that language.

1. Comte Paul Riant, "Le Changement de direction de la Quatrième Croisade," *Revue des questions historiques*, XXIII (1878), 114; Achille Luchaire, *Innocent III: la question d'Orient* (Paris, 1907), p. 97; Edgar H. McNeal and Robert Lee Wolff, "The Fourth Crusade," in *A History of the Crusades*, ed. Kenneth M. Setton, *et al.*, II (Philadelphia, 1962), 172; Hans Eberhard Mayer, *Geschichte der Kreuzzüge* (Stuttgart, 1965), pp. 175–177. In support of the same position: P. Mitrofanov, "Izmenenie v napravlenii chetvertogo krestovogo pokhoda" [The Change in the Direction of the Fourth Crusade], *Vizantiiskii Vremennik* [*Byzantine Chronicle*], IV (1897), 490; Leopoldo Usseglio, *I marchesi di Monferrato in Italia ed in Oriente durante i secoli XII e XIII* (Turin, 1926), II, 171.

235

been gained, but no one has offered a full and systematic consideration of the historiographical controversy as evolving by distinguishable stages toward a deeper and broader understanding of the events of 1201–1204.[2] Scholars who have returned to the fray have not wasted their time fruitlessly belaboring a dead question, but have made the question itself a living and growing thing. Their work has been profitable, and continued contemplation and discussion also promise to be valuable and even exciting.[3] We believe that the century-old controversy deserves review within this framework.

Until about mid-nineteenth century historians accepted at face value the testimony of Geoffrey of Villehardouin, marshal of Champagne, not only an eyewitness, but a member of the inner circle of decision-makers and a frequent envoy of the crusaders. His chronicle presents the attack upon Constantinople as the consequence of a series of chances, most notably the unexpectedly small number of crusaders arriving at Venice, their lack of funds to fulfill their contract with the Venetians, and the appearance in the west of the Byzantine Prince Alexius. Villehardouin's interpretation is called the "theory of accidents" by scholars, some of whom have accused him of being an "official" historian, who has sought to conceal what really occurred.

The theory of accidents has been under attack since about the middle of the nineteenth century by a succession of "treason" theorists who accuse Philip of Swabia, Boniface of Montferrat, Enrico Dandolo, or even Innocent III of betraying the crusade for their own political or economic ends. Philip was the heir of Hohenstaufen and Norman hostility toward Byzantium, the bitter foe of the pope, and the husband of a Byzantine princess whose dethroned father and brother sought restoration. Boniface

2. Ernst Gerland, "Der Vierte Kreuzzug und seine Probleme," *Neue Jahrbücher für das klassische Altertum und für Pedagogik*, XIII–XIV (1904), 505 ff. See also summaries of the debate in the following: Comte Paul Riant, "Le Changement de direction de la Quatrième Croisade," pp. 71–114; F. C. Hodgson, "Excursus on the Sources for the History of the Fourth Crusade," in *The Early History of Venice* (London, 1901), pp. 428–438; Heinrich Kretschmayr, *Geschichte von Venedig*, I, 1st ed. (1905); reprinted (Gotha, 1964), 479–489; A. A. Vasiliev, *History of the Byzantine Empire, 324–1453*, 1st Russ. ed. (1917–25); 2nd Eng. ed. rev. (Oxford, 1962), pp. 455–458; M. A. Zaborov, "Krestovye pokhody v russkoi burzhuaznoi istoriografii," [The Crusades in Russian Bourgeois Historiography] *Vizantiiskii Vremennik* [*Byzantine Chronicle*], IV (1951), 171–190; Sara de Mundo Lo, *Cruzados en Bizancio: la Cuarta Cruzada a la luz de la fuentes latinas y orientales* (Buenos Aires, 1957), pp. 85–97.

3. In the footnote where Luchaire's *dictum* is quoted with approval, McNeal and Wolff remark upon "the new and most interesting review of the subject by A. Frolow...." See below, pp. 270–273.

had family connections which drew him toward Constantinople, his father a Byzantine feudatory and two brothers married to Byzantine princesses, one of whom had aimed for the imperial throne. The Venetian doge, seeing the commercial privileges of his city threatened by Genoa and Pisa and seeking revenge and restitution for the massacre of 1171, also had reason to plot the overthrow of the Greeks. The pope, of course, harbored hopes for the healing of the schism in the church. The treason theorists generally do not point to only one of these culprits to the exclusion of others, but in making one or another dominant they admit of classification as advocates of Swabian or Venetian or some other responsibility. The treason theories often follow the national sentiments of the writers, who try to exonerate their own compatriots from any blame for the deviation.[4]

After about a half century of debate among proponents of the various treason theories and remaining champions of Villehardouin, there emerged about the turn of the century a modified theory of accidents, whose foremost advocate was Walter Norden. The modified theory of accidents is based upon the veracity of Villehardouin, but, believing that the marshal perceived only superficial causes, while ignoring deep-rooted historical movements, it attempts to place the conquest of Constantinople in historical perspective, especially in the framework of relations between the East and West. The selfish motives attributed by the treason theorists to the various principals are not ignored, but take their places in a pattern of events awaiting the concatenation of fortuitous circumstances of 1201–1204 to find its natural culmination in the attack on Constantinople.

Most recently a few scholars have attempted to shake off the political, diplomatic, and economic preoccupations of earlier historians in an effort to understand the motives of the crusading host in medieval terms. The insights of social psychology have been brought to bear upon the anonymous mass of crusaders to bring forth interpretations giving due weight to hagiography, eschatology, the cult of relics, the cult of poverty, and other medieval disciplines and fads. The effort to see events through the eyes of the mass of mute participants has been called interior history.[5]

4. On the contrary, Jules Tessier wrote to reclaim the honor of France by showing that the crusade was a French affair and that his countrymen were not dupes of German or Venetian conspirators. *La Quatrième Croisade: la diversion sur Zara et Constantinople* (Paris, 1884), pp. 4–5.

5. Paul Alphandéry, *La Chrétienté et l'idée de croisade*, 2 vols. (Paris, 1954–59), I, 81 and 186. See also Henri Berr in the "Avant-propos," in *ibid.*, I, xii–xiii.

This phase of the controversy over the Fourth Crusade, we believe, has barely begun to make its contribution toward the continuing and meaningful debate.

I. THE TREASON THEORISTS

A more critical attitude toward historical sources, as well as the contemporary vigor of nationalism and a new sense of economic forces in history, led many scholars in the second half of the nineteenth century to reject Villehardouin's account of the diversion. The attack on Constantinople was discovered to be the result of a plot manipulated by this leader or that, and Geoffrey the Marshal was castigated as an official historian, either a party himself to conspiracy or a dupe of those who were.

A transitional[1] role in the development of the treason theories was played by F. Hurter's work on Pope Innocent III. The Venetians in Constantinople had suffered under Manuel Comnenus, and Enrico Dandolo had lost his sight at the hands of the Byzantines, so the Venetians with Dandolo as doge were driven by desire to regain Venetian power and to obtain revenge.[2] On the other hand, Hurter rejected the Venetian-Egyptian treaty for the diversion of the crusade alleged by the continuator of William of Tyre. Although the Venetians took advantage of their opportunity to turn the crusade against Constantinople, Hurter doubts whether Dandolo had this goal in mind from the beginning.[3] Boniface of Montferrat, the leader of the crusade, perhaps also had his part in the diversion. Boniface had encountered the son of the dethroned Isaac

---

1. Some other historians had begun in a modest way to modify Villehardouin's account. E.g., Pierre Daru, *Histoire de la République de Venise*, 1st ed. (1819); 4th ed. (Paris, 1853). The diversion to Zara was caused by lack of funds (p. 196), and the deviation to Constantinople occurred by chance (p. 204). Venice, however, was instrumental in the diversion, although there was no Venetian-Egyptian treaty to that end (p. 205). See also Lodovico Sauli, *Della Colonia genovese in Galata* (Turin, 1831), pp. 31–32. Sauli found the Venetians motivated by desire for revenge and for commercial advantages. They were instrumental in drawing the crusading host into the plan for diversion. Sauli mentions the account of a Venetian-Egyptian treaty to divert the crusade, but does not place much credence in it. Some authorities give Sauli as the originator of the Venetian treason theory, e.g., Comte Paul Riant, "Innocent III, Philippe de Souabe et Boniface de Montferrat," *Revue des questions historiques*, XVII (1875), 325. Sauli treated the diversion problem incidentally, briefly and without serious discussion. He had no influence on the controversy.

2. Friedrich Hurter, *Geschichte Papst Innocenz III und seiner Zeitgenossen*, I, 1st ed. (1835); 2nd rev. ed. (Hamburg, 1836), 441–443.

3. *Ibid.*, I, 503.

Angelus, Alexius, who had fled in 1201 from the captivity to which he and his father had been subjected by his usurping uncle Alexius III.[4] Hurter believed that Boniface and Alexius had probably agreed on the restoration of the Byzantine prince and then had obtained Venetian support for the undertaking. Nonetheless, as Villehardouin had declared, the lack of crusaders who appeared at Venice to fulfill the treaty of 1201 was the origin of the failure of the Fourth Crusade to pursue its ostensible goal.[5] Hurter, in sympathy with the subject of his work, found Innocent strongly opposing any diversion, aiming solely for the destruction of Muslim power and seeking to avert the shedding of Christian blood.[6] In this he differed from Villehardouin, who minimized papal opposition to the diversion.

Although hints had earlier appeared that leaders of the Fourth Crusade had been moved by selfish political and economic interests to take advantage of the contingencies described by Villehardouin, the first genuine treason theorist positing a plot conceived in advance and led step by step to execution was Comte Louis de Mas Latrie.[7] Villehardouin, along with the other French a victim of Venetian duplicity, "did not know and could not see through the secret objective that the council of the Republic of Venice pursued." Instead of the marshal, Mas Latrie chose to rely upon Ernoul, a continuator of William of Tyre. The Syrian coast held little attraction for the Venetians, and they very much desired good relations with those lands through which Asiatic goods passed into the Mediterranean basin, especially Egypt. Venice therefore willingly accepted the sultan's offer of a treaty granting privileges in the port of Alexandria in exchange for the diversion of the crusade. Mas Latrie regarded the privileges later obtained by Venice from 1205 to 1217 as payment for the betrayal of Christendom. The favored position enjoyed by Venice in Constantinople for over a century had recently been threatened by privileges given to the Pisans and the Genoese; so the Venetians determined to divert the host to the Byzantine capital.[8]

4. *Ibid.*, I, 451. The *Gesta Innocentii, PP. III.*, in Migne, *PL*, CCXIV, cxl–clxi, provides Hurter's proof. The reliability of the *Gesta* on this point will be very important in the treason theories to be discussed. Similarly, the date of the flight of Alexius is crucial to the treason theories. Villehardouin placed his appearance in 1202, which would not have allowed time for the alleged plots to be developed.

5. *Ibid.*, I, 501.   6. *Ibid.*, I, 446.

7. *Histoire de l'île de Chypre sous le règne des princes de la maison de Lusignan*, 3 vols. (Paris, 1852–61), I, 161–164.

8. Mas Latrie, *Histoire de Chypre*, I, 161. Mas Latrie later edited the chronicle of Ernoul: Ernoul and Bernard le Trésorier, *Chronique*, ed. L. de Mas Latrie (Paris, 1871). The chronicle was probably written at Tyre and covered events in the East from 1183

A Venetian treaty with Egypt for the diversion of the Fourth Crusade seemed proved when Karl Hopf published his "Geschichte Griechenlands" in the J. S. Ersch and J. G. Gruber encyclopedia in 1867. He wrote:[9]

> We are in a position at length to clear up this dark point. Soon after Venice had made the alliance with the French barons for the Crusade, Marino Dandolo and Domenico Michieli, perhaps in response to an invitation from the Sultan, had been sent on an embassy to Cairo, and come to an understanding with them; the doge had declared himself a loyal friend to the son of Eyub. While the Crusaders were waiting impatiently to advance against the infidels the ambassadors had, on the 13th of May 1202, really concluded a treaty of commerce, which guaranteed to Venetians many privileges, granted them a quarter in Alexandria, and promised safety in person and goods to all pilgrims going to the Holy Sepulchre with the Venetians. The Emir Seadeddin was sent to Venice for ratification of this. The favourable conditions that Adel promised decided the fate of the Crusade.

Since the treaty was undocumented, Hopf's death shortly after his work appeared left scholars in the dark, but Hopf's great reputation for a short while convinced the scholarly world that he had discovered a new and important document.[10]

---

to 1229. Ernoul is the prime source of the alleged treaty between Venice and Egypt. The reliance of the Venetian treasonists upon his account is a serious weakness, since he cannot be taken as a knowledgeable source on this matter.

9. Karl Hopf, "Geschichte Griechenlands," in *Allgemeine Encyclopädie der Wissenschaften und Künsten,* ed. J. S. Ersch and J. G. Gruber, LXXXV–LXXXVI (Leipzig, 1867), LXXXV, 188. In the recent, but undated reprint of *Geschichte Griechenlands* as a separate book, it is p. 122. The English translation is that of Hodgson, *The Early History of Venice,* p. 429.

10. Hopf had worked for many years on Venetian sources. One of his major scholarly contributions was his edition of *Chroniques gréco-romanes inédites ou peu connues* (Berlin, 1873). His high standing in the world of scholarship is illustrated by the attitude of Comte Paul Riant, who knew that the treaty alluded to by Hopf was printed in *Urkunden zur älteren Handels-und Staatsgeschichte der Republik Venedig,* G. L. Fr. Tafel and G. M. Thomas (eds.), in *Fontes rerum austriacarum,* zweite Abtheilung, Bänden XII–XIV, (Vienna, 1856–57), II, 184–193; reprinted (Amsterdam, 1964), and that Hopf had altered the date and the name of one of the Venetian ambassadors. Riant tried to justify these changes, but finally concluded that the proof would have to come from Hopf's papers. "Innocent III, Philippe de Souabe et Boniface de Montferrat," *Revue des questions historiques,* XVIII (1875), 75. His faith in Hopf was unshaken: "Mais l'autorité incontestable de Hopf me paraissait pouvoir amplement suppléer—pour un point incident de la discussion générale que j'abordais—à toute autre guarantie." *Ibid.*

Hopf also found that the motivations of Boniface of Montferrat coincided with those of the Venetians, although it was they, and not he, who instigated the diversion. The young Byzantine Prince Alexius had fled from captivity to the West in 1201, and had met Boniface at Christmas of that year at the court of Philip of Swabia. The family interests and claims of the marquis led him to adopt the cause of the Byzantine pretender.[11]

A new candidate for the role of chief conspirator was found in Philip of Swabia by Eduard Winkelmann. Embroiled with the Welf faction in a struggle for the empire, opposed with all the power of the papacy, Philip saw in the diversion of the crusade to Constantinople an opportunity to improve his diplomatic position and thwart his foes. He and his accessory Boniface first discussed the use of the crusaders as early as 1200, when the marquis was in Germany on a mission for Innocent III. After his election as head of the crusade Boniface was again in Germany in 1201, at which time he met Philip's brother-in-law Alexius, who became an instrument for the development of the conspiracy. Winkelmann attempts to prove this meeting, which must be established in 1201 to allow time for the plot to ripen, by the testimony of the *Annals of Cologne* and the *Gesta Innocentii*.[12]

Winkelmann finds it difficult to explain how the struggling German king could divert the crusade. He concedes that Philip had not the financial resources to subvert the host with money. Boniface and Philip personally sought to win over the pope to the scheme, using without success the bait of the unification of the church. Only the Hohenstaufen's diplomatic ingenuity in dealing with the crusaders, according to Winkelmann, was responsible for his accomplishment.[13]

11. Hopf, "Geschichte Griechenlands," LXXXV, 191. In *Bonifaz von Montferrat und der Troubadour Rambaut von Vaqueiras* (Berlin, 1877)—edited after Hopf's death by Ludwig Streit—Hopf discussed Boniface's family claims and interests in Constantinople.

12. Eduard Winkelmann, *Philipp von Schwaben und Otto IV von Braunschweig*, 2 vols. (Leipzig, 1873–78), I, 524–525. The *Annales Coloniensis maximi*, Karolus Pertz, ed., *M.G.H., SS.*, XVII, 810, mention that Alexius appeared at Philip's court at the same time that Archbishop Siegfried went to Rome to be consecrated. There were two archbishops named Siegfried, however, Siegfried of Magdeburg, who was elevated in 1201, and Siegfried of Mainz, who was elevated in 1202. The *Gesta* states outright that Alexius was at Philip's court in 1201, where he met Boniface. See Gerland, "Der Vierte Kreuzzug," p. 510. (The present article had been accepted and copyedited before we read J. Folda, "The Fourth Crusade, 1201–1204. Some Reconsiderations," *Byzantino-Slavica*, XXVI (1965), 277–290. He argues convincingly for the early arrival of Alexius in the West.)

13. Winkelmann, *Philipp von Schwaben und Otto IV von Braunschweig*, I, 525–528.

In spite of the accusations of many scholars Villehardouin retained defenders, such as Natalis de Wailly, the admiring editor of *La Conquête de Constantinople*. Wailly staunchly defended the unique value of an account written by a participant in *la haute politique*. He accepted the theory of accidents with no reservations.[14] Naturally, he was most anxious to refute the contradictory testimonies of Ernoul and Robert of Clary. He argued vigorously and cogently against the authority of Ernoul, who was not a participant in the crusade and whose sources of information are suspect, refuting the Levantine chronicler's accusations against the Venetians. Robert of Clary, although honest and valuable for certain purposes, was never aware of what was happening in the top circles. His account perpetuates "*les vaines rumeurs de la passion populaire.*"[15]

Wailly's able advocacy of the theory of accidents provoked Comte Paul Riant's erudite exposition of Swabian responsibility.[16] Riant had worked extensively with the sources for the Fourth Crusade as well as carefully absorbing the work of his predecessors.[17] An attack on Constantinople by the Hohenstaufen had been building up for some years. Germany had never had good relations with Byzantium, and these had been worsened by the intervention of the Comneni in Italian affairs on the side of the Guelphs. Hohenstaufen imperial ideas came to full fruition in the mind of Henry VI, who yearned to dominate the world and would have taken Byzantium had he not died prematurely.[18] Riant thus accepted the Swabian theory of Winkelmann, but his development is far more elaborate than his predecessor's.[19]

Boniface of Montferrat was the chief agent of Philip of Swabia in the execution of his scheme. His election as leader of the crusade coincided

14. In Geoffroi de Villehardouin, *La Conquête de Constantinople*, ed. Natalis de Wailly, 1st ed. (Paris, 1870), pp. ix–x. Wailly later wrote: "Les récits s'enchainent et se justifient dans leurs moindres détails: c'est un témoin véridique et bien informé qui mérite d'autant plus de confiance qu'on ne peut le contredire sans contredire aussi la vraisemblance et la raison." *Conquête de Constantinople*, 3rd ed. (Paris, 1882), p. 438.

15. Wailly, in Villehardouin, *Conquête de Constantinople*, 3rd ed., pp. 432–433 and 443.

16. Riant, "Innocent III, Philippe de Souabe et Boniface de Montferrat," XVII, 321–375, and XVIII, 5–75; Riant, "Le Changement de direction de la Quatrième Croisade," pp. 71–114.

17. Riant was the editor of *Exuviae sacrae Constantinopolitanae*, 3 vols. (Geneva, 1877–1904), which gathered the primary sources describing the relics brought to the West after the sack of Constantinople.

18. Riant, "Innocent III, Philippe de Souabe et Boniface de Montferrat," XVII, 343–345.

19. "*La conquête de Constantinople serait, au premier chef, un oeuvre germanique.*" *Ibid.*, XVII, 331. (Italicized by Riant for emphasis.)

with the flight of young Alexius to the West in 1201.[20] Both proceeded to Germany where their meeting at Philip's court was said to take place. Riant embraces the testimony of the *Gesta Innocentii* that at this meeting Philip and Boniface concluded a treaty to establish Alexius on the throne of Constantinople with the aid of the crusading army. With somewhat more specificity than the scanty evidence will support, Riant has the three conspirators discuss the crusaders' lack of money to fulfill the treaty of transportation and their consequent vulnerability to manipulation. As leader of the crusade Boniface could place his army at the disposal of Alexius—and Alexius' real principal, Philip. The marquis and Philip would attempt to enlist the pope in their plan, but if this failed they would be forced to appeal to the barons to divert the crusade.[21] And so it happened as Philip devised.

While Boniface was Philip's most important agent, the cooperation of Venice was also essential. Riant relies heavily on Hopf's account of the Venetian role in the crusade, accepting the Egyptian treaty as proof of a Venetian betrayal.[22] He also draws upon Mas Latrie when he uses the privileges later granted to Venice by the sultan as evidence of a subsequent payment for the diversion. Like Mas Latrie and Hopf, Riant employs Ernoul for evidence of Venetian conspiracy, but he also turns to such diverse sources as Baudouin d'Avesnes, Galeotto del Carrotto, and Boiardo.[23] Committed by their treaty with the sultan to divert the crusade from Egypt, the Venetians were readily led to join in Philip's plan to enthrone his Byzantine brother-in-law. The crusaders' debt of 34,000 marks to Venice provided the opportunity.[24]

20. Boniface's election, according to Riant, was contrived by Philip Augustus. *Ibid.*, XVII, 351. According to Villehardouin, he himself proposed Boniface simply because he was a logical candidate. Geoffroi de Villehardouin, *La Conquête de Constantinople*, ed. and trans. Edmond Faral, 2 vols. (Paris, 1938–39), Sec. 41, I, 42. Nicetas Choniates reports that the flight of Alexius occurred during the rebellion of Manuel Kamytze, which Riant dates 1201. Because Nicetas' account is not strictly chronological, and because the rebellion occupied a period of months, the argument is not conclusive.

21. Riant, "Innocent III, Philippe de Souabe et Boniface de Montferrat," XVII, 352–356.

22. Accepting the authority of Hopf, he used May 13, 1202, as the date of the treaty and Marino Dandolo as one of the ambassadors. Like Wailly, he recognized that the treaty was identical with that published by Tafel and Thomas. *Ibid.*, XVIII, 70–72. Wailly subsequently objected to this arbitrary dating of the treaty and the attempt to discredit Villehardouin. "Note," *Revue des questions historiques*, XVIII (1875), 578–579.

23. Riant, "Innocent III, Philippe de Souabe et Boniface de Montferrat," XVII, 328. It is worth noting that Riant relied extensively upon chroniclers who were not eyewitnesses.

24. *Ibid.*, XVII, 362–363.

The hapless role of Pope Innocent in the Fourth Crusade is also discussed by Riant. Mistrusting the Venetians, Innocent only accepted their participation after Genoa and Pisa had refused. The papal confirmation of the treaty of 1201 imposed the condition that the crusaders would make "no attack against Christian powers." Toward Byzantium the pontiff's attitude was patient; above all else he wished to stay removed from palace rebellions.[25] Of course the pope wished for unity of the two churches, but he wanted unity rather "by a regular and certain manner than by the aid of an illicit and violent enterprise."[26] When Boniface and Alexius visited Rome in an effort to win papal support of their undertaking Innocent decisively refused.[27] He little realized how slight would be his influence upon the course of events. The pope's attitude toward the crusade remained firm, although after the conquest and the restoration of Isaac and Alexius he was forced to accept the *fait accompli*. Innocent at first thought the crusaders would proceed to Syria after taking Constantinople, but when it became evident that they would not he was profoundly troubled by the definite ruin of his projects.[28]

The execution of the plot without the cooperation of the pope required skillful maneuvering and great adaptability to unforeseen circumstances. The lengthy negotiations between the Venetians and the sultan, supposed by Riant to have occurred in 1202, explain the prolonged detention of the crusading army on the Lido and the difficulties encountered by the barons in contracting loans to meet their obligations to the republic under the treaty of transportation. In this sense the attack upon Zara also was a result of the treaty with the infidel.[29] The differences of the Venetians and the crusaders offered an excellent opportunity to Boniface, the chief agent of Philip for the diversion to Constantinople. After his arrival in Venice the marquis discussed with a small group the project for the restoration of young Alexius. The three barons were an easy prey, at the mercy of any scheme which promised to extricate them from their financial difficulties. At Venice they came to an agreement with Boniface which was later embodied in the treaty of Zara. The leaders of the crusade accepted the

---

25. *Ibid.*, XVII, 335–336. On the refusal of Genoa and Pisa, Riant is following Robert of Clary, who was not present, against Villehardouin, who was. See D. E. Queller, "L'Évolution du rôle de l'Ambassadeur: Les Pleins pouvoirs et le traité de 1201 entre les Croisés et les Vénitiens," *Le Moyen Age*, LXVII (1961), 488.

26. Riant, "Innocent III, Philippe de Souabe et Boniface de Montferrat," XVIII, 27.

27. *Ibid.*, XVII, 356–358. Riant's defense of Innocent is based upon the *Gesta*. He holds that the antipapal view reflected in some chronicles was created by Boniface. *Ibid.*, XVIII, 32–33.

28. *Ibid.*, XVIII, 61–66.   29. *Ibid.*, XVII, 363.

deviation to Constantinople as a necessary detour en route to the Holy Land.[30] Venice was won over by her fears for her commercial privileges in Constantinople, by the unpaid indemnities owed her for the massacre of 1171, and by the private hatred of Dandolo toward the Greeks.[31] Innocent III gambled away his opportunity to prevent the attack upon Greek Christians by attempting to use the threat of the crusading army to frighten Alexius III into accepting the unification of the churches.[32] While the pope played at diplomacy, the conspirators pre-empted the decision. The opposition of the lesser crusaders, an immense majority of whom wanted to proceed directly to the Holy Land, is evidence to Riant for the treason theory. Many of them suspected a German plot and deserted.[33] Those leaders (including Villehardouin) who signed the treaty of Zara agreeing to the diversion and others whose influence or silence was required betrayed their vows for money.[34] That remnant of the original host which had not sailed from ports other than Venice and had not defected from Zara became then the instrument of the Swabian plot to restore young Alexius.

Riant made by far the most complete analysis of the diversion problem to his time. Not only did he examine the motivations of the principal participants and the preparations for the diversion, but he carried the discussion through the capture of Constantinople. His documentation was exhaustive and his arguments imposing, if somewhat overly imaginative.[35]

Not all scholars found Riant's arguments compelling, and a variety of interpretations continued to flourish. Ludwig Streit returned to the Venetian treason theory. Although Streit was the literary executor of Hopf and adopted his point of view in general, he discovered from Hopf's notes that the alleged treaty of May 13, 1202, was in fact identical with the documents published in Tafel and Thomas, and that Hopf had made arbitrary alterations in the text. His discovery contributed to the ultimate discrediting of Hopf's testimony, although Streit himself believed in it,

---

30. *Ibid.*, pp. 364–366. Most authorities, following Villehardouin, place the proposal to attack Constantinople at Zara, although Alexius had approached the crusaders at Venice. They have Boniface joining the host for the first time at Zara.

31. *Ibid.*, p. 367.

32. *Ibid.*, pp. 373–374.

33. *Ibid.*, XVIII, 38–39. That large numbers of crusaders deserted because of their scruples against attacking Constantinople does not necessarily prove that they suspected a German plot.

34. *Ibid.*, p. 37.

35. August Baer, *Die Beziehungen Venedigs zum Kaiserreiches in der Staufischen Zeit* (Innsbruck, 1888), followed Riant's interpretation very closely from the flight of Alexius in 1201 until the end of the crusade.

merely substituting a later date.[36] The Venetian treason as Streit saw it
stemmed naturally from Byzantine-Venetian relations of the twelfth
century.

Five-sixths of Streit's work is devoted to developing the background of
the crusade before 1200. Although other authors had discussed briefly the
deterioration of East-West relationships which led up to the Fourth Crusade, Streit was the first to insist that the conquest of Constantinople be
placed firmly in historical perspective. Venice had grown great under
Byzantine patronage in the early twelfth century in exchange for the use
of the Venetian fleet to protect Byzantium against the West. Especially
during the early crusades Venice became the only mediating power
between the East and the West.[37] When the Norman, Roger of Sicily,
attacked Byzantium, the East was again dependent upon Venetian sea
power, and in return for Venetian help Manuel Comnenus in his chryso-
bull of 1148 gave the Venetians a large quarter on the Golden Horn.[38]
To counterbalance Venetian influence Manuel subsequently began to
favor Genoa and Pisa, and finally his jealousy of Venetian power led to the
attack on the Venetian quarter of 1171. Venice went to war over this
incident, but lost its fleet to storm and plague.[39] Once again in 1182 the
easterners attacked the Latin quarter. From that time the strife increased
between East and West; Norman and Italian attacks upon Byzantine
territories assumed the nature of a lasting conquest.[40] When Venice
finally joined the western powers against Byzantium, the danger to the
Eastern Empire became acute. In 1193 an eighty-four-year-old patrician
was elected doge, Enrico Dandolo, the redeemer of Venice. Dandolo
dreamed of the past glory of his city and awaited his opportunity to strike
for its restoration and expansion.[41] Venice had to suffer additional set-
backs, however, while Pisa threatened her control of the Adriatic and her
commercial predominance in Constantinople. The Greeks, according to

36. Ludwig Streit, *Venedig und die Wendung des vierten Kreuzzugs gegen Konstantinopel* (Anklam, 1877), pp. 3, 32, and 49. See Gabriel Hanotaux's summation of Streit's con- tribution, "Les Vénitiens ont-ils trahi la Chrétienté en 1202," *Revue historique*, IV (1877), 101.

37. Streit, *Venedig und die Wendung des vierten Kreuzzugs*, p. 6.

38. *Ibid.*, pp. 9–11. For a description of the Venetian quarter in 1148 and its subsequent development, see Horatio Brown, "The Venetians and the Venetian Quarter in Constan- tinople to the Close of the Twelfth Century," *Journal of Hellenic Studies*, XL (1920), 68–88.

39. Streit, *Venedig und die Wendung des vierten Kreuzzugs,* pp. 11–13. A predecessor of Streit's in discussing these matters was G. M. Thomas, "Der Doge H. Dandolo und der Lateinerzug gegen Konstantinopel," *Allgemeine Zeitung*, Munich, No. 356 (Dec. 22, 1875). Unfortunately this piece has proved inaccessible.

40. Streit, *Venedig und die Wendung des vierten Kreuzzugs*, pp. 16–17.

41. *Ibid.*, p. 21.

Nicetas, incited the Pisans against Venice. For this reason and others
—Venice had never received compensation for the incident of 1171
—Venetian-Byzantine relations were extremely bad at the end of the
twelfth century.[42]

Finally Streit begins a short discussion on the actual preparations for
the crusade. All the plans of the pope for the redemption of the Holy
Land crashed to the ground before the intrigues of the crafty and ambi-
tious doge. Dandolo saw that the time for vengeance and aggrandizement
had arrived, and even as he negotiated the treaty of transportation of 1201
the thoughts of the aged doge were dominated by his ducal oath to seek
the honor and profit of his fatherland. It was he who cleverly worded the
contract so that "no word of the document showed the unbeliever as the
enemy to be fought." First Zara and then Constantinople were to be
the goals of the crusade.[43] Streit was not concerned as much with the
working out of the deviation as with the preconditions which produced it.
He believed that he had proved that Dandolo was the moving force of the
diversion, and he concluded with a eulogy of the doge who extended the
greatness and the glory of his fatherland as "no other doge before him,
none after him."[44]

Shortly after the work of Riant and Streit, an unsettling article by
Gabriel Hanotaux appeared dealing with the Venetian treason theory
and particularly with Hopf's treaty between Venice and the sultan.
Wailly and Riant had already noticed the identity of Hopf's treaty and the
documents published in Tafel and Thomas, and Streit, working almost
simultaneously with Hanotaux, had shown some of Hopf's errors, but to
Hanotaux belongs the credit for proving conclusively that the alleged
treaty of 1202 did not exist.[45] No treaty could have been concluded by
Malik al-Adil in Cairo on that date, for he was not in Egypt, but in Syria.
As both Riant and Streit had noticed, moreover, Hopf had changed the
name of one of the Venetian ambassadors to Cairo from Pietro Michieli
to Domenico Michieli, since the former could not have been in Cairo on
May 13, 1202.[46] A hint of a more likely date is given in the first of the

42. *Ibid.*, pp. 22, 26–27.   43. *Ibid.*, pp. 27–29, 31–32.

44. *Ibid.*, pp. 33–34. Jules Tessier has criticized Streit for his eulogies of Dandolo.
Quatrième Croisade, p. 10. Streit was one of those who accepted Ludwig Sauli, *Della
Colonia genovese in Galata*, as the founder of the Venetian treason theory.

45. Hanotaux's appendix, added after the completion of his article and after receiving
from Riant a copy of Streit, credits Streit's findings. Gabriel Hanotaux, "Les Vénitiens
ont-ils trahi la Chrétienté en 1202," p. 101.

46. *Ibid.*, pp. 87–88; Riant, "Innocent III, Philippe de Souabe et Boniface de
Montferrat," XVIII, 70–72; Streit, *Venedig und die Wendung des vierten Kreuzzuges*, p. 32.
Hopf's unacknowledged alteration, "Geschichte Griechenlands," LXXXV, 188.

documents comprising the treaty which is dated by day and month, though not by year: *"Fuit scripta die decima nona Saben, mensis Martii."* In order to date the document it is only necessary to find when the nineteenth of Shaaban falls in the month of March. This only happened three times during the reign of Malik al-Adil: March 31, 1201; March 21, 1207; and March 9, 1208. Hanotaux concluded that the treaty was probably from March 9, 1208.[47] It was negotiated during a period of truce, when no crusade threatened the Holy Land and the sultan could allow safe-conducts to westerners.[48] Hanotaux also found evidence that Malik al-Adil did not assume the titles *Rex regum* and *Amicus atque delicium principis fidelium* until the year 604 (or 1207–1208 of the Christian era). The use of these titles in the treaty provides additional evidence against Hopf's early date.[49]

Hanotaux argues that the treaty was indicative of continuing good rapport between Venice and the Saracens, which had existed for years. Although he agrees that Venice had reasons for desiring the conquest of Constantinople, the treaty published by Tafel and Thomas provides no incriminating evidence against her.[50]

Hanotaux's argument against Hopf was carefully worked out and absolutely devastating. Hopf's treaty may no longer be cited as evidence of Venetian treason.[51] Hanotaux's article, combined with the background material provided by Streit, marks a turning point in the Venetian treason theory, for future treasonists were compelled to turn from a simplistic betrayal to a more sophisticated analysis of underlying trends and motives. It also offered a striking lesson on the necessity of careful documentation.[52]

Treason theorists, and particularly those emphasizing the German role, received a setback in V. Vasilievskii's analysis of the date on which young Alexius reached the West. On the basis of events surrounding the flight of Alexius in Nicetas' account, Innocent's letter of November, 1202,

47. Hanotaux, "Les Vénitiens ont-ils trahi la Chrétienté en 1202," p. 91. Riant also recognized a problem in dating, but counted upon Hopf's papers to explain it satisfactorily. "Innocent III, Philippe de Souabe et Boniface de Montferrat," XVIII, 74–75.

48. Hanotaux, "Les Vénitiens ont-ils trahi la Chrétienté en 1202," pp. 96–97.

49. *Ibid.*, p. 101. Combining the factors mentioned, moreover, appears to establish March 9, 1208, since the Muslim year 604 began on July 28, 1207.

50. *Ibid.*, pp. 98–100.

51. As McNeal and Wolff note in "The Fourth Crusade," p. 170, n. 44, "It is a surprise, however, to find it in Steven Runciman." *A History of the Crusades*, 3 vols. (Cambridge, 1951–54), III, 113.

52. Riant's article of 1878, "Le Changement de direction de la Quatrième Croisade," was an unsuccessful attempt to refute Hanotaux.

and Villehardouin's record of the meeting with the Greek prince, Vasili-evskii concluded that the flight of the young Alexius occurred in 1202. Time was lacking, therefore, for the laying of the plot posited by the treasonists.[53] The question of the date of the flight of young Alexius, however, was not terminated by the arguments of Vasilievskii, but still rages.

Wilhelm von Heyd, the historian of Levantine commerce, followed the Venetian treasonists on the Fourth Crusade, but in the light of Hano-taux's criticism. He accepts the arrival of young Alexius in the West in 1201 and a possibility that Philip and Boniface discussed a diversion. He praises Winkelmann's demonstration of the German's influence on the crusade, but he believes that Riant exaggerated Philip's role. The chief responsibility lay with the Venetians, who were guided by a sole motive, the defense of their commercial interests.[54] The treason took on a new cast, as Heyd looked deeper into the economic background. Although he did not realize it, Heyd was pointing toward a view of the diversion as a result of natural and persistent dispositions and policies, a view which was susceptible of synthesis with Villehardouin's theory of accidents.

That the primitive and discredited Venetian treason theory could still attain wide circulation, however, is proved by Edwin Pears's pseudo-scholarly *The Fall of Constantinople*. Apparently unaware of Hanotaux's article, he accepted without criticism Hopf's treaty of May 13, 1202.[55] He rejected Villehardouin as a suppressor of unpleasant facts, while following Robert of Clary, Ernoul, and Nicetas.[56]

In spite of the objections of critics, both capable and inept, the marshal of Champagne retained supporters for his theory of accidents. The most able defender of Villehardouin prior to Norden's important synthesis— and still a scholar well worth consulting—was Jules Tessier. In Tessier's eyes the Venetian and Swabian treasonists had portrayed the French

53. V. Vasilievskii, "Kritikcheskie i bibliografischeskie zametki" [Critical and Bibliographical Notes], *Zhurnal Ministerstva Narodnogo Prosveshcheniia* [Journal of the Ministry of Public Instruction], CCIV (1879), 337–348.

54. Wilhelm von Heyd, *Histoire du commerce du Levant au moyen âge*, 1st Germ. ed. (1879); trans. Furcy Raynaud and revised and augmented by the author (1885); reprinted, 2 vols. (Leipzig, 1936), I, 265–266.

55. Edwin Pears, *The Fall of Constantinople* (London: 1885), pp. 263–265. See the devastating review by Ch.-V. Langlois in *Revue historique*, XXX (1886), 411–412. The recent unsatisfactory vulgarization by Ernle Bradford, *The Sundered Cross* (Englewood Cliffs, N.J., 1967), follows Pears closely without noting his inadequacies and the greater part of the more recent literature on the subject.

56. Pears, *Fall of Constantinople*, p. 244.

crusaders, his own compatriots, as simple-minded dupes.[57] Villehardouin, *"notre vieux chroniqueur champenois,"* who stands against any such view, is still the only real authority for the Fourth Crusade.[58] The reduction of the role of his countrymen was an affront to the patriotic Frenchman. He discredited both Venetian and Swabian treason on the grounds that Alexius did not arrive in Germany in 1201, but in 1202, as reported by Villehardouin. Tessier rejected the evidence of the *Gesta Innocentii* as hearsay and that of Robert of Clary and the *Annals of Cologne* as suspect on all questions of dating.[59]

His discussion of the treaty of transportation of 1201 gives the first hint that this is more than a retelling of Villehardouin. Since the Christians in the Holy Land would be of little help to the crusaders, the barons and their envoys to Venice favored the Egyptian route, but most of the army desired direct transportation to the Syrian coast. In order to keep the crusading army intact the leaders concealed from the host their destination and no allusion to Egypt appeared in the treaty.[60]

Tessier exculpates, however, the chief actors singled out by the treason theorists for responsibility. The Venetians, far from being mistrusted by the pope, were his choice among the Italian sea powers, Pisa and Genoa being at that time in disfavor. Venice had received from Innocent a special dispensation from the embargo on trade with the Muslims of 1198. In Tessier's view there was excellent rapport between the Republic of San Marco and the Holy See.[61] The marquis of Montferrat is also exonerated of blame for the diversion. As Villehardouin reports, he was elected because he was a well-known figure and a natural candidate, and his choice aroused no dissatisfaction among the host. The arrival of Alexius in the West would naturally have come to his attention, but this does not prove him Philip's accomplice. Had he been Philip's agent and an adversary of Innocent, he would not have bowed to the papal wish that the leader of the crusade should not be present at the attack on Zara. Finally, his title as chief gave him no real power over the other leaders to divert the crusade.[62] The German king himself never took an active part in the course of events. Through Alexius he did envisage a means for uniting the

---

57. Tessier, *Quatrième croisade*, p. 12.   58. *Ibid.*, pp. 183–184.

59. *Ibid.*, pp. 135–142. On the *Gesta* and Clary he is absolutely right. Tessier bases his date of 1202 on the letter of Innocent, Nov. 16, 1202, to Alexius III, in which Innocent describes the length of time since he had seen the young Alexius. This same letter has also been used to prove the 1201 date.

60. *Ibid.*, pp. 49–50, 57–59, 61–62.   61. *Ibid.*, pp. 94–103.
62. *Ibid.*, pp. 174–176.

Greek church with Rome and the possibility of salvaging his desperate situation in Germany by winning the favor of the pope.[63]

Innocent himself was not as opposed to the deviation as historians had supposed.[64] Peter Capuano's decision to allow the attack upon Zara to prevent the dispersion of the host did not lead to his disgrace or the loss of his legatine powers, and the pope's letters show his continued confidence in the legate.[65] Innocent planned to use the threat of the crusading army to intimidate Alexius III, who had neither aided the Holy Land nor furthered the reunion of the churches. Although Innocent wanted no responsibility for the conquest of Constantinople, he was not displeased when it occurred.[66] He facilitated the absolution of the crusaders, sent French missionaries, and requested the University of Paris to send masters and doctors. The pope did not really regard the conquest, as Hurter believed he did, as a "deplorable event." Had he been able, he would have prevented the attack upon Zara, but for the conquest of Constantinople he merely wished to relinquish responsibility.[67]

It was only at Zara, not earlier, that the project of diversion to Constantinople began. The decision was made by a dozen French nobles, the chief leaders who had been partisans of the Egyptian route. The opposition of the Syrian faction had now made the earlier plan impossible, and the twelve hoped that Constantinople would arouse less resistance than Alexandria. Prince Alexius, moreover, offered to pay their debts and provide military assistance for the assault on the Holy Land. The deviation to Constantinople was not caused by a plot, but developed from the quarrel over the route of the crusade.[68]

P. Mitrofanov follows Villehardouin and Tessier very closely. Boniface was an obvious choice for leading the crusade, because of his family connections in the East and his political skill.[69] The affair of Zara was a practical idea of Dandolo which would keep the crusade together, although the rank and file were kept in the dark. While the description of the events follows Tessier closely, Mitrofanov does lay more blame on the Venetians, who exploited the poverty of the crusaders, but he does not

---

63. *Ibid.*, pp. 156–159 and 165.
64. *Ibid.*, p. 159.
65. *Ibid.*, pp. 192–193.
66. *Ibid.*, pp. 224–227.
67. *Ibid.*, pp. 237–238.

68. *Ibid.*, pp. 167–169. Francesco Cerone's "Il Papa e i veneziani nella quarta crociata," *Archivio veneto*, N.S., XXXVI (1888), 57–70 and 287–297, follows the interpretation of Tessier so closely that it does not require separate discussion.

69. P. Mitrofanov, "Izmenenie v napravlenii chetvertogo krestovogo pokhoda" [The Change in the Direction of the Fourth Crusade], p. 473.

see this as a plot and firmly rejects any alleged treaty with the sultan.[70] As for a German plot, he feels that this was substantially obliterated by Vasilievskii's article proving that the flight of Alexius occurred in 1202.[71] Unlike the other Russian writers who deal with the diversion problem, Mitrofanov is most definite in exculpating Pope Innocent.[72]

II. THE MODIFIED THEORY OF ACCIDENTS AND ITS OPPONENTS

The genuine political and economic insights of the treason theorists and the more sophisticated defense of the theory of accidents by champions of Villehardouin, such as Tessier, came to fruition before the turn of the century in a synthesis by Walter Norden, perhaps the most influential scholar in the history of the diversion question. The title of his work, *Der Vierte Kreuzzug im Rahmen der Beziehungen des Abendlandes zu Byzanz*, suggests his thesis: "The Fourth Crusade represents the dénouement of the old conflict between the West and Byzantium, when once it had become acute since the middle of the eleventh century."[1] Like Streit and Heyd before him, Norden places the Fourth Crusade in the perspective of historical relations between the East and West, but the earlier scholars had concentrated only upon Venetian-Byzantine relations and had been led to the Venetian treason theory. Norden's perspective was as deep as theirs, but broader, including not only the Venetians, but other leading participants in the crusade. Venetians, Hohenstaufen, and others did not find the idea of an attack upon Constantinople unprecedented or startling, and all the leading participants had reasons for desiring it, although none of them plotted a deviation. When fortuitous circumstances, however, presented the detour via Constantinople as a means of preventing the dissolution of the crusade the leaders possessed ample motivation for agreeing to it. We have dubbed this the "modified theory of accidents."

Norden was primarily interested in the background of the crusade, especially the history of the idea of a western attack upon Constantinople. Like Streit, Norden stresses Venetian naval power and commercial interests. Venice had offered her fleet to protect Byzantine territory, and in exchange had gained commercial dominance in the eastern Mediterranean. In the late twelfth century, however, Pisa and Genoa were challenging Venetian pre-eminence, and the republic's relations with

70. *Ibid.*, pp. 475–477, 485–487.   71. *Ibid.*, pp. 495–497.
72. *Ibid.*, pp. 499–504.
1. Walter Norden, *Der Vierte Kreuzzug im Rahmen der Beziehungen des Abendlandes zu Byzanz* (Berlin, 1898), p. 2.

Byzantium were badly deteriorating.[2] Her threatened privileges made Venice very susceptible to the lure of the Bosporus. The Norman dynasty in South Italy and Sicily had a long tradition of designs against Byzantium, and earlier crusaders, such as Odo of Deuil and the great Barbarossa, had contemplated the conquest of Constantinople.[3] Henry VI, combining the heritages of the Normans and the Hohenstaufen, dreamed of an empire embracing all Christendom, and his Byzantine rival was saved from attack only by Henry's premature death. Philip of Swabia, his successor, carried on the Hohenstaufen imperial idea, although his precarious situation in Germany did not permit him to think seriously of attacking Constantinople.[4] Alexius III blundered in violating Venetian rights in his empire and in failing to supervise properly his captives, Isaac and young Alexius.[5] Finally, the crusading army was attracted to Constantinople by the prospect of gain, of ending the problems posed by Byzantium for the crusades, of unifying the churches, and of restoring the rightful Byzantine emperor to the throne.[6] The participants were all eager for the conquest of Constantinople, but they conceived it as merely a stage in the campaign against the infidel.[7] There were no duped participants.

Norden carefully refuted the treason theories in a section entitled: "*Die Wendung des vierten Kreuzzuges gegen Konstantinopel war nicht das Werk einer Intrigue.*"[8] A Venetian plot could not be reasonably conjectured, because there were simply too many uncontrollable variables. If young Alexius, for example, had been able to carry out the treaty of Zara, the crusade would have proceeded against the unbeliever after enthroning him and Isaac, but unforeseeable circumstances made this impossible. Norden accepted Hanotaux's conclusion that there was no treaty between Venice and Egypt to divert the crusade, as Ernoul, trying to impose guilt *ex eventu*, contended. Norden believed that beyond the secret codicil of the treaty of transportation naming Egypt as the goal, or beyond its alternative, the detour via Constantinople, the Holy Land itself always remained the ultimate goal of the undertaking.[9] The Swabian theory, placing the blame upon Philip, who sought to thwart and embarrass the pope, was equally invalid. The *Gesta Innocentii*, upon which the Swabian theory is based, was written from an anti-German point of view, but

2. *Ibid.*, pp. 22–27.   3. *Ibid.*, pp. 13–21.

4. *Ibid.*, pp. 30–33.

5. *Ibid.*, pp. 35–36. Paolo Lamma has recently analyzed the conflict that grew between East and West in the twelfth century. *Comneni e Staufer: ricerche sui rapporti fra Bisanzio e l'Occidente nel secolo XII*, 2 vols. (Rome, 1955–57).

6. Norden, *Vierte Kreuzzug*, pp. 44–47.   7. *Ibid.*, pp. 39 and 47–48.

8. *Ibid.*, pp. 67 ff.   9. *Ibid.*, pp. 83–92.

neither it nor Innocent's letters speak of an antipapal design of Philip. The Hohenstaufen's supposed plan to thwart the pope by causing the crusade to miscarry could succeed only if Constantinople became its terminal objective, and Philip, like the Venetians, had no way of foreseeing the combination of circumstances which brought about this unlikely conclusion. The conquest of Constantinople, moreover, would achieve the union of the churches ardently desired by Innocent, Philip's foe.[10]

Innocent's own position on the conquest of Constantinople was a changing one. From the beginning he opposed the misuse of the crusade against the Christians of Zara and Constantinople, but his prohibitions went unheard.[11] Never had a Byzantine ruler shown less interest in uniting the churches than had Alexius III in the past three years, but Innocent did not trust the promises of the young pretender, nor did he wish to see him, the brother-in-law of his German enemy, on the throne of Byzantium.[12] With the taking of the city, however, Innocent's position was suddenly reversed, and he praised the Grace of God, who had performed so great a miracle. His change of mind was the acceptance of a *fait accompli*. Only when he finally realized that the host would never proceed to the Holy Land did he despair of the undertaking and place his hopes upon an entirely new crusade.[13]

Norden accomplished his goal of placing the Fourth Crusade in the framework of relations between the East and the West. This prohibits classifying him and his followers simply as adherents of Villehardouin's theory of accidents. Geoffrey's account is essentially truthful, but, for Norden, too superficial.[14] The marshal's version is based on mere coincidences, while Norden's "accidents" are set in a background of historical causation, long-term forces, and deep-seated motivations. This modified theory of accidents is not at all like the facile acceptance of Villehardouin by Wailly.

The view of Norden with minor variations has become extremely influential. One of the earliest to make use of his work and commend it was F. C. Hodgson, who follows Norden closely and rejects the alleged Venetian treaty with Egypt as "a libel."[15]

10. *Ibid.*, pp. 73–76.

11. *Ibid.*, pp. 95–99.

12. Walter Norden, *Das Papstum und Byzanz* (Berlin, 1903), pp. 147–149.

13. Norden, *Vierte Kreuzzug*, pp. 100–102.

14. Norden, *Papstum und Byzanz*, p. 153 n. 1. Norden follows Villehardouin on the facts, such as the arrival of Alexius in the West in 1202.

15. Hodgson, *The Early History of Venice*, p. 349 n. 1 and p. 355 n. 2.

F. I. Uspenskii offers an example of the mixture of the old treasonists with the modified theory of accidents of Norden. Because of his death in 1927 the third volume of his *Istoriia Vyzantiiskoi Imperii* did not appear until 1948, but its chapter on the Fourth Crusade was taken largely from his history of the crusades published in 1901. He deals with the background of relations of the Hohenstaufen and the Venetians with Byzantium,[16] but emphasizes the conspiratorial roles of Boniface, Philip, and Innocent. Boniface's meeting with Philip at Haguenau in 1201 and the 1201 date for the flight of Alexius are relied upon, as in the old treason theories.[17] Innocent's rescinding of the excommunication for the attack on Zara was an example of his "looking through his fingers" at the whole adventure.[18]

Heinrich Kretschmayr's still authoritative *Geschichte von Venedig* follows more closely Norden's path along the road of long-term East-West relationships. The immediate cause of the expeditions to Zara and Constantinople was the lack of money resulting from the defections of those who opposed Egypt as the place of debarkation. Alexius, who arrived in the West in 1202, provided an opportunity to salvage the undertaking. The Venetians were strongly motivated to grasp this chance, for they wished to re-establish their commercial domination in Constantinople and they saw no gain for themselves in Syria or Egypt.[19] The plan to restore Alexius and his father was probably authored by Philip, but carried out by the doge, as German and Venetian interests and policies coincided. Philip could give only diplomatic support, but he passed on his plan to the crusaders through Boniface. From this point Kretschmayr, like Streit, sees Dandolo as the decision-maker of the crusade, "*die leitende Persönlichkeit des Unternehmens.*" The pope's role is characterized as laissez-faire, since Innocent was compelled to allow to happen what he could not prevent.[20]

Achille Luchaire's much-cited work on Innocent III changed in many ways the interpretation of Innocent's part in the crusade as presented by Hurter. Luchaire's entire view was shaped by his belief that in the Fourth Crusade profane sentiments and material interests had a more prominent place than in earlier expeditions. Innocent was on good terms

16. F. I. Uspenskii, *Istoriia Vyzantiiskoi Imperii*, III (Moscow-Leningrad, 1948), 367–368, 372–373. Of course, Streit and Heyd before Norden had placed their Venetian treason theories in historical context.

17. *Ibid.*, pp. 367–369.

18. *Ibid.*, p. 371.

19. Heinrich Kretschmayr, *Geschichte von Venedig*, I, 282–287.

20. *Ibid.*, I, 289–294.

with the merchants of the Adriatic republic, even though he had not been able to persuade them to give up their trade with the Saracens. Venice was chosen to transport the crusaders, because only she could provide sufficient naval forces for such an army. The Republic of St. Mark did not betray the crusade, but acted simply as she had during the preceding century and as she would in that which followed. Luchaire accepted Villehardouin's assertion that Innocent confirmed the treaty of transportation *molt volentiers*. He believed that the *Gesta*, which seems to oppose Villehardouin's view of the confirmation, anachronistically attributed to Innocent *"une sorte d'instinct de divination."* [21] It is interesting that the modern biographer of the pope has rejected the propapal panegyric.

Innocent emerges as a practical statesman, maintaining the moral position of the church, while accepting the evil which he regretted but could not prevent, managing somehow to draw advantage from it.[22] Although the pope was unhappy about the attack upon Zara, he did not disgrace his legate, who, in an effort to keep the army together, refused permission to clerics who wished to abandon this pilgrimage gone awry. After the conquest of the Dalmatian port, because of his own intense desire to preserve the host, Innocent allowed the absolved crusaders to proceed in company with the excommunicated Venetians. He did not wish the conquest of Constantinople, but he allowed it to occur, realizing that all opposition was futile.[23] Innocent's letter to the Venetians after the fall of the city was very conciliatory, and the Venetians were shortly absolved, showing that the pope accepted the *fait accompli*.[24] On the surface the interests of the pope and Roman church were served by it. Beneath the surface, however, the interests of Rome had been "constantly sacrificed to those of the barons and the merchants."[25] Luchaire is not overly concerned with the diversion question, however, for "science has something better to do than to discuss indefinitely an insoluble problem."[26]

This advice to lay aside the question of the diversion might be followed by its author, since the focal point of his interest was the pope, whose role in the Fourth Crusade became more and more marginal, but other historians concerned more specifically with the crusade itself or with its principal characters have not been able to heed it. Since the turn of the century the majority of them have followed the lines laid down by Norden.

21. Luchaire, *Innocent III: la question d'Orient*, pp. 87–94.
22. *Ibid.*, pp. 125–126.   23. *Ibid.*, pp. 100–116.
24. *Ibid.*, pp. 127–128.   25. *Ibid.*, p. 141.
26. *Ibid.*, p. 97.

J. K. Fotheringham, for example, declared extinct the theory of a deep plot involving Venice and the Egyptians or the Germans.[27] His special interest, however, was the effort of Genoa to secure a share in the spoils after 1204; so he does not develop the diversion question.

Focusing on the city of Constantinople was Horatio Brown's article, "The Venetians and the Venetian Quarter in Constantinople to the Close of the Twelfth Century." Brown traced Venetian privileges in Constantinople as far back as 880. From the city on the Golden Horn, where she was granted a quarter in 1082, Venice extended her influence throughout the Levant. Byzantine jealousy of Latin intrusion produced a growing rift between the Venetians and the empire.[28] Brown analyzed the causes of the rift as: (1) the consolidation of the Venetian position in the Latin kingdom of Jerusalem; (2) the increasing desire of the Venetians to trade with the Normans, the ancient enemies of the empire and her Venetian allies; (3) the growing wealth and troublesomeness of the Venetian colony in Constantinople; and (4) the Emperor Manuel's need of funds, which he could acquire by a seizure of Venetian wealth.[29] Brown described the rift between Venice and Byzantium more fully than even Norden had done. The growth of Venetian influence in Constantinople led to disaster for the Greeks in 1204.

The treatment of the Fourth Crusade by Leopoldo Usseglio in his very scholarly study of the marquises of Montferrat also follows in the tradition of Norden, stressing the accidents which led to the deviation, but not neglecting the interests of Venice or the dynastic ambitions of Boniface. While the marquis had no preconceived plan and neither sought nor willed the poverty of the host, he saw the opportunity to serve his own cause and the cause of the Holy Land at one stroke. Seeing that the crusaders had agreed to attack Zara, Boniface, remembering his encounter with Alexius in Germany, proposed the diversion to Constantinople.[30]

27. J. K. Fotheringham, "Genoa and the Fourth Crusade," *English Historical Review*, XXV (1910), p. 33.

28. Brown, "The Venetians and the Venetian Quarter," pp. 68–72. Louis Halphen also described the Latin infiltration of Constantinople, creating hatred of westerners among the Greeks and leading to the conquest. "Le rôle des 'Latins' dans l'histoire intérieur de Constantinople à la fin du XIIe siècle," *Mélanges Charles Diehl*, I (Paris, 1930), 141–145. Reprinted in Louis Halphen, *A travers l'histoire du moyen âge* (Paris, 1950). See also E. Frances, "Sur la conquête de Constantinople par les Latins," *Byzantinoslavica*, XV (1954), 21–26, which stresses the internal weakness of Byzantium.

29. Brown, "The Venetians and the Venetian Quarter," p. 83.

30. Usseglio, *I marchesi di Monferrato*, II, 197–198. According to Usseglio, this proposal occurred at Venice, not at Zara, as reported by Robert of Clary. Henri Grégoire called

Venice too seized opportunities it had not sought in order to protect its investment in the enterprise and gain commercial advantage. Not love of lucre, however, but zeal for religion basically inspired the Venetians, as it did the crusaders from the North.[31] Despite the interests of Boniface and Venice in the conquest, there was no connivance. The negligence of the crusaders and their lack of money could not have been foreseen or brought about.[32] Had the crusade proceeded to Egypt or Palestine after wintering in Zara, the year of service to which the Venetians were obligated would have expired, and the host would have faced starvation on an enemy shore.[33] By inexorable necessity the fleet turned its prows toward the imperial city.[34]

In spite of the arguments of the treasonists and the attempt of Norden and his followers to synthesize these with the theory of accidents, the uncomplicated theory of accidents of Villehardouin retained some proponents, such as H. Vriens. The Venetian and Swabian theories were understandably irreconcilable with his position, but Vriens' rejection of Norden is somewhat more unexpected. Where Norden saw a growing conflict between the West and Byzantium as a cause for the assault upon Constantinople, Vriens saw conflict between the Christian powers (including Byzantium) and the Islamic, with the earlier issues dividing Byzantium and the West diminishing as the power of Byzantium declined.[35] Where Norden dwelt upon underlying motives, Vriens had no doubt that the original motives of the crusaders were pure.[36]

Vriens found three turning points in the crusade: the decision at Venice to attack Zara; the decision at Zara to restore Isaac and Alexius; and the decision at Constantinople to take the city and impose a Latin ruler. The crusaders were compelled by financial necessity to yield to the Venetian desire for the reconquest of Zara.[37] The decision to assist Alexius

---

Usseglio's work a "splendid book . . . , one of the most important contributions ever made to our Byzantine studies by a non-Byzantinist," in "The Question of the Diversion of the Fourth Crusade," *Byzantion*, XV (1941), p. 166.

31. Usseglio, *I marchesi di Monferrato*, II, 178.

32. *Ibid.*, p. 199.   33. *Ibid.*, pp. 211–212.

34. *Ibid.*, pp. 215–216. Usseglio also believed, following Riant, that it was useless "to go around in circles endlessly repeating again and again the same arguments . . ." with regard to the deviation. *Ibid.*, p. 171.

35. H. Vriens, "De kwestie van den vierden kruistocht," *Tijdschrift voor Geschiedenis* XXXVII (1922), 56.

36. *Ibid.*, p. 63.

37. Vriens pointed out that Zara was the best port for the exportation of Dalmatian oak needed by Venice for the construction of her fleets. *Ibid.*, p. 69.

was in no way unprecedented. Since the Second Crusade it had been customary to smooth a path for the crusaders through embassies, concessions to neutrals, and assistance in small internal questions.[38] Circumstances compelled the decision to take Constantinople the second time. The army was in a strange land, surrounded by enemies, and faced with an ally who had not fulfilled his obligations to them. After the death of Alexius IV the election of any Greek emperor would place on the throne an enemy of the Latins; therefore they had no choice but to seize the government for themselves.[39] None of these key decisions had as a necessary consequence any of those that followed, and the aim of the crusade, the Holy Land, remained constant. Unforeseeable contingencies decreed that it should never be achieved.[40]

The most vigorous modern defense of Villehardouin is probably that of his editor Edmond Faral in his article in the *Revue historique* of 1936. Faral's arguments centered upon Villehardouin's most controverted views. He argued for the marshal's assertion that Innocent confirmed the treaty for transportation *molt volentiers*. In Faral's view the author of the *Gesta* attributed to the pope miraculous divinatory powers by transferring a later papal prohibition against attacking Christians to May, 1201.[41] Papal absolution to the crusaders for the subsequent sack of Zara was freely given, because Innocent realized that they had been driven to the irreligious act by the Venetians.[42] A key point for the treasonists' attack upon Villehardouin is the date of Alexius' flight, and Faral attempted to defend Villehardouin's assertion that it occurred in 1202. The *Gesta* and Robert of Clary were quickly cast aside as unreliable sources, and the *Annals of Cologne* were declared not useful because of their mixed chronology.[43] Faral opted for a date in the summer of 1202. He relied upon

38. *Ibid.*, p. 72. Vriens believed that the pope allowed the diversion to happen in the hope of the conquest of Jerusalem with the help of a Byzantium reunited with Rome. *Ibid.*, p. 74.

39. *Ibid.*, pp. 80–81.

40. Vriens criticized Alexius IV and Villehardouin for the contributions their poor judgments made to the outcome. *Ibid.*, pp. 81–82.

41. Edmond Faral, "Geoffrey de Villehardouin: la question de sa sincérité," *Revue historique*, CLXXVII (1936), 537–539. For further discussion of Faral's arguments on this issue, see Donald E. Queller, "Innocent III and the Crusader-Venetian Treaty of 1201," *Medievalia et Humanistica*, XV (1963), 32–33.

42. Faral, "Geoffrey de Villehardouin: la question de sa sincérité," pp. 541–546. Faral maintained that Villehardouin's description of the absolution conformed to the "spirit" of the pontiff's letter and the interpretations of the Anonymous of Halberstadt and Gunther of Pairis.

43. *Ibid.*, pp. 547–549.

Nicetas, who, according to Faral, dealt with the flight in a section covering September, 1201, to August 31, 1202, mentioning it specifically in connection with events of 1202. Faral found additional evidence in the pope's reply to Alexius III's inquiry concerning events in the West, for, in his opinion, Innocent described the time between the arrival of Alexius and the presentation of his proposals at Zara as very short.[44] That the crusaders sent their reply to these proposals to Philip of Swabia was not, according to Faral, evidence of a German plot, but due merely to the extreme youth of Alexius.[45] Villehardouin's attackers had contended that he said little about the pope's disapproval of the diversion in order to shroud the impious nature of the deed, but Faral believed that the pope raised only token objections. The Greeks had not been disposed to accept Innocent's authority, and he was not strongly opposed to the conquest. Had he wished to prevent it, he would not have granted absolution to the crusaders for the sack of Zara. The "spirit" of Innocent's subsequent letters also shows his willingness to accept the deviation.[46]

Faral comes out foursquare for the sincerity of Geoffrey the Marshal, but he does, in conclusion, make a concession to the school of Norden. The deviation could not be explained solely in terms of a debt and the chance appearance of a fugitive prince. These could only have had the effect they did in a favorable milieu, and to this extent it is true that a *théorie des causes fortuites* cannot be held sufficient.[47]

If, since the work of Norden, Villehardouin has had friends, he also has had foes, a sizeable number of more-or-less unreconstructed treasonists.

One of the severest critics of the marshal of Champagne was Albert Pauphilet, who published in 1928 a study on "Robert de Clari et Villehardouin" declaring that the marshal was party to a plot to divert the crusade to Constantinople. Pauphilet obviously preferred the testimony of the sincere, though naïve, Robert to that of the disingenuous marshal of Champagne. Not through Villehardouin, who maintained a guarded silence, but through Robert do we learn of the meeting of Philip and Boniface in 1201 where the conspiracy took form. Villehardouin discussed only the military aspects of the attack upon Constantinople, not the political situation, which he astutely concealed. As one of the *hauts*

44. *Ibid.*, pp. 550–553.
45. *Ibid.*, pp. 554–556.
46. *Ibid.*, pp. 560–562.
47. *Ibid.*, p. 581. Jean Longnon in *Les français d'outremer au moyen âge* (Paris, 1929) was also willing to return to Villehardouin's theory of accidents. Longnon made few additions to Villehardouin's account besides adopting the idea of long-term tensions between the East and the West.

hommes implicated in the diversion Villehardouin cleverly wove a tissue of half-truth to conceal the conspiracy in which he and others were engaged.[48]

Among those who distrust Villehardouin, Byzantinists are prominent, probably because those sources with which they have a lifelong familiarity tend toward the treason theories.[49] Henri Grégoire sought to prove a treason centering upon Boniface, and a first step was a refutation of Faral's defense of Villehardouin. With some justification Grégoire contended that Faral rejected Robert of Clary with "contemptuous briefness." He also sharply criticized Faral's analysis of Nicetas. One source of difficulty was that Faral read Nicetas in translation. Additional problems arise from the Greek historian's chronology, for his treatment of the Kamytze rebellion and the causes of the diversion is not strictly chronological, as Faral had supposed. "The chronology may be correct within a particular story, and that is all." The relationship in time of the flight of Alexius to the Kamytze rebellion thus cannot be proved from Nicetas. Even if it could, the Kamytze rebellion occupied a longer period of time than Faral assumed, and the flight is described at an early stage of the rising. Nicetas treats the escape along with a discussion of the causes of the Fourth Crusade, not in chronological sequence. Nicetas actually favored an early date for the flight, probably the winter of 1201/1202, as do the *Annals of Cologne*, the *Gesta*, and the papal letter of November 16, 1202, to Alexius III. This is the same letter used by Faral to establish 1202 as the date of Alexius' flight. The contested passage reads: "Nos autem imperiali prudentiae aliter duximus respondendum, quod predictus Alexius *olim* ad praesentiam nostram accendens . . . ." *Olim*, according to Grégoire, would not mean that the pope had seen Alexius recently, but quite a long time before.[50]

48. Albert Pauphilet, "Robert de Clari et Villehardouin," *Mélanges de linguistique et de littérature offerts à M. Alfred Jeanroy* (Paris, 1928), pp. 559–564. His reasons for accepting Clary over Villehardouin are not convincing.

49. We do not mean to imply that Byzantinists ignore western sources or misuse them, but only that their basic views tend to be molded by the sources most familiar to them. It must be pointed out, however, that the Greek sources, Ernoul and the Chronicle of Novgorod cannot be expected to be as well informed upon a series of events occurring within the ranks of the westerners as the westerners themselves.

50. Grégoire, "The Question of the Diversion of the Fourth Crusade," pp. 158–166. Grégoire frequently stoops to utter contempt of Faral and assumes that his own arguments will simply terminate the discussion. Mayer finds Grégoire's argument unconvincing: " . . . aber das Argument ist zu spitzfindig und presst die Quelle zu sehr, zumal die Bedeutung von *olim* von der fernsten Vergangenheit bis zur fernsten Zukunft reicht." *Geschichte der Kreuzzüge*, p. 177.

An important adherent of the Swabian treason theory throughout his long career was Louis Bréhier. Alexius had fled to the West in 1201 and had met Boniface at Philip's court. Here they probably discussed the restoration of the Byzantine prince.[51] Even before the crusaders gathered at Venice the diversion had been planned. The secondary diversion to Zara was part of Philip's scheme, for he hoped to delay the crusaders while he sought papal sanction for the deviation to Constantinople. It was not difficult for Philip to persuade the Venetians to join in the conspiracy, since Venice had her own commercial interests to consider.[52]

The pope's deep desire was to restore the Holy Land to Christians and to this end he aimed every endeavor.[53] He had ratified the treaty of 1201 only with the reservations against attacking Christians given in the *Gesta*.[54] Innocent always opposed the deviation, but his protests arrived too late at Zara. Philip's plot prevailed over the pope's efforts to maintain the crusade against Islam.[55] Bréhier's points from first to last closely followed the Swabian theory of Winkelmann and Riant. Unlike the Venetian theory, which had gained in depth since Streit, Heyd, and Norden, the Swabian theory had changed very little. The contest between Philip and Innocent was prominent in all the Swabian treason theorists with the pope appearing as the unfortunate loser.[56]

In his recent *Cathedral and Crusade*, Henri Daniel-Rops also concluded that Philip of Swabia instigated the diversion as an antipapal measure: ". . . it seemed not unlikely that the scheme had been worked out between them [Philip and Alexius] and the notorious Ghibelline Boniface of Montferrat, lest a victorious campaign in Palestine should complete the triumph of Innocent III." Daniel-Rops takes into account, however, the influence of Norden and his followers, and holds that all but a few crusaders found reasons of their own to welcome the diversion.

51. Louis Bréhier, *L'église et l'orient au moyen âge: les croisades*, 1st ed. (1906); 6th ed. (Paris, 1928), p. 153. There is no citation for the discussion of Alexius' restoration, and Bréhier concedes that this is only a guess on the basis of subsequent events. Bréhier's work is extremely careless with regard to dates and details.

52. *Ibid.*, pp. 154–155. Bréhier accepted Hanotaux's refutation of the treaty between Venice and Egypt and believed that Venice was motivated by her underlying commercial interests in the Levant. On the entire diversion question Bréhier did not basically alter his views in later years. *Vie et mort de Byzance* (Paris, 1947), pp. 365–367.

53. Bréhier, *L'église et l'orient au moyen âge: les croisades*, p. 146.

54. *Ibid.*, p. 152.

55. *Ibid.*, p. 158.

56. See also René Grousset, *Histoire des croisades et du Royaume Franc de Jérusalem*, 3 vols. (Paris, 1934–36), III, 173, and *L'empire du Levant* (Paris, 1949), p. 443. In the latter, Grousset cites Bréhier as the source of his information.

Without their concurrence Philip's intent could never have been achieved.[57]

The old Swabian theory of Winkelmann and Riant has remained largely unchanged, although Daniel-Rops could work into it the long-term trends and underlying motives of the Norden tradition. The Venetian theory, on the other hand, has become much more cautious under the impact of decades of discussion, and it is usually a considerably modified version of Mas Latrie and Hopf which now appears.

The mellowing of the theory of Venetian responsibility can be illustrated in the work of Charles Diehl, a famous Byzantinist, whose writings on the subject span a period of thirty years. In *Une république patricienne* (1915) he gives the credit for the expedition largely to Dandolo. In a romantic spirit Diehl offers a eulogy to the aged doge:

> Ambitious, avid for glory for himself and still more for his country, he offers an admirable example of Venetian patriotism, capable of every self-sacrifice, careless also of every scruple when the greatness of the Republic was at stake.[58]

In *Byzance: grandeur et décadence* (1919), *Histoire de l'Empire Byzantin* (1919), and the *Cambridge Medieval History* (1923), Diehl was more reserved. While the Venetians had seized a good opportunity, all the other members of the crusade had numerous reasons for desiring the attack upon Constantinople, "haines religieuse, ambitions politiques, convoitises economiques, irréductible antagonisme de deux races et de deux mondes ...."[59] Over twenty years later Diehl wrote an article in the *Histoire générale* (1945), following the pattern laid in his earlier works. He did not attempt to prove that the Venetians planned the diversion as early as April, 1201, although Diehl still upheld a moderate belief in Venetian responsibility.[60]

Other Byzantinists also have been inclined to cast the Venetians as the prime movers of the drama of the fall of Constantinople. This is reflected in two of the most popular handbooks of Byzantine history, those of A. A. Vasiliev and George Ostrogorsky. Vasiliev modified the Venetian

57. Henri Daniel-Rops, *Cathedral and Crusade: Studies of the Medieval Church, 1050–1350*, trans. John Warrington (London, 1957), pp. 461–462.

58. Charles Diehl, *Une république patricienne* (Paris, 1915), pp. 47–48; our translation.

59. Charles Diehl, *Byzance: grandeur et décadence* (Paris, 1919), p. 255. *Histoire de l'Empire Byzantin* (Paris, 1919), pp. 242–255; "The Fourth Crusade and the Latin Empire," in *Cambridge Medieval History*, IV (Cambridge, 1923), pp. 415–418.

60. Charles Diehl, *Histoire du Moyen Age*, in Gustave Glotz (ed.), *Histoire générale*, IX (Paris, 1945), p. 125.

treason theory with many long-ripening motivations: desire to prevail in commercial rivalry, Venetian offense at the uncollected indemnity owed by the Byzantines, and personal animosity. Even so, "the central figure of the crusade was the doge of Venice, Enrico Dandolo ...." The Venetians had not made any treaty with Egypt, however, nor had they plotted with Philip, but their attitude toward Byzantium, arising out of years of conflict, was crucial to the diversion.[61] Here the influence of Norden is obvious in the emphasis on mixed and long-term causes, the natural development of events and the absence of praise or blame.[62]

Ostrogorsky's view was similar to Vasiliev's, although he was somewhat less willing to temper the theory of Venetian treason. That Dandolo was "entirely unmoved by the genuine crusading spirit" is a statement which is possibly incorrect or exaggerated, and is certainly simplistic. In spite of this, Ostrogorsky also considered more general causes, such as the growing secularization of the crusades and Latin hatred of the Greeks, which turned the crusade into "an instrument of conquest to be used against the Christian East."[63]

In the new *Cambridge Medieval History*, D. M. Nicol also finds the Venetians responsible:

> In the interminable controversy over the diversion of the Fourth Crusade, many have doubted the ulterior motives of Philip of Swabia, of Boniface of Montferrat, and of Innocent III. But few have tried to exonerate the Venetians. At worst the Doge of Venice stands out as the villain of the piece, at best as the only realist in the table of confused aims and misdirected ideals.[64]

There seems at least a partial truth in Nicol's statement that "in the end the decision rested with the Doge of Venice; for without his ships the crusade could sail nowhere." Nicol describes Innocent as curiously

---

61. Vasiliev, *History of the Byzantine Empire, 324–1453*, pp. 452–459.

62. Paul Rousset, *Histoire des croisades* (Paris, 1957), p. 213, agrees with Vasiliev's views.

63. George Ostrogorsky, *History of the Byzantine State*, 1st German ed. (1940); trans. Joan Hussey from the 2nd German ed. (1952) with revisions by the author (New Brunswick, 1956), pp. 367–368. Adolf Waas, *Geschichte der Kreuzzüge*, 2 vols. (Freiburg, 1956), I, 244–250, also declares the Venetians the prime leaders of the diversion. Although there was no official treaty with the sultan of Egypt, Venice hoped to receive her reward for diverting the crusade. Dandolo hated Byzantium, and Waas follows Ostrogorsky's characterization of Dandolo.

64. D. M. Nicol, "The Fourth Crusade and the Greek and Latin Empires, 1204–61," in *Cambridge Medieval History*, IV (Cambridge, 1966), 278.

hesitant. Like Tessier, he believes that the Fourth Crusade set out for Constantinople with the connivance, if not the blessing, of the pope.[65]

Unfortunately the views of many on the Fourth Crusade will be molded by Sir Steven Runciman's well-known *A History of the Crusades*, which fails to integrate generations of scholarship on the diversion question. Runciman adopts at first a view that curiously resembles the old and thoroughly discredited Venetian treason theory of Mas Latrie and Hopf:

> At the very moment when the Venetian government was bargaining with the Crusaders about the transport of their forces, its ambassadors were in Cairo planning a treaty with them in the Spring of 1202, after special envoys sent by Al-Adil to Venice had been assured by the Doge that he would countenance no expedition against Egypt . . . .

His footnote cites Ernoul, of course, and refers to Hopf's treaty, which "has been denied," but which Runciman seems extremely reluctant to give up.[66] On this question, however, Runciman shows little consistency, for he had just finished writing:

> The truth seems to be that while Philip of Swabia, Boniface and the Venetians all had separate reasons for desiring an attack on Constantinople, it was the accident of Alexius' arrival which made the diversion practicable.[67]

This sounds more like a modified theory of accidents. These views do not reconcile easily.[68]

In *The Eastern Schism*, Runciman follows the growing ecclesiastical conflict which grew into a popular antagonism. Again at one point he leans toward Villehardouin: "The actual course of the Crusade was due more to accident than to deliberate planning . . . ."[69] His description of

65. He also agrees with Tessier, however, that Innocent did not approve of the attack upon Zara. *Ibid.*, p. 280.

66. Runciman, *A History of the Crusades*, III, 113–114 and 113 n. 2. Hanotaux's devastating criticism of Hopf is not clearly acknowledged. It may be possible yet to present a case for a Venetian-Egyptian treaty, though it seems extremely improbable to the present authors, it but cannot be baldly asserted on the mere authority of Ernoul and the discredited treaty of Hopf without regard to the considerable learned literature on the subject. See McNeal and Wolff, "The Fourth Crusade," p. 170 n. 44.

67. Runciman, *A History of the Crusades*, III, 112 n. 2.

68. Hopf estimated the sending of the Venetian ambassadors to Cairo in the autumn of 1201. If the arrival of Alexius were essential to make a plot practicable, then his arrival in the West must be placed remarkably early.

69. Steven Runciman, *The Eastern Schism* (Oxford, 1955), p. 167.

events, however, does not follow Villehardouin. Philip and Boniface plotted to put young Alexius on the throne; the terms of the treaty of transportation were very high for the crusaders; and Boniface was elected at the suggestion of the French king. The pope was very unhappy about the deviation, and wished the crusaders to proceed as quickly as possible to the Holy Land.[70] So Runciman's view does not really resemble Villehardouin's.

William Daly, while subscribing to a Hohenstaufen-Venetian plot, has argued that the diversion was made possible only by the breakdown of the feeling of Christian fraternity between the Latins and the Greeks.[71] Although the conquest of Constantinople had been proposed on earlier occasions, these bonds of Christian fraternity had saved the Greeks.[72] By the Fourth Crusade, however, "ideals and material interests had parted company."[73] Daly emphasized, however, that the bulk of the crusaders were not aware of the conspiracy of their leaders and were opposed to the diversion. Their opposition, although ineffectual, was a continuing manifestation of the medieval peace movement.[74]

Despite the erudition of the Soviet historian M. A. Zaborov, his articles on the Fourth Crusade are tainted by Stalinist dogma. The diversion of the crusade was a result of the predatory machinations of western feudalism and the Roman Catholic church. Nineteenth-century advocates of the theory of accidents were supporters of French colonial expansion in the East, and more recent attempts to revive the theory of accidents are also apologies for contemporary imperialism.[75] Even Russian bourgeois historians, although they did not realize the force of economic motivation and the class struggle, led European historians by

70. *Ibid.*, pp. 145–147. Another contemporary treasonist is Aziz Atiya, who, however, distributes blame for "the disgraceful affair" liberally among Venetians, French, Flemings, and Germans. *Crusade, Commerce and Culture* (Bloomington, 1962), pp. 82–85.

71. William Daly, "Christian Fraternity, the Crusaders and the Security of Constantinople, 1097–1204; the Precarious Survival of an Ideal," *Mediaeval Studies*, XXII (1960), 78 and n. 114. We would not agree that historians now "generally admit that there was considerable prior understanding among a handful of the leaders." Daly cites Vasiliev, Bréhier, Ostrogorsky, Runciman, and Grousset, all Byzantinists except Grousset, an orientalist. It has already been mentioned that they tend toward the treason theories. None of them, moreover, offers an extensive and painstaking scholarly treatment of the subject.

72. *Ibid.*, pp. 55–56.

73. *Ibid.*, p. 78.

74. *Ibid.*, pp. 79–80. He explicitly follows A. Frolow.

75. M. A. Zaborov, "K voprosu o predistorii chetvertogo krestovogo pokhoda" [On the Question of the Prehistory of the Fourth Crusade], *Vizantiiskii Vremennik* [*Byzantine Chronicle*], VI (1953), 223–224.

clearing away the rubble of one-sided theories.[76] Since one of the themes of western historiography has been the justification of the papacy as a reactionary force supporting the capitalist order, Marxist-Leninist historians are obligated to expose papal intrigue as an important factor in the conquest of Constantinople.[77] He also takes considerable pleasure in arguing that still another representative of western imperialism, Philip Augustus, was instrumental in the election of Boniface for the purpose of diverting the army to Constantinople. The French king brought this about in support of his ally Philip of Swabia and possibly even possessed designs upon the Byzantine throne on his own account.[78]

Although unanimity is far from achieved, the contemporary weight of opinion seems to be with the modified theory of accidents. The prestige of the Pennsylvania *History of the Crusades* and the erudition and judiciousness of its chapter on the Fourth Crusade by Edgar McNeal and Robert Lee Wolff would suggest in themselves that the tradition of Norden occupies a favored place. Freddy Thiriet and Roberto Cessi are also among contemporary scholars subscribing to the modified theory of accidents.[79]

Thiriet has done a great deal of work with unpublished Venetian chronicles (largely of a later date), and he approaches the Fourth Crusade from this vantage point.[80] As a Venetian specialist, he quite naturally concentrates upon Venetian-Byzantine relations. During the reign of

76. *Ibid.*, p. 223; M. A. Zaborov, "Krestovye pokhody v russkoi burzhuaznoi istoriografii" [The Crusades in Russian Bourgeois Historiography], *Vizantiiskii Vremennik* [*Byzantine Chronicle*], IV (1951), 177–180.

77. M. A. Zaborov, "Papstvo i zakhvat konstantinopolia krestonostsami v nachale XIII v. K voprosu o roli Innokentiia III v peremene napravleniia chetvertogo krestovogo pokhoda" [The Papacy and the Conquest of Constantinople by the Crusaders in the Beginning of the Thirteenth Century. On the Question of the Role of Innocent III in the Diversion of the Fourth Crusade], *Vizantiiskii Vremennik* [*Byzantine Chronicle*], V (1952), 153–154. A. Ivanov, "Zakhvat Konstantinopolia Latinianami v 1204 godu" [Conquest of Constantinople by the Latins in the Year 1204], *Zhurnal Moskovskoi Patriarchii* [*Journal of the Patriarch of Moscow*] (1954), pp. 64–73, is little more than a retelling of Zaborov's tale with the latter's bias, but without his learning.

78. Zaborov, "K voprosu o predistorii chetvertogo krestovogo pokhoda" [On the Question of the Prehistory of the Fourth Crusade], pp. 230–232.

79. Other recent scholars who share this view include Helene Tillman, *Papst Innocenz III* (Bonn, 1954), and Mayer, *Geschichte der Kreuzzüge*. Although Mayer's work is merely a brief handbook, it is based upon a remarkably broad and accurate bibliographical knowledge.

80. Freddy Thiriet, "Les chroniques vénitiennes de la Marcienne et leur importance pour l'histoire de la Romanie gréco-vénitienne," *Mélanges d'archéologie et d'histoire. École française de Rome*, LXVI (1954), 241–292.

Manuel Comnenus (1143–1180) relations between the Venetians and the Greeks fluctuated between warm and cold, reaching a low point in the massacre of 1171. As the power of Manuel diminished, however, the influence of the Venetians increased. Dislike for the interlopers continued to grow during the last years of the dynasty, and in 1182 occurred another popular outburst. Friendly relations were restored under Andronicus Comnenus (1183–1185) and Isaac II Angelus (1185–1195), but then fell apart under Alexius III (1195–1203). Alexius' favoring of the Genoese and Pisans at Venetian expense was the cause of a deep rift between the merchant republic and the empire.[81] Although Venice was eager to join the diversion, Thiriet believes "the Fourth Crusade is a collective enterprise, the responsibilities for its deviation toward Constantinople are thus divided." He notes that the crusaders entered into negotiations with Philip concerning Alexius without even consulting their Venetian allies. Thiriet also realizes that religious motives were important, as well as political and economic, although he concentrates upon the economic interests of Venice in the East.[82]

Among those adhering to a modified theory of accidents in the tradition of Norden is the most eminent of Venetian historians Roberto Cessi, who offers a number of intriguing re-interpretations of the course of the Fourth Crusade.[83] Out of love for the city to which he has devoted an unbelievably long and fruitful career, however, Cessi takes on the role of Venetian apologist, attempting to exonerate them from all blame.

The point of debarkation of the expedition as agreed upon in the treaty of 1201 was Syria, not, as Villehardouin states, Egypt. The comment of Villehardouin reflects only his personal view, for no one in the Venetian government took notice of Egypt in connection with the Fourth Crusade, and, of course, the fleet did not in fact proceed to the mouth of the Nile.[84] Cessi also regards the pope's prohibition against attacking Christians contained in the *Gesta Innocentii* and the supposed Venetian

---

81. Freddy Thiriet, *La Romanie vénitienne au moyen âge* (Paris, 1959), pp. 51–56.

82. *Ibid.*, pp. 67–71.

83. "The Fourth Crusade, summoned to redeem the Holy Land, was led by an inevitable chain of events to Constantinople . . . ." Roberto Cessi, "Venice on the Eve of the Fourth Crusade," in *Cambridge Medieval History*, IV, Part 1 (Cambridge, 1966), 274. The same passage, however, refers to "Venetian inspiration" of the diversion, which, as we shall see, is quite contrary to Cessi's prevailing viewpoint.

84. Roberto Cessi, "L'eredità di Enrico Dandolo," *Archivio veneto*, Ser. 5, LXVII (1960), 2 n. 2; Roberto Cessi, "Politica, economia, religione," in *Storia di Venezia, vol. II, Dalle origini del ducato alla IV crociata* (Venice, n.d.), p. 451.

refusal to accept it as a malicious attempt to defame Venice.[85] The inability of the crusaders to fulfill their treaty with Venice led to an alteration of the legal relationships of the army and the Venetians with the latter assuming the cross and gaining a greater participation in the leadership and the expected profits. The debt of the crusaders to Venice should be paid out of the first conquests.[86] The attack upon Zara, however, does not appear to Cessi as a conquest imposed upon the crusaders as the price of their failure to pay their debt to Venice, but as part of a routine gathering of guarantees from Adriatic cities bound to Venice in which the crusading host was not originally to participate. Villehardouin's account of Dandolo's offer to the crusaders was another effort to cast odium upon the Venetians.[87] Dandolo stood cautiously aloof from the negotiations of the envoys of Alexius with the crusader chieftains. Finally, at Corfu, his concern for the situation of the Latins (and especially the Venetians) in Constantinople gained his adherence to the plan to restore Isaac and Alexius, and this was decisive in deflecting the crusade from Syria to Constantinople.[88] By grasping at last the opportunity presented to him to further Venetian interests in Constantinople, Dandolo crowned with his name the building that had been prepared stone by stone before him, even though this may have been accomplished, not so much by an act of his will, as by the imperative requirements of events.[89]

The chapter on the Fourth Crusade by Edgar McNeal and Robert Lee Wolff in the Pennsylvania *History of the Crusades* is a balanced essay judiciously weighing the various causes and motives involved in the crusade. Though the authors agree with Luchaire that the diversion is an insoluble question, they are as interested as any historians in attempting to solve it. Although they generally follow Villehardouin, they accept the interpretation of Nicetas which established the arrival of Alexius in the West in 1201. This would allow time for a plot to develop, but the authors neither find a conspiracy nor accuse Villehardouin of deliberately altering the date.[90] In the tradition of Norden, McNeal and Wolff believe

85. Roberto Cessi, "Venezia e la quarta crociata," *Archivio veneto*, Ser. 5, XLVIII–XLIX (1951), 11 n. 1.

86. Cessi, "L'eredità di Enrico Dandolo," p. 5 n. 2; Cessi, "Politica, economia, religione," pp. 452–453.

87. Cessi, "Venezia e la quarta crociata," pp. 26–27; Cessi, "Politica, economia, religione," pp. 453–455.

88. Cessi, "L'eredità di Enrico Dandolo," p. 4 n. 2; Cessi, "Politica, economia, religione," pp. 457–458; Cessi, "Venice on the Eve of the Fourth Crusade," p. 274.

89. Cessi, "Politica, economia, religione," pp. 466–467.

90. McNeal and Wolff, "The Fourth Crusade," pp. 170–172. See especially p. 172 n. 51.

that the attack upon Constantinople, while not premeditated, "coincided with the interest of Venice, of Boniface of Montferrat, of Philip of Swabia, and—to the extent that it placed a Roman Catholic dynasty and patriarch on the imperial and ecclesiastical thrones of Constantinople—of Innocent III as well."[91] The pope, however, probably did not actively participate in the diversion, but rather allowed it to happen.[92] The authors often decline to take a categorical position on controversial questions, and perhaps this is a result of a century of unresolved debate which has shattered all facile solutions.

The real contribution of the founders of the modified theory of accidents at the turn of the century can be seen in this recent and scholarly synthesis by McNeal and Wolff. Norden and Kretschmayr, particularly, marked a new trend in Fourth Crusade historiography. They avoided the judgmental attitudes of their predecessors and prepared the way for the more sophisticated views of most modern scholars.

III. THE INTERIOR HISTORY

An exciting new dimension to the continuing debate on the Fourth Crusade has emerged in recent years in the works of A. Frolow and Paul Alphandéry. The older issues are left behind, and a phase of the debate far more different from any of its predecessors than they are from one another has begun. Unsatisfied with the analysis of political and economic factors, Frolow and Alphandéry have sought to penetrate the minds of the crusaders—and especially of the anonymous mass—not in mid-twentieth-century categories of thought, but in those of the beginning of the thirteenth. Their quest for the true and, in the deepest sense, *historical* motivations of the crusaders has led them, especially Alphandéry, to an analysis of the psychology of the crusading movement.[1] More than just psychology, they have also exploited sociology, hagiography, astrology, and eschatology in their effort to understand the currents of thought and emotion moving the crusade. Alphandéry describes this approach as interior history.[2]

91. *Ibid.*, p. 169.   92. *Ibid.*, p. 176.

1. For reflections on the value of a psychological approach to history, review William L. Langer's presidential address of 1957 to the American Historical Association: "The Next Assignment," *American Historical Review*, LXIII (1958), 283–304.

2. Paul Alphandéry, *La Chrétienté et l'idée de croisade*, I, 81, 186. See also Henri Berr in the "Avant-propos," in *ibid.*, I, xii–xiii. Naturally a treatment of this nature tends to be more general in character than specific to the Fourth Crusade. This is especially true of Alphandéry, who ranges over the entire crusading movement.

In emphasizing the influence of sacred relics upon the motivations of the crusaders, Frolow has offered an approach to the problem of the Fourth Crusade too long blindly overlooked. Riant had perceived the importance of relics and he published relevant source material in his *Exuviae sacrae Constantinopolitanae*, but subsequent historians, preoccupied with modern nationalism and economic determinism, failed to seize this key to medieval mentality. The testimony of many chroniclers, among them Villehardouin, Robert of Clary, Gunther of Pairis, Matthew Paris, and Otto of St.-Blaise, reveals the crusaders' concern with relics and with Byzantium as the new center of the cult.[3]

Frolow begins with an able, but fairly commonplace political and economic approach to the problem. Discussing the deviation question in traditional terms, he aligns himself with Norden and other followers of the modified theory of accidents: he finds no reason to doubt Villehardouin's sincerity, but he incorporates a perspective of the era. Byzantium had long feared the encroachments of the crusaders, and the crusaders had long considered Byzantium an obstacle to the success of the crusade. Once Cairo rather than Jerusalem had become the immediate objective, more-over, there was nothing illogical in seizing Constantinople instead in an effort to assure provisions and lines of communications for the future campaign.[4] Frolow finds it difficult to admit that a small group of con-spirators could have been clever enough to dupe the mass of the crusaders.[5]

The most important contribution of Frolow is contained in the chapter entitled "Causes doctrinales," dealing with the cult of relics and the quest for salvation. The vow of crusaders from the beginning of the movement focused on the Holy Sepulcher, but through the poems of the late eleventh century and the pontifical letters and crusading sermons of the twelfth the goal was extended to the whole "province of Jerusalem" —the site of the Temple, the land of the prophets, the place of the Nativity and the earth that knew the imprint of the feet of Christ, of the miracles of the Gospels, and the mysteries of the Redemption. The warrior who

---

3. Frolow's contribution has recently received favorable notice from Mayer, *Ges-chichte der Kreuzzüge*, p. 175; Joan M. Hussey, "The Later Macedonians, the Comneni and the Angeli, 1025–1204," in *Cambridge Medieval History*, IV Part 1 (Cambridge, 1966), 246; Nicol, "The Fourth Crusade and the Greek and Latin Empire, 1204–1261," in *ibid.*, p. 280; and Daly, "Christian Fraternity," p. 79.

4. A. Frolow, *Recherches sur la déviation de la IVe croisade vers Constantinople* (Paris, 1955), pp. 28–29. Previously appeared as "La déviation de la 4e croisade vers Constantinople: problème d'histoire et de doctrine," *Revue de l'histoire des religions*, CXLV (1954), 168–187; CXLVI (1954), 67–89 and 194–219.

5. Frolow, *Recherches sur la déviation de la IVe croisade*, p. 5.

fell in battle for the earthly Jerusalem—or who died in the course of his pilgrimage—would gain by his valor and his sacrifice the heavenly Jerusalem. The Church Triumphant in the heavens would increase at the expense of the Church Militant on earth, tested in battle and diminished by casualties, as Innocent III believed. The mystical transference of the objective of the crusade to the Jerusalem that is above transcended the specific geographical goal of the land where Jesus lived and died. Especially as westerners discovered that the most coveted relics of the Sacred History were no longer in Jerusalem, but in Constantinople, it became possible to conceive the city on the Bosporus as the geographical objective of the crusaders' pilgrimage. Here, too, the army of God could assault the walls of the heavenly Jerusalem.[6] The quest for coveted relics easily combined with the crusaders' antipathy toward the Greeks to justify "pious larceny," so that Abbot Martin of Pairis, for example, felt no qualms in committing sacrilege to the end that the holy objects might pass into more worthy hands. The emphasis upon the relics in the sources, and especially in those texts which give an historical account only for the purpose of authenticating the relics, provides overwhelming proof of the importance of the cult.[7]

Frolow then begins to concentrate upon the most sacred of relics, the Holy Cross, the sign of the crusaders. The importance of the Holy Cross for the crusades is suggested by the song of the unfortunate children of 1212: "Domine Deus, exalta christianitatem *et redde nobis veram crucem.*"[8] At the time of the Fourth Crusade it was well known that the famous relic of the True Cross of the treasury of the Holy Sepulcher had disappeared. Some fragments had made their way to the West as prizes of the earlier crusades, but Constantinople was known to possess among its churches the most important extant collection of sacred wood. Frolow believes that the Latin clergy, seeking to inspire the disheartened crusaders after the failure of their assault of April 9, 1204, made use of their zeal for the Holy Cross to revive their spirits for a second effort.[9]

To further emphasize the importance of the relic of the primary instrument of the Passion, Frolow appends a chapter entitled "La Croisade et les guerres persanes de Heraclius." The seventh-century Byzantine emperor's attempt to regain Jerusalem from the Persians became associated after the event with the cult of the True Cross. The figure of Heraclius was depicted in icons with the figure of the Cross, with St. Helena (whom legend associates with the discovery of the True Cross), or

6. *Ibid.*, pp. 47–48 and 64.   7. *Ibid.*, pp. 54–55, 58.
8. *Ibid.*, p. 63.   9. *Ibid.*, pp. 69–71.

with Christ. In the popular mind his expedition came to be considered a "pre-crusade," and this conception in turn enforced the relationship between the cult of the Cross with the Holy War, the *Gesta Dei*.[10] Ironically, in 1204 the quest for the Cross led the crusaders to raise their arms against Heraclius' own capital.[11]

Frolow's analysis offers a serious attempt to combine iconography, hagiography, and psychology with the history of outward events. The documentation is thorough. His emphasis on the True Cross and the Heraclian tradition are highly suggestive, and his evidence on the general importance of relics in the minds of the crusaders is actually compelling.

Paul Alphandéry died twenty-odd years before his notes and manuscripts were placed in book form by his student Alphonse Dupront in the 1950s.[12] While Alphandéry, like Frolow, recognized the importance of relics, he also considered other religious and psychological factors affecting the crusaders. He searched after the collective consciousness of the masses, "*sur 'l'intérieur de l'esprit de croisade.*"[13] A religious historian, he saw the crusades as an integral part of the medieval church, as he emphasized by his title, *La Chrétienté et l'idée de croisade*.

The tumultuous movement of the unsung and sometimes unarmed host captured Alphandéry's lively imagination. In all the crusades there was constantly friction between the emotions of the masses and the calculations of the responsible leaders, and, in the crusades as a whole, as within a given crusade, the influence of the popular and aristocratic parties waxed and waned. The First Crusade lends itself readily to his approach, and, although he finds the official leadership at times dominant, his interpretation of the First Crusade as a popular movement is most convincing. In the Second and Third Crusades he sees the triumph of the aristocratic party with its practical and realistic concern for organization.[14] The practical preoccupations of the aristocratic leadership constitute an oft-told tale, which does not capture Alphandéry's vivacious inspiration. His interest revives, however, with the Fourth Crusade, in which he

10. *Ibid.*, pp. 72–76, 79–80.   11. *Ibid.*, p. 83.

12. Dupront maintains that "Seules quelques notes, et la bibliographie conçue comme instrument de travail et l'analyse de la matière, marque le temps écoulé depuis son élaboration." Alphandéry, *La Chrétienté et l'idée de croisade*, I, xxix. Dupront may be excessively self-effacing.

13. Berr, "Avant-propos," in *ibid.*, I, xv.

14. Virginia G. Berry, while recommending Alphandéry on the whole, criticizes in her book review his failure to find stronger elements of popular participation in the Second, Third, and Fifth Crusades; especially the Second, upon which she is expert. *American Historical Review*, XXXVII (1962), 90–91.

perceives a strong regeneration of the old popular enthusiasm. The popular element waxed even stronger, of course, in the ill-starred Children's Crusade and the Shepherds' Crusade, in which the poorer host became completely dominant. Alphandéry enthuses over the re-emergence of popular fervor, for he sees in it the heroic and epic character of the crusades. A strong reflection of his interests and sympathies is shown in his comment on the Fifth Crusade: "La Croisade réfléchie, préparée, devient la Croisade différée et definitivement remise à plus tard ou à jamais."[15]

Alphandéry endeavors to find the reason, the necessity, the religious character of the conquest of Constantinople, to reintegrate it into the "living Crusade."[16] Fulk of Neuilly has great significance, for Alphandéry not only lavishes attention upon the popular preacher in the Fourth Crusade, but opens his "Introduction" to the entire work with Fulk. Fulk represents the popular and mystical element to which Alphandéry was dedicated. The popular preacher sought to purify society, because only through such purification could the crusade succeed and the heavenly Jerusalem be won. He adopted the methods of the eleventh- and twelfth-century eremites—popular and vehement preaching against sin and power. He began by preaching against luxury and usury, and by leading prostitutes from their lives of sin into marriage by supplying them with suitable dowries.[17] In reality Fulk was more than a mere preacher of the Fourth Crusade, for he epitomized the changing values of society and the crusading movement. This change had been heralded by Bernard of Clairvaux with his loving preoccupation with the human and historical Jesus. St. Bernard's new piety dwelling upon the helplessness of the infant, the humility of the man, and the agony of the Cross formed a new Christology.[18]

The poor and suffering Jesus of this new Christology offered a key to Fulk, following his teacher Peter Cantor, for the purification of the church and the idea of the crusade.[19] Poverty, the incarnation of sanctity, had been an important factor in earlier crusades (especially in the First), but had never been so dominant as in the Fourth Crusade. It is possible

15. Alphandéry, *La Chrétienté et l'idée de croisade*, I, 4.

16. *Ibid.*, II, 76–77.

17. *Ibid.*, pp. 49–55.

18. *Ibid.*, pp. 64–65. Harnack's *Das Mönchtum* is credited with tracing the development of piety in the twelfth century and Bernard's role in this movement. Adolf Harnack, *Das Mönchtum*, 7th ed. (Giessen, 1907). Notice the relationship between the emphasis on the human and historical Jesus and the cult of relics.

19. *Ibid.*, II, 67.

that Fulk preached a crusade strictly reserved to the poor. If so, this most holy work, which would assure paradise to those who accomplished it, could be achieved only by the poor. They alone were elected for the privilege.[20]

Eschatology also had a role in the idea of the crusade. The last days, according to prophecy, were to be preceded by the coming of Antichrist, and his advent in turn required as a previous condition the Christianization of the land of promise.[21] Toward 1200 millennial movements were again announcing the destruction of the world and the reign of Antichrist.[22]

A concept of mystical unity of the universe also shared in the composition of the idea of the crusade. Through pilgrimages, especially to Jerusalem, had arisen the notion of a center in the middle of the land, a navel of the world, the place where the great mystery concerning the Christian universe and its salvation was worked out. Geographically and mystically the universe was ordered about this holy place.[23] The campaigns to seize Jerusalem were a:

> . . . living expression of unity. Unity of Christian power which ought to lay low every enemy . . . ; unity of Christian peace and surely unity of man, . . . on the double plane of his own existence and of his relations with a supernatural world.[24]

The crusades sought the ultimate unity of the end of the age, the destruction of evil and the reign of God. Before unity could be accomplished, however, Jerusalem must be firmly in Christian hands. The Muslims, the Greeks, and even the Albigensians stood in the way of this unity. It was little wonder that the crusaders, imbued with the mission of preparing the earth for the reign of eternity, should proceed with zeal against these foes. The relationship between the church and the crusade was not, therefore, fortuitous, but essential. The church and the crusades were two sides of a single coin.

Alphandéry has sought in the Fourth Crusade, as in the entire crusading movement, a new dimension. To view the diversion in terms of treason theories, as a triumph of selfish passions upon the fervor of the crusade, is to impose modern stereotypes upon the past.[25] Insofar as a political and economic interpretation of the crusade is meaningful, Alphandéry would largely accept the modified theory of accidents of Norden and his followers.

20. *Ibid.*, I, 1.   21. *Ibid.*, p. 40.
22. *Ibid.*, II, 71–72.   23. *Ibid.*, I, 38.
24. *Ibid.*, II, 236; our translation.   25. *Ibid.*, p. 76.

His work reveals much more, however, something new and exciting. He has tried to view the collective consciousness of the crusaders, not just of the leading barons, but of the masses. He has attempted to grasp the medieval mind on its own terms and not with the political and economic orientation of most modern historians.[26] He is subject to criticism for the overzealous enthusiasm of an innovator, but he and Frolow have opened vast new fields of inquiry for crusade historiography.

CONCLUSION

The inability of historians to arrive at a definitive solution to a complex problem of motivation and responsibility ought not dismay modern scholars, hopefully rid of the scientism of the past. The discussion of such issues goes on endlessly, and quite properly, for every new scrap of evidence and every new insight deepens our awareness of the problems and our ability to deal with them in sophisticated terms.

The historiography of the Fourth Crusade has long since abandoned the superficial theory of accidents of Villehardouin. Since the mid-nineteenth century a succession of able scholars has called our attention to the political, economic, and ecclesiastical aims which motivated the Venetians, Philip of Swabia, Boniface of Montferrat, and Innocent III toward Constantinople. Whether or not there was actually a prior conspiracy in which one or another of these parties took the lead (although the present authors believe that there was not) remains open to debate, but the treason theorists have provided us the insights and evidence necessary for a more comprehensive view of the diversion question than we previously possessed. Taking full account of this contribution, the advocates of the modified theory of accidents, following Norden, introduced a new era in the historiography of the Fourth Crusade. They reached back in time for evidence to show that the route toward Constantinople presented itself to the crusaders as a perfectly natural one. The occasion for taking it, as Villehardouin had stated, arose as a consequence of a series of contingencies, but each of the leading participants faced the occasion with a background which inclined him to regard it as an opportunity to pursue long-range aims and interests. Norden and his followers extended the view of the diversion question in time, but did not really change its essence. The interior history theorists of recent years have

26. The treason theorists were guilty of imposing modern values upon the crusades to the neglect of medieval values, and Norden and the followers of a modified theory of accidents only broke away from this fault in small measure.

introduced a qualitative change in the question. The narrower interests of states and of leaders are set aside, and an attempt is made to examine the minds and actions of the mass of the crusaders. Hagiographical, millennial, and eschatological causes for the diversion are found operative.

The world of scholarship should be grateful that Riant's and Luchaire's advice that the diversion question should be dropped has not been followed, and historians should not attempt to obey more recent injunctions to that effect. The pursuit of the question of the diversion of the Fourth Crusade through its various stages has not been a waste of the talents of the fine historians who have engaged in it, but has resulted in a fruitful dialogue through which scholarship has been progressively enlightened.

PHILIP THE FAIR
AND THE JOURS OF TROYES

John F. Benton

California Institute of Technology

PHILIP THE FAIR
AND THE JOURS OF TROYES*

When Philip the Fair, fortunate in both his marriage and his inheritance, combined the office of count of Champagne with that of the king of France, he extended the control of the monarchy east to the borders of the Empire and presented his officials with the task of assimilating a feudal principality almost as large as the duchy of Normandy. The ease with which Philip swallowed such a large bite is attributable to the long experience of royal administration in Normandy. One of the most efficient ways the French kings had found to control their new duchy was to send men from Paris to be masters of the high court, the Exchequer, and Philip repeated this procedure in Champagne.[1] The purpose of this paper is to investigate how Philip reconstituted and administered the judiciary of Champagne, the precise timing of his changes, and whether his county court was rivaled by a parallel court of the barons of Champagne which embodied provincial opposition to his centralization.

After the middle of the thirteenth century, about the same time the royal court of Parlement became stationary at Paris, the count of Champagne routinely held his judicial assemblies in the city of Troyes. These days of judgment therefore came to be known as the *Jours de Troyes, dies Trecensis*, or as we might say, the sessions of Troyes. In the early fourteenth century popular usage distinguished these sessions from other, lesser days of court (such as those of the foresters) by calling the high court of the county the "Grands Jours," and by the early fifteenth century the adjectives *grand* and *magnus* were routinely used in government documents. In the

* The following pages are dedicated to Professor Joseph R. Strayer, in gratitude for his continuing instruction, encouragement, and inspiration. The research upon which this paper is based was greatly facilitated by a Guggenheim Fellowship in 1963–64 and grants from the Johnson fund of the American Philosophical Society and the American Council of Learned Societies, for which I wish to express my appreciation. I am grateful for the special assistance of Mlle Elisabeth Dunan of the Archives Nationales.

1. On the masters of the Exchequer see Joseph R. Strayer, *The Administration of Normandy Under Saint Louis* (Cambridge, Mass., 1932), pp. 92–93. The administrative effects of the acquisition of Normandy and Languedoc are freshly analysed by Strayer in his Presidential Address to the Medieval Academy in 1968, to appear in *Speculum*.

time of Philip the Fair and his predecessors, however, the official name of the court was simply the Jours of Troyes.[2]

In the period before 1284, when the county of Champagne was independent of French control, judicial sessions were held at Troyes as often as three times a year, frequently at the great religious festivals when the count held court in the cathedral city, but our records are too fragmentary to suggest any pattern, and perhaps the Jours had no fixed calendar.[3] The men who attended this court were a mixed lot. The great barons were rarely present, and the idea that the seven peers of Champagne sat in these sessions with the count is a myth.[4] Some of the more important men of the county attended ex officio. In the absence of the count the governor of the county was the president of the court. The marshal came often, as did the seneschal, the lord of Joinville. A few other barons were present at some sessions, but usually the nobles at court were not great lords in their own right. Although they were men of some substance and experience, these lesser nobles were not wealthy or powerful enough to avoid court service. In the period we are considering, attendance at the court of the county, like attendance at the English Parliament, was still more a burden than a privilege. In addition to the nobles, some churchmen were often present, sometimes an abbot or two, and usually a few lesser clerics. The *baillis*, tne major administrative officials of the county, appeared regularly, probably both to give advice and to defend their own actions. For

2. For what little is known of the Jours under the independent counts of Champagne see Henri d'Arbois de Jubainville, *Histoire des ducs et des comtes de Champagne*, 6 vols. in 7 (Paris, 1859–67), IV, 576–577, and Félix Bourquelot, *Études sur les foires de Champagne et de Brie*, 2 vols. (Paris, 1865), II, 258–261. The accounts of the commune of Provins refer to the *"Grans Jours a Troies"* in 1306 and 1308 and the phrase *"in diebus Trecensibus magnis"* appears in the accounts of the chapel of Notre-Dame of the cathedral of Troyes in 1333; see Maurice Prou and Jules d'Auriac, *Actes et comptes de la commune de Provins* (Provins, 1933), with an index (Montereau, 1935), pp. 204 and 214, and Bourquelot, *Études*, II, 270 n. 4. *"Les jours du gruyer"* are mentioned in Auguste Longnon (ed.), *Documents relatifs au comté de Champagne et de Brie*, 3 vols. (Paris, 1901–14), III, 451 L.

3. Arbois de Jubainville, *Histoire*, IV, 577. For other dates see Prou and d'Auriac, *Actes et comptes*, pp. 23, 24, 43, 58, and 60.

4. The old story is repeated by Jean Longnon in Ferdinand Lot and Robert Fawtier, *Histoire des institutions françaises au moyen âge*, 3 vols. to date (Paris, 1957——), I, 131, citing Arbois de Jubainville, *Histoire*, II, cxxi–cxxii. The text printed by Arbois de Jubainville is from the collection of a seventeenth-century antiquarian, the Abbé Decamps. Apparently both Decamps and Pithou (cited *ibid.*, p. cxxii n. 4) based their statements on a decree of March 4, 1404, printed in the *Ordonnances des rois de France*, 22 vols. (Paris, 1723–1849), VIII, 636. The text, of value for showing the rights of the peers at the opening sessions of the Jours under Charles VI, of course tells us nothing of the courts of the independent counts. See Bourquelot, *Études*, II, 262–263.

example, twenty-one people are known to have attended a session in 1276: two barons (the marshal and Joinville, the seneschal); five knights, including one of the guards of the fairs of Champagne; two abbots; six clerks; the four *baillis*; a burgess of Provins who was the other guard of the fairs; and an unidentified person.[5]

The men who composed the court of the Jours in the 1270's had long had experience in delivering justice without the oversight of the count. Thibaut IV had become king of Navarre in 1234, and since then the counts of Champagne had often been absent in Spain. After Count Henri III died in 1274, Champagne was held in trust by his widow Blanche of Artois and her second husband Edmund of Lancaster, who found it easier to govern the county by delegation than in person. The role of the count in the proceedings of the court was therefore restricted. A few barons and abbots, aided by a small number of other nobles and clerics and by the administrative officers, were responsible for dispensing justice and declaring the law. The members of this court were not elected, and they could be called representative of the county only in the most generous sense of virtual representation. Except for a few clerics, they had acquired their legal training in the school of experience. We have no grounds for saying that they were not fair or did not do their duty in preserving the customary law. In fact, we know too little of the court to assess its efficiency or its fairness. Presumably, however, the job done ,by the haphazard collection of courtiers who sat in the Jours of Troyes could have been done as well by any group of honest men who knew the local law, and men with more extensive judicial training and experience could have done it better. When Philip the Fair destroyed the provincial autonomy of the court and staffed it from Paris, he probably improved it greatly.

A review of the chronology of Philip's acquisition of Champagne will help make clear the way in which the monarchy changed the composition and function of its high court. Although Champagne was not definitively attached to the royal domain until 1361, the county came under royal control and administration when Philip the Fair married the heiress of Champagne, Jeanne of Navarre. The marriage was assured by a treaty of May, 1275, between Philip III and Blanche of Artois, widow of the last count of Champagne; this agreement stipulated that Blanche's daughter Jeanne should marry one of King Philip's two oldest sons and gave the little girl into the king's care to be raised. Shortly after making

5. See Appendix III. Some of the members of other courts before 1284 are recorded in *L'ancien coutumier de Champagne*, ed. Paulette Portejoie (Poitiers, 1956), pp. 165–167 (1270), 171–173 (1270), 174–175 (1271), and 148–150 (1278).

this agreement, Blanche married the only brother of King Edward of England, Edmund of Lancaster, who held the guardianship of the county until 1284. On August 16 of that year Jeanne, not yet twelve, married Prince Philip, who was then sixteen. A little over a year later, on October 6, 1285, Philip III, then forty, died as he was returning from his ill-fated crusade against Aragon, and the young count and countess of Champagne became king and queen of France.[6]

For the next twenty years Philip ruled Champagne directly, but only by virtue of his wife's position as countess. When Jeanne died in April, 1305, her rights to the kingdom of Navarre and the county of Champagne and Brie passed to her eldest son Louis, who was then fifteen years old. After his mother's death Louis could style himself count of Champagne, and in January, 1310, after he had reached nineteen, he bought his brothers' rights in the inheritance of their mother and had them do homage to him.[7] It is not certain, however, to what degree Philip permitted his son to gain experience by exercising authority in Champagne, or how soon Louis assumed complete responsibility for the administration of the county. The death of Jeanne of Navarre also raised the problem of the possible separation of Champagne from direct royal control, a problem which was to trouble the monarchy greatly in the fourteenth century. If—as actually happened—Louis died leaving only a female heir, the succession to the kingdom could pass either to his daughter or to his brothers, but there was no question that unless special arrangements were made the right to Champagne should properly go to his child.[8] With the advantage of hindsight we can see that the last ten years of his reign provided time in which Philip could prepare for the day when once again Champagne might be bound to the monarchy only by ties of vassalage, and we may try to determine whether this consideration actually affected his policy.

This summary shows that before 1314 royal control of the county had passed through four stages. After May, 1275, when an eventual marriage of the heiress to a royal prince was anticipated, authority in the county was held by Blanche of Artois and Edmund of Lancaster. Then came the

6. Arbois de Jubainville, *Histoire*, IV, 440–456.

7. *Registres du Trésor des Chartes: Inventaire analytique*, pub. under the direction of Robert Fawtier (Paris, 1958——), I, No. 1451. According to the customary law of Champagne a boy could inherit at age fifteen; see Portejoie (ed.), *Coutumier*, art. 5, p. 148.

8. Unfortunately, there has been no detailed study of the acquisition of Champagne by the monarchy since that of Denis François Secousse, "Mémoire sur l'union de la Champagne et de la Brie à la couronne de France," *Mémoires de l'Academie des Inscriptions et Belles-lettres*, XVII (1751), 295–315.

period of fourteen months between August, 1284, and October, 1285, when Philip III supervised the administration for his teenage son. The third period, when Philip IV ruled both France and Champagne, began in October, 1285. Finally, after the death of the queen in 1305, Prince Louis was nominally count but acted more or less under his father's direction.

The degree of royal influence on the composition of the high court in the first period is not certain. In theory Edmund of Lancaster or his lieutenants should have been free to choose their own courtiers without any direction from the king. But two clerks closely connected with the Parlement of Paris, Master Anseau de Montaigu and Florent de Roye, are known to have attended a session of the Jours in 1278, and it has therefore been suggested that during the minority of Jeanne of Navarre, Philip III began the practice of sending commissioners from Paris to attend the provincial court.[9] Before concluding that the king regularly or even frequently sent representatives of the Parlement to the Jours, however, we should examine the nature of the case in which the two royal clerks were involved. A vital question at issue between the king and Edmund of Lancaster was the age at which Jeanne would reach her majority, when Edmund would lose his guardianship. Any determination of the age at which girls could inherit property in Champagne was therefore critical to the monarchy. And it was just such a case, in which the court of Champagne declared that a girl's wardship ended when she had reached eleven, that brought the royal clerks to Troyes.[10] Our record tells us only that these men were present, and not whether they acted as judges, advocates, or simple witnesses. We do know that their attendance was later of special importance to the king, for at a hearing on March 11, 1284, they testified about the majority of Jeanne of Navarre.[11] This special case is therefore a poor basis on which to build a theory that Philip III made a practice of sending Parisian masters to the Jours during Jeanne's minority.

Our next question is whether Philip III altered the established relationship between the Parlement and the Jours in some other fashion. Under Louis IX it had been extremely rare for cases from Champagne

9. Emile Chénon, "L'ancien coutumier de Champagne," *Nouvelle revue historique de droit français et étranger* (année 1907), p. 317; see also Chénon, *Histoire générale du droit français public et privé*, 2 vols. (Paris, 1926), I, 691, and Fawtier in Lot and Fawtier, *Histoire*, II, 470. For encapsulated biographies of the two men see Portejoie (ed.), *Coutumier*, p. 149 nn. 4–5. Florent de Roye came to be one of Philip IV's experts on the affairs of Champagne. He probably was not a native of Champagne but came from Picardy, for St. Florentius was the principal patron of the church of Roye (Somme).

10. Portejoie (ed.), *Coutumier*, art. 5, pp. 148–150.

11. *Les établissements de Saint Louis*, ed. Paul Viollet, III (Paris, 1883), 166–168.

to be heard before the Parlement and quite difficult to get a ruling that the royal court had any jurisdiction over cases which belonged in the Jours. In 1267 when the abbot of Saint-Urbain of Joinville brought charges against the lord of Joinville, the Parlement sent the case back to the court· of Count Thibaut, who had claimed jurisdiction, and in 1269 the royal court heard charges made against the count of Sancerre by the abbot of St. Germain of Auxerre only because the matter was ruled to be personal and not feudal.[12] Two other cases show that during this period the count of Champagne was well treated in the royal court, for when the count claimed that royal *baillis* had encroached on his jurisdiction, Parlement ruled against the *baillis*.[13]

The court of Philip III appears to have made no radical change in St. Louis' policy of respecting the judicial rights of the count of Champagne. There was, it is true, an increase in the number of cases between the count and royal vassals or religious houses under the king's guard recorded in the *Olim*, those invaluable registers of the early Parlements, but this was probably only a result of a general increase in litigation.[14] In a conflict of 1279 between Count Edmund and the abbey of Sainte-Colombe of Sens, Parlement ruled that it had jurisdiction because the abbey was in the king's guard, but in the same year the court told the monks of Saint-Jean of Laon that if they wanted to bring a case against the lord of Joinville over the priory of Ragecourt, they should complain to the count of Champagne.[15] In fact, Parlement under Philip III remained quite sensitive about usurping the authority of the Jours. In 1283 the dissatisfied children of a certain Jaillart appealed a decision of the *bailli* of Provins to the Parlement on the grounds of denial of justice. Jean of Acre, Count Edmund's lieutenant, in turn demanded that the case should be returned to the court of Champagne. Finally, *with the agreement of the officials of Champagne*, the court decided that the appeal should be settled by the bishop of Dol and the abbot of Saint-Denis, but it clearly stated that no future rights of the heir of Champagne should be prejudiced "and the court of France should through this procedure acquire no new right." The exceptional treatment of this case shows that in the time of the independent

12. *Les Olim*, ed. Arthur Beugnot, 4 vols. (Paris, 1839–48), I, 677, vi, and 756, xi. Of course cases between the count and other royal vassals were heard in Parlement; see *ibid.*, I, 657, xix, and 759, xix.

13. *Ibid.*, I, 420, viii, and 639, xiii.

14. *Olim*, II, 103, xviii; 126, lix; 169, xliii; 178, xxiii; 197, iv; and *Essai de restitution d'un volume perdu des Olim*, ed. Léopold Delisle, in Edgard Boutaric, *Actes du Parlement de Paris*, 2 vols. (Paris, 1863–67), I, 338, Nos. 234 and 235; 353, nos. 335 and 339; 370, no. 465; 372, no. 475; 374, no. 487; 375, no. 494; 385, no. 525.

15. Delisle (ed.), *Essai*, p. 358, No. 380, and *Olim*, II, 137, xxiv.

counts there was no regular procedure for appeal to Parlement from Champagne, and that the court of Philip III respected this independence.[16]

The Parlement of Philip III did discuss some matters involving Champagne, not to take up cases which the count claimed as his own, but for administrative purposes and in occasional cases of voluntary jurisdiction. As has been said before, the agreement of 1275 had assured that eventually Champagne would come under royal control, and the king therefore had an interest in the administration of the county. This interest explains why in 1278 the Parlement ordered the marshal of Champagne to pay the money fiefs which he owed (presumably so that arrears would not build up) and to cease excessive exploitation of the woodlands.[17] And in 1281 Edmund's lieutenant Jean of Acre used the Parlement rather than the Jours as the proper setting in which to return the charters which he had confiscated from the commune of Provins.[18] Foreseeing that the monarchy would increase its role in the county, a few litigants voluntarily brought their cases before the royal court for settlement. In 1282 the chief financial officer of the county, Renier Accorre, and some money-changers of the fairs of Champagne by mutual consent moved their conflict from the Jours to the Parlement.[19] And in the following year the burghers of Provins went to Paris as well as to the Jours to complain that the *prévôt* had knocked down their judicial ladder used for displaying criminals.[20] It is noteworthy, however, that the settlement of this second case came from the Jours rather than from Parlement. Philip III appears to have protected his future rights in Champagne without showing any special desire to infringe the judicial autonomy of the county.

For the story up to this point we have only scattered sources of information about the Jours, but starting in the fall of 1284 there is more information, though not nearly enough. The reason for this improvement is that a clerk marked the beginning of Prince Philip's power in Champagne by starting a new register of the proceedings of the Jours of Troyes. This register, which carried the record of the court up to 1295, and a second volume which went up to 1299, did not survive the fire of the Chambre des Comptes in 1737, but before they were lost Nicolas Dongois, Du Cange, Nicolas Brussel, and other antiquarian historians had copied

16. *Olim*, II, 228, vi; cf. Portejoie (ed.), *Coutumier*, art. 39, pp. 193–194. Arbois de Jubainville, *Histoire*, IV, 578–579, in using this case as evidence of the principle of appeal, does not do justice to the hesitations of the royal court.

17. *Olim*, II, 119, xxxvii; see also 223, iii.

18. *Ibid.*, II, 177, xix.

19. *Ibid.*, II, 214, xxxviii. Possibly the changers felt that Renier had too much influence in the county for them to receive à fair hearing in the Jours.

20. Prou and d'Auriac, *Actes et comptes*, pp. 59–60.

extracts which we can use today.[21] If the complete registers had survived, we would know almost as much of the Jours of Troyes under Philip the Fair as we do of the Parlement of Paris.

Brussel's extracts tell us of the composition of the court which gathered at Troyes in early December, 1284.[22] Twenty-five names are recorded, of which many are of men known to have attended the court before. The marshal of Champagne and Joinville, the seneschal, head the list. Abbot Robert of Montiéramey was there, as he had been in 1276, though this time with a different abbot as a colleague. Among the administrative officials were the tax collector of the county, a guard of the fairs, a former chancellor, the *baillis* of Sens and Troyes and the former *bailli* of Vitry, and among the clerks we find the familiar names of Anseau de Montaigu and Florent de Roye. In addition, however, the court contained a number of men new to Champagne but previously associated with the Parlement, including the great noble Simon de Clermont; an experienced royal administrator, Gautier de Chambly, archdeacon of Coutances; the archdeacon of Bayeux; and other men who had worked together in Paris. The influence of the royal court on the Jours of Troyes was not yet paramount, but it had begun.

Whether young Philip the Fair exercised any personal influence in this session is a question which, like so many others concerned with his role in government, is tantalizing.[23] The new count was represented in court by a proctor, and we do not have the evidence to determine if Philip was actually present.[24] It would be hard in any case to see the prince through the crowd who attended the Jours, but we simply cannot tell whether Philip or his father's courtiers should be considered responsible for decisions of unusual severity in two feudal cases.

Pierre de Bourlemont was in trouble with the count for a number of reasons, particularly because he had broken an oath of peace made earlier to the abbot of Mureaux, and he therefore had to make a special petition to do homage for Bourlemont and Rorthey. Philip's proctor at first

21. See Appendix I, pp. 303–304.

22. Appendix II, No. 1.

23. For the most successful effort to date to solve the mystery of Philip's political personality see Joseph R. Strayer, "Philip the Fair—A 'Constitutional' King," *American Historical Review*, LXII (1956), 18–32.

24. The accounts of Provins show that the king (of France or of Navarre?) was at Troyes on Oct. 13, 1284; see Prou and d'Auriac, *Actes et comptes*, p. 65. In November, Philip issued a charter as king of Navarre for the abbey of La Barre (British Museum add. chart. 1391) which was dated at Paris. The fact that the lord of Bourlemont did homage at the Jours does not necessarily mean that Philip was there to receive it.

opposed this petition, and then after the lord of Bourlemont was finally permitted to do homage, his fiefs were taken into the count's possession. Gautier de Chambly, a member of the royal court, and Guillaume de Prunay, a local noble, were then appointed to make an investigation. The final result was that Pierre was condemned to pay a fine to the count of Champagne and damages and expenses to the abbot of Mureaux.[25] The second case is one in which the court exacted an even heavier penalty for what seems like a relatively minor offense. Henri de Grandpré, who held the guard of the abbey of Chéhery along with the rest of the county of Grandpré in fief from the count of Champagne, had been paid by the monks to permit them to abjure his guard and place themselves under the protection of Philip III. Since this increase of the king's power was to the detriment of the county of Champagne, Philip's proctor demanded that all the fiefs of the count of Grandpré should be forfeited. Count Henri sought a delay to take counsel, and after this was denied, he requested a hearing at Chéhery, which was granted. At this point our extract breaks off, but we need not assume that Henri escaped his punishment, for in 1287 the county of Grandpré was in Philip's hands.[26] Rigorous exercise of his legal rights seems to have been a part of Philip's government from the very beginning.

In the spring of 1285 Philip III began his crusade against Aragon, taking Prince Philip with him. He left Champagne in the care of two guardians: Joinville, a native of the county and a trusted adviser of about sixty; and Gautier de Chambly, a courtier who had sat in Parlement as early as 1262, had been St. Louis' chaplain, and was to become bishop of Senlis at the end of the year. When these guardians held a session of the Jours of Troyes after Easter, they were assisted by six men who were paid wages for their attendance. Besides four clerks, including Florent de Roye, there was the abbot of Montiéramey, formerly chaplain to Count Thibaut V, and a distinguished old baron of Champagne, Gilles de Brion, who had been governor of the county in 1261. This court was therefore balanced between men from Champagne and men who owed their primary loyalty to the royal court. In this transitional period the influence of Paris was apparent but men from the county still played a significant part in the court of the Jours.[27]

---

25. Appendix I, No. 11.

26. *Ibid.*, No. 3. For what little is known of the annexation of Grandpré, see Longnon, *Documents*, III, 54 n. 1.

27. Appendix II, No. 2. On the abbot of Montiéramey and Gilles de Brion see Arbois de Jubainville, *Histoire*, IV, 459 and 531.

Once his father was dead, Philip changed the composition of the court even more. Under Philip III, as we have seen, Joinville had headed the administration of the county, but Philip the Fair did not cherish the advice of his sainted grandfather's old friend, and between 1285 and 1291 Joinville's name does not appear as a member of the Jours. Gilles de Brion died in 1287, so that his disappearance from the court cannot be· attributed to Philip. But the systematic exclusion of men of stature from the county is clearly showed by the elimination of the abbots from Champagne. For years under Philip the Fair no major ecclesiastic from the county was included among the "masters holding the Jours of Troyes."[28]

After 1285 almost without exception the new judges came down from Paris, and they were regularly men who sat in the Parlement. Nobles from Champagne were notable by their absence; in the first years of Philip's reign the only noble layman in the court was usually Guillaume de Grancey, the head of the second most important feudal house in Burgundy.[29] The dependence of the Jours on the Parlement of Paris was finally spelled out for all to see by an ordinance issued in 1296, which declared that twice a year at the end of the sessions of Parlement four members of that court should be delegated by the king or the president of Parlement to attend the Jours of Troyes; these four were to be a prelate, a baron, one of those who issued judgments, and one other member of the council.[30]

Under Philip the Fair, the court of the Jours changed not only its membership but its procedure, for there is an obvious difference between a court with a handful of judges and one composed of over twenty people. The earlier practice, which continued through the first session of Prince Philip's Jours, was for a large number of people of differing status to meet together as an undifferentiated court. While the opinion of a minor

28. As will be seen later, the abbot of Montiéramey was present at a session of the Jours in 1286, but not as a master. In 1296 Guichard, abbot of Montier-la-Celle (and later the famous bishop of Troyes), was the next ecclesiastic from Champagne known to have a seat at the Jours. See Appendix II, Nos. 14–16.

29. For the genealogy of the family of Grancey see Ernest Petit, *Histoire des ducs de Bourgogne*, VI (Dijon, 1898), 537–546, and the chart following p. 548. Guillaume was a member of the judicial council of Burgundy in 1285 and sat in the Parlement of Paris in the same year; see *ibid.*, p. 330, No. 4737, and Portejoie (ed.), *Coutumier*, pp. 207–209.

30. Charles Victor Langlois, *Textes relatifs à l'histoire du Parlement* (Paris, 1888), pp. 161–167. The date of this ordinance in the spring of 1296 was established by Léon L. Borrelli de Serres, *Recherches sur divers services publics du XIIIᵉ au XVIIᵉ siècle*, 3 vols. (Paris, 1895–1909), I, 339–347.

noble would not carry the weight of that of a baron, all present were thought to have been involved in the common decision. But as early as the spring court of 1285 there was a distinction between the people who were paid to hold the court and others who simply attended the sessions. We cannot be certain that the payment of a few people to be "masters" of the court was an innovation, but it is likely that this practice was newly introduced in Champagne on the model of Parlement and the Exchequer. The difference between the new and the old forms of the Jours is shown by a charter of 1286 which lists five people who held the court for the king, and then names thirteen others who were present, including the abbot of Montiéramey, two *baillis*, the mayor of Provins, and two local lawyers.[31] Those who were "present" might give advice, and they could testify later to what had happened at the session, but they were not responsible for the judgment of the court. Physically this court of 1286 may have appeared no different from its predecessors, but within a few years the status of the masters was enhanced by special furniture, for in 1288 the *bailli* of Troyes paid a little under one *livre* "to make the seats for the masters at the Jours of Troyes."[32]

The new administration changed the Jours from a nonprofessional feudal court to one run by specialists. A few experienced men were paid from the income of the county for their services as a panel of judges and their expenses in making the journey, if they had to come from Paris. Sessions were held on a more orderly schedule, usually with one meeting in September and one in the spring; some lasted for over three weeks, though not all the masters stayed the whole time.[33] Cases were regularly heard *bailliage* by *bailliage*, in a fashion similar to the *dies balliviarum* at Paris. A clerk kept a written register, more informative and detailed than the *Olim* and not divided into separate sections for *arresta* and *inquesta*.[34]

As a professional court the Jours of Troyes, like the Exchequer of Normandy before it, became a delegated branch of the Parlement of Paris. It was no more necessary for a master of the court to be from Champagne than for a *bailli* to come from the region in which he served, and perhaps it was believed that judges from outside the county would be more

31. Appendix II, No. 4.
32. Longnon (ed.), *Documents*, III, 87.
33. The judicial sessions therefore did not coincide with the two accounting terms, which ended the week after Christmas and the Sunday before the feast of St. Mary Magdalen (in July). On the time individual masters spent at the Jours, see Appendix II, Nos. 2, 9, and 19.
34. This summary of procedure in the Jours is based on the reconstruction of the existing fragments of the lost first register in Appendix I.

impartial and render better justice. Others among those present could advise them on the customary law of Champagne, or they could refer to the custumal of the county, which may well have been prepared to meet the needs of the new masters.[35] The law was presumed to be local, but the judges came and went.

Since Philip was both king and lord of Champagne and the same judges sat in the Jours and the Parlement, there was little reason to maintain a rigid separation of the jurisdictions of the two courts. Royal vassals and churches under royal protection had the right to bring their cases to Paris, and in some instances it seems to have been a matter of convenience or timing whether a case was heard in Paris or Troyes. In 1289 the Parisian court referred a dispute between Joinville and the abbey of Saint-Urbain to the court at Troyes, and when the masters of the Jours were unable to reach a decision because Joinville challenged the authenticity of a charter, they adjourned the dispute "to the next Jours of Troyes or to the coming day of the barons [i.e., the time at Parlement reserved for baronial cases]." The matter was finally settled in Paris.[36] Again in 1289, when the count of Bar failed to answer their summons, the master of the Jours ordered him to appear "at the next day of the barons at Paris."[37] These cases concerned barons and therefore might easily be heard at Paris, but lesser people could also bring their complaints about affairs in Champagne directly to Parlement. We have no reason to think that the masters of Parlement wanted to aggrandize their jurisdiction, but once plaintiffs had appeared before them, it probably seemed simpler to settle the matter on the spot than to refer it to Troyes.[38] The masters of the Jours may also have referred difficult cases to the larger and more important court at Paris. Without fuller records it is hard to tell why a matter like the question of the royal right to collect *mainmorte* should have been decided in Paris rather than Troyes.[39] But whatever the reasons for them, cases from Champagne became sufficiently common

---

35. Portejoie argues convincingly (*Coutumier*, pp. 9–11) that the custumal was completed shortly after 1295, and was perhaps prepared by the *bailli* Guillaume du Châtelet.

36. Appendix I, No. 67. The Parlement of St. Martin 1289 decided against Joinville and declared that Saint-Urbain was under the king's guard; see Delisle (ed.), *Essai*, p. 425, No. 720. The monks of Saint-Urbain renounced Joinville's guard in a charter of October, 1288, printed in Jules Simonnet, *Essai sur l'histoire et la généalogie des sires de Joinville* (Langres, 1876), pp. 201–204.

37. Appendix I, Nos. 73–74.

38. For complaints taken to Parlement see *Olim*, III, 91, xxxviii; III, 206, xxxi; Delisle (ed.), *Essai*, p. 455, No. 880.

39. *Olim*, II, 440, xxiv; cf. Delisle (ed.), *Essai*, p. 442, No. 800; p. 446, No. 833.

that the county was allotted a specific time in the schedule of the Parlement along with the *prévôté* of Paris and the *bailliage* of Sens.[40]

The blurring of jurisdictional lines was an encouragement for litigants dissatisfied by their treatment in Troyes to try again in Paris. After the masters of the Jours had judged that the possession of the lepers' hospital of Montmirail belonged to the nunnery of Saint-Jacques of Vitry and not to the bishop of Châlons, the bishop appeared before the Parlement of St. Martin of 1289 and complained that the royal officials had *de facto* and improperly transferred the possession of the hospital. The masters of Parlement then heard the testimony of the royal officials who were present and judged in the bishop's favor, annulling the transfer. In the following Parlement of Pentecost 1290, however, the abbess of Vitry had her turn and testified that the action had been taken following a formal decision of the court of Troyes, and after seeing the judgment of their colleagues, the Parisian masters returned possession to the abbess.[41] About the same time Parlement had to judge a case between the abbey of Saint-Pierre of Oyes and Lord Jean de Châteauvillain concerning his rights of guard over the abbey. Although the *Olim* does not specify who made the complaint, we may presume that the abbey initiated the action in Paris. Jean maintained his rights by claiming that the guard of the abbey had been granted to him by the court of the Jours. Some of those who had held the Jours and were present in the Parlement then stated that Jean had been granted the guard of the abbey on such terms that if the abbey was dissatisfied it should not have recourse to the royal court.[42]

In these two cases the bishop of Châlons and the abbot of Oyes seem to have counted on a certain lack of communication between the masters of the two courts, and during his first hearing the bishop did indeed find that the masters present in Parlement were unaware of what had happened before in the Jours. Both parties hoped for a better judgment than they had received before, but I think it is significant that the *Olim* does not say that either one was making an appeal. In informal terms, they were complaining, rather than asking for a formal reconsideration of the decision reached in Troyes. During this period of the reign of Philip IV the Parlement exercised authority in Champagne, but

40. The schedule for early 1309 is published in Langlois, *Textes*, pp. 181–182, and *Registres du Trésor des Chartes*, I, No. 864. We do not know how early the county of Champagne had a place in the *dies balliviarum*, but it is interesting to see that it was scheduled after Louis became count.

41. *Olim*, II, 292, xii, and 301, viii.

42. *Ibid.*, 289, v.

it does not seem to have reduced the Jours to the position of "a simple court of first instance."[43]

While there is no evidence of formal appeal from the Jours to the Parlement in the period before the death of Jeanne of Navarre,[44] there are several instances recorded in the *Olim* of appeals to Paris from the court of the guards of the fairs. The first of these occurred in 1296, when the decision of the guards was upheld. In 1304 there were two appeals, one of which was denied and the other accepted. And then in 1306 there were four appeals, in three of which the judgments of the guards were reversed. It is possible that this high percentage of reversals in 1306 was associated with the fact that in the same year Parlement found one of the guards guilty of peculation.[45]

The final period of Philip's reign is the one for which we have the least evidence of the working of the Jours. Only one list of the masters of the court of Troyes survives from the period after the death of the queen, but that list fortunately can be dated about 1311, after Louis had bought out his brothers' rights in the county.[46] This precious document shows that even after the heir apparent had become count, masters of Parlement were still sent to Troyes to hold the Jours, and it seems safe to assume that throughout his reign Philip or his officials appointed the masters of the Jours from Paris. In this important matter Philip's practice does not seem to have changed.

But the separation of the offices of king and count did call for some recognition of the judicial distinctiveness of the county.[47] It is hard to be certain which cases should have been tried where, but after about 1306 the number of cases coming to Paris from Champagne without explana-

43. The phrase is Beugnot's in *Olim*, II, p. xiv. Beugnot has, I think, misinterpreted the scope of the order to all the king's *baillis* and guards of the fair which he cites in support of his argument. Such an order was quite properly made in the royal court, since contractual letters agreed to outside the fairs could be made outside the county as well as in Champagne. While on occasion it was convenient for the Parlement rather than the Jours to treat matters from Champagne, at this time there was no advantage in reducing the authority of the Jours. Orders to the guards of the fair or the *baillis* of Champagne could also easily come from the Jours; see Appendix I, Nos. 24, 27, 35, 44, 45, 53.

44. Except for the unusual case of 1283 cited in n. 15.

45. *Olim*, II, 411, xxiii; III, 144, xiii; 154, xxxii; 200, xxii; 204, xxix; 209, xxxvii; 216, xlvii; and for the peculation of the guard Hugues de Chaumont, III, 207, xxxiv.

46. Appendix II, No. 20.

47. One important change was that fines levied in the county now went to Louis and not to his father. See *Olim*, III, 775, lxi (which refers to the earlier time in which "dominus Rex comitatum Campanie ad manum suam immediate tenebat") and *Registres du Trésor des Chartes*, I, No. 653.

tion seems to have declined sharply. In 1308 the king declared expressly that an interminable conflict between the commune of Provins and the nuns of Faremoutiers, an affair which had been heard in both Paris and Troyes, should be settled in his son's court of Champagne.[48] And, as will be seen, appeals from the decisions of the guards of the fairs no longer went directly to Paris but had to be taken to the Jours.

At the same time that a greater effort was made to distinguish between the jurisdiction of the king and the count, a new principle was introduced into the relationship between the Jours and the Parlement—the recognition of a formal right of appeal. In 1307 a case involving the abbey of Saint-Pierre of Bèze and some burgesses of the abbey was taken to the Parlement from the Jours by the mutual consent of the interested parties. In this case the word "appeal" was not used, and the matter seems to have been one of voluntary jurisdiction, perhaps taken to Parlement because the abbey was in the duchy of Burgundy.[49] But finally in 1310 a disappointed litigant, one Jean Cristo, appealed from the guards of the fairs to the Jours and then formally appealed to the Parlement against a judgment he considered *"falsus et pravus."*[50] In 1312 there were three more cases of formal appeal, including one from the guards to the Jours to Parlement and another from the *bailli* of Vitry to the Jours to Paris. The third appeal is the most interesting, for it is the only one in which the judgment of the lower court was reversed. Erard de Nanteuil had brought suit against some alleged serfs, who produced letters of franchise which convinced the masters of the Jours that the defendants were free. Erard then brought a suit for false judgment to the Parlement, where the Parisian masters reviewed the testimony and declared that the judges of the Jours had made a poor decision and should therefore pay a fine to the Parlement.[51]

This chronological survey permits a more precise answer to the old question of whether the Jours was a court of first instance or had final jurisdiction. No one principle applies to the whole period under study. Louis IX fully respected the judicial autonomy of Champagne, and Philip III permitted only a few cases to come before his court with the consent of those involved. As long as he was both count and king, Philip IV recognized no formal principle of appeal, but in practice he tolerated some confusion of the jurisdiction of his two courts. And finally, when his

48. *Registres du Trésor des Chartes*, I, No. 829.
49. *Olim*, III, 228, viii.
50. *Ibid.*, p. 575, lxx (the case is repeated on p. 615, cviii).
51. *Ibid.*, II, 573, viii; III, 765, li; 784, lxx.

son became count, Philip's masters met the immediate problem of separate courts and the possible eventual separation of Champagne from the crown by permitting (and perhaps even encouraging) appeals from the Jours to Parlement. In the latter part of his reign Philip treated the Jours as a delegation of Parlement by appointing the judges, but also established the right of appeal. In this the practice of Champagne was different from that of Normandy, for appeals from the Exchequer seem to have been quite unusual, and by the charter of 1315 they were finally banned.[52] But Normandy was firmly part of the royal domain and Champagne might possibly be lost to the monarchy. Throughout his kingdom Philip the Fair showed no intention of leaving any of his vassals free from judicial review, even if this supervision meant that for Champagne the officials of King Philip had to reconsider cases they had already settled for his son as count.

The preceding account has shown that royal control of the judicial system was from the start of Philip's reign so strong and pervasive that there was no opportunity for provincial opposition to develop. Most previous writers on the Jours of Troyes have thought differently and have maintained that there was an alternative Court of the Barons which to some degree resisted Philip's centralization and attempted to preserve the old feudal and provincial traditions of Champagne. This concept of two different courts was introduced in 1727 by Nicolas Brussel, who described a *"Cour des Barons"* as the ordinary court of the county and the *"Cour des Grands Jours"* as an extraordinary court.[53] Brussel's view was challenged by his contemporary Lévesque de la Ravallière, but unfortunately La Ravallière's learned history has remained unpublished and has had little influence.[54] The more easily available and seemingly authoritative opinion of Brussel was followed by Arthur Beugnot, Théophile Boutiot, and Arbois de Jubainville, and Félix Bourquelot was exceptional in contradicting it.[55] The dissident view of the distinguished historian from Provins has been either dismissed or ignored by modern authors, however, and Brussel's concept of two separate courts appears today in our legal

52. Strayer, *Administration of Normandy*, p. 16 n. 2; Strayer shows (p. 14 n. 2) the same interchange of cases between the provincial court and Parlement that can be seen in Champagne. For the Norman charter see Isambert, *Recueil général des anciennes lois françaises*, 29 vols. (Paris, 1822–33), III, 51, art. 13.

53. Nicolas Brussel, *Nouvel examen de l'usage général des fiefs en France*, 2 vols. (Paris, 1727; reissued with altered title page in 1750), pp. 249–251.

54. B. N., Coll. de Champagne, t. 67, fols. 11–12.

55. *Olim*, II, pp. ix–xiv; Théophile Boutiot, "Recherches sur les Grands Jours de Troyes," *Mémoires de la Société académique . . . de l'Aube*, XVI (1852), 405–446; Arbois de Jubainville, *Histoire*, IV, 565–566; Bourquelot, *Études*, II, 259–260.

and historical handbooks.[56] Moreover, in her meticulous edition of the custumal of Champagne published in 1956, Paulette Portejoie presents additional evidence in support of the theory of parallel courts, which she describes in this way:

> After the highest court of Champagne had become an outgrowth of Parlement, the barons of Champagne, who had been eliminated, independently formed another court, as if the old Grands Jours had been split apart, forming on the one hand a court composed of masters of Parlement and on the other a court of the barons.[57]

The belief in the existence of separate courts is based on three different arguments. The first, which seemed conclusive to Brussel, is that the register of the Jours in two places referred to the *dies baronum* or "day of the barons," which he thought meant the court of the barons of Champagne.[58] As has been seen, however, the "day of the barons" was the time at Parlement reserved for baronial cases. Brussel knew that the term *dies baronum* had referred to Parlement in the past, but he thought that it no longer had that meaning in the days of Philip IV. In this he erred, for the three examples Du Cange gives for *dies baronum* all refer to a period of time at Parlement, and two are from the reign of Philip the Fair. In addition, in the late thirteenth century the accounts of the commune of Provins tell of sending officials to the *Jours au barons* at Paris. Furthermore, the register of the Jours itself specifically states that the *dies baronum* took place at Paris. This phrase therefore provides no basis for a theory of a baronial court in Champagne.[59]

The second argument, fundamental to the discussion of Portejoie, is based on a set of decisions recorded in the custumal of Champagne. One of these, article 57 of the new edition, is the settlement of a conflict between Hélissande d'Arcis and her brothers over the division of the inheritance of Chacenay. It is dated the week after Pentecost of a year which seven manuscripts give as 1287 and one as 1281, and it concludes with the statement: "A cest jugement faire furent Messire de Joinville senechaux de

56. Chénon, *Histoire générale*, I, 691; Lot and Fawtier, *Histoire*, II, 470.

57. Portejoie (ed.), *Coutumier*, p. 6.

58. Brussel, *Nouvel examen*, pp. 249–251; cf. Appendix I, Nos. 67 and 73.

59. Two of the texts in Du Cange, *Glossarium*, s.v. *dies baronum* (ed. Henschel, II, 846) are edited in Delisle (ed.), *Essai*, p. 413, No. 678, and p. 428, No. 724. See also Langlois, *Textes*, p. 108; *Comptes royaux, 1285–1314*, ed. Robert Fawtier and François Maillard, 3 vols. (Paris, 1953–56), II, 373, No. 20503; and Prou and d'Auriac, *Actes et comptes*, pp. 69 and 76.

Champagne, et tuit li autres qui sont nommé au jugement devant cestue." There are no names included in the immediately preceding article, but article 55 of Portejoie's edition ends with the names of Joinville and seven other nobles, including the lords of Jully, Chappes, and Broyes, plus Guillaume du Châtelet, a man who served as *bailli* in a number of places and Pierre de la Malmaison, at one time *bailli* of Vitry. Article 55 is undated, but on the basis of the reference to "the preceding judgment" in article 57, Portejoie assigns it to the week after Pentecost of 1287.[60]

If we could trust the date of 1287 given to article 57 and if article 55 were of the same date, then the existence of a separate Court of the Barons, rivaling the Jours of Troyes after Philip came to power, would be established. Bearing in mind that the court of the Jours was convened at Troyes the week after Ascension in 1287, let us try to imagine the circumstances under which this baronial court would have been held. Since it began just ten days after a session of the Jours, Hélissande d'Arcis and the others who brought their cases before it were deliberately avoiding the court favored by the king and his justices. Since Philip had dropped Joinville from the Jours since 1285, we must give the seneschal credit for courage, if not audacity, for presiding over a competing court. And we must note that in laying down this challenge to the king, Joinville did not surround himself with hot-headed young nobles, but called upon some of his oldest friends and companions, for seven of the nine men are known to have sat together in a session of the Jours seventeen years before.[61]

My own conclusion from this evidence is not that a remarkable group of old-timers held court in Troyes concurrently with the Jours or just a few days after its masters had ridden off to Paris, but that the custumal as we have it now contains one or perhaps two errors. The most obvious explanation of the problem is to suggest that we do not have the original arrangement of the articles, and that the reference to "the preceding judgment" refers to article 10, a case concerning Hélissande's brother Erard d'Arcis, which was judged by Joinville *"qui lors gardoit Champagne"* and four other men. The date given in the custumal is 1284, but it is likely that this case is from the spring or summer of 1285. That is also a

---

60. The two articles are printed in Portejoie (ed.), *Coutumier*, pp. 220–222. The editor assigns both to the same date on p. 7. It is hard to date article 55 from its references. The latest reference I have found to Guichard de la Porte, at one time mayor of Bar-sur-Aube, is an act of 1279, Aube, arch. dép., 3 H 41.

61. For the session of the Jours the week after Ascension, 1287, see Appendix II, No. 6. For members of the court in 1270 see Portejoie (ed.), *Coutumier*, pp. 165–167 and 171–173. Article 22 (pp. 175–176) contains a list of members of the court identical to article 55. It is undated, but for unexplained reasons Portejoie assigns it a date of 1271 on p. 7.

likely date for a case involving Hélissande d'Arcis and her brothers to have been tried by the Jours before the question of the succession of Chacenay was taken to Parlement in the winter of 1285. In fact, the dates given in the custumal are so uncertain that no argument should be based on them without supporting evidence. To answer this second argument briefly, it is probable that the date of article 57 is wrong and should be 1285, and in any case, the connection between article 57 and article 55 is tenuous.[62]

The third argument cannot be challenged in such a categorical fashion as the first two, for it is true that there was a place for nobles from Champagne in the judicial administration of the county after 1285. The custumal of Champagne contains the record of four court sessions between 1287 and 1290 held outside of Troyes and independently of the assizes of the *baillis*, and shows that the masters of the Jours were not present at these courts but that some nobles from Champagne were. Although it is accurate to refer to these meetings as baronial courts, it would be misleading to think of them as sessions of an institutionalized Court of the Barons which had split off from the Jours of Troyes.[63]

One of these courts was held at Val-des-Escoliers and two were at Châteauvillain; no location is given for the fourth, but it judged the rights of the chapter of Châteauvillain and very likely took place there. The reason why these cases were heard by nobles from the region of Chaumont, rather than at the Jours of Troyes or the court of the *bailli* of Chaumont, is to be found in the special nature of the two places. To begin with the more certain case, Val-des-Escoliers, or more precisely a meeting place named Les Etaux in a field near the Augustinian priory on the banks of the Marne, was the point on the border at which the count of Champagne customarily did homage to the bishop of Langres and where, "according to the custom of the march," conflicts between the two territories were to be heard. The custumal of Champagne tells of two disputes between the *bailli* of Chaumont and the bishop of Langres which

---

62. The extent to which the articles of the *Coutumier* have been shuffled is shown by the editor's table on pp. 231–232. For the date of article 10 see Appendix I, note 8. Portejoie has shown (p. 207 n. 2) that article 50, in which the Parlement settled the succession of Chacenay, must be of 1285 and not 1283, as the custumal has it. See also Delisle (ed.), *Essai*, p. 400, No. 585. Bourquelot, *Études*, II, 261, used a copy of the custumal which gave the date 1281 to article 57. He was therefore spared this problem. I have not been able to determine that any of the men named in article 55 were actually dead in 1287, but Pierre de la Malmaison had surely retired by that time, for he last appeared as *bailli* of Vitry in 1276.

63. These cases are in Portejoie (ed.), *Coutumier*, pp. 168–170, 187–188, 197–198, 209–214. Portejoie calls these decisions "arrêts de la Cour des barons, fonctionnent concuremment avec les Grands Jours royaux" (p. 7).

were brought before a court of nobles and churchmen of the border region on February 20, 1290. Agreement was reached on one of the issues, but the court divided on the other, which therefore had to be sent to Parlement for settlement. This court was convened simply because neither the Jours nor the court of the bishop of Langres had jurisdiction, and because it was the custom to try to avoid the expense of litigation in Paris by local settlement if possible.[64]

We know less about the other three cases, two of which concerned Châteauvillain, and the other of which involved someone from Arc-en-Barrois. We do know a little, however, about the peculiar feudal position of the seigneury of Châteauvillain and Arc. This once unified fief had split off from the county of Bar-sur-Aube in the eleventh century, and in an unexplained fashion became divided between its two powerful neighbors, with its lord owing homage to the count of Champagne for Château-villain and to the duke of Burgundy for Arc.[65] The attempt to settle cases from this seigneury in courts in which men from both Champagne and Burgundy were present probably resulted from this feudal split. In sum-mary, these four courts recorded in the custumal were not sessions of the baronage of Champagne per se, but meetings of the nobles of border regions, in what we might call "courts-in-march," to settle cases in which neither neighboring lord had full jurisdiction. In one particular instance, when no settlement could be reached locally, the case then went to the Parlement at Paris.

Once we are in a position to eliminate from the historical record the phantom court of the baronage of Champagne created by Brussel, the process by which Philip the Fair took over the judicial system of Cham-pagne and subordinated it to the Parlement can be seen as simple, effective, and unchallenged. The jurisdictional barrier which had been maintained scrupulously by Louis IX and somewhat less rigorously by Philip III began to crumble when young Philip brought Parisian courtiers to his first session of the Jours in the fall of 1284, and it was destroyed when Philip made the Jours a professional court with masters sent down from Paris. The people of Champagne came before Philip's justices because there was nowhere else to go, and by the end of Philip's reign the Jours of

64. On the location see Jean François Lemarignier, *Recherches sur l'hommage en marche et les frontières féodales* (Lille, 1945), pp. 168, 172–173. The record of the case which was not settled locally and which came before the Parlement of Candlemas 1291 refers to the customary meeting place of *Scella* or *Scallis*, which I take to be a corruption of *Stalla*, *Stallis*, for *Les Etaux*. For the case, which contains a reference to the custom of the march, see Delisle (ed.), *Essai*, p. 436, No. 770.

65. Eugène Jarry, *Provinces et pays de France, III: Bourgogne* (Paris, 1948), p. 252 n. 50.

Troyes had become even more a branch of Parlement than the Exchequer of Normandy.

One of the paradoxes of French history is that the duchy of Normandy, subject to the monarchy since the early thirteenth century, emerged from the middle ages with stronger provincial institutions than the county of Champagne, which was not definitively attached to the crown until 1361. By the early sixteenth century the old Norman Exchequer had grown into the Parlement of Rouen, while in Champagne the Jours of Troyes withered away and the county remained under the jurisdiction of the Parlement of Paris.[66] Although Rouen and Troyes are about the same distance from Paris, the Norman city became a provincial capital, while Troyes was subject to the influence and administration of the central government and Champagne became a province without a capital.

The reign of Philip the Fair was a turning point in the development of the two provinces, and the explanation of the greater dependence of Champagne contains an ironic element. When Philip Augustus conquered Normandy, its administrative and judicial institutions were independent of the monarchy and there was a clear demarcation between the rights and obligations which were Norman and those which were French. Since the king replaced his predecessor by conquest, the simplest way for him to govern his new territory was to keep the institutions separate but to replace the administrators with men loyal to his court. The feudal history of Champagne before its acquisition was quite different, for its counts never had the independent power of the Norman dukes, and the western frontier of the county was permeable to royal influence. People from Meaux, for instance, could go more easily to nearby Paris than to Troyes, and since the king exercised considerable feudal authority in the county, many religious houses and some lay vassals found it advantageous to invoke the king's power against the count. Even before Philip the Fair became count there were plenty of excuses for royal administrators to act in Champagne, while there was no reason for a royal agent outside Normandy to interfere with another agent of the king inside the duchy.

When Philip became both king and count, there was no longer an independent administration with an interest in opposing royal influence. There was also pressure within Champagne to take cases to the more

---

66. Sessions of the Grands Jours were held intermittently in Troyes until 1409. Apparently documentation to show what happened to the high court of the county under Isabelle of Bavaria and the Burgundians has not survived. In 1431 representations from Troyes were sent "aux prochains Jours de Sens et de Champagne, à Poitiers." See Théophile Boutiot, "Nouvelles recherches sur la cour des Grands Jours," *Annuaire administratif, statistique et commercial de l'Aube* (1870), p. 83.

powerful court, and litigants on expense accounts (like the communal officials of Provins) undoubtedly preferred to plead in Paris rather than in the moribund city of Troyes. The flow of cases from Champagne to the Parlement could only have been checked if the government of Philip IV had made an effort to prohibit it, as Philip III had earlier attempted to limit the cases coming to Paris from provinces which had royal *baillis*.[67] But Philip the Fair, count only in his wife's name, had no reason to build a strong local judicial system in Champagne. The masters of the Jours were not recruited from the county but sent from the royal court, and cases could be judged in Troyes or Paris as convenience dictated. Finally, when it was apparent that the monarchy might not be able to appoint the masters of the Jours indefinitely, Philip established the right of appeal from the Jours to the Parlement, a principle it was not necessary to impose on Normandy. The great centralizer of medieval France subordinated the Jours but permitted the Exchequer to remain relatively independent because in his day the monarchy had a firmer hold on Normandy than on Champagne.

67. Langlois, *Textes*, p. 95, art. 1.

APPENDIX I

REGISTERS OF THE COURT OF THE JOURS

Two registers of the court of the Jours of Troyes were once kept in the *Chambre des comptes* at Paris. One of these—we do not know which—was described in an inventory of the registers of the *Chambre de Champagne* made in 1489 as a volume of 190 leaves of parchment, bound in white leather on boards, with five nails in each board, and labeled on the cover: "*Arresta antiquitus prolata ad magnos dies Trecenses seu registrum ipsorum arrestorum.*"[1] Later users recorded the dates of the two registers; one went from 1284 to 1295, the second from 1296 to 1299. Du Cange quoted this second volume once,[2] and anonymous antiquarians listed some of the nobles and masters of the Jours named in it, but only the earlier volume was the subject of careful study.

D   Nicolas Dongois, who wrote a treatise *De l'origine des Grands Jours* in 1666, systematically extracted from the first register in an appendix which he entitled *Jours de Troyes tenus sous Philippe Le Bel depuis 1284 Jusques en 1291*. The treatise is now preserved in the Archives Nationales as U 749, and the appendix exists in two copies in U 749 and U 750. The second copy is more clearly written and is the one cited here as MS D. At the time Dongois used it the register was already badly damaged, and he had to conclude his extracts at 1291 with the comment: "Il est impossible de rien dechifrer de tout le reste du registre." Quite possibly Dongois marked the material he extracted in some way, for the cases he thought interesting were often copied again, particularly by Brussel.

The great scholar Charles du Fresne Du Cange also made use of the registers of the Jours in the seventeenth century, either directly or through the intermediary of his friend Vyon d'Hérouval, auditor of the Chambre des Comptes. Du Cange quoted from the registers in his *Glossarium* and in the *Histoire de S. Louys*. He may also have been responsible for the copying of a list of "Chevaliers Champenois denommez aux Assises de

C   Champagne, qui sont en la Chambre des Comptes de Paris." This list is on fols. 54–55 of B. N., MS fr. 9501, which came from the Du Cange collection and is labeled on the first folio "Mss. duCange 1226." The list for the first volume, which can be checked against the extracts, is incomplete

1. Longnon (ed.), *Documents*, II, 575.
2. *Glossarium*, s.v., *dies magni Trecensis*.

and not entirely accurate, but in turn it provides a check on the folio numbers given elsewhere. It ends at fol. 111 in 1289, and no foliation is given for the names from the second volume. This manuscript also contains on fols. 37–38*v* a list of the "Maistres des grands Jours de Troie, Envoyes et Deputez par les Comtes de Champagne, et par les Roys de France. Ensemble ceux qui les ont assistez dans les Jugemens. Tirez de deux Vol. des Assises de Champagne de la Chambre des Comptes de Paris, et du vieux Coustumier de Champagne." It is cited hereafter as MS C.

A   The list of the "Maistres des grands Jours de Troie" copied in C also appears on fols. 377–380*v* of B. N., n. a. fr. 7412. This volume of notes and extracts was formerly MS 82 of the collection of the Abbé Decamps and is cited in Appendix II as MS A.

B   Possibly the second register had disappeared from the Chambre des Comptes by the early eighteenth century, but the first register remained in the *dépôt des Terriers*, where it was used extensively by another auditor of the Chambre des Comptes, Nicolas Brussel. Brussel's *Nouvel examen de l'usage général des fiefs en France*, which was first published in 1727 and reissued with a new title page in 1750, contains our longest extracts from the first register. It is cited hereafter as B. Brussel noted that the manuscript was badly damaged by moisture, forcing him to leave some blanks or to provide tentative readings in parentheses, and his book contains no extracts later than fol. 112*v*. I have not been able to find the manuscript of Brussel's transcription, but apparently copies not included in his book were available to Lévesque de la Ravallière, who noted:

> Mr Brussel a ecri[t] à la fin des titres qu'il a extraits du registre, f° 119, apres le titre des arrests qui furent rendus en l'an 1289: "Le registre n'est plus susceptible d'extraits pour son grand endommagement de pouriture; il paroit qu'il va jusqu'environ l'an 1295. Il s'y trouve l'ordonance autrefois faite pour tenir les grands jours de Champ^e avec les instructions aux comissaires, mais elle est aussi presqu'entierement mangëe de pourriture."[3]

L   It is not clear whether La Ravallière also had access to the original manuscript before the great fire of the Chambre des Comptes in 1737 or depended on copies, but his work contains material from the register not otherwise available. His essay and notes on the Grands Jours are in B. N., Collection de Champagne, t. 67, fols. 8–18, and t. 133, fols. 420–422, and his notes on Provins are in t. 26. All this material is cited as L.

3. B. N., Coll. de Champagne, t. 67, fol. 12.

These materials and a few other sources of information on the decisions of the court of the Jours permit the very limited reconstruction which follows of the first part of the first register of Philip's court. Most of the material is available in Brussel's book, but since his dating and foliation are not always accurate, a systematic ordering of his extracts provides a useful check and much more precision. Material not available in print has been quoted in full, but otherwise I have given only analyses. Personal names and other information not in the text have been supplied in square brackets at their first appearance in each entry. I have attempted to make the analyses detailed enough for the reader to follow the procedure or significant arguments, but have summarized as much as possible. Place-names in this and the following appendixes are identified in the index.

EXTRACTS FROM THE FIRST REGISTER

Session Beginning November 25, 1284

fol. 4   1. The daughters of the late Jean de Montréal failed to appear against Beatrice, duchess of Burgundy, and were placed in default. Their brothers, who were present and were therefore permitted to submit a new petition, requested that the duchess be summoned to the next session of the Jours of Troyes, which was granted. For the continuation of the case before the Parlement of Paris in 1292, see *Olim*, II, 343, xxii; Jean's daughters were Agnes, wife of Odo Bezors, lord of Villarnoult, and Beatrice, wife of Jacques, lord of La Roche-en-Brenil, and his son was Gui de Montréal.— B, p. 238 n.

fol. 10*v*   2. Agathes de Damery claimed that her husband held all the property which belonged to her and her children by her first marriage and did not permit them to have any income from it, but made those who administered it for her appear before the church court. The *bailli* of Vitry was ordered to make a settlement between the parties, and if this was not possible to take the property into his possession and administer it for her.

Dicebat domina Agathes de Damery quod maritus suus tenet omnes hereditates et bona ipsius et liberorum suorum ex primo cubili suo procreatorum, nec permittit quod habeant aliquod commodum de eisdem, et omnes illos qui ex parte dominae praedictae colunt hereditates et bona facit coram judice ecclesiastico conveniri, ipsos fatigando laboribus et expensis. Quare petit quod subveniatur eidem et liberis[1] et quod de bonis predictis eisdem sua necessaria ministrentur. Injunctum est baillivo Vitriaci quod vocet partes et eas inter se concordet, ut maritus uxorem suam et liberos secum revocet et ipsos modo debito tractet, et quod eisdem de bonis praedictis commoda ministret, et si alterutrum istorum nolit facere, capiat baillivus de bonis praedictis et de eisdem ministret sufficienter dictae dominae et liberis suis supradictis.—D, fol. 21v.

fol. 12v   3. The proctor of the count of Champagne charged that although Count [Henri] of Grandpré held his county, including the guard of the abbey of Chéhery, directly from the count of Champagne, the count of Grandpré had sold permission to the abbey of Chéhery to enter the guard of the king of France, to the detriment of Champagne. The proctor therefore requested that all the land of the count of Grandpré be confiscated and adjudged to the count of Champagne. The count of Grandpré requested a delay to take counsel, which was denied, but he was granted a hearing at Chéhery on the following February 11. On this case, see above, p. 289.—B, 808–809 n.

fol. 17   4. Concerning the claim of Lord [Jean] de Chappes that Duke [Robert II] of Burgundy had threatened violence to the village of Essoyes, which he held in fief from the count of Champagne, the *bailli* of Chaumont was ordered to protect the property the lord of Chappes held from the lord of Champagne.—B, p. 238 n.

fol. 17   5. Concerning the request of Lord Jean de Norrois that Duke [Ferri III] of Lorraine, who had announced hostilities with him, should make him an oath of peace (*asseguramentum*), the court agreed that the duke should be told in writing to keep peace with the lord of Norrois.—B, p. 239 n.

1. MS: *libelis.*

fol. 17*v*   6. Lord Erard de Grand proposed a division through sale of the forest of Grand, which he held in equal shares with the count of Champagne and Duke [Ferri III] of Lorraine. The court ordered that the duke be addressed on this matter, and that if he consented, the forest should be sold.—B, p. 239 n.

fol. 17*v*   7. The court ordered that whenever the officials of the count of Champagne retained in their villages any serfs of lords who were vassals of the count, the *bailli* should determine why the serfs wished to be in the jurisdiction of the count of Champagne and report what he found to the court.— B, p. 269 n.

fol. 17*v*   8. Concerning the request of Gui de Virey-sous-Bar, knight, that he be permitted to bear arms for the defense of his home, the court ordered the *bailli* of Troyes to determine if Gui had just cause to bear arms against persons who were not in the jurisdiction of the count of Champagne, and if so, to grant him permission to bear arms.—B, p. 230 n.

December 4, 1284

fol. 17*v*   9. At the request of Guillaume du Châtelet, formerly *bailli* of Chaumont, the court ordered Lord Pierre de Bourlemont to make an oath of peace to Guillaume in full court at the Jours of Troyes, in the presence of many witnesses (see Appendix II, No. 1).—B, p. 859 n; D, fol. 22.

December 5, 1284

fol. 17*v*   10. Lord Pierre de Bourlemont renewed his oath of peace to the abbot of Mureaux[2] in full court at the Jours of Troyes in the presence of many witnesses (see Appendix II, No. 1). —B, p. 859–860 n.

fols.   11. The proctor of the count of Champagne argued that
17[*v*]–18   Lord Pierre de Bourlemont should not be received in homage for Bourlemont and Rorthey because, among other reasons, he had broken the oath of peace he had made about five years before to the abbot of Mureaux, and which he had

---

2. Brussel erroneously modernized *Miroaut* as the name of the abbey of "Mirevaux."

renewed about three years before. It was finally agreed, with
Pierre's consent, that he should be received in homage by the
count of Champagne, but that this homage would not
prejudice the proctor's case against him. After Pierre had
done homage, his fiefs were taken into the count's seisin, and
Gautier de Chambly and Guillaume de Prunay were named
as auditors to make an inquest for the court. Brussel added
that Pierre was later condemned to pay a fine to the count
and damages to the abbey.—B, pp. 862 and 862–863 n; cf.
B, p. 814.

Session Beginning April 8, 1285[?] [3]

fol. 18v   12. Lady Mathilda, wife of Gilo Fuiret, requested the
            return of her own inheritance, which had been confiscated
            by the officials of the king of Navarre because of her hus-
            band's crime; Count Edmund of Lancaster had granted her
            this dispensation during his guardianship. The *bailli* replied
            that according to the customs of Champagne, she should not
            enjoy her inheritance during her husband's lifetime.[4] The
            court declared that she should have the same dispensation
            Edmund had made.—B, pp. 218–221.

fol. 21v   13. Erard de Dinteville, squire, stated that when he began
            to build a fortified house in some of his allodial land in
            Champagne, for which he had recently entered the homage
            of the count of Champagne, he had been prevented by
            officials of the king of France acting at the request of the
            bishop of Langres [Gui II], although there were many other
            such houses held in fief from the count in the same allod. The
            court declared that the count of Champagne should prose-
            cute his rights concerning this fortified house in the next
            Parlement of Pentecost, and Erard was ordered to be present
            to defend his rights against the officials of the king of France
            and the bishop of Langres.—B, p. 385 n.

fol. 21v   14. The prior and canons of Belroy, of the order of Val-
            des-Escoliers, complained that they were no longer receiving

3. Brussel places case No. 12 in the session of April 8, 1285, but dates Nos. 13 and 14
in 1284. According to C, fol. 54, the year 1285 began somewhere between fol. 21 and 24.
4. On this principle see Portejoie (ed.), *Coutumier*, p. 57.

a *muid* of grain granted them from certain granges, which the count of Champagne had later given to the duke of Lorraine (see below, No. 23). The *bailli* was ordered to make an investigation and to do right.—B, p. 240 n.

Session Beginning April 8, 1285

fol. 23   15. The lady of Saint-Remy [-en-Bouzemont?] requested the return of property taken from her by order of the *bailli* of Vitry for fines imposed by her on some of her men, who claimed to have appealed to the officials of the king [of Navarre] for false judgment and denial of justice. After a hearing the court ordered that the goods be returned and the lady permitted to do justice to her men, unless they pursued their appeal.—B, p. 266 n; D, fols. 22–22*v*.

fol. 23   16. Lord [Henri] de Hans stated that according to an agreement made between himself and [Thibaut V], king of Navarre–count of Champagne,[5] the burgesses of Hans did not have the right to settle in the towns of the count of Champagne without losing their property in Hans. Although the burgesses of Hans made a contrary claim, the court declared that the king-count did not guarantee the property of burgesses coming to his towns from Hans.—B, pp. 1014–1015 n; Du Cange, *Glossarium*, s.v. *percursus*.

fol. 26[6]   17. Henri de Saint-Benoît-sur-Vanne, knight, requested the return of his serfs held in the royal prison at Troyes for debt, claiming that his men could not make obligations without his special permission. The *bailli* replied that his men and all men of any condition in Champagne could engage in trade and make contracts with their own goods. After hearing these statements, the court declared that it would not hear the knight's case.

Petebat Henrions de Sancto Benedicto miles homines suos de corpore sibi reddi et deliberari qui in prisione regis Trecis detinebantur pro debitis in quibus se obligaverant per litteras balliviae ut dicebatur cum omnibus bonis suis;

5. See Arbois de Jubainville, *Histoire*, VI, No. 3453.
6. Folio supplied from C, fol. 54.

dicens dictus miles quod ipsi homines non poterant se obligare nec eorum bona alienare sine ipsius licentia speciale, baillivo pro rege dicente quod tam ipsi quam alii homines cujusque conditionis in toto comitatu Campaniae possunt de bonis suis mercari et contrahere et ratione contractuum se per litteras obligare. Auditis hinc inde propositis, pronunciatum est dictum militem non esse super hoc audiendum. —D, fol. 22v.

fol. 28   18. In a case between the king of Navarre and the lord of Crécy-en-Brie [Gaucher V de Châtillon], by order of the court an inquest was made on the right to collect mainmorte from bastards and on the ownership of servile bastards in the village of Artonges. The inquest showed that these rights belonged to the lord of Crécy, and the *bailli* was ordered to withdraw his injunction.—B, p. 956 n.

Session of August 1285

19. The proctor of the commune of Provins complained that, contrary to the charter granted to the commune by the count of Champagne,[7] the officials of the count were preventing the commune from collecting fines up to 20s. from those coming to Provins from outside the town. After seeing the charter the court ordered the *bailli* of Troyes to permit the commune to collect these fines.—Prou and d'Auriac, *Actes et comptes*, p. 282.

Uncertain Session, Probably in 1285[8]

20. Lord Erard d'Arcis brought suit against Henri l'Armurier and Thibaut de Saint-Antoine, both of Troyes, because they

7. This charter of Thibaut V of 1268 was confirmed by Prince Philip and his wife in February, 1285; see Félix Bourquelot, *Histoire de Provins*, 2 vols. (Provins, 1839–40), II, 416–417 and 432.

8. The custumal names the masters and dates this case in 1284. For this date to refer to the old style calendar, there would have had to have been a session of the Jours between March 11, when the masters Joinville and Gautier de Chambly took up their duties as guardians after the king's departure from Orléans, and Easter. Since no such session is recorded in the accounts of Champagne for the first half year of 1285 (see Longnon [ed.], *Documents*, III, 27–28), the date should probably be corrected to 1285 (N.S.). There is no way to tell whether this case was tried in the April or the August session.

had purchased houses and other property at Sacey and Thénnelières from serfs held in fief by Erard. The court declared that the defendants could not make these purchases and that Erard should have them.—Portejoie (ed.), *Coutumier*, art. 10, pp. 155–158.

Session Beginning January 27, 1286[?][9]

fol. 27[?][10] 21. Lord Henri de Hans was ordered to name a guardian (*tutor seu curator*) for his cases, both for and against him, since he claimed to be continually ill. If he failed to do so, his goods were to be administered in justice by the *bailli* of Vitry.—Brief analysis in L, t. 67, fol. 11.

fol. [?][11] 22. The court declared that the woman who married the son of the lord of Hans did not have to pay relief, since the marriage was void because at the time it was constituted the son had entered holy orders.

Curia declaravit quod quaedam femina quae duxerat in virum filium domini de Hans non tenetur ad solvendum rachatum pro eo quod dictum matrimonium nullum fuit ex eo quod dictus filius tempore constituti matrimonii erat in sacris ordinibus constitutus.—D, fols. 22*v*–23.

Session Beginning April 22, 1286

fol. 33 23. The prior and canons of Belroy declared that Lambert le Bouchu, chamberlain of Champagne, had granted them an annual revenue of two *muids* of grain from the granges of Beaurepaire, La Grange-au-Bois, Arrentières, and Rouvre,[12]

9. This date is uncertain and puzzling. D, fol. 22*v*, places the session "in quindena festi Sancti Remigii 1286" after that "in quindena Pasche 1285" and before that "in crastino octave Pasche anno 1286." Although in Champagne the year normally began at Easter, this position suggests that in this instance the year had already changed. L places this case "aux jours de la S. Remy 86."

10. C, fol. 54, places a case concerning "Henricus dom. de Hans senior" in 1286 on fol. 27. L gives no folio.

11. Dongois records this case "in quindena festi Sancti Remigii 1286." On the problem of dating and placement see the notes to the preceding case.

12. For this charter of January, 1232, see Charles Lalore, "Notice sur le prieuré de Belroy," *Mémoires de la Société academique . . . de l'Aube*, LI (1887), 184.

that three of these granges had come into the possession of Count Henri III of Champagne, and that the count had granted two of them to Duke [Ferri III] of Lorraine in the settlement of the dowry of his sister [Marguerite of Navarre]. They therefore requested that the duke's son Thibaut be ordered to pay them the revenue from the two granges of Arrientières and Rouvre. Thibaut's proctor responded that the granges had been assigned free of obligations. The court ordered that Thibaut should pay the grain to the priory, without prejudice to his right to bring an action against the lord of Champagne (cf. above, No. 14).—B, pp. 241–242 n.

fols. 34–35   24. The court declared that when the guards of the fairs, acting by reason of their office and in conformity with the customs of the fairs, had imprisoned a debtor attached to the fairs (*de corpore nundinarum*) at the request of any merchant, if the debtor left the prison without the assent of the merchant, the guards (and the lord of Champagne whom they represent) should be obliged to pay the merchant the sum for which the debtor had been imprisoned.—Du Cange, *Glossarium*, s.v., *custodes nundinarum Campaniae*.

Uncertain Session in 1286

fol. 39   25. Lord Thibaut de Broyes and the abbot and community of Saint-Pierre of Oyes made mutual oaths of peace in the presence of the court.—B, p. 857 n.

fol. 39   26. Borgine, daughter of Huard Baudier, accused the lady of Chassins of holding her father in prison on suspicion of the murder [of Philippe de Moncel] and of hanging him without proper procedure and sufficient evidence, wherefore she requested that his body be taken down from the gallows and his property be released to her. The lady replied that Huard, her serf, had been judged with the counsel of good men for a murder committed in her jurisdiction. The court decided that Borgine's accusation should not be taken up.—B, p. 222; for details see *ibid.*, pp. 228–229 n.

fol. 39*v*   27. The *baillis* were ordered to investigate the property acquired by churches in their districts. If they found that grants of real property had been confirmed by the king [of Navarre] and had been held for a sufficiently long time, they were to leave the churches alone. Otherwise, they were to deal with the churches as best they could, and to refer their settlements to the king for approval.—B, p. 666 n.

fol. 39*v*   28. The proctor of the abbot and community of Saint-Médard of Soissons stated that the church was obliged to pay annually 20 *livres* for the *gîte* of Damery and 10 *livres* for that of Cierges when the king did not stay there in person, but that when the king came to those places, they had to pay all the expenses of his stay. The proctor complained that although the recent visit of the king had cost them 100 *livres tournois*, they were still required in the same year to pay the stated 30 *livres*, which they requested be returned. The court granted the request.—B, p. 566 n.

Session Beginning November 8, 1286

fol. 40   29. In an inquest and local hearing in a case which Oudin Louchat had brought against Perrin Fumon, knight, concerning the plaintiff's status, Oudin had sufficiently proved that Perrin's mother had freed him. The court therefore declared that Oudin was to remain a royal serf in the same fashion as he had been a serf of Perrin.[13]—B, p. 934 n.

November 15, 1286

30. The court declared in favor of the abbey of Jouy in a case concerning its mills.—B. N., MS lat. 5467 (cartulary of Jouy), p. 201; Bourquelot, *Études*, p. 262.

fol. 43   31. After a man had been murdered in the town of Meaux, his widow was charged with the crime and detained in the royal prison. Since she was a serf of Saint-Faron at Meaux, the abbey claimed the right to judge her. The *bailli* replied

13. Presumably Oudin had been freed without royal authorization, thereby reducing the fief Perrin held from the king.

that the king held all the rights of justice in Meaux. The court declared that the woman should be handed over to the monks.—B, p. 223 n.

fol. 43*v*   32. The proctors of Saint-Quiriace of Provins, of the abbey of Rebais, and of the Temple and its treasurer at Laon and its men at Provins claimed that by grant of the count of Champagne their men at Provins were freed of all exactions, and that the royal officials were unjustly compelling them to pay taxes on cloth and other goods. The royal officials and the mayor and commune of Provins replied that these taxes, established by ordinance,[14] were not placed on persons but on goods, and therefore should be paid by all. The court ruled that in spite of the objections of the churches, the ordinance should remain in effect.—L, t. 26, fol. 115.

Procuratores S. Quiriaci Pruvinensis, abbatis et conventus Resbacensis et Templi ac thesaurarii Laudunensis suo et hominum suorum Pruvini, commorantium nomine, dicebant contra Regem, majorem et communitatem de Pruvino, quod cum homines predicti ipsarum ecclesiarum et thesaurarii sint per privilegia comitum Campaniae sibi concessa liberi et immunes ab omni taillia, et gentes domini Regis ipsos compellant ad solvendum de quolibet panno persico duodecim denarios, de radiato, sex denarios, et quasdam alias redevancias quotiens vendunt pannos seu alias mercaturas contra libertatem suam veniendo, petibant homines suos in sua libertate remanere et gaiges dictorum hominum propter hoc capta.

Sibi reddi, et per jusdici, gentes domini Regis et majorem et communitatem predictam non habere jus talia faciendi, gentibus domini Regis et majore et communitate praedicta in quantum tangit seu tangere potest quemlibet ipsorum e contrario dicentibus, quod olim de voluntate et assensu comitis Campaniae, archiepiscopi et majoris partis burgensium et ministrorum marchandisiorum de Pruvino fuerat ordinatum, quod quilibet (quantumcumque privilegium haberet) de pannis quos venderet et mercaturis quas faceret, solveret redevancias supradictas, quare cum ista onera

14. For Henri III's regulations of 1273 see Longnon (ed.), *Documents*, II, 78–79.

fuissent imposita personis sed mercaturis, hoc non erat contra privilegia eorumdem et debebant adsolvendum compelli. Auditis omnibus hinc et inde, pronunciatum est per arrestum quod non obstantibus propositis ex parte procuratorum S. Quiriaci, Resbacènsis et Templi et thesaurarii, ordinatio praedictorum comitis et archiepiscopi cum burgensibus de Pruvino in suo robore remanebit.

fol 44   33. Having seen the letter of manumission at the king's pleasure granted to Henri l'Armurier [of Troyes] by the king, the court declared that his wife [Marie] was free of the *jurée*[15] for as long as the king should please.—B, p. 921, marginal note.

fol. 49   34. Jean Banloquiers, a royal burgess [at Passavant], declared that Geoffroi de Louppy-le-Château had unjustly disseized him of the house and goods left him by his mother. Geoffroi, seconded by the proctor of Count [Thibaut II] of Bar-le-Duc, pleaded that the case should be tried in the court of his lord, the count of Bar. The court declared that the count should not have jurisdiction over the movable goods, and that it would determine the location of the real property and make a later decision concerning it. Consequently Geoffroi contumaciously left without giving a response. The *bailli* of Vitry was ordered to put Banloquiers in possession of his movable goods (cf. No. 60).—B, pp. 937–939 n.

Session Beginning April 14, 1287

fol. 50   35. The court forbade all the *baillis* and *prévôts* of Champagne and Brie to sell the offices of sergeants or mayors, or to permit them to be sold to anyone, until they should receive a special order to the contrary from the king. If they did otherwise, they were to be severely punished.—B, p. 242 n.

fol. 50v   36. The men of Lord Gui de la Neuville-aux-Bois complained of injuries Gui had done them contrary to their charter. Gui responded that he was not bound to reply to

15. At Troyes the *jurée* was a tax of six *deniers* per *livre* on the assessed value of movable property and two *deniers* per *livre* on real estate. In the 1270's it produced a revenue of about 1500 *livres* a year. See Longnon (ed.), *Documents*, II, 13 D.

this charge of his serfs, since it did not concern default of
justice or false judgment. The court declared that the case
should be returned to Gui's court, and ordered him to do no
injury to the plaintiffs and to observe their charter in order
to avoid royal action because of his default.—B, p. 267; D,
fols. 23–23v; L, t. 67, fol. 12.

fol. 51   37. The monks of Montier-en-Argonne claimed to be under
the guard of the count of Champagne.—B, p. 814.

Uncertain Session in 1287

fol. 53[16]   38. Lord [André] de Saint-Phal, knight, pleaded that the
land of Courgerennes, which had formerly been held by
Lord Gautier de Courgerennes, knight, and which had been
confiscated by the king for Gautier's crime, should be held
in fief from him, but that it had had no vassal or tenant since
Gautier's death.[17] The court declared that if the land was
held in fee, André should have a vassal, and if it was held in
villenage, he should have a tenant.—B, p. 155 n.

fol. 53   39. Jean du Plessis-lés-Chaast had captured a thief and
hanged and condemned him; later the *bailli* of Troyes had
the body removed and hanged from the royal gallows. The
bailli was ordered to determine whether the thief had been
captured in the territory of royal justice or in that of Jean's.
—B, p. 222; D, fol. 23v.

fol. 54   40. Lord Jacques Mauferas [of Turgy], knight, complained
that a year before he had been beaten and wounded by Jean
Boutauz [of Lignières?], knight, and his accomplices, who
had also beaten one of his servants and stolen his sword. Jean
responded that he was under the jurisdiction of the lady of
Lignières and sought to have the case heard in her court; he
was seconded in this by the lady of Lignières. The royal
proctor replied that the officials of Champagne had juris-

16. B gives the folio as 53 and the date as 1286. The folio is confirmed by C, fol. 54.
17. Gautier was condemned and his brother banished as early as Pentecost, 1285. Up
to Christmas, 1287, their lands paid the king over 112 *livres*. See Longnon (ed.), *Documents*,
III, 35.

diction of all nobles of Champagne with respect to their movables and in criminal cases. The court declared that before going further the matter should be referred to the king, that the *bailli* should seek more information, and that Jean should remain in the royal prison at Troyes.—B, pp. 231–232 n; D, fols. 23v–24.

Session Beginning May 22, 1287

fol. 57   41. The viscount of Bar-sur-Seine complained that the *bailli* of Chaumont had seized a certain serf whose dues he had fixed (*abonaverat*) with the authorization of the lady of *Honneriis*,[18] from whom he held the serf. The *bailli* stated that since the lady held the serf from the king and the agreement to fix his dues had been made without royal authorization, the serf should belong to the king. The court declared that henceforth the viscount should receive from the serf no more than the sum agreed upon and the king should receive the rest of his payments as the viscount had before.—B, p. 935.

fol. 60   42. Two daughters of Huard Baudier brought the same charges against the lady of Chassins as Borgine had before (No. 26), and the lady made the same defense, requesting that the case not be taken up, particularly since the court had ruled against a similar charge brought by one of the daughters. The court declared that the charge should not be taken up, but ordered the *bailli* of Vitry to free the daughters' maternal inheritance, which had been seized by the lady of Chassins, to seek more information, and to submit a sealed report at the next session of the Jours.—B, p. 224; cf. D, fol. 26.

Session Beginning September 9, 1287

43. The court ordered the *bailli* of Troyes to permit the free entry of wine being taken into Troyes for the use of the

18. I cannot identify any place in Champagne named *Honneriis* or Honnières. Possibly Brussel made an error for *Lyneriis*. The family of Lignières had once held the office of viscount of Bar-sur-Seine; see Alphonse Roserot, *Dictionnaire historique de la Champagne méridionale* (Langres, 1942–48), pp. 114–115.

Hôtel-Dieu-le-Comte of Troyes, since such wine did not have to pay portage. He was also ordered to see that justice was done with respect to the prebend in Saint-Etienne of Troyes, which the brothers of the Hôtel-Dieu claimed belonged to them and had been unjustly retained by the dean and chapter of Saint-Etienne.[19]—Printed by Philippe Guignard, *Les anciens statuts de l'Hôtel-Dieu-le-Comte de Troyes* (Troyes, 1853), pp. 104–105, from an eighteenth-century copy in Aube, arch. dép., Lay. 5. D. 19.

fol. 61   44. The court ordered that all those guarantors of debts (*personarii*) held in prison for debt who wished to hand over their goods, both movables and real property, should be freed, no matter whether the debts had been recorded by the *baillis* or not. This order was made without prejudice to the rights of the fairs of Champagne.—B, pp. 243–244 n; D, fol. 24*v*.

fol. 66*v*   45. The court ordered that in every place where there should be a mayor the *baillis* of Champagne and Brie should establish an appropriate person, that no other sergeants should remain in the office of mayor, and that the mayors should engage in no other service except that of their districts, for which each should answer in the assizes of his *bailli*.—B, p. 243.

46. The court recorded an offer of concord made to Lord [Jean] de Chappes by Lord Erard d'Arcis and Lord Guillaume de *Gant*, knight.[20]

Erard d'Arcies pour luy et pour Monsieur Guillaume de Gant, chevaliers, lequel Messire Erars prenoit en main, cet offre que Erars d'Arcies ha faite a Monsieur de Chappes.

Premierement Messire Erars se doit mettre en la prison de Monsieur Guillaume de Juilly, et le terra s'il velt autretant en prison et en telle prison comme il tint Monsieur de

19. In the twelfth century the founder of the Hôtel-Dieu, Count Henry I, had granted it "annualia quoque prebendarum Sancti Stephani quocumquemodo prebenda vacet vel muttetur exceptis prebendis personatuum," Aube, arch. dép., 40 H layette 1.

20. Dongois gives neither date nor folio, but apparently the entry should precede Nos. 47 and 48.

Chappes. Et ce fait, quand il istrera hors de prison, il s'en doit aller outre la mer d'Angleterre au rapport de Monsieur de Juilly, et ce fait, il s'en doit aller à Saint Jacques en Galice et à Nostre Dame de Vauvert et a Saint Nicolas de Varangéville, et de ces choses faire il est à la requeste de Monsieur de Juilly ou son commandement; et ce faisant li ditz Erars et le ditz Guillaume ont bonne paix à Monsieur de Chappes et à tous les siens et quittent de toutes choses dou temps passé jusques aujourdhuy.—D, fols. 24–24*v.*

fol. 68   47. Through the testimony of Jean de Villeblevin, Gilles de Compiègne, Jean l'Esquallot, and Pierre de Chaource, the court recorded the mutual oaths of peace (*assecuratio*) made by Lord Erard d'Arcis and his party and Lord [Jean] de Chappes and his party. These oaths had been made in full court at the Jours of Troyes a year before.[21]—B, p. 857 n.

48. Lord [Jean] de Chappes maintained that after he had made an oath of peace (*aseurement*) with Lord Erard d'Arcis, the two of them had made a concord (*pais*). Their later hostilities had therefore broken the concord but not the oath. The court ruled in favor of Jean, declaring that he should be fined for breaking the concord [and not punished for the more serious crime of breaking an oath of peace].— Portejoie (ed.), *Coutumier*, art. 30 (dated 1287), pp. 182–185.

fol. 68   49. The court determined that the mayor and counsellors of Provins had sufficiently proved their right to a pillory (*scala*) and declared that one should remain there, without prejudice to the rights of the king.—L, t. 26, fols. 112–112*v*, giving date and folio; B. N., Coll. Dupuy, t. 761, fol. 49; Grillon entered the text in the "Cartulary" of Provins (Provins, Bibl. mun., MS 89), fol. 45, with the date 1283; printed from this last source in Prou and d'Auriac, *Actes et comptes*, p. 62.

21. Among those of whom the court was to enquire further was the "Senescallus de Biaucaria tunc Baillivus de Calvomonte." This statement indicates a step in the career of Jean de Champrupin not otherwise recorded; see François Maillard, "Mouvements administratifs des baillis et des sénéchaux sous Philippe le Bel," *Bulletin philologique et historique du Comité des travaux historiques et scientifiques* (année 1959), pp. 408–411. Jean l'Esquallot and Pierre de Chaource were guards of the forests of Champagne; see Longnon (ed.), *Documents*, III, 50 and 58.

Visa apprisia facta super hoc quod major et scabini de Pruvino dicebant se esse et fuisse in bona saisina faciendi et habendi scalam a tempore dominorum Campaniae predecessorum domini Regis apud Pruvinum in medio vico ante Domum Dei Pruvinensem ad ponendum ibidem malefactores, jurantes in honesta juramenta, et justiciandi eosdem in scala sive puniendi secundum loci consuetudinem et secundum delictorum quantitatem, inventum fuit et probatum dictos majorem et scabinos vel juratos intentionem suam sufficienter probasse: quare pronunciatum fuit per curiae consilium quod ibidem prout esse consueverat, salvo jure domini Regis, scala fiet et remanebit.

Uncertain Session in 1287 (O. S.)

fol. 69   50. Jean de Fay charged that Jean Raymond [a prominent citizen of Provins] had beaten and threatened him, and he requested that Jean Raymond be fined. Jean Raymond replied that the case should not be taken up, since Jean de Fay had brought similar charges before the court of the *bailli* of Troyes at the assizes of Provins, where Jean Raymond had been released by judgment of the court. Jean de Fay replied that Jean Raymond had broken the judgment of the court, since he was supposed to submit any later grievances to arbitration. The court declared that Jean de Fay's case should not be taken up.—B, p. 237 n.

Session Beginning May 3, 1288

fol. 71   51. The *bailli* of Vitry had not made the investigation into the case of Huard Baudier requested earlier by the court (No. 42) because of a transfer of office.[22] The new *bailli* was directed to make a sealed report at a later session of the Jours.—B, p. 225 n.

fol. 73[?][23]   52. The abbot and community of Saint-Memmie-lés-Châlons stated that although they had made use of their

22. Pierre Saymel was named *prévôt* of Paris and replaced as *bailli* of Vitry by Jean de Champrupin in late 1287 or early 1288; see Maillard, "Mouvements," p. 411.
23. Brussel gives the folio as 37, but the date suggests that the figures were reversed.

burgess rights (*burgesia*) in Châlons and had received burgesses in their tenures since time immemorial, paying 40
livres tournois a year to the count of Champagne for this,[24]
now the *bailli* of Vitry and the bishop of Châlons were inter-
fering with these burgess rights; they therefore petitioned for
relief. The court ordered the *bailli* to permit the abbey to
enjoy its burgess rights, notwithstanding the constitution
[passed in the Parlement of Pentecost 1287].[25]—B, p. 903 n.

fol. 73*v*   53. The court ordered that debtors bound by notarial
letters and jailed by reason of their personal obligations
should be released from prison if they gave the judges a
claim on all their forthcoming inheritances for the satisfaction of their debts, that debtors bound by notarial letters
should be able to prove through acceptable witnesses that
they had paid their debts, that notaries should not do their
work outside of castles, and that the *baillis* should prevent
notaries from making or receiving obligations which were
against the law.—B, pp. 244–245 n.

fol. 74   54. The court recorded the terms of the concord (*paix*)
made between the relatives of Raolin d'Argers and the
Hermit of Stenay. The Hermit gave the friends of the dead
Raolin 100 *livres* to establish a chapel for him, and his son
Girard was obliged to go overseas and bring back letters
testifying to the journey.—Du Cange, *Dissertations sur l'histoire de Saint Louis* in *Histoire de S. Louys* (Paris, 1668), pp. 337–
338, reprinted among other places in *Glossarium*, ed. Henschel,
VII, 125.

Uncertain Session in 1288

fol. 79   55. Lord Jean de Bourlemont, knight, and Jean de Gondre-
court-le Château, squire, and their supporters made mutual
oaths of peace.—B, p. 857 n.

24. According to the accounts of 1287 and 1288 the abbey paid the count 40 *livres* a
year for "garde" or "taille"; see Longnon (ed.), *Documents*, III, 53*E* and 91*H*.
25. For the text of this constitution see César Chabrun, *Les bourgeois du roi* (Paris,
1908), pp. 135–144.

Session Following September 14, 1288

fol. 79v   56. The prior of Gimont was condemned to a fine of 60 *livre tournois* because he had appealed from a judgment made in the assizes of the *bailli* of Chaumont to the masters of the Jours of Troyes, but had then made peace with the *bailli*, renounced his appeal, and approved the judgment.—B, p. 237 n; D, fol. 25.

57. The court ordered that all of the acquisitions made by the church of Saint-Quiriace of Provins more than forty years before should remain in their hands without impediment, but all acquisitions made more recently should remain in the hands of the king.[26]

Auditis rationibus decani et capituli Sancti Quiriaci super acquestibus ab eisdem factis, quos impedium receptores Campaniae, injuste ut asserum: dictum et ordinatum est per Curiae consilium quod omnes acquestus suos quos fecerunt ultra quadraginta annos, penes ipsos absque impedimento remanebunt; omnes autem alios quos fecerunt quoquomodo infra quadraginta annos, penes dominum regem remanebunt, et de praemissis receptores se informabunt.—D, fols. 25–25v.

fol. 80v   58. Two men of Grand who had made a concord between themselves after arming for a judicial duel, as reported by the *bailli* of Chaumont, were ordered to pay 30 *livres* apiece to the royal tax collectors.—B, p. 989 n.

fol. 87   59. The *bailli* of Vitry made a partial report on the case of Huard Baudier (cf. No. 51), but since the lady of Chassins was ill, as certified by the court, the matter was prorogued until the next session of the Jours. The *bailli* was ordered to hear witnesses from both sides and to submit a complete sealed report.—B, p. 226 n.

fol. 87   60. Geoffroi de Louppy-le-Château, squire, charged that Jean Banloquiers, whom he claimed to be his serf, had made an oath of peace to another man in his presence, that he had

26. Dongois gives no folio but places this case in the same term as No. 56.

imprisoned Banloquiers for breaking this oath, and that
Banloquiers had escaped from his prison. He therefore
requested that Banloquiers, as his serf and subject, be
returned to him for examination. Banloquiers replied that
for about three years he had been in conflict with Geoffroi
over his mother's property (see No. 34), that never before
had Geoffroi brought this charge, that he was a royal burgess
living at Passavant, and that he was prepared to defend his
burgess right against anyone in the king's court. The court
ruled that Banloquiers did not have to answer this charge [in
Geoffroi's court], but that if Geoffroi wished to have him
brought before the *bailli* of Vitry, the *bailli* should render a
judgment which might not be appealed to the court of
Champagne.—B, pp. 939–940 n.

fol. 89   61. Lady Christine de Bar requested that since Miles de
Jaucourt had been found guilty of the murder of her son, as
certified by the local *bailli*, Miles should be called before the
king's justice and given the appropriate punishment. The
court instructed the *bailli* to take Miles, said to be a cleric,
outside of Holy Church, to hand him over to the bishop of
the place for punishment, to confiscate all the property which
Miles possessed at the time of the murder, and not to proceed
to a hearing on the disposition of that property without the
king's special order.—B, p. 233.

fol. 90*v*   62. Lord [Jean] de Joinville complained that the *bailli* of
Chaumont had taken over the justice of Joinville and had
prevented him and his men from exercising justice there. The
bailli responded that he had done this properly because of a
denial of justice, since after two men had made oaths of
peace before the royal *prévôt*, one of them with the help of
accomplices had beaten and wounded the other in the town
of Joinville, and the justice of Joinville had not acted to
apprehend the malefactors or to restrain them. The lord of
Joinville admitted these facts, but claimed that the *bailli* did
not have the right to interfere with his justice, since he was a
noble castellan, that the *bailli* had not summoned him to his
assizes on the charge of denial of justice, and that the *bailli*
could not try his case or interfere with his justice without a

sufficient summons.[27] The court declared that the cognizance of the alleged case of broken oaths of peace should remain with the *bailli*, that he should return the authority to exercise justice in Joinville to its lord, and that he should not permit the lord of Joinville to be molested.—B, pp. 865–866 n.

fol. 91   63. The court ordered the *bailli* of Troyes to permit the lord of Jully [Guillaume I] to collect the *jurée* from his serfs married to female serfs of the lord of Champagne in the same fashion that the lord of Champagne customarily collected it in those places where the men lived. Concerning the request of the lord of Jully to divide their children and to collect *taille à merci* from these men as he had before their marriages, the *bailli* was ordered to determine the local customary practice and to submit a sealed report at the next session of the Jours.—B, 923 n.

Session Beginning March 17, 1289

fol. 93v   64. One of the daughters of Huard Baudier requested that the report of the *bailli* of Vitry on her father's case be considered and a judgment made. The lady of Chassins, who appeared in person, argued that the case should be dropped. The court agreed to consider the case (cf. No. 59).—B, p. 227 n.

fol. 94v   65. Pastorelle de Verdun, who claimed to be a burgess of the lord of Champagne, complained that the Thirteen Justices of Verdun had unjustly confiscated her goods and had refused the request of the *bailli* of Vitry that they return them. The Thirteen Justices, although summoned by the *bailli* to appear at this session of the Jours, had not appeared, and therefore Pastorelle requested restitution of her goods with damages and expenses. The *bailli* was instructed to make restitution to Pastorelle from the goods of people from Verdun staying in Champagne if he could find them, but that if the Thirteen Justices wished to appear in his

27. Portejoie (ed.), *Coutumier*, p. 74, explains that since the oaths were made before a royal *prévôt*, the lord of Joinville could not be blamed for failing to act in a matter in which he did not have competence. But this was not the defense Joinville actually made.

assizes, he was authorized to do justice to the parties as reason dictated.—B, p. 920.

fol. 95   66. In the case between Ermengarde, daughter of Huard Baudier, and the lady of Chassins (cf. No. 64), the court declared that neither the court of Champagne nor anyone else could make any demands on the lady of Chassins for her execution of Huard Baudier, but that if the dead man were alive (*se cieus vesquesit qui est mort*), the court would charge him as guilty of Huard's death.[28] Consequently Huard's body was to be taken down from the gallows publicly and buried in a cemetery, if it was acceptable to the church, and the lady of Chassins was ordered to deliver to Ermengarde all the goods Huard had possessed on the day of his trial.—B, pp. 228–229 n; D, fols. 26v–27.

fol. 97   67. Lord [Jean] de Joinville requested a review of the inquest made on the guard of the abbey of Saint-Urbain of Joinville, which had been referred to the court of Champagne by order of the court of France. The *bailli* of Chaumont replied that the inquest should not be reviewed until a judgment had been made on the authenticity of the charter which the monks had offered in proof and which the lord of Joinville declared false. The court ordered that the matter should be reviewed at the next session of the Jours or at the coming day of the barons [at Parlement], and the proctor of the abbey was ordered to bring the charter with him to that judgment (see above, p. 292 and note 36).—B, pp. 249–250 n; cf. *ibid.*, p. 814.

Unspecified Session in 1288 (O. S.)

68. Pierre de la Ferté was condemned to pay a fine of 10 *livres tournois* for breaking an order of the court.—Brief analysis in L, t. 67, fol. 11.

28. In this amazing decision the court was obviously straining to fit an equitable judgment into the framework of the law. The reason for the argument actually used was not made clear. Nowhere in the previous record was it stated that the plaintiffs had claimed that Huard had acted in self-defense or that the dead man was in any way at fault.

Session Beginning September 9, 1289

fol. 101   69. The mayor and town counsellors of Monthois, who claimed that their charter granted them the customs of Beaumont-en-Argonne, requested the right to try their burgess, Baudier de Donzy, who had been arrested by the *bailli* of Vitry.[29] The *bailli* replied that Baudier had done great injury to the officials of Champagne, and that he had voluntarily accepted the *bailli*'s jurisdiction and then broken away while on the way to prison. Moreover, the burgesses of Monthois offered in proof only an inquest made by the Council of Forty of Beaumont, and not the text of the charter itself. The court deferred the case until the next session of the Jours, when it could see the charter or its authentic transcript, and Baudier was given his choice whether to be delivered on bail to the burgesses of Monthois or kept in the royal prison. The court also declared that a judgment it had rendered earlier in a case between the lady of Corbon and certain men of Monthois concerning their status applied only to those men and was without prejudice to the present case.— B, pp. 926–928 n.

fol. 101   70. The court ordered the *bailli* of Vitry to fine and punish anyone who challenged its earlier judgment in favor of the lady of Corbon against certain men who claimed burgess rights at Monthois.—B, p. 928 n; L, t. 67, fol. 11.

fol. [?][30]   71. After the Thirteen Justices of Verdun agreed to make full restitution of her goods to Pastorelle de Verdun through the agency of the *bailli* of Vitry, on condition that she guarantee the amount, Pastorelle was unable to do so. The court ordered the *bailli* to keep her goods and to administer them to provide for her necessities and the costs of prosecuting her case (cf. No. 65).—B, p. 921 n.

fol. 106[31]   72. Lord Guillaume de Grancey, knight, complained that burgesses from Bar-sur-Aube were occupying servile tenures

29. This charter is not recorded in Edouard Bonvalot, *Le tiers état d'après la charte de Beaumont* (Paris, 1884); on the principle of local trial see p. 398.

30. Brussel dropped a digit and gives the folio as 10*v*. The session is indicated, however.

31. Although Brussel dates this case in 1288, the folio is confirmed by C, fol. 54*v*.

in his village of Couvignon. The court ordered the *bailli* of Chaumont to seize the produce of the property held by the burgesses and bring it into Couvignon. The *bailli* was then to ask the burgesses if they wished to submit to his judgment in this matter, and if not, he was to protect the lord of Grancey in doing justice himself.—B, pp. 917–918 n.

fol. 106 73. The court ordered the *bailli* of Chaumont to direct Count [Thibaut] of Bar to return to Balduin de Tour, squire, his house of La Tour-en-Woëvre, which Balduin claimed to hold from the lord of Champagne.[32] And since the count of Bar had been summoned to this session of the Jours and had not come or excused himself, the *bailli* was ordered to summon the count to appear at the next day of the barons at Paris [i.e., the Parlement of Pentecost 1290].[33] —B, p. 250 n.

fol. 106*v* 74. The *bailli* of Chaumont was ordered to go to Count [Thibaut] of Bar, who had been summoned to this session of the Jours and had not appeared, to request a truce with Hugues Bekait, knight, who had complained to the court of Champagne. If the count alleged a just cause for not keeping peace with Hugues, the *bailli* was to summon him to appear against Hugues at Paris.—B, p. 858.

fol. 106*v* [?][34] 75. The *bailli* of Chaumont was ordered to direct Duke [Ferri III] of Lorraine to make amends for the injuries done to the sergeants and *prévôts* of Champagne. If he refused, the *bailli* with an armed band was to seize the goods of the duke wherever he could find them and the persons of those who had done the injuries and to take vengeance to maintain the honor of the king.[35]—B, pp. 245–246 n; D, fol. 27*v*.

32. La Tour-en-Woëvre was a fief of Champagne; see Longnon, *Rôles des fiefs du comté de Champagne* (Paris, 1877), No. 1341.

33. He did not appear there either; see Delisle (ed.), *Essai*, p. 430, No. 744.

34. Brussel gives the folio as 186*v*, but both he and Dongois place this case in the September term of 1289.

35. In May, 1289, Philip assumed the guard of the possessions of the chapter of Toul on the left side of the Meuse, while Ferri had renewed his safeguard of the chapter two months before. Perhaps these events explain the violence discussed here. See Fritz Kern, *Acta Imperii* (Tübingen, 1910), No. 62, and Jean de Pange, *Catalogue des actes de Ferri III* (Paris, 1930), No. 891.

Session Beginning September 10, 1290

fol. 112v   76. Ermengarde, daughter of the late Huard Baudier, acting with the approval of her husband, stated that her suit for the rehabilitation of her father's memory had cost her 100 *livres tournois*, and she therefore pleaded that the lady of Chassins should pay her this sum (cf. No. 66). She added that her two brothers-in-law had agreed to pay half the expenses of the suit and pleaded that they should be ordered to pay what they owed. The lady of Chassins replied that since the brothers-in-law were her serfs, the case should be tried in her court. The court declared that the lady of Chassins should not have jurisdiction of this case, but should answer the petition. —B, pp. 268–269 n.

Uncertain Session in 1290[?]

fol. 114[36]   77. Jean de Joinville, lord of Reynel, made an agreement with his father Jean de Joinville, concerning the land of Reynel, which he had inherited after the death of his mother Alix de Reynel.—Du Cange, *Généalogie de la maison de Joinville*, p. 22, in *Histoire de S. Louys*.

fol. 115[37]   78. Geoffroi de Joinville came into conflict with the king of Navarre concerning a female serf.—*Ibid.*, p. 14.

36. Du Cange gives the folio as 114 and the date as 1288. Probably the error is in the date. The seneschal and his son endowed candles at Alix's tomb in November, 1290; see H.-François Delaborde, *Jean de Joinville* (Paris, 1894), Nos. 577 and 585.

37. Du Cange gives the folio as 115 and the date as 1288. Presumably the error is again in the date.

APPENDIX II

MEMBERS AND MASTERS OF THE JOURS OF TROYES UNDER PHILIP THE FAIR

The sources of information about the members of the court of the Jours are the two registers which were once in the Chambre des Comptes, the accounts of Champagne, the custumal of the county, a royal ordinance, a memorandum of Parlement, and a few miscellaneous charters. Of all these records only the custumal was written years after the events it relates. The custumal is therefore of lesser authority than the other materials, and where it is in conflict with them or unsupported, it should be considered suspect.

The names of those attending the Jours are given here with the fullest titles which appear in any of the cited sources, and additional information is added in brackets. All dates have been converted to the Gregorian year. The sigla of the manuscripts are explained at the beginning of Appendix I.

1. 1284, term of St. Catherine (November 25)

Hugues [III] de Conflans, marshal of Champagne
Jean de Joinville, seneschal of Champagne
[Simon II de Clermont], lord of Nesle
Lord Gilles de Brion
Matthieu, *vidame* of Chartres
Lord [Guillaume I] de Jully
Lord Jean de Braisne
Lord Guillaume de Villarcel [guard of the fairs of Champagne]
Lord Henri de Saint Benoît-sur-Vanne
Lord [?] of Breuil
Lord Jacques de *Verna* or *Beona*[1]
[Robert], abbot of Montiéramey
[Guillaume ?], abbot of Montiérender
Master [Gautier de Chambly], archdeacon of Coutances
Master Etienne, archdeacon of Bayeux
Master Jean de Vassoigne
Master Jean . . . [Baras ?]

1. These are the readings of D and B respectively.

Master Anseau de Montaigu
Master Guillaume d'Outremer
Vincent de Pierrechastel, formerly [chancellor of Champagne]
Florent de Roye
Renier Accorre [tax collector of Champagne]
Oudard de Neuville, *bailli* of Sens
Guillaume d'Alemant [*bailli* of Troyes]
Hugues de Chaumont, formerly *bailli* of Vitry
And many more.

Based on two different lists in the first register, fol. 17v in B, pp. 859–860 n; D, fol. 22; cf. C, fol. 37v, and A, fol. 378.

2. *1285, term of two weeks after Easter (April 8)*

Those paid wages specifically for attending the court are marked with an asterisk, and the number of days of service is noted in parentheses. The two guardians, who presumably presided, were paid separately.

Lord Jean de Joinville, who then guarded the county
Master Gautier de Chambly
*Master Jean de Vassoigne (17 days)
Gilles de Compiègne
*Florent de Roye (19 days)
*[Robert], abbot of Montiéramey (11 days)
*An unnamed clerk [possibly Gilles de Compiègne]
*Master Jean Baras (16 days)
*Lord Gilles de Brion (9 days)

In addition Renier Accorre was paid expenses for his clerks (13 days), and wages were also paid to Count Philip's proctor, Pierre de Beaumont.

The first five names are those recorded in the *Coutumier* for case No. 20, Appendix I. The accounts, printed in Longnon (ed.), *Documents*, III, 27–28, record the wages paid to those attending the session beginning April 8, 1285.

3. *1285, August 3*

No names are recorded except those of the guardians, Jean de Joinville and Gautier de Chambly.

Prou and d'Auriac, *Actes et Comptes*, p. 282.

4. *1286, term of the week after All Saints (November 8)*

Taking the place of the king (*tenentes locum domini Regis*):
Brother Arnoul de Wisemale
Master Simon Matiffas, archdeacon of Reims[2]
Master Gautier de Chambly
Master Jean de Vassoigne
Gilles de Compiègne

Present on November 15:
[Robert], abbot of Montiéramey
Guillaume d'Alemant, *bailli* [of Troyes]
Renier Accorre
Chrétien de Provins
Master Guillaume de Beaumont
Lord Jean de Broyes
Lord Guillaume d'Erbloy
Gautier de Durtain, mayor of Provins
Guillaume Raymond
Gautier, viscount of Saint-Florentin
Lord Gilles, his brother
Master Jean de Taillefontaine
Master Jean de Vandeuvre
Guillaume du Châtelet, *bailli* of Sézanne
And many others.

Appendix I, No. 30.

5. *1287, undated session*

Jacques de Boulogne, archdeacon of Thérouanne
Robert de Harecourt, treasurer of Poitiers
Gilles de Compiègne

These three names are given a separate listing under 1287 in C, fol. 37*v*, and A, fol. 378*v*. They are probably taken from the first register for the sessions beginning April 14, 1287.

6. *1287, Tuesday after Ascension (May 20)*

Jacques de Boulogne, archdeacon of Thérouanne
Robert de Harecourt, treasurer of Poitiers

C, fol. 37*v*, and A, fol. 379.

2. Became bishop of Paris in 1290.

7. 1287, term of the day following the Nativity of the Virgin (September 9)

Those paid for their expenses in attending the session are marked with an asterisk.

Lord Gautier de Chambly, bishop of Senlis [?]
Brother Arnoul de Wisemale, of the Knights of the Temple
*Gilles de Compiègne
*Florent de Roye
Lord Jean de Villeblevin, *bailli* of Troyes
Lord Jacques de Boulogne, bishop of Thérouanne [?]
*Lord Guillaume de Grancey
*Lord Robert de Harecourt, treasurer of Poitiers
*Lord Philippe de Givancourt
*[?], chancellor of Meaux[3]
*Master Rich[ier], paid a salary for preparing *arrêts*
*Gencien   ⎫
             ⎬ tax collectors of Champagne
*Renier Accorre⎭

The first six names are from a case recorded in the *Coutumier*, Appendix I, No. 48. Since Gautier de Chambly and Jacques de Boulogne are not named by other records, it is possible that the custumal is in error on these two names. In its heading for the session, the register names only three masters, Arnoul de Wisemale, Guillaume de Grancey, and Robert de Harecourt. For this record see B, p. 247 n; D, fol. 24*v*; BN, Coll. Dupuy, MS 761, fol. 49; and C, fol. 37*v*, and A, fol. 379. The comparison of the list with the accounts (Longnon, [ed.], *Documents*, III, 51) shows that not every master was paid for his services from the treasury of Champagne, and that on occasion people who were not listed in the register as masters were paid for attending the Jours.

8. 1288, term of Monday before Ascension (May 3)

G[autier de Chambly], bishop of Senlis
Master Gilles Lambert[4]
Lord Guillaume de Grancey
Gilles de Compiègne

First register, printed in B, p. 247 n; cf. C, fol. 37*v*, and A, fol. 379.

9. 1288, term beginning Wednesday of the week after the Nativity of the Virgin (September 14)

Those paid for their expenses were:

*G[autier de Chambly], bishop of Senlis

3. Quite possibly Simon Caumy; see *Obituaires de la province de Sens*, ed. Auguste Longnon and others, 4 vols. in 5 (Paris, 1902–23), IV, 60 F.
4. Became dean of Saint-Martin of Tours.

*Lord Guillaume de Grancey
*Gilles de Compiègne (23 days)
*Master Richier, his clerk

Longnon (ed.), *Documents*, III, 88; first register in B, p. 247 n; D, fol. 25; C, fol. 38, and A, fol. 379. Only the first three were listed in the register as holding the Jours.

10. 1289, term of Thursday before mid-Lent (March 17)

Lord and Master Simon Matiffas, archdeacon of Reims
Brother Arnoul de Wisemale, knight of the Temple
Lord Guillaume de Grancey
Gilles de Compiègne
Oudard de la Neuville, *bailli* of Senlis

First register, fol. 93 in B, pp. 247–248 n, and D, fol. 25*v*.

11. 1289, term of the day after the Nativity of the Virgin (September 9)

G[autier de Chambly], bishop of Senlis
Master Jean de Vassoigne, archdeacon of Bruges in the church of Tournai [5]
Lord Guillaume de Grancey
Gilles de Compiègne, of the household of the king of France
Oudard de la Neuville, *bailli* of Senlis

First register in B, p. 248 n; D, fols. 27–27*v*; C, fol. 38; and A, fols. 379–379*v*.

12. 1290, term of Sunday after the Nativity of the Virgin (September 10)

Lord Guillaume de Grancey, knight
Master Etienne Becard, dean of Sens
Gilles de Compiègne
Oudard de la Neuville, *bailli* of Senlis
Master Guillaume, chancellor of Champagne

First register, fol. 111, in B, p. 248 n; D, fols. 27*v*–28; and C, fol. 38, and A, fol. 380.

5. The register read "Magistrum Joannem de Vaissona brugensem Archidiaconum in Ecclesia Carnotensi." The correction was made by Portejoie (ed.), *Coutumier*, p. 158 n. 7. He became bishop of Tournai in 1292.

13. 1291, term of Sunday of the Nativity of the Virgin (September 9)

Lord G[autier de Chambly], bishop of Senlis
Lord Etienne Becard, dean of Sens
Lord Pierre, dean of St. Quentin[6]
Arnoul de Wisemale, brother of the Knights of the Temple
Master Martin, chancellor of Champagne[7]
Jean de Joinville, seneschal of Champagne
Oudard de la Neuville, *bailli* of Senlis
. . . de Mondidier, clerk of the king of France

First register in B, p. 248 n; D, fol. 28; C, fol. 38; and A, fol. 380.

14. 1296, Monday before St. Peter (February 20)

G[uichard], abbot of Montier-la-Celle of the diocese of Troyes[8]
Jean [de *Manstrole*], cantor of Bayeux
Denis, cantor of Paris

These three men issued a charter as "Dies Trecenses pro domino Rege Francie tenentes" in February, 1295 (O. S.); L, t. 67, fol. 10, and Bourquelot, *Études*, II, p. 266 n. 11. For the date see Prou and d'Auriac, *Actes et comptes*, p. 98. All three names appear in the following list.

15. 1296, unspecified term

G[uichard], abbot of Montier-la-Celle of the diocese of Troyes
Master Jean [de *Manstrole*], cantor of Bayeux
[Master ?] Denis, cantor of Paris
Jean de Montigny, sent and commissioned by the king to hold the Jours with:
Lord [Jean] de Joinville
Philippe le Convers ⎱ royal clerks
Jean de Dammartin ⎰
Florent de Roye, *bailli* of Vitry[9]

Second register in C, fol. 38, and A, fol. 380.

6. B: S. Quiriacii; D, C, and A agree that the church is that of St. Quentin. Canon Michel Veissière has kindly informed me that the dean of St. Quiriace of Provins in 1291 was Etienne Paillard.

7. B: *Camerarius*; D: *Cancellarius*; CA: *Chancelier*. Martin was chancellor in 1288; see Longnon (ed.), *Documents*, III, 83.

8. Elected bishop of Troyes in 1298.

9. Possibly an error, for Florent de Roye is not otherwise named as a *bailli*; see Maillard, "Mouvements," p. 430.

16. 1297, Tuesday after the first Sunday of Lent (March 5)

G[uichard], abbot of Montier-la-Celle
J[ean de *Manstrole*], cantor of Bayeux
Etienne, archdeacon of Bruges in the church of Tournai
Lord Gui de Néry
Lord Simon de Marchais, knight of the king
Lord Oudard de la Neuville

From the second register in C, fols. 38–38*v*, and A, fols. 380–380*v*.

17. 1298, the twentieth day after Christmas (January 13)

[Guichard], abbot of Montier-la-Celle
*J[ean] de *Manstrole*, cantor of Bayeux
[Etienne], archdeacon of Bruges [in the church of Tournai]
[Master Guillaume Bonnet], treasurer of Angers[10]
Oudard de la Neuville

Second register in C, fol. 38*v*, and A, fol. 380*v*.* The accounts of Jean de *Manstrole* for attending the Jours of Christmas, 1297 (O.S.) are noted in Fawtier (ed.), *Comptes royaux*, I, No. 436.

18. 1298, Monday after the Exaltation of the Cross (September 15)

[Guichard], abbot of Montier-la-Celle
[Jean de *Manstrole*], cantor of Bayeux
[Master Guillaume Bonnet], treasurer of Angers

Second register in C, fol. 38*v*, and A, fol. 380*v*.

19. 1299, Monday after Ascension (June 1)

Jean [de la Grange], bishop of Meaux
G[uichard], bishop-elect of Troyes
*Master Pierre de Belleperche, canon of Auxerre (18 days)[11]
Master Nicolas de Châlons, canon of Sens ⎱
Master Philippe le Convers, canon of Noyon ⎰ royal clerks
Lord Simon de Marchais, knight of the king

10. Elected bishop of Bayeux in 1306. For the identification of the treasurer of Angers, see Fawtier (ed.), *Comptes royaux*, I, Nos. 3143–3146.
11. Became bishop of Auxerre in 1306.

Master Martin de la Chambre, chancellor of Champagne, archdeacon of Lisieux

Second register in C, fol. 38v, and A, fol. 380v.* The payment to Pierre de Belleperche for the term before Pentecost, 1299, is noted in Fawtier (ed.), *Comptes royaux*, I, Nos. 3148, 3152.

20. *1311 (or possibly 1312), term of two weeks after St. John (September 12)*

[Jean de Savigny], bishop of Nevers
[Gui de la Charité], bishop of Soissons
[Jean d'Auxy], cantor of Orléans
Master Denis de Sens, [dean of Saint-Etienne of Sens]
Lord G[uillaume] de Nogaret
Lord Hugues de la Celle, [lord of Fontaines]
Bernard du Mès
Pierre de Dicy

Langlois, *Textes*, pp. 178–180. For the date see Borrelli de Serres, *Recherches*, II, 320.

APPENDIX III

SESSION OF THE JOURS IN 1276

The record of a court which met in the count's palace at Troyes on February 1, 1276, was entered in thirteenth-century handwriting on the verso of a sheet inserted at the beginning of the *Petit Cartulaire* of the Hôtel-Dieu of Provins. The text does not have the form of a charter and is clearly a copy, since it leaves blanks for several names. It suggests the existence of some sort of register of the decisions and members of the court of the Jours before the accession of Prince Philip, which could have been used by the compiler of the custumal of Champagne. It is noteworthy that this text names twenty-one members of the court; if the compiler of the custumal used records as full as this one, he selected those names most likely to be familiar to his readers and consequently created a distorted picture of the composition of the court.

The cartulary is now at Melun, archives départementales de Seine-et-Marne, H Supplément, Grand Hôtel-Dieu de Provins, A 13*. The text is on fol. 1*v*.

Anno domini m° cc° lxx° quinto in vigilia purificationis beate Marie, in aula regia Trecensi, recto regali iudicio adiudicaverunt amovere impedimentum quod excellentissimus Theobaldus ultimus quondam rex Navarre, Campanie et Brie comes palatinus, posuerat sua propria voluntate et de facto in annualibus prebendarum capelle sue aule Provini datis et litteratorie concessis ab antecessoribus suis fratribus et pauperibus Domus Dei Pruvini, hiis agentibus et presentibus: domino Hugone de Conflans, marescallo; domino Johanne de Joinville, senescallo; abbate de Altovillari;[1] abbate Monasterii Ariame;[2] domino Radulpho de Toreta, canonico Meldensi; magistro Matheo de ... ; magistro Ansello ... ; magistro Rufino; domino Henrico Tuebuef; domino Petro de Vilecer, milite; domino Guillermo, fratre eius;[3] domino Eustachio de Escuri; domino Guillermo pivole de Paciaco; Christiano dicto Ursi; magistro Johanne; Garsie;[4] quatuor ballivis, videlicet domino Petro de

1. Thomas de Moiremont was abbot of Saint-Pierre of Hautvillers in 1276.
2. The abbot of Montiéramey in 1276 was Robert.
3. At this time Guillaume de Villarcel was one of the guards of the fairs; see Elizabeth Chapin, *Les villes de foires de Champagne* (Paris, 1937), p. 255.
4. Probably Garsie Sanchez, notary; see Arbois de Jubainville, *Histoire*, IV, 541.

Maladomo,[5] domino Guillermo de Joiaco,[6] Guillermo dicto Alexandre,[7] Guillermo dicto ... [probably du Châtelet];[8] et Guillermo Remondi dicto.[9] Quorum consilio et mandato predictus magister Matheus dictum impedimentum [sic] in presentia et generali audientia multorum die predicta in aula Trecensi existantium predictum impedimentum in annualibus capelle aule predicte Pruvini positum generali et sententia et generali iudicio amovisse et de predictis annualibus dictis fratribus et pauperibus dicto iudicio licentiam dedit deserviendi et percipiendi quotiensusque fuerit oportuum [sic].

5. *Bailli* of Vitry; see Portejoie (ed.), *Coutumier*, p. 167 n. 6.
6. *Bailli* of either Meaux or Chaumont.
7. *Bailli* of Troyes and Provins; see Roserot, *Dictionnaire*, p. 1525.
8. *Bailli* of either Meaux or Chaumont; see Portejoie (ed.), *Coutumier*, p. 10 n. 28.
9. Guillaume Raymond, a prominent citizen of Provins, was the other guard of the fairs at this time; see Chapin, *Villes*, p. 255. Arbois de Jubainville (*Histoire*, IV, 486) omitted the preceding name and therefore included him as one of the four *baillis*.

INDEX OF PERSONS AND PLACES IN THE APPENDIXES

References to people are given following baptismal names, when these are known. Places in or near Champagne are identified, and cross references given to people from those places; but people from outside Champagne or its environs are not listed under their place of origin or office. Unless the name of a *bailli* is supplied in the text, *baillis* are listed only by the place of office and year. All entries are to items and appendixes and not pages; those not preceded by a Roman numeral refer to Appendix I. (Abbreviations used are as follows: ar., arrondissement; c., canton; cne., commune; ch. l., chef-lieu; dep., department; dioc., diocese.)

Agathes de Damery: 2

Agnes, wife of Odo Bezors, lord of Villarnout: 1

Alix de Reynel, wife of Jean de Joinville: 77

André de Saint-Phal: 38

Anseau, master: III

Anseau de Montaigu: II, 1

Arcis-sur-Aube (Aube, ar. Troyes, ch. l. c.): *v.* Erard d'

Argers (Marne, ar. and c. Sainte-Menehould): *v.* Raolin d'

Arnoul de Wisemale, of the Knights of the Temple: II, 4, 7, 10, 13

Arrientières (Aube, ar. and c. Bar-sur-Aube): 14, 23

Artonges (Aisne, ar. Château-Thierry, c. Condé-en-Brie): 18

Balduin de Tour: 73

Bar [?]: *v.* Christine de

Bar-le-Duc (Meuse, ch. l. dep.): *v.* Thibaut II, count of

Bar-sur-Aube (Aube, ch. l. ar.), burgesses of: 72

Bar-sur-Seine (Aube, ar. Troyes, ch. l. c.), viscount of: 41

Baudier de Donzy, of Monthois: 69

Beatrice, duchess of Burgundy: 1

Beatrice, wife of Jacques, lord of La Roche-en-Brenil: 1

Beaumont-en-Argonne (Ardennes, ar. Sedan, c. Mouzon): 69

Beaurepaire (Aube, ar. Troyes, c. and cne. Piney): 14, 23

Belroy, priory of Val-des-Escoliers (dioc. Troyes): 14, 23

Bernard du Mès: II, 20

Borgine, daughter of Huard Baudier: 26, 42

Bourlemont (Vosges, ar. Neufchâteau, c. Coussey, cne. Frébecourt): 11; *v.* Jean de, Pierre de

Breuil (*Brolium?*), lord of: II, 1

Brion-sur-Ource (Côte-d'Or, ar. Montbard, c. Montigny-sur-Aube): *v.* Gilles de

Broyes (Marne, ar. Epernay, c. Sézanne): *v.* Jean de, Thibaut de

Burgundy: *v.* Beatrice, duchess of; Robert II, duke of

Châlons-sur-Marne (Marne, ch. l. dep.): 52; bishop of, 52; *v.* Nicholas de

Champagne, *baillis* and *prévôts* in general: 7, 27, 35, 44, 45, 53; chamberlain: *v.* Lambert le Bouchu; chancellors: *v.* Guillaume, Martin de la Chambre,